The Question of Christian Philosophy Today

PERSPECTIVES IN CONTINENTAL PHILOSOPHY
John D. Caputo, Series Editor

1. *Deconstruction in a Nutshell: A Conversation with Jacques Derrida*, edited and with a Commentary by John D. Caputo
2. Michael Barber, *Ethical Hermeneutics: Rationality in Enrique Dussel's Philosophy of Liberation*
3. Michael Strawser, *Both/And: Reading Kierkegaard—From Irony to Edification*
4. *Knowing Other-wise: Philosophy at the Threshold of Spirituality*, edited by James H. Olthuis
5. James Swindal, *Reflection Revisited: Jürgen Habermas's Discursive Theory of Truth*
6. Richard Kearney, *Poetics of Imagining*, second edition
7. Thomas W. Busch, *Circulating Being: From Embodiment to Incorporation—Essays on Late Existentialism*
8. Edith Wyschogrod, *Emmanuel Levinas: The Problem of Ethical Metaphysics*, revised edition

The Question
of Christian Philosophy
Today

Edited by

FRANCIS J. AMBROSIO

Fordham University Press
New York
1999

Copyright © 1999 by Fordham University Press
LC 99–052875
ISBN 0–8232–1981–X (*hardcover*)
ISBN 0–8232–1982–8 (*paperback*)
ISSN: 1089–3938
Perspectives in Continental Philosophy, no. 9

Library of Congress Cataloging-in-Publication Data

The question of Christian philosophy today / edited by Francis J.
Ambrosio.
    p.   cm — (Perspectives in continental philosophy ; no. 9)
   "Presented at a symposium held at Georgetown University,
September 24–26, 1993"—Introd. Includes bibliographical
references and index.
   ISBN 0-8232-1981-X — ISBN 0-8232-1932-8 (pbk.)
   1. Christianity—Philosophy. I. Ambrosio, Francis
J. II. Series.
BR100.Q47   1999
230′.01—dc21
                                  99-052875

Printed in the United States of America

CONTENTS

Acknowledgments   vii

Introduction   ix

I
EVOKING THE QUESTION

1. Back to the Future?   3
   William J. Richardson

II
ENCOUNTERING THE TRADITION

2. History of Philosophy as Tutor of
   Christian Philosophy   37
   Marilyn McCord Adams

3. Secular Philosophy and Its Origins at the Dawn of
   the Modern Age   61
   Louis Dupré

4. Original Sin: A Study in the Interaction of
   Philosophy and Theology   80
   Robert Merrihew Adams

5. The Problem of Christian Philosophy   111
   Adriaan Peperzak

6. A Theological View of Philosophy: Revelation
   and Reason   142
   David Tracy

III
OF WHAT AVAIL?

7. Lonergan and the Measures of God   165
   Patrick A. Heelan, S. J.

8. Metanoetics: Elements of a Postmodern
   Christian Philosophy   189
   John D. Caputo

9. "Divine Woman/Divine Women": The Return of the
   Sacred in Bataille, Lacan, and Irigaray   224
   Amy Hollywood

10. "Christian Philosophy": Hermeneutic or Heuristic?   247
    Jean-Luc Marion

IV
PHILOSOPHIZING AS A CHRISTIAN

11. Philosophy and Existence   267
    Jean Ladrière

V
A CONCLUDING ROUNDTABLE DISCUSSION

VI
IN RESPONSE

12. On Seeing Fra Angelico's San Marco *Annunciation*:
    The Place of Art   313
    Francis J. Ambrosio

About the Authors   363

ACKNOWLEDGMENTS

The editor wishes to thank the many individuals who contributed materially and collegially to make the symposium possible. Michael J. Collins, Dean for Summer and Continuing Education at Georgetown University, provided the principal funding for the event as well as indispensable administrative support for all of the organizational and logistical details of the event. These were handled with skill, care, and grace by Ms. Emma Harrington, Director of Special Programs. Additional financial support came from the Dean of Georgetown College, Robert B. Lawton, S.J., the Office of the Executive Vice President for Academic Affairs, and the Philosophy Department of Georgetown University under the leadership of its chair, Professor Wayne Davis, who enthusiastically encouraged the plans for the Symposium in their early stages. The President of the University, Leo J. O'Donovan, S.J., graciously hosted a dinner for the speakers on the first night of the Symposium. Deborah R. Warin, Director of Continuing Education at Georgetown, performed the challenging task of editing the transcripts of the Question and Answer sessions and the concluding Roundtable discussion with patience and sensitivity so as to preserve the vitality of living conversation without sacrificing clarity of expression.

Finally, I wish to express my gratitude to the late Thomas P. McTighe, professor of philosophy at Georgetown for more than forty years, to whom this volume is dedicated and who from the first time I mentioned the idea of the symposium to him through its conclusion was a source of encouragement, creativity, and sound judgment as well as warm good humor and wry insight. Thank you, Tom.

INTRODUCTION

The essays contained in this volume were presented at a symposium held at Georgetown University, September 24–26, 1993, entitled "The Question of Christian Philosophy Today." Together with excerpts from the question-and-answer sessions that followed each presentation and the concluding Roundtable discussion involving all the presenters, these essays document the proceedings of that event. Beyond that, it is possible, I believe, to discern in them something of the meaning of that event, and something of its spirit, as experienced by those who took part in it. Many participants testified that the conversation prompted by both the formal and the informal dynamics of the symposium sustained a sense of timeliness, a certain recognizable warrant of the significance of its claims upon them. From the beginning, a palpable doubt, expressed in different ways by several speakers and many of the participants, made its power felt and had a distinct effect on the way the conversation unfolded. Was there really a question here? Was there life in this question still, for us, here, today? How could that be possible? What could be the point? Like the products of Penelope's loom, the presentations were interwoven with a strand of "guilty consciousness" that foresaw the intention, the necessity, to undo in the night what had been done in the day. The experience of the symposium was one of double-doing, and from that experience, explored and compounded from session to session, there gradually emerged a recognition that, in fact, this was a warranted question; there was a real dialectic at work between present doubt and the weight of tradition and effective precedent, between hesitation and hope. For that very reason, it became clear that a genuine dialogue was possible. It could not be decided in advance what the outcome would be, or what it was possible to say regarding Christian philosophy today, or how anything could be said. It emerged, however, that, despite doubt and uncertainty, people wanted to find out. This was a timely question, because the conversation it invited was wanted and needed. In that sense, it could be freely and truthfully undertaken and enjoyed.

The symposium was fortunate to be given, early on, a potent and evocative image of this sense of timeliness. William Richardson, speaking on the first evening, began his presentation by asking his listeners to look carefully at the projected image of Giorgione's *The Three Ages of Man*, which hangs in the Pitti Gallery in Florence, Italy, and is reproduced on the cover of this volume. He went on to suggest that in the picture as a whole, but particularly in the enigmatic expression and gaze of the old man at the left of the group, he recognized the way this experience of being in question looks on a human face. He asked us to see the question and to see it as our own, to recognize ourselves in the picture this question opens to our view.

I would like to suggest that this volume be read from the perspective this image offers us and Bill Richardson articulates and develops in his essay, "Back to the Future." To facilitate adopting that perspective, the essays are grouped here and sequenced in an order different from their order in the actual symposium program. After "Back to the Future," the second section, "Encountering the Tradition," includes five essays that attempt individually to help situate and establish the present context of the question of Christian philosophy. The third section, "Of What Avail?" comprises four essays that address in their own distinct ways the possibility of a genuinely timely Christian philosophy. The fourth section, "Philosophizing as a Christian," offers one instance of the form an individual response to the question or the look on the face of Giorgione's old man might take. Finally, the fifth and sixth sections, "A Concluding Gathering," and "In Response," offer two distinct types of reflection on the experience of the symposium.

To further suggest the possibility of adopting the viewpoint Richardson has suggested, a brief prelection of each of the papers might be in order. Without wishing to limit the possible interpretations, a point of focus can be anticipated for each.

Evoking the Question

If there is still any point in saying that any picture is worth a thousand words, then we might well begin to appreciate that point as it emerges in the strategy William Richardson employs to initiate the development of the symposium. Called on to "evoke the question [of Christian philosophy today] in its fullest and most radical terms and to bespeak its timeliness for the symposium audience," Richardson responds with a performance that honors the fundamental lesson about philosophical existence and conversation which Plato taught masterfully once for all: namely, that it is a *dramatic event*. Philosophy occurs when life really becomes a question and is allowed to show itself as such. In what amounts to a master stroke of philosophical dramatic imagination, Richardson lets a painting, *The Three Ages of Man* by Giorgione, act as the dramatic metaphor that links his own personal experience of the question of the symposium happening to him on a cloudy-bright Good Friday afternoon on a bridge over the Seine after a visit to a painting exhibition, and is the plot structure by which his essay unfolds. Through this metaphor he enacts the meaning of the claim his contribution makes on us: to think about how there opens up another, different possibility between, on one hand, "Christian philosophy" as a body of ideas and, on the other, "Christian philosophers" as a combination of two distinct characteristics in a single person: philosophizing as a Christian.

After introducing his central image, Richardson carefully situates his own reflection in the context of both the Continental and the Anglo-American concern with and response to the question in the twentieth century. From this consideration there emerges not only the frame of the debate in its traditional and contemporary modes but also a sharply focused glimpse of the painting's capacity to help us enter into the history of the question for ourselves. For Richardson takes the three figures together as an image not only of the tradition, including its current issues and debates, but also of the question about the tradition that grows out of the experience of living in and through the twists and turns of its "plotting."

Richardson singles out three elements of the grouping for special consideration: the text under discussion, the personal nature of the subjects involved in the dialogue, and the gesture of the master, which suggests the function of metaphysical thinking in the tradition. Using these issues he introduces the relevance of voices such as those of Nietzsche, Derrida, Foucault, Lacan, Heidegger, Lyotard, and Marion. From each issue seen through the experienced eyes of the old man the question of truth emerges, particularly the question of what binding truth-claim can speak out of texts whose fabric separates and frays within the economy of difference; from the issue of personal nature the question of the person emerges, of how Christian philosophy can ever come to grips with the radical antihumanism of postmodern thinking; and, finally, from the issue of the role of metaphysics comes the question of history, particularly the question of the relation of Time and Being that Christianity claims is given a uniquely privileged resolution in the Incarnation of Jesus Christ. In this regard, Richardson gives special attention to the response of Jean-Luc Marion in *God Without Being*, and goes on to suggest what Richardson says he sees as "one more step in the direction that Marion's proposal has opened up": a sketch of Richardson's conception of what it means "to philosophize as Christians." What Richardson has to say in developing this suggestion is intended not as an answer but only as an opening up and bringing to light, a "clarifying" of the question. But in that light, under the penetrating gaze of the old man's eyes, something else comes to light, belonging not to any individual but to the subject itself and to us all in relation to it—resistance, the resistance to experiencing the question as addressed to us, individually and communally, personally. " 'I resist being looked at in that way and asked so directly: Well and good, but what about you? Where do you stand? Or will you walk away?' " That resistance is the impulse that sets the rest of the symposium to work.

ENCOUNTERING THE TRADITION

Speaking from the perspective of one educated "at Cornell in the early 1960s and by life in America's analytical philosophy circles since," Marilyn McCord Adams offers a pointed focus on the "Francophone" controversy that developed between Gilson and Van Steenberghen sixty years ago regarding the challenges of Christian philosophy in the twentieth century. Using a sketch of the battle lines drawn in that debate, Adams pursues a tactic first employed perhaps by Plato in his *Protagoras*: offering a characterization of philosophy and philosophers by exploring the dimensions and dynamics of the process of education which its nature requires. In her contribution, "History of Philosophy as Tutor of Christian Philosophy," she speaks autobiographically of her professional upbringing in the "borderline 'abusive home'" of Anglo-American analytic philosophy. Avoiding caricature and recrimination, and recognizing a range of good intellectual and professional habits that that pedagogy inculcated, she allows herself to become explicitly conscious of the thin "ontological diet" on which she learned to subsist and its deficiency for nourishing the commitments and intuitions for which her identity as a Christian would naturally have hoped a hardier fare. Her metaphors, carefully balanced and with a ring not only of familiarity but also of truth for many of her colleagues, give a new and timely appropriateness to Anselm's characterization of *fides quaerens intellectum*. It is in this context that she suggests that many, or even most, of us who are concerned with the question of Christian philosophy today and who have grown up in the analytical school "will be helped in recovering our identity as *Christian* philosophers by putting ourselves to school in the history of Christian philosophy in the Middle Ages." One thousand years of richly textured tradition that prized analytical rigor, yet resisted artificial structures within the identity of its teachers and pupils, can, Adams argues, serve as a tutor and guide to the development process wherein we learn first to "try on for size" the ways of thinking and the issues that together formed the philosophical identities of great persons who could serve as "role models" and from whom we can learn not just by imitation, but also by recapitulating for ourselves their achievement of learning to think for themselves as Christians. Unspoken throughout her essay is the invitation to those of her colleagues who were brought up and now have gained their maturity in other "philosophical households," especially the modern European metaphysical tradition or contemporary postmodern heritage, to allow themselves to become conscious both of their relationship to the analytical tradition and of the dynamics that have shaped the philosophical pedagogy by which they themselves have been formed. Adams seems to say to us all that, as Christian philosophers, we all need to spend our day as Hippocrates did, listening to and reflecting on the pedagogies that are continually shaping our philosophical souls.

In the second symposium essay, Louis Dupré continues to probe the historical roots of the issue, asking why it is that Christian philosophy has become a question today. He sketches the historical process that led to a separation between the tradition of religious thought proper and the autonomous, purely rational philosophy that emerges at the beginning of the modern age. While philosophy might yield the notion of transcendence, it cannot, he argues, lend it a positive content. This it can acquire only from an actual encounter with religious belief, so that in dealing with this specifically religious content, philosophy must be satisfied to reflect on a *given*, nonphilosophical experience or on a positive faith. Although classical Greek and medieval philosophy succeeded to a large extent in holding these two in a vital and creative tension, Dupré discerns a tendency in modern philosophy to blend and confuse metaphysics with the philosophy of religion, either ignoring the possibility of real transcendence or incorporating it in an autonomous metaphysics, but in either case closing off the possibility of a Christian philosophy proper. Dupré introduces as his central thesis the notion that this apparent new impossibility is a consequence of a fragmented vision of the real, in which cosmic, anthropic, and transcendent elements became divorced from one another and destroyed the ancient sense of universal harmony. More specifically, he argues that the notion of the "supernatural," relegated to the status of a detached scaffolding, became extraneous to the realm of being proper to philosophy when the concept of *nature*, both human and cosmic, became separated from the constitutive relation to transcendence that supported its meaning and value. In the second section of his essay, Dupré examines in detail two foci of the tensions within traditional Christian philosophy that eventually split apart, creating the fissure between the natural and the "supernatural." The first is the transmission of the Aristotelian theory of causality from its original vital contact, which Aquinas maintained even after it gained the ascendancy in his expression over the Platonic elements in his thought, to a far more mechanical and schematic notion in which the relation of Creator to creation was reduced almost exclusively to that of efficient cause. The second and more damaging fracture, according to Dupré, was introduced by nominal thought—it is significant that he excludes Ockham from complicity in this regard—into the understanding of divine freedom. He argues that nominalist theology transformed the concept of God's *potentia absoluta* and its relation to the *potentia ordinata* in such a way as to make plausible a view of nature as a closed system of secondary causes fully equipped ιο act without special divine assistance and, hence, ultimately detachable from any divine "superstructure." The development of "natural theology" in the sixteenth and seventeenth centuries, which began as an attempt to reclaim the domain of transcendence for the new philosophy of the modern age, ended up a misguided foundationalist project. Faith and grace were conceived and explained as "building on" the foundation of nature, but the foundation was viewed as providing that basis independently, so that the relation ceased to be either original or organic. This recognition leads Dupré in the essay's third section to call for a restoration of Western thought's "ontological unity," through a fundamental rethinking of our philosophical approach—"a new kind of metaphysics" such as Nicholas of Cusa initiated in the fifteenth century. Although this subject is left undeveloped in Dupré's essay, he clearly points the way toward issues that later symposium contributions would consider: the overcoming of the "baneful" absolute priority of the subject, the crucial issue of the difference that arises within freedom, an ontology of immanent relation and "finite transcendence," especially with regard to the place of revelation in Christian philosophy, and the nature of the distinction between theology and philosophy.

Robert Adams's symposium contribution is motivated by an interest in studying the complex dynamics that characterize the interplay of Christian theology and philosophy as they have operated historically, insofar as they can be discerned by carefully probing at least one important nexus of those dynamics: Kant's treatment of the subject of original sin. As Adams makes clear at the outset, however, and again in his conclusion, such an interest has a hermeneutical relevance that extends beyond historical comprehension to a recognition of its application for our contemporary understanding of the way such questions are playing themselves out in our own society and ways of thinking. Citing the importance of Reinhold Niebuhr's work, which he styles as "at once social criticism, political ethics, and Christian apologetics," Adams argues that behind Niebuhr's most famous project, his exposition and rehabilitation of the doctrine of original sin, stands Kant's treatment of the subject and the view that the topics of sin and forgiveness belong both to the Christian tradition and to a treatment of *Religion Within the Limits of Reason Alone*. Although one might argue that this view of Kant's is itself idiosyncratic or, at least, peculiar to his historical situation, Adam's analysis of the roots of Kant's position in the contrast of the Scholastic approach of Aquinas, based on a faculty psychology, with Melanchthon's version of the Reformers' view, which departs from the medieval style of thinking about the will and responsibility, reveals a philosophical issue central to both ethical theory and the issue of human personhood. Through a careful and detailed account of the similarities and differences of Kant's view with these two influential predecessors concerning the relation between voluntariness and our responsibility for motivational states—especially our deepest motivation, which Kant refers to as our "ultimate subjective ground of choice"—Adams offers a lucid demonstration of what Gadamer might refer to as *wirkungsgeschichtliche Bewußtsein* (historically effected consciousness) working itself out in the human dialogue between theological and philosophical concern and understanding for a genuinely shared subject matter. Adams's reflection reaches a double climax in relation to the question of the symposium. First, it invites us to consider the implications of its historical reflection on our contemporary consideration of the nature of human moral agency and personhood. Second, it provokes us to confront the fact that from the Middle Ages to the early modern period "important parts of the development of conceptions of the voluntary and of moral responsibility . . . took place in the context of discussions of original sin." As Adams draws his conclusion that it would be "fatuous" to expect to comprehend these philosophical developments apart from the context of their embeddedness in a theological question, the stage is set for the reflection that later symposium contributions will give to the implication of this conclusion for our own participation in the dialogue between these two abiding human concerns: the philosophical and the religious. The question of the possibility and promise of philosophizing as a Christian emerges as the central focus of Adriann Peperzak's essay, "The Problem of Christian Philosophy." The strength and value of his contribution lies in the gentle but firm spirit of irony Peperzak is able to bring to the discussion of three questions that formulate the problematic character of his theme. First, he asks "What is philosophy and how is a philosopher engaged in it?" Finding the path to a satisfactory response blocked by peculiarly modern assumptions which obscure the original features of philosophical existence as a passionately committed way of life, he gradually works to gain a view of philosophy in which the relationship among wisdom, life, and theory is restored to the integrity it genuinely enjoyed in so much of the practice of classical and medieval philosophers and to which many developments in postmodernist thought promise at least the possibility of a return. At the core of this integrity, Peperzak identifies an openness to human affectivity as responsive and responsible which both capacitates and requires an involvement with life which takes the form of a process of purification and, as such, is appropriately viewed as a spirituality.

Peperzak's second thematic issue concerns what we should understand by the word *Christian*. Again, the ironic tone of the response leads us first to consider all that is not (yet or fully) Christian as mysteriously yet inseparably a part of whatever is Christian. Here he evokes the ambiguity that is characteristic, though in different ways, of the Incarnation as the content of faith and of human sinfulness as the enemy of faith. As a consequence, the life of Christian faith, too, is a process of purification that rejects sin by forbidding "idolatry," any absolutization or infinitization of human culture. It is in this parallel of philosophy and Christian faith as human experiences of a process of purification—different in their original commitment, self-understanding, and practice, yet connected by this passionate involvement and responsibility—that Peperzak discerns an opening for the practice of an authentic Christian philosophy.

Thus is he led to consider his third question concerning the connections between philosophical and Christian moments in a person who makes both commitments. Here the negativity of irony passes over cautiously to the more hopeful but no less ironic suggestion of a logic of integration of the two, in which a transformation of both the life of Christian faith and the life of philosophy occurs, allowing both to honor the determinacy of their original *Yes* or *Amen*, while entering into a growing intimacy of lived commitment and mutual effective recognition. Lest this hope sound like too facile a nostalgia for the "marriage of faith and reason," Peperzak insists on the limits as well as the difficulties of such a process of integration. Nevertheless, behind his conclusion that "A post-postmodern renaissance of Christian spirituality in philosophy is necessary" stands the author's demonstrated conviction that it is also possible.

In "A Theological View of Philosophy: Revelation and Reason," David Tracy focuses attention more sharply on two points—one, the theological category of revelation; the other, philosophical hermeneutics—in an attempt to illustrate one way in which theology can and, indeed, must relate in significant ways to philosophy, insofar as a revelation-constituted understanding of faith as knowledge is a meaningful cognitive claim. Arguing that the philosophy of religion, as a distinctly modern development, has the effect of losing the Christian emphasis on divine self-revelation through the Incarnate Word, Tracy explores the opposing constraints that fideism and rationalism, in all their protean forms, introduce into the effort to reconcile the legitimate claims of both philosophy and theology to interpret the possibility of a form of human knowledge which arises in faith. He then goes on to offer a theological construal of revelation as an event of divine self-manifestation in the event and person of Jesus the Christ. Focusing on three elements of this notion of revelation—event, manifestation, and Word—he shows how hermeneutic philosophy can make a contribution to our comprehension of the notion of revelation which goes beyond merely analytic classification to genuine development. Tracy identifies two distinct dynamics in the hermeneutical dialectic of the Word: as Logos, the Word is disclosive manifestation; as Kerygma, the Word is disruptive proclamation. This distinction not only allows for a way of understanding all the classic dichotomies of Christian theological self-understanding—for instance, incarnation/

cross, sacrament/word, analogy/dialectic, love/justice, participation/distance, and the like—but also serves to make unmistakable the necessarily hermeneutic character of Christian faith: the written texts called Scripture assure that the Christ of the present Christian community is the same Christ testified to by the apostolic witnesses as the decisive self-manifestation of God and humanity. What is revealed in and through Christ as manifested in the witness-word of Scripture is a new possibility for human existence: Love. Faith is a knowledge born of revelation that God is Love and human beings are loved creatively and redemptively by God, and are therefore empowered and commanded to love in their turn. Through revelation, Tracy concludes, all Being is now known as gracious.

For Tracy, hermeneutics is a particularly appropriate way of understanding Christian existence as participation in the knowledge of faith. He identifies five specific elements that this appropriateness comprises: (1) hermeneutics accords priority to "possibility" over "actuality"; (2) it takes history and human historicity with full seriousness; (3) it offers an understanding of truth as manifestation which, unlike coherence or correspondence theories, is fruitful for a view of revelation as the event of God's self-manifestation; (4) it clarifies, through its emphasis on textuality, the role of form as the imaginative embodiment of a possible mode of being in the world; and (5) through its dialogical model of understanding, it opens the way to an ethics of understanding the Good and the gracious transformation of all Being by Love. Tracy concludes by suggesting two general dynamics that could characterize the interpretation of hermeneutic philosophy and a Christian theology of revelation. First, theology can offer the possibility of reconstructing the basic categories of hermeneutic philosophy in accordance with the Form of Christian revelation, the person of Jesus Christ. Second, hermeneutics provides a new way to clarify, challenge, and even connect theology's understanding of revelation as manifestation of a *reasonable*, even if formerly unimagined, possibility for human existence. Finally, Tracy suggests that hermeneutics can also offer a way to reestablish an effective connection between theology and spirituality through its commitment to thinking (recollection) as an ontological element of being in the world and to dialogue (prayer as conversation) as the most fundamental of disciplines.

OF WHAT AVAIL?

In his symposium contribution, Patrick Heelan identifies Bernard Lonergan, S.J., as one of the few philosopher/theologians of our time who has written with genius on both the philosophy of science and the philosophy of religion and made a significant contribution to the discussion—or, more precisely, to the appropriate method for a discussion—of whether through a common method with science one could arrive at a theology of the Christian God. In *Insight* he, like Aquinas, failed to resolve the question. Later, in *Method in Theology* and other works, he came to address the elements missing from *Insight*. Heelan proposes to show that if the apparatus of *Method in Theology* is applied to complement *Insight*, one has at hand both a truly sophisticated philosophy of natural science and a method in theology that embraces both the natural sciences and theology.

Heelan argues that a philosophy of science according to *Insight* would be enriched by adopting the hermeneutical modes of inquiry studied in *Method*. The former comprises 'data,' 'insight,' 'judgment,' and 'decision.' The latter comprises 'conversion,' 'horizon,' 'history,' and the structure of 'belief.' The latter are especially pertinent to the study of scientific decisions made during phases of laboratory experimentation. He also proposes that theology should add the empirical/rational modes of *Insight* to the hermeneutical modes of *Method* in its search to express the scientific and philosophical grounds of a faith community. While the hermeneutical modes traditionally focus on the literary and historical sources of a faith community, such as its scriptures, rituals, and the documents of its Magisterium, the empirical/rational modes study existing communities of faith on the model of *Insight*. These involve the identification of true communities of faith, and the use of traditional criteria such as the 'spiritual senses' that are used within the context of the institutional life of the community.

Heelan does not argue that a contemporary theology pursued

in this way would guarantee that the natural and social sciences reveal the God of the Bible. What it shows is merely that if, as Lonergan supposes, there is a common philosophically understood method underlying theology and science, then using that method within the established traditions of Christian life and practice, scientists who are Christian and theologians who respect the processes of science should be able to share reliable experiential, intellectual, and rational knowledge both of nature, the subject matter of the natural sciences, and of the Christian Trinitarian God, the subject matter of the Christian religion, crossing back and forth with ease the frontier between science and theology.

In his essay, "Metanoetics: Elements of a Postmodern Christian Philosophy," John D. Caputo takes up questions remarkably closely aligned with those Richardson raised. His working hypothesis is that, if we have eyes to see and ears to hear, we can discern deep affinities between the themes and concerns of postmodernism and those of the New Testament. In a bold stroke, Caputo announces that by "Christian philosophy" he means, "at least minimally, thinking philosophically within the context and the framework of the New Testament," where that "context" functions as a way of being in the world whose categories we philosophers need and want to understand. Caputo dubs the endeavors to achieve such an understanding a "hermeneutics of the Kingdom," asserting thereby that the traditional distinction between faith and reason is, in this new dispensation, to be suspended, placed under *epochè*. This amounts to a contemporary "de-Hellenization" of the Greek contribution to "Christian philosophy," an exposure to its Jewish "other" which nonetheless allows it to be more itself. Appealing principally to Heidegger and Levinas, Caputo argues that contemporary postmodernist thought characteristically "goes back, in part, to originally philosophico-religious projects that are motivated by a reading of biblical sources." He develops a view of the New Testament in which the distinction between philosophy and theology is muted in favor of a reading of Scripture that offers an "alternate categoricality" in which the categories of onto-theology are simply not in play.

This development proceeds in three steps: a generalized metanoetics, the kingdom of anarchy, and being and time in the king-dom. (That these three steps are closely aligned with Richardson's three questions is left to the reader to verify for him- or herself.) The first task is to establish a generalized sense of what "metanoetics" would mean as a way of thinking that especially emphasizes change or "conversion"—literally, chang-ing one's "mind," one's way of thinking, and changing it in such a way that it itself eventually turns into a change of heart, or perhaps even that mind and heart become interchangeable—thereby suggesting in advance an idea that Caputo thematizes as the New Testament portrayal of a "kingdom of metamorphosis." Underscoring the New Testament's preoccupation with "bodies" and particularly with their needs and maladies, Caputo argues that in Jesus's kingdom of metamorphosis *metanoein* and *thera-peuein* always went hand in hand and that these two dynamics of existence necessarily came together in the process of immersing (*baptizein*) one's whole self, heart and mind, in the cleansing element of transformation. Once it has been entered, however, this transformed element of existence displays itself as a king-dom of anarchy, the principal rule of which is that, in general, rules are suspect. The distinction between *phronesis* and *kardia* parallels, in Caputo's view, the difference between, on one hand, ethics as the thoughtful, prudent application of the general rules to particular situations and mercy, on the other, as the suspension of the rules altogether. Forgiveness, the first and only law of the kingdom, is precisely anarchic: it does not look back to first prin-ciples so as to apply them to past deeds, but, rather, looks ahead to what the change of heart announced by *metanoia* promises. This leads Caputo to his third step: a consideration of the tempo-rality of forgiveness, the new relation of time and being in the kingdom of metamorphosis, where what is most real about things is not their permanent structure, their deep essence, but what happens to them. To know the reality of this kingdom is to say of it, "Let it happen; may it come!" Caputo concludes by chal-lenging his readers to consider whether it might not be precisely the way of thinking that postmodernism and the New Testament show signs of sharing that could make Christian philosophy pos-sible today.

One ironic effect of the symposium, especially for those involved in its organization but also in the experience of the participants, was the way it called attention to a difficulty in evoking the question of Christian philosophy particularly in regard to one ineluctable aspect of its timeliness: the need and the desire to engage in dialogue the concerns and contributions of contemporary feminist thought. Far from being solely a theoretical issue, the actual difficulty appears most tangibly in finding participants capable of bringing these two concerns close enough together in their own experience and thought to enter readily and effectively into the conversation. So, more by way of default than by choice, the symposium took place without including a presentation that deliberately set out to address the question of Christian philosophy today from a feminist perspective.

It stands as a double irony, then, that for the publication of the symposium proceedings, we are able to include an essay that, though not presented as part of the original event, directly evokes and speaks out of the voice that was lacking then. The essay by Amy Hollywood, entitled "Divine Woman/Divine Women: The Return of the Sacred in Bataille, Lacan, and Irigaray," attempts to suggest how radical the disruption of our experience of the question can become once the possibility is raised of deconstructing both its traditional and its contemporary reception following the traces of the masculine and patriarchal exclusions that are inscribed in its language and imagination. Hollywood's essay invites us to consider, through reflection on the nuanced interactions of the thought of Bataille, Lacan, and Irigaray, just how open the possibilities for renewing the question of Christian philosophy today might be and, at the same time, how formidable the difficulties.

In "Christian Philosophy: Hermeneutic or Heuristic?" Jean-Luc Marion makes a contribution notable both for the clarity and forthrightness of its affirmation of "Christian philosophy" as an undertaking and for the radical originality of the way he proposes to understand what that undertaking means. His essay can well be seen as an imaginative meditation on Richardson's characterization of the possibility of "philosophizing as a Christian." At the same time, Marion's study engages Caputo's conception of Christian philosophy as a "radical hermeneutic of the Kingdom" and offers an alternative model at once closer to the heuristic method of Husserl's phenomenology yet in solidarity with Caputo's direct appeal to the Jesus of the Gospel as the ultimate "fact" of revelation.

The study unfolds as an argument for a different construal of Étienne Gilson's definition of Christian philosophy from the one Gilson himself defended. Gilson argues that Christian revelation intervenes as an "indispensable auxiliary of reason," not because it offers to reason themes that otherwise would be inaccessible to it, but because it offers a radically original interpretation of them in the light of the revelation of Christ. Marion identifies widespread historical and contemporary evidence of philosophical practice that could well be viewed as conforming to this hermeneutic model of Christian philosophy, but goes on to propose three telling objections to so understanding it: to reduce Christian philosophy to a hermeneutic amounts to (1) denying it the level of philosophy; (2) branding it as arbitrary; and (3) reducing faith to its *preambula.*

Marion proposes, as a complement to the purely hermeneutic view of Christian philosophy, an extended understanding of the sense in which revelation can be an auxiliary to reason, not simply as a new interpretation of phenomena that are already visible, but also as making visible of phenomena that would have remained invisible without it. Using Pascal's threefold distinction of the order of charity, the order of spirit, and the order of the flesh, Marion argues that the order of charity, which is revealed in the person and life of Jesus, is genuinely a "new creation" that cannot be known from within either of the other orders and contains "facts" they do not. The heuristic of charity provides phenomena discovered by revelation and offers them not only to theology but to a philosophy that would examine them under the natural light of reason. The example he offers is a reflection on what it means to see the face of another person. In this sense, Marion argues, "Christian philosophy" compromises theology as much as philosophy, because its concept, the Incarnation, is intrinsically contrary. The acceptance of this scandal requires faith, but its acceptance makes it possible to "philosophize as a Christian." This proposal, startling in its inversion of the traditional relation of the elements of nature and grace as they are viewed working in Christian philosophy, is elaborated in Marion's careful consideration of four possible objections to it. He concludes with a hopeful suggestion that a Christian philosophy which is done by introducing and discovering phenomena that come from a heuristic of charity, as revealed in Christ but now inscribed historically in the world, could contribute in a determining way to a transformation of philosophy already under way at the close of our century which would restore its original dedication to "its forgotten ambition of loving wisdom."

PHILOSOPHIZING AS A CHRISTIAN

In the essay by Jean Ladrière the work of the symposium reaches its climax. Although its author would certainly dismiss any claim to finality or privileged uniqueness regarding methodology, the essay nevertheless earns by its performance our recognition of it as an exemplary fulfillment of the best legitimate hopes of all the participants. Gathering many of the themes of other speakers, Ladrière undertakes to lay out before us, not an argument for the possibility of a fully articulated and reconciled "Christian philosophy," but an enactment of that possibility in its basic and essential elements, fully self-conscious of its challenge and task, yet never allowing itself simply to rest in this awareness but pressing, almost relentlessly, onward to their realization. Here we have a warrant for the truth-claim of Christian philosophy, offered in the achievement of the harmony of *logos* and *ergon*, word and deed, which is the credential identified by Plato for recognizing the philosophical authenticity of Socratic existence: its manifest human integrity.

A CONCLUDING ROUNDTABLE DISCUSSION

Perhaps the most remarkable aspect of the symposium as an event was the way in which it concluded: with a gathering, indeed, of fragments, but fragments for which the participants found ample reason to be grateful. What they found and how it transformed their experience and opened their eyes to new possibilities for meaning in the question of Christian philosophy today is presented here in their own words.

IN RESPONSE

In place of a conclusion, and in the spirit of attempting to continue the conversation the symposium initiated, the final contribution to this volume is a paper inspired by and attempting to realize some of the promptings that I took from the proceedings. Entitled "On Seeing Fra Angelico's San Marco *Annunciation*: The Place of Art," it follows the example set by William Richardson in his "Back to the Future" presentation and begins with another painting, a fresco, that can be seen in the city of Florence. Using an explicitly interdisciplinary method, it offers a hermeneutic approach to understanding the "place" of art in human existence, exploring the possible philosophical significance of "Incarnation" for understanding more generally how the Divine "takes place" in history.

I
Evoking the Question

Giorgione: *The Three Ages of Man.* Pitti Gallery, Florence. Reproduced by permission.

1

Back to the Future?

William J. Richardson

FIRST A WORD OF *apologia*. When Frank Ambrosio first invited me to participate in a symposium on "The Question of Christian Philosophy Today," my first reaction was "Oh, no, not again—we have already been through that. Only a year ago an entire issue of *The Monist* was devoted to the problem [1992]. What more is there possibly to say?" But then the second paragraph of his letter read: "Specifically, I would invite you to deliver one of the opening addresses, the goal of which would be to evoke the question itself in its fullest and most radical terms and to bespeak its timeliness for the symposium audience." The task, then, would be not to answer the question but simply to formulate it "in its fullest and most radical terms." But this would mean confronting squarely my own initial resistance to the question which others might, indeed, share. Obviously, this was more than an invitation—it was a challenge, a challenge from which one could not walk away. But if, with whatever bravado, one says yes to such a challenge, one awakes the following morning with the frightening question: Good God, what have I said yes to? How can anyone do all that in a short space of time?

I dealt with the question, as one might expect, by ignoring it (though it never really went away), until a rainy day last spring in Paris. It was early one Friday afternoon, and the work of the week that brought me there had just been finished. What to do with the afternoon? On one hand, it was a golden opportunity (and foreseeably the only one, for I was about to return home) to see at the Grand Palais the celebrated exhibition "The Century of Titian: The Golden Age of Venetian Painting." On the other hand, this was not just any Friday—it happened to be Good Friday. In other times and climes, Good Friday had always been the

occasion for recollection and for rereading St. John's story of the
passion—of Jesus before Pilate, his last words on the cross, and
so forth. But this was a unique opportunity to see a unique exhibit, and there are worse ways of spending Good Friday than by
looking at how Titian and Tintoretto portray their vision of the
passion. So, with that little fix for my sense of guilt, off I went
to the Grand Palais.

The exhibition was extraordinary—the reviews, even in
America, had been glowing—but there was one painting in particular that captured me and drew me back again and again. It
was not, in fact, by Titian but by one of his contemporaries, a
certain Giorgio Barbarelli, better known simply as Giorgione.
The painting fascinated me—I didn't know why. It was only afterward, crossing the Seine on the way home—the same Seine
that the Romans knew (same and not the same, a river is a
river)—that I experienced a kind of epiphany. The rain had
stopped and the whole city was ablaze with sunshine. Behind me
was the Grand Palais and the Renaissance; in front was the gilded
dome of Napoleon's tomb covering the decayed remains of the
Enlightenment; to the right was the Eiffel Tower, monument to
the soaring hopes of science and technology; and down to the
east, the twin towers of Notre Dame that were already old and
weather-worn when Descartes was a little boy. Suddenly, in a
flash, I felt the way I imagine St. Thomas felt when he pounded
the table, saying, "That ought to settle the Albigensians," for I
punched the air and said, "That ought to settle Frank Ambrosio."

To try to evoke the question of Christian philosophy today "in
its fullest and most radical terms," I would like to recapture, if
possible, that moment and try to articulate the experience. But,
to do this, I must display the picture and let it serve as visual
metaphor for what I have to say. This means (alas!) resorting to
a visual aid. I do so with misgivings, for surely philosophers are
above such things as visual aids. Unfortunately, there is no other
way to say what I think should be said except within this frame.

The painting at the beginning of this essay hangs in the Pitti
Gallery (Florence) and is entitled *The Three Ages of Man*. My
strategy with regard to it is quite simple. I propose to talk about
the two figures on the right, then the one on the left: with regard

to the former I shall speak about Christian philosophy as an historical phenomenon; with regard to the latter, about the question
today. I shall conclude with a few remarks of my own that will
attempt no more than to let the question be a question.
First, an historical note. See in the painting, if you will, the
crest of Renaissance humanism in Italy: at the beginning of the
sixteenth century, while Giorgione and Titian were working in
Venice, Leonardo was in Milan, Michelangelo in Florence, and
Raphael in Rome. But they, and others like them, were only expressing in art form the exuberant, uninhibited delight in all
things human, typified by the celebrated hymn to the dignity of
human being (premodern, of course) by Pico della Mirandola as
he imagines God the Father saying to newly created Adam:

> I have set you [O Adam] at the center of the world, so that . . . the
> molder and maker of yourself, you may fashion yourself in what-
> ever form you shall prefer. . . . O supreme generosity of God the
> Father! O highest and marvelous felicity of man! To him it is
> granted to have whatever he chooses, to be whatever he wills.[1]

As for the painting itself, early critics saw in it the depiction
of a music lesson (music was a familiar theme for Giorgione
and resonated nicely with the Neoplatonic spirit of the age). The
musicality being discussed by the figures on the right would have
become meaningless to the old man, who would have lost his
ability to hear it. For my own part, the two figures on the right
suggest, rather, the whole complex nature of philosophy as *traditio* that, in fact, insinuated itself into Christian discipleship itself
as this was handed on from generation to generation.

If you can accept that conceit, the basic structure of the philosophical tradition, it seems to me, would remain constant while
the elements involved in it would vary greatly over time. One
could even conceive of divine revelation itself as following this
paradigm, where the disciple would be the believer (or the believing community), the master the Spirit of Jesus, and the text
the meaning of Christ's message in different moments of history.
The gesture would be pointing out, by whatever method the

---

[1] Cited in J. H. Plumb, *The Horizon Book of the Renaissance* (New York:
American Heritage, 1961), p. 330.

Spirit chooses to use, what Vatican II called "the signs of the times." In purely human (that is, philosophical) terms, the paradigm suggests, to me at least, the pedagogical (that is, radically interpersonal, dialogical, developmental) character of the philosophical *traditio*: there is the disciple, the master, his gesture of interpretation, and the text to be understood, sedimented, as it is, by a past, and to be revealed in its meaning for the present of any given period of time.

For primitive Christianity, philosophy—that is, the purely human search for wisdom as pursued by the Greeks—had no part in its pedagogy. We know that St. Paul dismissed it as "folly" (1 Cor. 1:20), but when it came time (as early as the second century) for Christians to understand their faith, to explain it and defend it against misconceptions, the apologetes—and after them, the Fathers generally—soon reached accommodation with the wisdom of the Greeks. Thus, St. Justin the Martyr describes how he had looked in vain for wisdom among the Greeks (Pythagoreans, Plato, Aristotle, Stoics), but found it only in the revelation of Christ, where he found unity in place of their fragmentation. For him, the role of master was played by the friends of Christ and by the prophets; the texts to be interpreted were the works of the Greek philosophers themselves, which took on adequate meaning for him only after his conversion. It was thus that he discovered that all truth, whatever is "well said," "belongs to us," that is, is seminated by Eternal Truth still to become Incarnate.[2] Thus, his *Second Apology* was the *magna charta* of a Christian humanism still in advent at the time.[3] But nary a word about "Christian philosophy."

In fact, the formula had no special cachet before the twentieth century in France. Even Pope Leo XIII, in his encyclical *Aeterni Patris* calling for a renewed study of St. Thomas, did not use the term, although his English translator, in supplying an English title for the encyclical ("Encyclical Letter on the Restoration of

---

[2] St. Justin Martyr, *La philosophie passe au Christ: L'oeuvre de Justin: Apologie I et II; Dialogue avec Tryphon* (Paris: Éditions de Paris, 1958), pp. 111–12.

[3] Étienne Gilson, *The Spirit of Mediaeval Philosophy* (New York: Charles Scribner's Sons, 1932), p. 27.

Christian Philosophy"), imputes it to him.[4] Let that suggest how for the contemporary mind the two were conjoined and Neoscholasticism was born.

"Christian philosophy" became a *cause célèbre* only after Émile Bréhier, the eminent historian, first in his *Histoire de la philosophie* (1927) and then in a series of lectures in Brussels entitled "Is There a Christian Philosophy?" answered with an unqualified *no*. Étienne Gilson, already preparing his Gifford Lectures that we know as *The Spirit of Mediaeval Philosophy*, responded with a roar, and the debate was on.

Gilson was an historian, and his research into the roots of Descartes had opened up for him the entire Middle Ages, especially the worlds of Augustine and Thomas Aquinas. Both of these, Gilson found, had his master (Augustine: Plotinus; Aquinas: Aristotle) whose distinct method helped each understand the texts that articulated the intellectual and spiritual crises of his time. Obviously, the two had much in common. If they differed, it was chiefly, it seems, in their conception of human nature. For Augustine, this was an historical concept—nature as he had experienced it and found it described by Paul, nature fallen and redeemed by grace which illumined the intelligence in such fashion that faith and reason functioned as one. For Thomas, it was a metaphysical concept, derived from Aristotle, permitting him to distinguish between nature and grace, reason and faith, philosophy and theology, where, by reason of that distinction, philosophy would enjoy a clear autonomy all its own.

Especially through Augustine, Aquinas, and their followers, Christianity did play a decisive role, Gilson argued, in the formation of certain new philosophical conceptions (for example, the idea of creation, of the person, and, somehow or other, of being itself as *esse*). Gilson's thesis, then, was clear: "I call Christian every philosophy which, although keeping the two orders [of faith and reason] formally distinct, nevertheless considers the Christian revelation as an indispensable auxiliary to reason."[5] "Indispensable auxiliary" here were the neuralgic words.

---

[4] Pope Leo XII, "*Aeterni Patris*: Encyclical Letter on the Restoration of Christian Philosophy," *One Hundred Years of Thomism: Aeterni Patris and Afterwards—A Symposium*, ed. V. C. Brezik (Houston: University of St. Thomas, Center for Humanistic Studies, 1981), p. 173.

[5] Gilson, *Spirit of Mediaeval Philosophy*, p. 37.

Mention should be made, too, of at least one other major figure in the controversy: Maurice Blondel. For Blondel, everything turns on reason's discovery of its own insufficiency, which leaves it open to receive divine revelation without being able to demand it as a right.[6] Whether or how God actually fills up that emptiness, philosophy by itself cannot say. Such would be the function of the "supernatural." Only a revelation by God could tell us about it—but this is where philosophy stops and faith begins. Is Blondel's thought here still philosophy rather than theology—albeit a Christian one? That became part of the debate. In any case, his position rallied to its support several wise heads who found it congruous not only with the tradition of Augustinian dynamism but also with the Thomistic notion of a natural desire for the beatific vision. At the very least, then, Blondel helped to nourish the subsequent controversy of the 1950s about the gratuity of the supernatural which culminated in Pope Pius XII's 1950 encyclical, Humani Generis.[7]

Gilson's position did not go unchallenged. The most representative voice of opposition was, perhaps, that of Fernand Van Steenberghen (Louvain). He saw the influence of Christianity on philosophy through its salutary effect on philosophers. First of all, for the Christian philosopher there is the help that grace brings to the exercise of his powers—"grace of office," as we say—to facilitate his endeavors. Psychologically speaking, there is the stimulus that comes to the philosopher from the new problems that faith poses: questions of creation, the soul, immortality, and so on. Furthermore, if fides quaerens intellectum characterizes the theologian's task, the philosopher is challenged to offer the theologian an efficient instrument to work with. Finally, faith offers the philosopher a constant point of reference on the journey—Leo XIII called it a "friendly star,"[8] to be understood at least in the negative sense: a sign that any philosophical position that in principle would exclude the possibility of faith has no

---

[6] See O. Blanchette, "Blondel's Original Philosophy of the Supernatural," p. 11 (typescript, 1993, Philosophy Department, Boston College, Chestnut Hill, Mass.).

[7] Pius XII, The Encyclical Humani Generis: With a Commentary by A. C. Cotler (Weston, Mass.: Weston College Press, 1951).

[8] Leo XIII, "Aeterni Patris," p. 182.

hope of success. In short, Christianity offers the philosopher a congenial ambience for her work, but this changes neither the principles nor the methods of her philosophizing. In a word, the influence of revelation upon philosophy is no more than indirect. For Van Steenberghen, "there are 'Christian philosophers' but [there is] no 'Christian philosoph[y].'"[9]

Such, in general terms, was the state of the question on the eve of World War II. Today, over fifty years later, after the further precisions by John Wippel, Leo Sweeney, Joseph Owens, Germain Grisez, and others, there seems little more to add. After the War, there was a new burst of philosophical energy. In France, a return to early Christian sources led by the Dominicans (Le Saulchoir) and the Jesuits (Fourvière), enhanced by Blondel's thinking, reinvigorated the nature/supernature debate. In Innsbruck and Rome, the impact of Maréchal's transcendental Thomism was beginning to be felt through the work of Rahner and Lonergan. In America, the leadership of Gilson was strongly felt through the influence of the Mediaeval Institute (Toronto) which reverberated broadly in the United States. In Louvain, where the Higher Institute of Philosophy was one of the first fruits of *Aeterni Patris*, there came to its traditional commitment to Aristotle, Thomas, and the philosophy of science a new opening toward the non-Scholastic, specifically phenomenological/ existential, world through the establishment of the Husserl Archives, under the vigorous leadership of Henry Van Breda. The delicate balance between respect for the old and attention to the new was brilliantly exemplified by the work of Albert Dondeyne, whose *Christian Faith and Contemporary Thought* (1958), responding to the challenge of Pius XII's *Humani Generis*, was the very model of astute Neo-Thomism opening its arms toward the thought of the day. For his readers Dondeyne became a master, as Thomas had been for him, showing by his own innovative gesture how a careful reading of new texts in conjunction with the old could be enlightening for both. In particular, Dondeyne's opening to phenomenology represented a breakthrough on two fronts: first, Dondeyne gave a new sense to Kant's Copernican

---

[9] Fernand Van Steenberghen, "La philosophie en chrétienté," *Revue Philosophique de Louvain*, 61 (1963): 577.

revolution, making it possible to understand the phenomenologist's claim that there is no world without human being, and no human being without the world—a position excoriated by some critics as "antirealist," but in a phenomenological perspective perfectly coherent and orthodox;[10] and, second, Dondeyne underlined the new importance of historicity in our thought processes, and, hence (by implication), the historicity of the truth they discern. At any rate, this kind of openness, together with a fresh spirit of ecumenism, encouraged Christian graduate students to specialize in non-Scholastic thinkers. Hegel, Husserl, Heidegger, Sartre, Merleau-Ponty, Wittgenstein, Whitehead, Peirce, James, and Dewey all became subjects for specialization. Most perceived this not as an abandonment of Scholasticism but, rather, as an effort to expand it. There was also a feeling of confidence that Thomism had come of age and was ready to engage in dialogue with non-Scholastic thought—not, indeed, to proselytize it but at least to mingle with it comfortably at convention smokers, if nowhere else.

As of 1960, then, Christian philosophy appeared to be largely a Western European—in fact, Roman Catholic—phenomenon that drew its strength from the metaphysical tradition of Neoscholastic Thomism but largely ignored, and was ignored by, the philosophical world of Anglo-American thought that surrounded it. That can no longer be said today. For now there is a strong Anglo-American form of Christian philosophy that must be accorded a highly respected place in any discussion of "Christian philosophy today." I am referring to a strictly American version that has emerged out of the Calvinist inspiration of the Dutch Reformed Church, and found institutional form in the rapidly growing membership of the Society of Christian Philosophers, with its official journal, *Faith and Philosophy*, giving ample evidence of the movement's intense intellectual vitality. To characterize the movement, I shall speak of one of its most illustrious members, whose work may be taken as representative of the direction that many others have been inspired to follow: Alvin Plantinga (John A. O'Brien Professor of Philosophy at the University of Notre Dame).

---

[10] Alvin Plantinga, "Augustinian Christian Philosophy," *The Monist*, 75 (1992): 300–302.

Plantinga is all American: American-born, -bred, and -trained. Coming from a devout Midwestern family, he did the bulk of his undergraduate work at Calvin College (Grand Rapids), where serious questions about how philosophy and religious faith relate to each other were an important part of his intellectual formation and reinforced a deeply personal religious commitment. Graduate study began at Michigan and ended at Yale, where the richly diversified department of the 1950s left him well trained but cool, to say the least, toward what he experienced as "metaphysics." But his personal philosophical style did not develop until his first teaching job at Wayne State University. There, young, enthusiastic colleagues whose formation bore the marks of Wittgenstein, Chisolm, Wilfrid Sellars, and the like helped him find his own way to "do what philosophers do" with hard-bitten rigor and analytic cogency.

In his published research, Plantinga has pursued his abiding religious concerns under the guise of a philosophical theology and apologetics. In his first book, *God and Other Minds*, for example, he argues that it is as epistemologically respectable to believe in the existence of God as it is to believe in the existence of other minds. To the objection that the fact of evil in the world is logically inconsistent with the existence of a good God he responds that this would be the case only if this good God had not chosen to create human beings capable of free choice (the so-called Free Will Defense of God's existence). Inevitably, this opens up the whole problem of God's concurrence with free acts, his knowledge of counterfactuals ("futuribles," as the metaphysical tradition used to call them), and, eventually (at least in the debates that followed), the whole problematic of "middle science" in God, thus resurrecting the Molina–Bañez debate of the sixteenth century (which metaphysicians had thought was safely resting in peace), examined now logically with new and pressing relevance.

Plantinga's master of preference in all this, he tells us, is John Calvin. Calvin's postulate, deriving from a long Augustinian tradition, was that God has implanted in humankind a tendency, or *nisus*, to believe in him: "There is within the human mind, and indeed by natural instinct, an awareness of divinity . . . a tacit confession of a sense of deity inscribed in the hearts of all."[11] Accordingly, belief in the existence of God, in the right circumstances, would be as "natural" as belief in the truths of logic.[12] Given this much, the task of Christian philosophers would be to use all their resources, including what comes from Christian teaching, to explore the philosophical depths of the Christian experience: for instance, epistemic problems (problems of knowledge, of belief, of warrant and justification); the nature of mind; the question of God and his attributes, his knowledge and power; the nature of nature and the laws of human conduct; the meaning of causality, of necessity, and so on[13]—in short, all the problems of the most classical metaphysics, thought through, however, in the Augustinian mode according to a new and very powerful, nonmetaphysical method. And presiding over all this is the single question with which the entire enterprise began: What difference does being a Christian make to being a philosopher today?

Taken in the sum, then, what can be said of Christian philosophy as a phenomenon of history? Incubated within a faith that sought an intelligence of itself, it was through the nourishment of that faith in Thomas Aquinas that philosophy awoke to the possibilities of its own autonomy. The meaning of that autonomy will be understood differently in keeping with the way one understands the notion of human nature itself, whether according to Augustine, or Aquinas, or Gilson, or Blondel, or Calvin. Its exercise would vary according to the charism of the thinker, the principal master he chooses, the texts on which he meditates, and the methodology he follows. The autonomy of Christian philosophizing, then, could, in principle, adapt to almost any style of philosophical thinking, provided the process not exclude the faith that first nurtured it. Such a style could be historical research (Gilson), speculative metaphysics (Rahner, Lonergan, Blondel), hermeneutics (Ricoeur, Gadamer), existentialism (Marcel), transcendental reflection (Maréchal), phenomenology (Dondeyne), dialectical thinking (Fessard), logical analysis/metaphysics

---

[11] John Calvin, *Institutes of the Christian Religion*, trans. F. L. Battles (Philadelphia: Westminster, 1960), I.iii.43–44.

[12] See Alvin Plantinga, "Advice to Christian Philosophers," *Journal of Christian Philosophers*, 1 (1984): 262.

[13] See Plantinga's "Augustinian Christian Philosophy," 308–12.

(Plantinga), or any other form one may wish to mention. The issues that could engage this autonomy are as broad as Christian humanism itself (*homo sum, humani nil a me alienum* [Terence]), but, in terms of urgency, some are more pressing than others (what makes a human being human? and when? how can it possibly relate to God? and so forth). Taking all this together, can we call this set "Christian philosophy"? Certainly not, if by philosophy we mean some kind of monolith. Instead of "Christian philosophy," let us speak rather of the unity of Christian philosophizing: the unity comes from the truth that is sought, whether through the light of revelation or of reason or, in fact, of both— truth that every Christian believes can never be untrue to itself. Its diversity would come from the kaleidoscopic, kerygmatic, not to say kairotic, gifts of those who pursue it.

If Christian philosophy be conceived this broadly, in what sense is it in question today? That is what we have to ask the old man, for the question is in his eyes. What do those eyes tell us?

To begin with, how old is he? Well, he's not *that* old—age is a state of mind. But he has seen a lot more than the other two, and that's what makes the difference. He knew the 1950s and the echoes of *Humani Generis*. He has been through the 1960s—has seen not just the assassinations, the VietnamWar and the turmoil, but Vatican II, *Humanae Vitae*, the break in the phalanx of the Roman Catholic consensus whereby Thomistic Neoscholasticism began to lose its place of privilege as the sole bastion of Christian philosophizing. The diversity of the 1950s begot a new pluralism; the quest for historicity discovered in hermeneutics a new methodology to legitimize it; theologians began to exercise an unaccustomed eclecticism (Kant, Fichte, Schelling, Hegel, Husserl, Heidegger, Whitehead, even Karl Marx—all became legitimate dialogue partners); new questions demanded new answers, such as those concerning the role of Marxism in effective social change, the demands of feminism, the expectations of multiculturalism. All this the old man has seen. During the 1970s and 1980s he watched the struggles over dissent within the Roman Church; now in the 1990s he is aware that another encyclical, *The Splendor of Truth* has appeared (more recently, *Faith and Reason*), and with them come new challenges to the autonomy of Christian philosophizing about what makes human beings human, what constitutes the law of their nature, and so on. All this the old man is aware of as he looks toward those who pose the question of Christian philosophy today: he has been chastened by time. What, then, is said by his eyes? I guess each must read it for him- or herself. For my part, I do not see him turning away from the other two in a spirit of disapproval. Rather, there is something compassionate, perhaps even protective, in the look. Certainly, he would have no time for triumphalism or complacency on their part, or for a cronyism that would be content to talk *about* the modern world but only *to* one another—but I see no disaffection in his eyes.

Nor is he turning away, I take it, because he has become tone deaf to their harmonies. Rather, he seems to be attuned to other sounds, the dissonant sounds/signs of the times—our times, no longer modern but postmodern times. For whatever is to be said about the sociology of the 1960s, philosophically speaking, the most decisive movement of the past thirty years has been, I submit, the shift toward what the jargon of the day in America calls "postmodern" thinking. What does that mean? Unfortunately, all we can do briefly is evoke a vague sense of it. Originally "postmodern" referred to a literary, architectural, artistic movement. In terms of philosophy, the best approximation is to recall the history of autonomous reason from Descartes to Jürgen Habermas which is referred to normally as "modernity": it is marked by the celebration of *logos*/reason as a kind of gathering into one. Its ideals are unity, continuity, clarity, identity, order, system, totality, closure. Postmodernity, whether in the form of art, literature, architecture, or philosophy, would be, as I understand it, the inversion—even the subversion—of all that. It celebrates disunity, discontinuity, difference, disorder, undecidability, incompleteness, the impossibility of anything's being whole. I suspect that the old man is deeply aware of this mindset, and one of the questions to be read in his eyes would be: How do you Christian philosophers respond to the challenge of postmodern thought? For every aspect of the constellation on the right has, in the era of postmodernism, come under attack. Let me try to suggest the dimensions of the problem by polarizing a

few brief remarks around three elements of that constellation that
we have already been contemplating: the text under discussion,
the personal nature of the subjects involved in the dialogue, and
the demonstrative gesture of the master that suggests the function
of metaphysical thinking in the Christian tradition.

First, the text! Text, and textuality, and contextuality have
taken on new meaning since philosophy (and literary theory)
have made the so-called "linguistic turn" in our thinking. The
major figure here is Jacques Derrida, and the term that characteristically identifies his thought is *deconstruction*. The term reveals
the fundamental influence of Heidegger on him. As a general
context, recall how the later Heidegger began to think Being as
Language in its origins. "Deconstruction" is Derrida's translation of Heidegger's earlier term, *Destruktion*, Heidegger's attempt to retrieve in the history of metaphysics the primordial
experience of Being, out of which metaphysics arose. For Derrida, what had to be deconstructed was metaphysics as centered
in the notion of being as presence, being understood as something static, immobile, monolithic. Metaphysics is a "centrism,"
then, which he designated (because of the importance of the
Greek *logos* [reason/language] for metaphysics) as "logocen-
trism." Language plays a central role in all this, but logocen-
trism, he observed, showed a striking tendency, from Plato on,
to consider spoken language as somehow more fundamental than
written language. This is manifest as well in Saussure, the father
of contemporary structural linguistics. Studying Saussure, Derrida could easily accept Saussure's conception of language as a
system of signs, distinguished from one another always and only
by their mutual opposition to—that is, *difference* from—each
other. But a closer analysis, especially of Saussure's understanding of the relation between language as spoken and language as
written, permitted Derrida to suggest a new way to think about
language in still more radical fashion as a primordial kind of
writing:

This concept can be called *gram* or *différance*. The play of differences supposes, in effect, syntheses and referrals which forbid, at
any moment or in any sense, that a simple element be *present* in
and of itself, referring only to itself. Whether in the order of spo-

ken or written discourse, no element can function as a sign without referring to another element which itself is not simply present. This interweaving results in each "element"—phoneme or grapheme—being constituted on the basis of the trace within it of the other elements of the chain or system. This interweaving, this textile, is the text produced only in the transformation of another text. Nothing, neither among the elements nor within the system, is anywhere ever simply present or absent. There are only, everywhere, differences and traces of traces.[14]

Différance here is spelt with an *a* instead of an *e* (notice that one can't detect that by sound but only by sight) to suggest that, derived from the Latin *differre*, *différance* means both "differ" and "defer," that is, "displace." The work of deconstruction, then, would be to read texts of whatever kind in the light of the *différance* out of which they are woven:

[In deconstruction] I try to respect as rigorously as possible the internal, regulated play of philosophemes or epistimemes by making them slide—without mistreating them—to the point of their nonpertinence, their exhaustion, their closure. To "deconstruct" philosophy, thus, would be to think—in the most faithful, interior way—the structured genealogy of philosophy's concepts, but at the same time to determine—from a certain exterior that is unqualifiable or unnameable by philosophy—what this history has been able to dissimulate or forbid, making itself into a history by means of this somewhere motivated repression.[15]

The consequences of this endeavor are far-reaching. The "economy" of *différance* is irreducible. It has no center, it has no author, it precedes all signifiers. As for what is signified by these signs (that is, meaning), any conception of stability or identifiable unity of meaning is dismissed as the seductive lure of the metaphysics of presence. Hence, the perennial hope of such a metaphysics to discern some meaning independent of all function of language is an impossible—though perhaps inevitable—dream.

The "rationality" . . . which governs a writing thus enlarged and radicalized, no longer issues from a logos. Further, it inaugurates

[14] Jacques Derrida, *Positions*, trans. A. Bass. (Chicago: The University of Chicago Press, 1981), p. 26.
[15] Ibid., p. 6.

the destruction, not the demolition but the de-sedimentation, the de-construction, of all significations that have their source in that of the logos. Particularly the signification of *truth*.[16]

What is left of truth, then, when deconstruction is over? Derrida admits, after putting in question the "value of truth" in all its forms (that is, as conformity, as certitude, as *aletheia*, etc.), that we nonetheless "must have [it]."[17] "Paraphrasing Freud, speaking of the present/absent penis (but it is the same thing), we must recognize in truth 'the normal prototype of the fetish.' How can we do without it?"[18]

If the old man, concerned about Christian philosophy, looks into the future and sees this happening to the texts by which it is constituted, is it any wonder that there is a troubled question in his eyes?

But there is another question there, too. It concerns the nature of those who engage in the reading of texts. For the Christian tradition, disciple and master are understood as persons, that is, autonomous subjects—not as Pico della Mirandola would understand that term, but, rather, in the sense that Christian humanism gives to it today. But for the postmodern mind, the human subject itself is under attack. For Derrida, if *différance* is irreducible, then without an author it is without a subject, too, if by subject one understands a conscious, speaking subject. For a self-conscious subject would be one that is present to itself and that could appear at best only as an effect of *différance*:

> The subject, and first of all the conscious and speaking subject, depends upon the system of differences and the movement of *différance*; . . . the subject is not present, nor above all present to itself before *différance*; . . . the subject is constituted only in being divided from itself, in becoming space, in temporizing, in deferral.[19]

Under pressure, Derrida will claim that he has never denied the existence of the subject but has sought only to probe the suppositions that the notion of *différance* illumines about the subject's

---

[16] Jacques Derrida, *Of Grammatology*, trans. G. Spivak (Baltimore: The John Hopkins University Press, 1974), p. 10.
[17] Derrida, *Positions*, p. 105.
[18] Ibid.
[19] Ibid., p. 29.

relation to the other-than-itself. But even if the subject be conceived as the transitional focal point of self-differentiating *différance*, how much stability can this ongoing self-deferral have to
engage in serious dialogue or commit itself to a search for a truth
that is anything more than a fetish?

But the postmodern assault on the subject does not come simply from the slippage of deconstruction. It comes also from Michel Foucault. By his archaeological and genealogical analyses
of discursive practices in society, he moves away from self-cen-
tered language toward an impersonal perspective in which the
notion of a constituting ego becomes inessential. For Foucault,
"Humanism represented the incarceration of human beings
within a specifically modern system of thought and practice that
had become so intimately a part of them that it was no longer
experienced as a series of confinements but was embraced as the
very substance of being human."[20] In this way Foucault's thought
becomes "antihumanist." And he confidently predicted that our
present understanding of man would prove to be a transient one,
doomed to "be erased, like a face drawn in sand at the edge of
the sea."[21]

And postmodern antihumanism comes in a still different guise
from those whose claim it is to probe the deepest dimension of
the subject—the unconscious. I am speaking of Freud and his
most representative contemporary interpreter, Jacques Lacan.
Freud's great discovery, and it has marked the entire century,
was that there is another center of human experience besides the
conscious one, and this other center, the unconscious, according
to Lacan, is structured like a language. The conscious subject,
then, would be spoken by this Other of language; indeed, the
subject is conceived to be an effect of the language of the unconscious. But this language is ultimately just a chain of signifiers
that has no unity of its own and cannot bestow unity on a subject.
For him, a subject is that which is referred by a signifier to another signifier.[22] All experience of unity in the subject is, in La-

---

[20] J. Bernauer, *Michel Foucault's Force of Flight: Toward an Ethics for
Thought* (Atlantic Highlands, N.J.: Humanities Press, 1990), pp. 8–9.
[21] Michel Foucault, *The Order of Things: An Archaeology of the Human Sciences* (New York: Pantheon, 1971), p. 387.
[22] See Jacques Lacan, *Écrits* (Paris: Seuil, 1966), p. 840.

can's terminology, "imaginary." We get a sense of Lacan's own acceptance of this dis-unified, antihumanistic subject from the following:

> If I am a psychoanalyst, I am also a man, and as a man my experience has shown me that the principle characteristic of my own human life, and, I am sure, that of the people who are here . . . is that life is something which goes, as we say in French, *à la dérive.* Life goes down the river, from time to time touching a bank, staying for a while here and there, without understanding anything. . . . The idea of a unifying unity of the human condition has always had on me the effect of a scandalous lie.[23]

Another question in the old man's eyes, then: How can a Christian philosophy ever come to grips with the radical antihumanism of postmodern thinking?

But the part of the postmodern mind most disconcerting for the Christian philosopher is its antimetaphysical bias. Let the role of metaphysics in Christian thinking be suggested by the demonstrative gesture of the master, for the philosophical style that has characterized the Continental tradition of Christian philosophizing has been most often, though not always, metaphysical. The dominant figure here in the attack on metaphysics is Heidegger. Perhaps the best way to understand him in the present context is to recall his explicit criticism of the very notion of Christian philosophy.

In the opening session of his 1935 lecture course published as *Introduction to Metaphysics* (1935)—shortly after the debate in France had appeared in print—Heidegger was attempting to introduce his listeners to his own question about the meaning of Being as different from beings (what he called the ontological difference) by recalling the question with which he had closed his lecture "What is Metaphysics?" and which had been formulated by Leibniz: "Why are there beings at all, and why not rather nothing?" For Leibniz, the question was, indeed, a metaphysical question: What is the bedrock foundation among beings

---

[23] Jacques Lacan, "Of Structure as an Inmixing of an Otherness," in *The Structuralist Controversy: The Languages of Criticism and the Sciences of Man,* ed. R. Mackey and E. Donato (Baltimore: The Johns Hopkins University Press, 1972), p. 190.

for the existence of other beings?—and the answer would be some supreme being that served somehow as ground for all the rest. It was this metaphysical question à la Leibniz that a believing Christian, as believing, Heidegger claims, could never pose:

> Anyone for whom the Bible is divine revelation and truth has the answer to the question "Why are there beings rather than nothing?" even before it is asked: everything that is, except God himself, has been created by Him. . . . One who holds to such faith can in a way participate in the asking of our question, but he cannot really question without ceasing to be a believer and taking all the consequences of such a step. He will only be able to act "as if."[24]

From the standpoint of faith, then, Leibniz's question is "foolishness," but philosophy is this very foolishness. "Christian philosophy," then, is *ein hölzernes Eisen*—"iron [made of] wood," a contradiction in terms. Really to ask the philosophical question signifies: "a daring attempt to fathom this unfathomable question by disclosing what it summons us to ask, to push our questioning to the very end. Where such an attempt occurs, there is philosophy."[25] The point is clear, but, for my own part, I have never found it absolutely decisive. For when, a few pages later, Heidegger defines what he means by "question," he defines it as "to will [not 'wish'] to know," where "to will" means "to be resolved" (*Entschlossenheit*), and "to know" means "to be able to stand in the truth, . . . to stand in the manifestness of beings, to endure [*bestehen*] them."[26] If to question is to will-to-know, in this sense—that is, to be resolved to stand in the truth of beings—why is it impossible for a believer (like Aquinas versus the Albigensians) to will-to-know as radically, albeit differently, as one who does not believe?

Heidegger's position here does not proceed from any disrespect for religious faith or for a conceptualizing reflection upon it that we call "theology." Faith, as he understands it, is not a set of doctrines but a life, a new life lived in union with the crucified

---

[24] Martin Heidegger, *Introduction to Metaphysics*, trans. R. Manheim (New Haven, Conn.: Yale University Press, 1959), p. 7.
[25] Ibid., p. 8.
[26] Ibid., pp. 20–21.

God. Reflection on such a life will develop its own form of conceptuality that, however systematic it may become, will remain as historical and factical as the life itself.[27] But for this it does not need the structure that philosophy supplies. This is an old thesis of Heidegger's. In a course called "Introduction to the Phenomenology of Religion" (1920–21), he had focused on the factical, performative, historical aspect of the faith of the early Christians, lived in the imminent expectation of Christ's second coming (for example, 1 Thess. 4:13ff.). The following semester, in a course called "Augustine and Neoplatonism" (1921), he showed how Augustine articulates the performance character of that life through the analysis of time in the tenth book of the *Confessions* but later resorts to Neoplatonic metaphysical language that freezes life into a kind of static endurance. For example, Augustine talks about "beatitude" as a *fruitio Dei* in a kind of eternal repose. But "if the experience of God is interpreted as *fruitio Dei*, if God is 'enjoyed' as the 'rest' of the heart, then it is forced out of the unrest of the factical-historical life and frozen in the vitality that [makes it what it is]."[28]

Early in his career, then, Heidegger took metaphysics, as he understood metaphysics, to be the natural enemy of theology, as he understood theology, and we understand better how for him Christian philosophy could be a contradiction in terms. It becomes an easy step to see how he would claim that Aristotle's definition of metaphysics as the question about "beings as beings" was fundamentally ambiguous. It could mean the question about "beings" in their generality (that is, ontology) or about beings in their ultimate ground (that is, a supreme being of some kind) (that is, theology) and so is onto-theo-logical in its very structure. The question, "Why are there beings at all and why not rather nothing?" is an ontotheological one; the god in question is the god of philosophers, not at all the one "before whom David danced," God of faith. Heidegger's own question is other: Whence comes the ontotheological structure of metaphysics in

---

[27] Heidegger, *Phänemenologie und Theologie* (Frankfurt: Klostermann, 1970), pp. 23–26.
[28] See O. Pöggler, *Martin Heidegger's Path of Thinking*, trans. D. Magurshak and S. Barber (Atlantic Highlands, N.J.: Humanities Press, 1987), p. 28.

the first place? How does it emerge out of Being in the temporality of its self-disclosure, itself emerging from a still more original
Event (*Ereignis*), the Event that appropriates Being to Time and
Time to Being through what has been disclosed to us as the ep-
ochal history of ontotheology? How can Christian philosophy
survive all that? How do Christian philosophers think about the
relation between the Incarnate Word of their religious faith and
the Event of the ontological difference? This, I suggest, is a third
question that may be found in the old man's eyes.

To be complete, we should show how these concepts, characteristic, to be sure, of Continental thought, are instantiated in the
American context under the guise of contemporary liberalism,
but that is a vast subject better left for another day. The challenge
to Christian philosophy that the old man sees is, I think, that of
the postmodern mind, but in fairness we should admit that not
everyone agrees it is worth responding to. Some might say that
postmodernism is a fad that, like other fads, will pass. The autonomy of Christian philosophers should make them independent,
too, of fads. In his inaugural address as O'Brien Professor of
Philosophy at Notre Dame, Plantinga had this advice for Christian philosophers:

> Christian philosophers are the philosophers of the Christian com-
> munity. But the Christian community has its own questions, its
> own concerns, its own topics for investigation, its own agenda and
> its own research program. Christian philosophers ought not merely
> take their inspiration from what's going on [elsewhere], attractive
> and scintillating as that may be. . . . If they devote their best efforts
> to the topics fashionable in the non-Christian philosophical world,
> they will neglect a crucial and central part of their task as Christian
> philosophers.[29]

In fact, Plantinga had other philosophical fads in mind, but
there is good reason to believe he would feel the same way today
about postmodernism. In any case, I cite him because that is a
defensible position to take and a caution that should be heard.
For my own part, I believe that postmodernism is more than a
fad. The floodwaters have run too high and spread too far for us

---

[29] "Advice to Christian Philosophers," 255.

to expect that, if and when they recede, the old familiar terrain will ever look the same again. There are few areas of contemporary thought that have not been affected by it, from theology to the philosophy of science. And if we don't feel ready to tangle with the high priests of this movement from Nietzsche to Lyotard, at the very least we are challenged to rethink those effects and reformulate our responses to them in areas of our immediate concern. There is a put-up or shut-up element in the old man's eyes that challenges us both as philosophers and as Christians, and refuses to let us walk away from a meeting like this with no more than a nostalgic pledge of allegiance to a lovely idea whose time is gone.

In saying this, I do not mean to imply that no one has addressed the problems I mention. In fact, some of the most creative thinkers in this area are members of this symposium and we will have the opportunity to hear directly about their work. If I may allude to one in particular, I hope without embarassment, it would be to Professor Jean-Luc Marion, whose work most directly relates to the perspective I have been presenting. In *God Without Being*, a book well known in Europe but only recently available in English,[30] he squarely addresses the question with which I concluded my remarks about Heidegger: How are we to think the God of the Christian faith in reference to ontotheology and the Event of the ontological difference? He argues that philosophical concepts concerning the "God" of the metaphysical tradition have indeed served as idols of one sort or another. But the anti-idolatrous thrust of a genuine Judaeo-Christian experience run profoundly counter to such language—in fact, counter to the language of the ontological difference as such, helpless as it is to articulate what in its own terms is admittedly unthinkable. Words like "is" and "being" do not, cannot, pertain to this God as revealed. He is not only beyond metaphysics but also beyond the ontological difference, and must be thought of simply as "God without Being."

To emphasize the point visually, Marion writes God thus conceived with a St.-Andrew's cross superimposed upon it: God-

---

[30] Trans. Thomas A. Carlson (Chicago: The University of Chicago Press, 1992).

the crossed-out [of ontological difference] God. Since, for the Christian believer, this God is also the Word of the Father who died on a cross, the crossed-out God is also the cruci-fied God, the same as he of whom John writes, "God is love" (1 John 4:8). When Marion comes to articulate his conception of this God, he meditates the notion of God as *agape*: love is pure giving, and human being, in responding, need not "think" through the idols of philosophical thought but simply accept this love in return. This has become possible through the God-Man who was nailed to a cross, of whom John writes, "God is love" (1 John 4:8). Marion's analysis permits him, then, to distinguish between the giving of Christian *agape* (where words like "is" and "being" are meaningless) and the giving (*es gibt*) of Heidegger's appropriative Event. This whole move is a tour de force that we can't follow further, but it is a full-scale assault on the problem the old man sees. The question it leaves us with, though, is this: What has become of the autonomy of philosophy? Are we back with Augustine doing theology again as *fides quaerens intellectum?*

But that permits the old man's eyes to say: So what? What difference would that make anyway . . . today . . . in parlous times like our own? So, to end as we began, I would like to take one more step in the direction that Marion's proposal has opened up and return again to the pattern of discipleship on the right to think of the master again as the Spirit of Jesus, pointing out for the Christian philosopher the meaning of another text that has become part of the liturgy of Good Friday, also taken from St. John. It reads:

> "So you are a king, then," said Pilate. . . . "Yes, I am a king. I was born for this, I came into the world for this: to bear witness to the truth; and all who are on the side of truth listen to my voice. [or: For all who are on the side of truth, it is my voice that they hear]" [John 18:33–38].

In the simplest terms, I take this to mean that, for the Christian, the original "splendor of truth" is the Incarnate Word, the Suffering Servant standing before Pilate. Any search for truth is a search for him, who, the previous evening, had said simply, "I am the truth" (and "way" and "life") (John 14:6). Any discovery of truth, then, is somehow an identification with him, whether or not this is announced, or recognized, or even intended. This is the case, of course, for any searcher anywhere and pertains rather to the *noema* of the Christian revelation. In the noetic order and more precisely, the Christian philosopher would be one who acknowledges this fact, accepts it as a statement of his or her faith and a sign of—and sign on (like the St. Andrew's cross)—the meaning of his or her work. This fact would be the "friendly star" Leo XIII spoke of—a negative guide, to be sure, but, positively too, a reminder that human truth of whatever kind is a sign that the Incarnate Word is there. To search for truth as a Christian philosopher, utilizing all the tools of one's trade, is to make a profession out of bearing witness to Jesus's own witness to truth. The tools of the trade include all the discipline of method, precision in understanding, and rigor of criticism of which one is capable. And it is through the use of these tools that the philosopher assumes the responsibility for the autonomy that makes us what we are.

If we could accept this conception of what it means to philosophize as Christians, we would have, I suggest, a fresh context within which to deal with some of the issues facing us today. For one thing, it would be unnecessary to identify some unity of philosophical thought as Christians by expanding a synthesis already achieved; such a unity to be sought lies in the truth of the Incarnate Word, always already in advent. For the *traditio* of Christian philosophizing must be thought as coming not out of the past but out of the future and through the past. That is why Christian thinkers may be untroubled by charges of "creative antirealism" or "historical relativism," for adventive thinking like Dondeyne's can find in the efforts of contemporary thinkers whatever truth may be gleaned from them, however subtle or hidden it may be. This is the way that truth itself may be thought in its historicity without our losing all sense of its absoluteness. The classic philosophical problems that have occupied Christian thinkers over the years (for example, the human being–God relationship, with all that this implies) would lose none of their vigor; they would simply become historically contextualized and need to be rethought with a fresh conceptuality, chastened by— even enriched by—the critique of a metaphysics of presence.

This conception of philosophizing as Christians would permit us to live peacefully with a peculiar paradox of our time that sees the distinction between philosophy and theology understood and respected, but at the same time somehow transcended, when it sees a first-class philosopher like Jean-Luc Marion end up doing theology and a first-class theologian like Michael Buckley in his comprehensive study, *At the Origins of Modern Atheism*,[31] end up doing, in effect, philosophy. Calling it "philosophical theology" does not make it any less philosophical for that. But whichever hat each wears, the effort, given the complexity of the issues, is a joint one in a diversified but common endeavor to move slowly toward the articulation of one ultimate truth, which can never be contained in any set of formal propositions, no matter who articulates them.

Finally, this conception of Christian philosophizing as bearing philosophical witness to the truth of the Incarnate Word permits us to acknowledge as specifically Christian the work of those whose energies are absorbed in discerning the elusive truth in non-Christian thought, such as, in our day, is called "postmodernism." They are not dispensed, of course, from the critical function of the philosophical enterprise, but their first task is to make this truth accessible to other philosophers in the Christian community so that these, in turn, may examine its promise. That is one more advantage to philosophizing as a Christian: the endeavor belongs to an entire community of thinkers whose unity is based on the belief that it is the Incarnate Word who really is truth in its ultimacy, a truth that is always already still to come.

That is the essential of what I wanted to say. But will it "settle" Frank Ambrosio? Probably not! It may, indeed, rather unsettle him, for I suspect he would like to have heard something more (or at least different) about what Christian philosophers should be doing in their courses in order to transmit "Christian values," or what be the orientation of philosophy departments should be in those colleges and universities that call themselves "Christian" today. But those are curriculum issues or policy issues that concern not simply Christian philosophy but Christian humanism as such and the role that philosophy plays in its transmission.

---

[31] (New Haven, Conn.: Yale University Press, 1987).

These are important questions, appropriately raised at Georgetown University, the oldest of such institutions in America still
making the claim today, itself heir to a special educational tradition whose ideal was to preserve the best of Renaissance humanism as defined, not by a vision of the First Adam, fantasized by
Pico della Mirandola, but in terms of the Person of the Second
Adam, the Suffering Servant, the "splendor of truth" as he stands
before Pilate in the Gospel according to John.

But these are other questions, larger questions, than the "willing to know" that concerns this symposium. They must be left
for another venue. For now, the question seems clear enough: it
lies in the old man's eyes. Why this resistance to the question? I
guess because the eyes are so relentlessly penetrating. I resist
being looked at in that way and asked so directly: Well and good,
but what about you? Where do you stand? Or will you walk
away?

But I was asked to evoke the question, not to answer it. That is
what a symposium is for. For my part, I must settle for small
gains and be content with that: to describe one glittering moment
while crossing the Seine, with Notre Dame down toward the east,
and talk about pictures in a gallery . . . on a Good Friday afternoon.

QUESTIONS AND ANSWERS

Q: I thought that your talk went really not to the heart of the
matter but to the absolute extreme of what is possible for a Christian philosophy. And I was absolutely fascinated by this, but I
have two questions: They are innocent questions.*
    The first one is about what you would call modernity, and the
second about postmodernism. Now, about the modern period,
you said that perhaps we should speak not about Christian philosophy, because it becomes such a multifarious, analogous concept, but about Christian philosophizing. But then my question
is, What is the difference between this kind of Christian philoso-

---

* Editor's note: As becomes clear in the following remarks, the questioner is
one of the symposium speakers, Louis Dupré.

phizing and someone who is simply a Christian and who does philosophy? To make it more concrete: the example of our illustrious teacher Dondeyne—what did he accomplish? You said he expanded Neoscholasticism. Indeed he did, to a point where there was no Neoscholasticism left when he was through with it. I went into Marx, you went into Heidegger, others went into Merleau-Ponty. What had this to do with Christian philosophy? Nothing! We were Christians. I wish I were a Christian philosopher, but I'm not. I'm a Christian who philosophizes, and I don't think that is really the question of Christian philosophy.

The second question involves a clarification about postmodernism. I obviously liked very much what you said, particularly at the end; I found this very moving personally. But one can go along with the other [postmodernism] only so long, and beyond a certain point names lose their meaning, including the name of Christian philosophy. In this case, not so much the word *Christian* as the word *philosophy*.

Let me just refer to one concrete example that you brought up, and please correct me if I misinterpret you, because that might well be the case. Let us take first the case of Derrida: the notion of *différance*, a deferral, which you point to as central in your exposition of Derrida. Now, I see this, not as something postmodern in the sense of antimodern, but as the extreme of modernity, because what we have in the notion of *différance*, if I understand it correctly, is a constant deferral from one to the other in a world that remains absolutely closed, where there is no room for transcendence whatsoever. I don't mind that the subject is abolished because that is the original sin of modernism, of modernity, and I think that postmodernism rightly reacts to that. But I am afraid of postmodernism when it has reduced everything, not to a subject and its achievements, but to the achievement itself. I think that is already started with Marx, who said, "Let us do away with this romantic talk about the self. Let us look at the *praxis*." Well, here we have the *praxis*, we have the closed universe in which we operate. But there is no we and there is no I.

I wonder how far you can go along with that—not just with Derrida; you give other examples—without giving up the notion of philosophy, in this case Christian philosophy, for something else? It is not enough, it seems to me, that we say, in the face of a postmodernist philosophy that breaks down any kind of metaphysical barriers, that nothing is left except the crucified God. This is an act of faith, but this is not philosophy. You and I draw a salary for teaching philosophy, but, more important, you and I are Christians who are trying to do philosophy, and this is our vocation. The question is, At what point does that vocation lose its meaning by giving in to something of which we must say: this is so absolutely different from what we set out to do that we no longer understand how it could possibly be congruous with the very notion of philosophy in a sense that makes a Christian philosophy possible? As I said, this is not a criticism, but a question.

A: I understand. Your questions are very relevant, and I appreciate the justice of them. I'll try to respond. Basically, you asked three questions. First, with regard to the modern period and Dondeyne's openness to it: What is left? He liquidated Neo-scholasticism, you claim. The second refers to postmodernism and our relationship to it, for example, in Derrida. Third, you talk about the personal responsibility of each of us as teachers of philosophy and as Christians.

I tried to address those, perhaps not precisely enough. With regard to the openness of Scholasticism, this was a response of which Dondeyne was an example (although there are certainly others at Louvain and elsewhere, but he is the most striking one), in which there was an openness to the world that philosophy, specifically phenomenology, made available, and he discerned that there was truth in phenomenology. His response to that was to discern as best he could and make that truth available to others. He was not responsible for the destiny of the world or for the work of the Holy Spirit; he was not responsible for what happened in the course of history. The best he could do—and it was already a great deal—was to read St. Thomas, read Merleau-Ponty, and try to find some accommodation between them. To the extent that he discerned truth and revealed it to others, that's already an achievement. And without that openness, who knows where you or I would be at the moment? We cannot measure futuribles, of course, but the fact of the matter is whatever has been done through us over the years owes a large debt to people like Dondeyne who opened us up to other worlds, and to the truth of other worlds.

In the last part, I was trying to make room for the fact that access to the truth, provided it's undertaken as a profession of commitment to the Incarnate Word of truth, is enough to make one a Christian philosopher. I was trying to make room precisely for those who would not call themselves such, but whose work is profoundly coherent with the insights of Christian philosophy insofar as their work has made accessible to us the contemporary world. Though it's presumptuous perhaps to say so, I'm not sure that Paul Ricoeur, for example, would want to call himself a Christian philosopher. He is a Christian who philosophizes, certainly, and a fine one. But I wanted to leave room for him to make that option, to say in the privacy of his own conscience, of course, whether or not he would want to declare himself: "This is what I want to do. This is what gives meaning to my life, to pursue the truth in philosophy, no matter where I find it, in the name of disclosing a truth which ultimately derives from the truth of the Incarnate Word that is still to come." Therefore, it makes room for a kind of anonymous appurtenance to the task of Christian philosophizing to the extent that one is willing to make one's own that profession, which I intended to make fairly precise and quite demanding. But it does entail that profession of faith, at least in the private forum of the meaning of one's life and the meaning of one's profession as a philosopher in the course of one's life.

As for Derrida himself, I don't feel qualified to take the discussion very far, especially in the presence of others who are much more familiar with him, and much more qualified to address the question in detail. My sense of Derrida himself is that, in the extremity of his language, there is a distinct sense at times of an experience of the other which would not correspond to a classical definition of transcendence as it comes out of the Middle Ages, but which is an experience of otherness that he finds congenial with the work, say of Emanuel Levinas, and which does not exclude him from the citizenry of those who at least respect the possibility that this other can be more than it appears to be at any given moment. There is a distinct strain in Derrida that lends itself to interpretation as a kind of mysticism that has been discerned by some of his readers, a kind of mysticism that goes back into the Hebraic tradition, sometimes in the Eastern tradition. At least the possibilities of his thought are such, it seems to me, that allow this as a question. And in allowing it as a question, and respecting the integrity with which he pursues it as a question, it seems to me a profoundly Christian task. To the extent that his discerning of the complexity of the issues that he deals with, to the extent that he actually has put his finger on something in the reading of texts that we did not know before and has sharpened our vision of them, this has enlivened our philosophical perception in such a way that he is here to stay, it seems to me. And I think our task as Christians is to try to discern what there is of truth, and potentially of truth, in the insights his studies made available.

Third, you speak of our task. You say you are not a Christian philosopher. Well, it depends on how you define that. You are not doing Christian philosophy, I take it, as it was done in the tradition and in the way you were describing some of those historical figures this afternoon. You are not doing Christian philosophy in the manner of Alvin Plantinga, but you are doing Christian philosophy today at least as a very, very, clear-minded and exigent reader of Christian philosophy, who is making that available to us. And to the extent that you offered a gift to us, and a very rich one for which we are all very grateful, this seems to me to be profoundly Christian philosophy, but only if you can broaden the notion sufficiently to make it include historicized thinking that takes seriously the advent of what is already still to come. In responding to that, it seems to me you do very well what I've been trying to suggest is a legitimate form of Christian philosophizing that is available to us today. As far as the integrity with which we respond to a vocation of that kind, it seems to me that to try to discern truth as it emerges in others by reason of a profession of philosophy constitutes us as Christian philosophers, at least sufficiently for the issue that I was trying to present this evening.

Q: I admired your capacity to articulate your position, and I have listened with a lot of interest today. I have the same questions that I suppose a number of us have, and that were articulated by Professor Dupré. I am a Christian, I teach philosophy, I try not only to teach but to philosophize, and my question comes basically to this. Is there not in philosophy a further point beyond thinking, which is a particular way of living? Is there not perhaps the closure of thinking philosophically today and of teaching philosophy with loving in a certain way in the world, so that we live as an intellectual and thereby show that Christianity is possible for people who think?

A: I agree completely. The thrust of my own thinking is to conceive of the task of Christian philosophizing as more than simply a communication of information. I would take the metaphor that I suggested this evening much further and conceive the Christian philosopher as witnessing to Jesus. The task of a Christian as such is to bear witness to the presence of the Incarnate Word in his life, in himself, as himself, which self, in this function of philosophizing, is witnessing to the truth, insofar as he can discern it, through the instruments that philosophy makes available.

Therefore, it seems to me that the task of Christian philosophy does indeed go beyond simply an enterprise on a conceptual, purely intellectual level; it involves precisely a commitment to this Incarnate Word, however discrete one may make that commitment, no matter how privately one lives it out. But, certainly, this is the effort of the Christian philosopher, precisely as being in the world as someone whose responsibility is not simply to a classroom or to a text, but an entire culture of which he is a representative and to which he testifies by the integrity of his own work. Certainly, this is a task which seems to me to characterize not only philosophizing or teaching, but human living as well. It's in these terms that I would extend the function of philosophizing to the deeper dimension of life itself, as you are suggesting. So I would make your suggestion very much my own and would try to orchestrate my own thought more completely and more explicitly in those terms in order to give your own proposal as rich a background as I possibly could.

Q: Your presentation seems to me startling in its breadth of conception and also its candor about the vocation of being a philosopher quite personally, and so I, for one, am very hesitant to ask a question. My reaction was rather meditative or appreciative than questioning at the end, but you wouldn't be satisfied with that. So, speaking not as a philosopher but as a renegade theologian who has now moved to another office, at least temporarily, I find that the programmatic and personal suggestion you are making about the philosopher's interior vocation, if he or she is a Christian, to bear witness to the Incarnate Word raises very serious questions for theologians. You speak eloquently of the Incarnate Word as a Suffering Servant, who is come, but yet to come. It seems to me that the pluralistic vocation of a Christian philosopher may be given all the more credit by the fact that theology recognizes more and more that an incarnational center is inadequate, and that a paschal and also eschatological dimension of Christology must be recovered. It's my conviction that in the general Western populace, this is not the case. It is the case in Latin American countries and in parts of our own culture where liberation movements are centered, but we tend still to think of Christ as God's Incarnate Word living among us, not as a Suffering Servant whose sufferings are being completed, and who is, indeed, to come in countless cultures for thousands of years ahead. This might fit better with the program of postmodern thinkers, might fit better in deconstructions of the illusions of holistic syntheses and nice harmonies.

So, I guess what I am suggesting is that, from the theologian's side, the notion of Christ as the Incarnate Word is an immensely valuable conception of the reality of Christ, but it's very partial. He is indeed the Suffering Servant, crucified and risen, who is to come, but who is not even himself, not real, without the people in whom he is suffering and the people in whom he will suffer. And to discern where the suffering is most critical, and where it should be responded to, seems to me the task of the Church, far more than it recognizes, and a critique of the Church's doctrinal program much more than it recognizes, but also a very valuable context for what the interior vocations of philosophers might be thought to be.

I hope I haven't been too obscure, but my basic suggestion is that you are appealing to a Christology which I hope will not become too Christocentric, too incarnational, too timeless.

A: Well, thank you. I am certainly sensitive to the dangers that you are suggesting, but you are thinking of it in terms of the broader perspective of the Church itself. And the conception that

I was presenting was one that I hope was not too ideological, but certainly took account, at least in my thinking even if it was not sufficiently explicated, of the historicity of the fact of the Incarnate Word *in our own time*. I meant to suggest, by that allusion, the fact that this is incarnation in our culture, and in the problems of our time, and in the destiny for which we are responsible in this short space of time that's given to us. When you speak of the instantiation, if that's the proper word, of the Incarnate Word in the suffering multitudes who are hungry for truth, and all that implies in social, political, theological, and spiritual terms, I am inclined to say that what you say is true, but you're describing a task for the Church, and if it's a task for philosophy, it's only insofar as the philosophizing of Christians is performed in a way that does service to the Church. The task of philosophy is quite limited, you know, given the expense of the task of redemption insofar as its effectiveness is to be carried out in the panoply of time. That was what I was trying to suggest by distinguishing between philosophy and the function of philosophy in humanism, and now I would extend that notion of humanism to the broader perspective of the task of the Church itself to make possible that human beings become more human by reason of its own apostolic task. But that takes the enterprise beyond the limits that I was considering tonight. I was simply talking about philosophy, and my purpose was really to try to suggest that the task of Christian philosophizing goes beyond extending a synthesis; it means creating a unity and doing it by the means that I suggested. In any case, it is a function of the Church to philosophize, and the task of philosophers who wish to engage in that task of the Church to serve the Church in that way.

II
Encountering the Tradition

2

History of Philosophy as Tutor of Christian Philosophy

Marilyn McCord Adams

"Christian Philosophy"? An Oxymoron?

The "Francophone" Controversy

SIXTY YEARS AGO A DEBATE raged in France over the very possibility of Christian philosophy.[1] Étienne Gilson began with historical data unearthed in his wide survey of medieval and early modern philosophy, with the existence of individual Christian philosophers, on one hand, and the discernible influence of Christian ideas on the evolution of Western philosophy on the other.[2] He concluded that these facts were best described by the Augustinian tradition, which treats faith and reason within the individual Christian not as accidentally associated and uncoordinated (like the white and the musical in Callias), but as functionally united in his or her philosophizing[3] in such a way that faith itself is

---

[1] This drama, although played out in many of the participants' works, is focused and well summarized in Étienne Gilson's "Séance du 21 mars 1931: La notion de philosophie chrétienne," *Bulletin de la Société Française de la Philosophie*, 31 (1931): 37–85; and in Fernand Van Steenberghen, "La IIe journée d'études de la Société Thomiste et la notion de 'philosophie chrétienne,'" *Revue Néo-Scolastique de Philosophie*, 35 (1933): 539–54.

[2] Cf. his "Séance du 21 mars 1931," 37–39.

[3] Thus, Gilson writes in ibid., 45: Thomas "sait que la foi est la foi et que la raison est la raison, mail il ajoute que la foi d'un homme et la raison du même homme ne sont pas des accidents incoordonnés d'une même substance. Le réel, c'est à ses yeux l'homme lui-même, unité profonde, indissociable en éléments justaposés comme seraient les fragments d'une mosaïque, ou la nature et la grâce, la raison et la foi, ne sauraient fonctionner chacune pour soi comme dans un mécanisme dont les morceaux auraient été achetés au magasin de pièces détachées. Si donc un homme chrétien philosophe, et s'il s'exprime vraiment dans sa philosophie, celle-ci ne saurait manquer d'être une philosophie chré-

fruitful in spawning rational breakthroughs. Augustine's *credo ut intelligam* and Anselm's *fides quaerens intellectum* reflect this conviction.[4] Moreover, Gilson reflects, such Christian philosophizing will characteristically and optimally issue in such integrated results that it will not be possible to separate out the "Christian" from the "philosophical" parts, to determine where philosophy leaves off and theology begins.[5]

In insisting on the possibility—indeed, actuality—of Christian philosophy, Gilson focuses on individual philosophers who were Christians (that is, on the agents), on the inner psychological processes of their thought, and on putative content influences on Western philosophy by Christian dogma. By contrast, Fernand Van Steenberghen's attention is on the autonomous methodology

---

tienne. Et elle sera, de bout en bout, à la fois chrétienne et philosophique, sans qu'on puisse l'analyser en éléments dont chacun équivaudrait à la négation du tout."

[4] "Le propre du chrétien, c'est d'être convaincu de la fécondité rationnelle de sa foi et d'être sûr que cette fecondité est inexhaustible. C'est la, si l'on y prend garde, le sens vrai du credo ut intelligam de saint Augustin et du fides quaerens intellectum de saint Anselme: un effort du chrétien pour tirer de sa foi en la révélation des connaissances de raison.

"Et c'est pourquoi ces deux formules sont la vraie definition de la philosophie chrétienne. . . ." Hence, historically, it is verifiable: "Ce sont des philosophies, puisqu'elles sont rationnelles, et elles sont chrétiennes, puisque la rationalité qu'elles ont apportée n'eût pas été conçue sans la christianisme. Pourque le rapport entre les deux concepts élémentaires soit intrinsèque, il ne suffit pas qu'une philosophie soit compatible avec le christianisme, il faut que le christianisme ait joué un rôle actif dans la constitution même de cette philosophie. Il y a bien des éléments compatibles avec le christianisme chez Platon et chez Aristote, il n'y a pas trace chez eux de philosophie chrétienne, mais on expliquerait difficilement sans le christianisme ce qu'ont ajouté à leurs philosophie celles de saint Augustin et saint Thomas d'Aquin" (ibid., 48).

[5] "Si cela est vrai, il faut nécessairement que la philosophie chrétienne soit chrétienne en tant que philosophie. S'il en était autrement, la notion ne serait pas seulement sans contenu propre, elle serait en contradiction avec l'unité fonciere du sujet concret qu'elle exprime. *Il résulte donc de là que toute philosophie chrétienne sera traversée, imprégnée, nourrie de christianisme comme d'un sang qui circule en elle, ou plutôt comme d'une vie qui l'anime. On ne pourra jamais dire qu'ici le philosophique finit et le chrétien commence; elle sera chrétienne intégralement et philosophie intégralement, ou elle ne sera pas.* Ce ne sont pas ici des concessions secondaires faites à la position augustinienne du problème, mais la reconnaissance ouverte du fait, que cette position est la vrai position du problème et que la réalité qu'elle définit est bien la realité à expliquer.

"Seulement reste à se demander si la description correcte de la réalité à expliquer qui vaut à son explication" (ibid., 46; emphasis added).

of philosophy as a discipline, when he takes the opposite point of view. While conceding Gilson's data, he insists that "philosophy is a scientific effort which attempts a general explanation of reality *insofar as it is an object of natural human knowledge*," a discipline whose principles, methods, and conclusions are "strictly rational."[6] To be sure, faith might have an indirect and accidental effect on a Christian's philosophizing, by establishing the internal peace, serenity, and love of truth required for research. Like the cinema or a walk in the park, revelation might suggest ideas or angles for nuancing a concept.[7] Nevertheless, Van Steenberghen urges, Christians can and should abstract from faith-claims for the sake of argument or subject them to methodological doubt and critical reflection. Besides, he promises, such philosophizing independent of dogma will bear the welcome fruits of overcoming the intellectual isolation between believers and unbelievers, and of furnishing philosophy with an instrument for use in its speculations.[8]

Van Steenberghen's position responded to a particular situation in European academe. At the end of his essay, he complains that—in the circles in which he was moving—Catholic philosophy was suffering from a great confusion and conflation of theology with philosophy, a malady that he traced to the absence of strict and rigorous philosophical methodology.[9] Reading between the lines, one suspects his target was those Thomists who took the 1898 papal proclamation as an excuse to make dogma not only a negative test of philosophical results (no true philosophy

---

[6] "la IIe journée d'études de la Société Thomiste et la notion de 'philosophie chrétienne,'" 539–54, esp. 543–46.

[7] Ibid., 546–47.

[8] Ibid., 545–46.

[9] "*Aujourd'hui encore, bien des philosophes catholiques, déformés par la theologie, ne parviennent pas à s'imposer une methode strictement philosophique.* Du coup les theologiens, mal informés de la signification précise des conclusions philosophiques, en font un usage malheureux dans l'interprétation du donné révélé. *Nous souffrirons beaucoup plus de la confusion de la philosophie et de la theologie que de leur isolement.* Bien souvent, notre philosophie n'est déjà que trop chrétienne, en ce sens qu'elle intègre des éléments empruntés à la révélation ou à la theologie, sans les assimiler selon les exigences de ses methodes rationnelles. Dès lors il faut se garder de favoriser, par l'usage d'un vocable inexact, une tendance contre laquelle il importe au contraire de réagir" (ibid., 554).

can contradict true doctrine) but also the dispenser of positive philosophical (viz., Thomistic) content. Van Steenberghen rightly identifies such authoritarianism as inimical to the spirit of philosophy (as St. Thomas would be the first to agree) and counters with the remedy of enforcing Aquinas's own division between philosophy and theology as disciplines. All parties to the "francophone" dispute agree that each field is rational in that it is susceptible to development and presentation in geometric form, beginning with axioms, postulates, definitions, distinctions; deriving theorems via sound arguments; rebutting objections; and so on. The difference is that the fundamental principles of philosophy are evident to the natural light of reason, theses to which every properly trained, rationally competent human being could be brought to agree; while theological "axioms" could never be recognized by unaided natural reason, but must be disclosed by the supernatural light of revelation. However much a Christian may believe the tenets of revealed theology, he or she is not allowed *qua philosopher* to smuggle in any of these claims as premises in strictly philosophical arguments. Rather, *qua philosopher* he or she must play by the rules of logic and follow rationally self-evident principles wherever they may lead.

Skeptical Realism and the Nature of Philosophy

Ironically for me, after threatening to make a career of refuting Gilson on Ockham, I find myself sharing Gilson's Augustinian intuitions about the nature, possibility, and desirability of Christian philosophy.

In any event, Van Steenberghen's position is unavailable to me for philosophical reasons, because I reject the classical foundationalism that he shares with Gilson (and perhaps Aquinas) in favor of skeptical realism about philosophical positions. I count myself a realist about philosophical/theological theories in that I believe (contrary to Carnap) there is some fact of the matter, prior to and independently of what we think, believe, or conceive of in our theories. I am a skeptic, however, because I believe that the defense of any well-formulated philosophical position will eventually involve premises that are fundamentally controversial and thus unable to command the assent of all reasonable persons. Because I do not believe there are any rationally self-evident principles from which philosophical conclusions of any interest could be drawn, I am unable to use Van Steenberghen's "epistemic accessibility" criterion to separate philosophical sheep from theological goats (to decide, for example, that "all is matter" and "all is mind" are philosophy, while "God the Father begets God the Son" or "God the Son assumed a complete individual human nature" is not).

Accordingly, I prefer a *content* criterion, which identifies claims or theories as philosophy on the basis of whether they are at least in part *about* philosophy—whether they make use of philosophical conceptual machinery in their formulation, stake out positions on philosophical issues, and so forth—quite apart from the issue of whether or not they are self-evident or demonstrable (in ways that I claim nothing of philosophical moment is). Thus, just as Goldbach's conjecture, which may or may not be provable within mathematics, is nonetheless a proposition in mathematics, because it is a thesis about mathematics; so I claim transubstantiation is as much a philosophical theory as mind/body dualism, because it involves claims about the nature of accidents and their relation to substances. Medieval formulations of the doctrine of the Trinity and the Incarnation are also philosophical in this sense, even though they fail to meet Van Steenberghen's epistemic accessibility criterion. So, for that matter, are most of Aquinas's *Summae*.

The Method of Coherence

Corollary to this outlook, I conceive of the task of philosophy as that of mapping the problems by formulating the alternative positions as fully as possible. The philosopher's job will involve conceptual analysis and argumentation to clarify the interrelations among the various claims and the costs and benefits of alternative approaches. Each philosopher will have a certain set of intuitions that draw him or her in the direction of one set of premisses or another, and he or she will have a particular commitment to develop that particular theoretical outlook so thoroughly and rigorously as to exhibit it as a viable competitor in the theoretical marketplace. But demonstrative proofs and disproofs—such as the notion that idealism is true and materialism false—will not be in the offing.

Thus, I embrace coherence, not as a theory of what truth consists in (as a realist, I believe truth to be constituted by correspondence with the facts), but as a method of pursuing truth. My assumption is that human reason's best chance at truth is won through the effort of integrating our data with our many and diverse intuitions into a coherent picture with theoretical virtues of clarity, consistency, explanatory power, and fruitfulness. The task is difficult, because our materials are so complex and pull in many different directions. It is dynamic, because the twin desiderata of consistency and richness force many trial adjustments and alterations before a satisfactory organization, mastering complexity with simplicity, is achieved. The assignment is also fluid, because data and intuitions that strike us as bedrock at one time may become less entrenched later, and vice versa, forcing "Copernican revolutions" in our outlook.

Coherence as a method of discovery is scarcely novel. Arguably, it is the way the human mind naturally functions. Developmental psychology, for example, compares human organisms to little scientists, with improving abilities to organize the booming, buzzing confusion of inputs into a stable self/world picture. Initially our "scientific" abilities are crude, and the resultant theories involve wild oversimplifications, which are readily contradicted by insistent data, leaving the individual scrambling to begin again. As the individual matures along cognitive and emotional dimensions, her theories improve, managing wider ranges of data with greater simplicity, successively approximating an adult point of view. Philosophizing this way is only one dimension of a more comprehensive human activity.

Coherence in Christian Philosophy

To return to the issue of Christian philosophy: I agree with Van Steenberghen that being done by a Christian is not enough to make the philosophy itself Christian (what we might call the "agent criterion" is insufficient). Rather, on my view, philosophy is Christian insofar as it involves an integration of faith commitments and intuitions with philosophical ones. Consequently, the Christian character of philosophy is a matter of degree and fluctuates along several parameters. "Involves" is ambiguous as between (*a*) content and (*b*) process. (*a*) A Christian philosopher's metamathematics will almost certainly fail to be distinctively Christian, because of the almost universal content-irrelevance of his or her credal convictions to his or her proof-strategies. By contrast, it would be surprising if ethical theory remained untouched by worship of the *summum bonum*. Other variables concern (*b*) the thinker's process. (i) Some Christians rigidly compartmentalize their theoretical activities and their religious beliefs, lest the one enter in to infect or contradict the other. (ii) Some allow religious and theoretical intuitions to interact at the conscious level but regulate the manner of their interplay in different ways. Whether in general or in relation to a particular issue, Christ may stand against philosophical culture or represent its teleological completion; hover above, pull in paradoxical tension with, or transform it.[10] Thus, creationists and opponents of women-in-office allow certain readings of Scripture and Church pronouncements to trump any other considerations, while liberals are accused of converting (reducing) Christ to a sponsor of the politically correct. Both William of Ockham and Julian of Norwich exhibited a high tolerance for tension, sincerely endorsing both what Mother Church proclaimed and their own philosophical intuitions or visionary insights, while claiming not to understand how to reconcile the two. Aquinas and Anselm recognized Christ as Wisdom Itself, the author and integrator of all intellectual inquiry, yet far transcending any human efforts. Again, (iii) results will vary according to how explicitly the investigator identifies a notion as Christian or otherwise: some pagans are "very close to the Reign of God," and Christians are often unwitting pagans in their attachments; either way, their theories would look different if such allegiances were fully out in the open, and the shock of such implicit commitments would provoke many to change their minds!

Gilson's portrait of the Christian philosopher takes a high degree of integration (viz., the "functional unity" of faith and rea-

---

[10] Here I borrow the provocative and influential classification of H. Richard Niebuhr in *Christ and Culture* (New York: Harper, 1951).

son) for granted. Van Steenberghen implausibly tries to have it both ways, when he concedes the psychological "subjective" influence of faith on the individual, while insisting that Christians can (as much as anyone else) and should observe the methodological autonomy of philosophy. For method is meant to govern practice and so—in this case—to influence the psychological process involved in philosophizing. For my part, I doubt the universal wisdom of Van Steenberghen's advice to Christian philosophers: namely, that they bend their professional efforts to pursuing true philosophy in abstraction from their faith commitments. While denying that anything of interest is rationally self-evident or demonstrable in Van Steenberghen's sense, I nevertheless agree that all philosophers need to know how to distribute burdens of proof appropriately and that Christians can do this as well as others can. But trying to develop my philosophical theories while confining myself to those intuitions, principles, and data that seculars share could enforce an intellectual compartmentalization that obstructs my philosophical creativity and caricatures my perspective. (I will suggest that this is precisely what happened for many Christians schooled in the Anglo-American analytic tradition over the last forty years (see "History of Philosophy in Christian Philosophical Formation," below). Van Steenberghen does not think this can happen, because he imagines that true philosophy will always be related to theology as prolegomenon and instrument. But what if for some Christians contents drawn from "revealed" theology (doctrines of the Trinity or Incarnation, for example) turn out to be the integrating keystones of metaphysics or value theory, in abstraction from which other principles seem unmotivated? Arguably, this was true for St. Bonaventure.[11] I agree with Gilson that the history shows philosophical intuitions and faith commitments reciprocally interacting within the great Christian philosophers, so that sometimes philosophy adjusts to revelation (as when medieval Aristotelians modify substance/accident ontology to explain how transubstantiation is possible); otherwise doctrine bends (as

---

[11] This is argued by Zachary Hayes, O.F.M., in *The Hidden Center: Spirituality and Speculative Christology in St. Bonaventure* (New York: Paulist Press, 1981); and Ewert Cousins, *Bonaventure and the Coincidence of Opposites: The Theology of Bonaventure* (Chicago: Franciscan Herald Press, 1978).

when biblical attributions of passions to God are "explained away" to accommodate Greek philosophical views that the perfect must be simple, immutable, and impassible).

Thus, according to my *process* criterion, philosophy will be the more truly Christian the more open the thinker is to letting religious and philosophical beliefs affect each other, not simply as negative tests on each other, but as positive givens and desiderata alike demanding places in the theoretical mosaic (say, the way colors and mental acts figure as empirical entities, phenomena to be preserved for Scotus and Ockham).

CHRISTIAN FORMATION, SPIRITUAL AND PHILOSOPHICAL

Developmental psychology has popularized the notion that human selves come into existence full of potential—with certain built-in physical, cognitive, and affective instincts, tendencies, propensities—but radically in need of human rearing and education to develop and coordinate these possibilities, to bring them to full flower. Moreover, we are built to become ourselves by copying a series of others who strike us by turns as good approximations. Thus, we are significantly shaped by adult caretakers and the wider social context, because they furnish models for imitation, set the exercises that develop the capacities, give constant negative and positive reinforcement, and teach us ways we can and ought to be.

Aptly enough, spirituality takes a page from psychology: just as, by nature, we cannot become human without being reared by humans, so we cannot become Christian without Christian education. Christian spiritual formation is a process that involves the whole self, training emotions, disciplining choices, focusing patterns of thought. It trains unconscious and conscious, body, mind, and spirit. Moreover, we know that these dimensions of the self (however variously identified) interact with one another. It is an illusion to think that what goes on in one has no effect on the other. *How* they are allowed to interact—whether there is an attempt to compartmentalize or a permission of free and open exchange—makes a big difference. But, either way, the dimensions affect one another in ways more and less beyond our control. This means that spiritual formation involves not only the training of a given dimension, but also disciplining their *coordination*. In certain people, one or another dimension will be overdeveloped while growth in the other is stunted. One sort of training may come to the fore at a given period of life only to be succeeded by another emphasis. "Getting a human spiritual act together" is a long process even (because it involves our cooperation) for the Holy Spirit of God!

Important for present purposes is the fact (explored by Piaget) that intellect is one of the several dimensions along which humans develop. Apophatic spirituality to the contrary notwithstanding, I cast my vote with Augustine, that intellectual formation—or, for those called to philosophize, philosophical formation—is part and parcel of spiritual development. Of course, some people are "born" philosophers, simply original in their capacity to raise and skills to pursue philosophical questions. Most of us require mentors and models, however, to teach us how. Again, someone trained in philosophy and converted to Christianity (such as Clement of Alexandria and St. Augustine) might simply invent wholesome ways of interrelating them. Most of us will learn how to coordinate faith and philosophy better and faster if we can number Christian philosophers among our teachers.

HISTORY OF PHILOSOPHY AS TUTOR AND GUIDE

Past Giants as Ego Ideals

Undoubtedly, I am biased in my insistence that, ideally, history of philosophy should be part of everyone's philosophical formation. I recognize, of course, the counterexample of brilliant philosophers who have made significant contributions without ever having read a line of Plato, Ockham, or Descartes. Yet, such exceptions prove the rule, because every culture is transparent to some insights and blind to others. Even if we give some credit to the myth of progress, we should still admit that earlier ages may have been more sensitive to some features of reality that ours obscures. Sometimes we will find problems approached from different angles—for example, human evaluation by frameworks of purity/defilement or honor/shame instead of modern-style moral responsibility; physical reality analyzed by hylomorphic rather than atomic theory. Sometimes we find altogether different questions raised—for example, about the possibility, intelligibility of change. Where problems are the same, historical probes will help us fill out the conceptual map of possible solutions, to place our own intuitions in relation to well-developed competitors. The effort of getting inside another position to understand how it works fosters intellectual flexibility and heightens our sense of our own creative possibilities.

Most American philosophy curricula walk a line between acknowledging the educational value of the history of philosophy and insisting that not every philosopher is called to become an historian of philosophy. Usually, they include surveys of Greek and modern classical (more rarely medieval) philosophy that everyone is required to take, as well as special history of ethics courses. Out of this canon, most schools select several that majors, and graduate students, are made to study again and again. At Cornell in the 1960s, the favored few were Locke, Berkeley, and Hume. There were special courses on British empiricism as well as single-author seminars. In addition, they were repeatedly consulted in topical courses, whether about personal identity, perception, causality, or value theory. For many Catholic universities, Aristotle and Aquinas would loom large, while, elsewhere, Kant and Hegel would hold sway. Whoever the heroes are, they are offered to us as philosophical "ego ideals," whose manner of thought we are invited to enter so deeply that we can think their thoughts after them. At an intermediate level at least, we "become" them enough to predict with accuracy what they would say on a wide range of issues. Educationally, we are "trying" past figures "on for size" to check their intuitions and methods for philosophical fit. Well-designed curricula would include sufficient variety and contrast to give students a good sense of whom they do and do not "want to be like when they grow up" philosophically.

Moreover, in philosophical formation as in human development generally, "hero-worship" should be "just a stage." Psychological cannibalism is a means by which we humans naturally discover who we are. But however close the model, our growth will be stunted if we content ourselves with trying to be somebody else. Rushing to put on our ideals, we at first accentuate the positive, overestimate how well they fit. In time we become aware how their shoes pinch us and where their coats sag and bag. Our focus shifts as we begin to differentiate ourselves by questioning and disputing authority. (Of course, where the match is very bad, the whole process is or should be accelerated; if not, serious damage to the pupil's philosophical spirit is risked.)

Universities in the High Middle Ages understood well how constructive this differentiation process is, when they enshrined the *quaestio* and *disputatio* as official methods of instruction.[12] The *quaestio* takes familiarity with *auctoritates* for granted, but its effort is no longer minute exegesis or determination of what the author really meant. Rather, canonical texts are used to formulate questions, and spotlight attention is on the substantive issues themselves. The *determinatio* called the Master to formulate *his own* position, while replies to *pro* and *contra* forced him to articulate where he agreed, where took issue with his great predecessors, and why. Even if we eventually join "a school"— become Thomists or Humeans, Whiteheadians or Wittgensteinians—and spend our careers elaborating the leader's vision; even if we are called to history of philosophy and take a decade or two figuring out what the past giant really meant by what he or she said and why, we will have to pass beyond the "ego ideal" stage, be ready, willing, and able to think philosophically for ourselves. The reason is simple: while all past philosophical giants were intellectually formed by their education, they became great by moving beyond it to become independent-minded. We will not be able finally to imitate them unless we gain a measure of independence from them, are willing to dispute and argue with them ourselves!

---

[12] Cf. Bernard C. Bazan, "Les questions disputées, principalment dans les facultés de theologie, de droit, et de médicine," *Les questions disputées et les questions quodlibétiques dans les facultés de théologie, de droit, et de médicine* (Turnhout, Belgium: Brepols, 1985), pp. 15–149; Stephen F. Brown, "Key Terms in Medieval Theological Vocabulary," in *Méthodes et instruments du travail intellectuel au Moyen Âge*, Études sur le vocabulaire intellectuel du Moyen Âge 3 (Turnhout, Belgium: Brepols, 1990), pp. 82–96.

History of Philosophy in Christian Philosophical Formation

Late nineteenth- and early twentieth-century scholarship showed how Christians are rightfully numbered among the "greats" of Western philosophy: Augustine, Anselm, Abelard, Aquinas, Scotus, and Ockham were not simply copying and garbling what Greek philosophers had already said, but also exhibiting their own creative and integrative philosophical genius. At the very minimum, medieval philosophy needs to be reintroduced at the level of general philosophical survey to acquaint students with the range of philosophical roles that God has been seen to play, and should be broached with the coherence, simplicity, and explanatory power afforded by theological theories, for example, of necessity and value. These facts remain underappreciated in high places (even by prominent historians of philosophy in outstanding graduate departments), and the resulting ignorance shows itself in caricatures of modern classical figures as well as of the philosophical issues involved.

A fortiori, it follows that past Christian philosophers (preferably several who systematically disagree with each other) belong in the intermediate-level "privileged" canon of thinkers to whom Christian philosophy majors return again and again. For many, if not most, they will be natural philosophical "ego ideals" with whom the student may explore philosophical problems with a Christian's sensitivity to what sort of philosophical options and assumptions happily cohere with theological commitments, and may try out methods of coordinating faith with philosophy. My generalization is not universal, because some Christians may, for one reason or another, be philosophically more in tune with non-Christian thinkers, identifying with whom may lay the ground for fresh integrations (as, for example, happened with Christian existentialists and phenomenologists earlier in this century).

History of Christian Philosophy as Therapeutic

There is a further, sociological reason for securing a place in the canon for the history of Christian philosophy, however. Sixty years ago, Van Steenberghen felt that French and Belgian Catholic philosophy was suffering from an overbearing influence of theology. Models of *Christian* intellectual identity seemed easy to come by. Unfortunately, he felt, many Christian philosophy professors had forgotten how to be *philosophical*. His plea was for Christians, whose faith has borne the fruits of peace of mind, to set their scientific hearts on "true philosophy" and put themselves to school in the rigorous rational methods shared by their secular and unbelieving colleagues.

The climate in Anglo-American circles of analytic philosophy for the last thirty or forty years has been quite the reverse. Fathered by the positivism of A. J. Ayer, nursed by the ordinary language analysis of J. L. Austin and Gilbert Ryle, and schooled by Wittgensteinism, British analytic philosophy invited Christians who wanted to be philosophers to shoulder a variety of semantic burdens of proof. We were summoned, not to prove the existence of God, but to show cause why anyone should regard the notion of disembodied personality (whether of God or the departed) as intelligible. (One of my UCLA colleagues still boasts, albeit good-naturedly, of being a "semantic agnostic"!) Empiricist and verificationist biases so thinned the metaphysical resources that the machinery needed to formulate doctrines of the Trinity or the hypostatic union were simply unavailable. Alternatively, we were offered the chance to keep our religious language and practice at the price of signing on for some antirealist construal of it (whether à la Braithwaite, Hare, or Wittgenstein). If the intelligibility of individual claims was granted for the sake of argument, it was often to mount a variety of arguments that theism was riddled with contradictions (for example, between divine eternity and divine personality, between divine omniscience and divine immutability and/or divine and created freedom; between evil and the existence of an omniscient, omnipotent, and perfectly good God). In many prominent graduate departments, the presumption was (and still is) that theism (much less Christianity) is positively irrational.

Brave and ingenious Christian philosophers responded with "defensive apologetics," which allowed the challenger to set the terms of the debate and counted itself successful if it could use the atheologian's philosophical beliefs to discredit his own case. Strategically, it sought to limit exposure and, so, rarely brought into play any more Christian beliefs than the opponent had already identified. Tailored to a climate of "methodologically principled" hostility to religion, it has absorbed enormous amounts of (indeed, for a time, virtually monopolized) our philosophical energy. And it has the twin vices of its virtues: by fixing our gaze outward, it seduces Christian philosophers into spending more time mapping the implications of our opponents' positions than understanding and developing our own, and by this very measure engenders a culpable ignorance of the genuine internal difficulties our beliefs entail. In my opinion, an especially pernicious example is the river of ink spilled over the "abstract" logical problem of evil (which defends the logical compossibility of divine existence with the occurrence of some evil or other) while dismissing concrete horrors as merely "pastoral" and closeting our darkest family "secret"—the doctrine of hell!

For better and worse, philosophy is "trendy," blown by doctrinal winds. Eventually, analytic philosophers rediscovered *de re* modalities and acknowledged the possibility of necessary existence. Mind/body dualism acquired respectability with Kripke's endorsement. Metaphysics and theory-building reappeared. At the methodological level, several prominent Christian philosophers shifted from discharging to displacing and reversing burdens of proof by insisting that, for example, many Christian beliefs are "properly basic." Yet, precisely because it is metatheoretical, this epistemological "reformation" does not demonstrate how to integrate faith with philosophical contents.

Over the last twenty years, the founding of the Society of Christian Philosophers has combined with new post–Vatican II alliances between Roman Catholic and other Christian philosophers to foster more constructive enterprises. Yet, at times, our discussions of the Trinity, Incarnation, atonement, and the Bible threaten both to reinvent the wheel and to fall into well-worn ditches, because training in the rigors of Anglo-American analytic philosophy have so effectively cut us off—sociologically as well as psychologically—from professional reflection on our traditions. To paraphrase Heidegger, Christian philosophers who engage in but do not study the history of Christian theology and philosophy are bound to repeat it! Yet, the syllabus of problems requires such subtlety and complexity, the contemporary polemical context mixes old and new with such rapid change, that we cannot afford simply to take our time and rehearse past mistakes. At least some of us, perhaps many or most, need to school ourselves in the Old Masters, climb up on the shoulders of giants, the better to nuance our own distinctively flavored Christian philosophical insights to this present age.

Of course, I paint in broad strokes here. Much that has been done under the rubrics of "defensive apologetics," "reformed" epistemology, and constructive Christian philosophy has been careful, insightful, clarifying, and path-forging. My focus is not on individual contributions but on the collective posture and movement of those of us Christian philosophers who have grown up in analytic circles. My drift may be best captured by returning to the analogy from developmental psychology.

In varying degrees, Anglo-American analytic philosophy of the last thirty or forty years has been a borderline "abusive home" for Christian philosophers and philosophy. It has not been the worst of homes, to be sure, for it offered an environment structured by well-defined limits and regulations, where philosophical elders spent long afternoons sharpening our wits to cut fine-grained distinctions, training our vision to logical structure, drilling us in succinct articulation: "Say what you mean, and mean what you say!" Ever-vigilant aunts and uncles were immaculate housekeepers, kept the rooms spare and austere, ready for momentary inspection, with basements checked hourly for murky thoughts, attics ruthlessly cleared of trunks of outmoded nonsense, closets aired daily to banish ghosts of past philosophical confusions. In such a household, we Christians appeared as messy children with a penchant for clutter, children whose lively imaginations ran to explore basement, attic, and closet. To civilize us into their ways, our elders had to be very strict on our logical grammar, severely limit our playtime activities, daily lock us up to do our homework in minimalist rooms. They were well-meaning and conscientious in following out their child-rearing philosophy. But their efforts to rear us adoptees into their image failed in varying measures to recognize who *we* are—philosophers, to be sure, with not only native but also much acquired taste for rigor, but with metabolisms geared to somewhat richer ontological diets. As parents, they were, to differing degrees, uncomprehending and so could teach us how to say only a distorted fragment of what *we* really mean.

Our early years in the house that analytic philosophy kept were spent learning the environment, imitating adopted-family ways, trying them on for size, learning how to survive, and even winning some favor from the adults in charge. In adolescence, we collectively felt the "misfit," and we began to spar and answer back, and poke holes in our mentors' arguments, as maturing apprentices are wont to do. "Defensive apologetics" was our speed, because we had been given no time and no place to examine the positive content of our religious intuitions—for the most part, had not been allowed, found, or learned any philosophical language to express them. Eventually, success bred confidence; recognizing natural siblings within our adoptive family fired courage to marshal the skills learned at Aunt Analysis's knee for a deeper challenge—not simply of isolated arguments here and there, but also of some fundamental premisses of our philosophical upbringing. Forming our own separate household within the larger family (the Society of Christian Philosophers), we first claimed our freedom of speech, tried to share with each other so much that our childhood had left philosophically unspoken. While retaining a decided taste for order and tidiness, many of us also fantasize a shift in decor from Danish modern back to something more Victorian.

My point is that most of us cannnot exactly remember what grandma's house really looked like, because we rarely, if ever, saw it and more often heard only disparaging things about its dark, ugly, overstuffed furniture and florid vases and carpets. Our accent sounds odd, our grammar eccentric, because we are trying to teach the language to ourselves. Happily, some individual family members are whizzes at language, while others have a flair for design; still other cousins have grown up in friendlier homes, and we are now discovering one another and learning from one another's experience. But, as with other sorts of one-sided development, therapy helps to bring out and integrate those closeted and undernourished dimensions of our philosophical selves. We need to establish a transference, identify new "ego ideals," to model different styles of integrating our new birth-family traditions with the philosophical personalities we have already become.

This time my shamelessly biased suggestion is more specific, but once again responds to Gilson's cue: some—perhaps many or most, but not all—of us Christians who grew up philosophically in the analytic school will be helped in recovering our identity as *Christian* philosophers by putting ourselves to school in the history of Christian philosophy in the Middle Ages. Like us, medieval Christian philosophers were trained to rigorous argument, sharp distinctions, technical precision. (Their example proves that it is not analytical method that has cramped our style, so much as the positivism, verificationism, antirealism, and so on that have accompanied it.) Like analytic philosophers since the mid-1970s, Augustine, Anselm, Aquinas, Bonaventure, Scotus, and Ockham all aimed for systematic positions on metaphysics, epistemology, action and value theory, and theology. Yet, their academic environment fostered, even demanded, the articulation of theological positions, and, where relevant and possible, their integration with philosophical intuitions. Spanning a thousand years, their coterie offers variety both of method and of substance. Even where our philosophical sympathies are wildly divergent, chances are good that we will be able to find some whose conception of their project we can comfortably try on for size and perhaps even borrow or share. Interacting with them carries the further benefit of widening the scope of our collegiality, makes us concrete beneficiaries of the philosophical communion of saints.

Conclusion

To be both philosophical and Christian is a great blessing. Like most divine benefits, it challenges our creativity: how to relate the two? History, both remote and recent, shows how conscientious persons have responded, allows us to survey the varieties and range of their successes and failures. Temptations and pitfalls, as well as inducements and advantages, differ markedly with time and place. Van Steenberghen spoke out of his Francophone experience in the late 1920s and early 1930s, and his firm word warned many Catholic philosophers away from dangers that threatened there and then. By contrast, my suggestions are formed by my philosophical education at Cornell in the early 1960s and by life in American analytic philosophy circles since. My commendation of the history of Christian philosophy as a tool of philosophical re-formation may fall on ready ears among those who have traveled similar paths. Yet, effective spiritual direction cannot be codified in universal generalizations, but must be carefully nuanced to each particular person. The guide must walk a narrow path of trying to learn from experience without expecting that everyone's journey will match his or her own. I believe Van Steenberghen overgeneralized with his advice to those who are both Christian and philosophers. Despite my numerous disclaimers, I am probably guilty of this as well.

QUESTIONS AND ANSWERS

Q: I think we see immediately that philosophy is going to be one of the wild cards in this symposium. I'd like to ask you two questions.

A medieval person would find it perhaps difficult to distinguish between theology and what you seem to be calling Christian philosophy, because you defined it as integrating your Christian insights or Christian beliefs with your philosophical ones. That's exactly what the medievals would call theology. Now, I am not sure how clearly you want to distinguish Christian philosophy from the enterprise of theology, which, at least in St. Thomas and the others, was the attempt to begin from revelation and then use philosophical insights to develop it. I don't see exactly how your Christian philosophy is different from that. I think it should be different.

My second concern is about whether or not it is enough to view philosophy just as articulating a coherent viewpoint. It would seem to me that you have gone further in your own exposition. You seemed to envision articulating coherent beliefs that would give you a positive vision of the universe—not demonstrable, but more than just coherent: a positive illuminating vision one would like to hold as real.

A: I guess I don't want to distinguish between Christian philosophy and theology any more sharply than St. Anselm does. I think that you are right to zero in on the fact that Anselm's posture in that regard is different from St. Thomas's, but I also think that there is a distinction between Christian philosophy and theology as they have been practiced since. In many parts of theology, philosophy is not the methodology of theology. Therefore, you could have a theology that would be biblical theology, for example, which would not be particularly philosophical any more than any view about anything would be philosophical.

I don't see a great need to make that distinction. St. Anselm's example is the one that has inspired me, and he doesn't make a sharp distinction between philosophy and theology. Of course, he wasn't working in a period where disciplines had been developed; he wasn't working in a university system, and so on. But I think that he was, of course, able to distinguish between arguments whose premises were apt to be accepted by various of his opponents, and those that weren't, and I certainly think that Christian philosophers need to be skilled at figuring out which of their arguments, and which parts of their theories, are apt to be coherent with the assumptions and intuitions of non-Christian philosophers, and so I think that kind of skill is very helpful.

I think, in the circles in which I have been moving, that there has been a lot of harm done by compartmentalizing. And since some of the things that we believe as Christians do involve taking a position about metaphysical issues, as well as value theory issues, it seems to me that to bracket them might not necessarily be the most creative way to proceed, and certainly the enforced bracketing that went on when I grew up philosophically was very unhelpful.

Now, you're quite right that I don't think that coherence is all there is to a philosophical theory. I think that coherence as a method of pursuing truth is a method that attempts to integrate the intuitions you find positively attractive into a coherent worldview, which would also have other virtues such as simplicity, explanatory power, consistency, and the like. So, I'm not just saying, "Well, so long as it's coherent, I'll go for it." No, I'm going to try to make my intuitions coherent, and so I come up with a coherent theory that appeals to me on the level of commitment, both intellectual and practical.

What I mean when I say that I'm a skeptic is that I do not think that, if we were all basically careful in formulating our beliefs, all fundamental disagreements in philosophy could be settled. That was what I had in mind. I don't think that we are going to get very much out of what "the natural light of reason" will reveal to all. I guess that is part of what motivates my position and also my lack of interest in St. Thomas's division. I have the impression that he was much more optimistic than I am about what "natural light" could yield, about the amount of agreement there could be about interesting philosophical claims. Once you begin to think that fundamental philosophical disagreements might be unsettlable, that proofs are not available to us, then the idea that what we should be trying to do is develop our intuitions into coherent theories as best we can has a little more appeal. At that point, a concern for what is provable and what is not drops away, because you don't think the starting points are provable.

Q: My question is about the method of coherence, with which I am sympathetic. What would you see as the sort of locus of formulating a coherent theory which is going to be a competitor among other coherent theories? Is it the individual, or is it perhaps a school, or possibly a tradition of thought? What you just said seemed to suggest it is the individual. It seems, however, more in accord with what the medievals thought, that the locus might be the community, particularly if, as you said, Christian life and thought requires some spiritual formation. One does not expect to have all the intuitions just because one professes Christianity. Rather, one attaches oneself as a novice to thinkers and teachers who live in that tradition. This changes the picture: the tradition or the community is going to be the locus of this theory-building rather than the individual.

A: Well, I think that's a fair point. Of course, part of the developmental analogy, and my recommendation that we go back and study history, do in a way presuppose what you make explicit: it is a rare person, if there are any such persons, who are "hatched philosophical" without having been trained. Philosophical problems are so hard to formulate, much less to develop positions and answers to them, that it takes decades, over centuries, to do so. The idea that it should be any different for us is naïve; I agree with that. I think that, of course, it is a collective effort, and whether we like to admit it or not, we are formed by our community. Nonetheless, the individual participant is, in some sense, always doing that job within him- or herself. But you are quite right; it is a good point.

Q: This is a question about your skepticism and combining that with the idea of coherence. If I make my life's goal as philosopher to develop my intuitions into a coherent whole, as I look around the philosophical community, I see that there are thousands of other philosophers all striving to do the same thing. Yet their intuitions are just wildly and completely different from mine, particularly on religious topics. So, I ask myself: why should I bother? Why go through all this excruciating pain if I don't think that ultimately I can reach a demonstrable (within probabilistic limits) truth, something that it is really reasonable for me to hold by this procedure, and reasonable for all others if they would just see it properly, too? If not, why should I do it?

A: Why should you do it? Well, I guess I think that is part of what it is to be human. We have two choices. We can either think confusedly or we can try to figure it all out and get it straight, as far as we can. Based on the actual record of philosophy, it seems to me very unlikely that we are going to reach an agreement. In fact, it's almost certain that we're not, insofar as a skeptic can say anything that is in some aspects merits the word *certain*. Nevertheless, there are communities that share intuitions and that can work together to try to get their ideas clearer and formulate the picture that captures them. It seems to me that that is the only way we have to get at truth, and we do have a yen for it. So, what can we do?

Q: You are still seeing it as a way that is open to us. It seems to me that you are granting that this might get us to the truth.

A: It might, but we'll never know, at least this side of the grave, but perhaps never. I will never know whether it was you who got to the truth, or whether it was I who got to the truth, or, more likely, that we both saw something very important, but we didn't get it all into focus. I think that's the more likely result.

Q: Well, then, why shouldn't we go into other fields where it looks more promising for us to arrive at some truth at least. Why muddle about in fields like philosophy? Why not just go out and have fun?

A: Well, this is the way I do have fun! Isn't that true of you, too?

Q: Professor, for the sake of some clarity, could you tell us a doctrine, a concept, or an argument that could be strictly denominated as Christian philosophy and that wouldn't fall into Christian theology? I think the conference hinges on this issue.

A: One might try to give an epistemic criterion of what counts as philosophy as opposed to theology. That is what many have done—for example, Van Steenberghen, at least as I understand it—and as people take Aquinas to have done. But if you're a skeptic about proving philosophical theories, then that criterion is not available to you. Then one asks, "Well, what would be a criterion of what counts as philosophy?" One answer would be that it's a content criterion. Is it about philosophy? Is it about what's real? And how would we would know that? And what would be the appropriate way to value that? And so on. It seems to me that everything I would count as Christian theology in that sense could be included in Christian philosophy as well from my point of view.

Q: Then, would you count the doctrine of Creation and Incarnation as part of Christian philosophy?

A: Certainly, I think it makes a big difference in metaphysics whether you affirm those beliefs or not. I'm not alone in that idea; it made a big difference in medieval metaphysics. They had to wrestle with the understanding of the relation of substance to accident in order to account for the assumption of an individual human nature by the Divine Word, and to account for the idea that the accidents could exist without inhering in a substance. In my view, this actually inspired a metaphysical advance on their part. Certainly, it makes a philosophical difference whether you think that the world exists by the necessity of its nature, or you think it is made out of nothing. So, I take those to be very substantive positions in metaphysics, even though they are not demonstrable. But then, in my view, mind/body dualism isn't demonstrable, and hylomorphic union isn't demonstrable, and idealism isn't demonstrable either, and those would have been thought to be noncontroversially philosophical theories. So, I am blurring, but I think I'm not doing any more than Anselm did, so I feel I'm in good company.

Q: You keep mentioning Anselm, and you talked about the study of historical persons in philosophy. Can you say something about the value of study of Anselm?

A: The real reason I chose Anselm is that I think he provides an example of somebody whose philosophical method is close to what I think is right, in that he is somebody that thinks that, at bottom, intellectual inquiry is a manner of prayer, a kind of prayer. Now, that is to be distinguished from saying, "Okay, God, I'm going to sit down and do philosophy now, so please help me out to think clearly." He prays those prayers, too. But in this other sense, the *Proslogion* is, I think, the centerpiece. There, intellectual inquiry itself is represented as a prayer in which the thinker addresses God and badgers God with all the questions, and arguments, and objections, and so on, that come to mind. Then there's a pause followed by a divine disclosure, after which the human inquirer tries to articulate what has been disclosed. After trying to articulate in human language what has been disclosed, to raise questions, and problems, and difficulties, and so on in the usual philosophical manner, all addressed to God in the second person singular, the cycle is repeated: there is a pause, there is disclosure, and then a further attempt to articulate. So, that seemed to me to be at the heart of a correct process for doing philosophy for Christians, or it captured my imagination anyway. Intellectual inquiry, when you strip it of all of its many disguises is a *Proslogion*: it is speaking to God, who discloses. That's my fascination, I guess. I also think, however, that Anselm had a very wonderful metaphysical vision of the relation between divine goodness and creatures, and I'm very interested in trying to understand his picture of the priority of goodness over being, that goodness explains being, instead of the other way around. That is very alien to my philosophical upbringing, but I want to get inside and understand it.

3

Secular Philosophy and Its Origins at the Dawn of the Modern Age

Louis Dupré

THE "QUESTION" OF CHRISTIAN PHILOSOPHY

WHY IS IT THAT CHRISTIAN PHILOSOPHY has become a question? The following contribution is intended to do no more than define that preliminary problem. I shall sketch the historical process that led to a separation between religious thought proper and the emergence of an autonomous, purely rational philosophy at the beginning of the modern age. It would be inaccurate to state that before the modern age the two had always been united. Indeed, the notion of a philosophy independent of religious expression appeared with Aristotle. I mean, not that Aristotle's philosophy was secular—he called it theology—but that with him, one might argue, it became autonomous. Its arguments were, for the most part, developed independently of an admittedly religious context. I say "admittedly" because he did introduce the idea of God, but that idea was, at least in the case we remember best, presented at the outcome of a rational process. It is the one to which Whitehead alludes: "Aristotle found it necessary to complete his metaphysics by the introduction of the Prime Mover—God. . . . After Aristotle, ethical and religious interests began to influence metaphysical conclusions."[1] In line with this idea, Whitehead argues elsewhere that the time has come to secularize once more the idea of God in philosophy.[2] This secularization, I believe, was

---
[1] Alfred North Whitehead, *Science and the Modern World* (New York: Macmillan, 1989), p. 156.
[2] Alfred North Whitehead, *Process and Reality* (New York: Harper & Row, 1960), p. 315.

accomplished, at least in principle, centuries ago, and it has created major problems in dealing with the question Husserl claimed was more important than any other in philosophy: namely, the question of God. Obviously, the problems did not arise from a lack of interest. I doubt whether philosophy has ever talked more about God than in the modern age. Yet Christian philosophers of an earlier age would have experienced difficulties in recognizing modern philosophical theology. To begin with, the idea of God is one that the philosopher has not invented, but received from a religious faith and, contrary to Whitehead's claim, I believe that the time has come to acknowledge that debt. "The philosopher encounters this idea; he is not its author. . . . The God of philosophy is from the start a theft and a blunder. One pretends that it is the property of philosophy, whereas it has been borrowed from religious life."[3] Before moving into the historical issue, let us briefly consider this methodological one.

Philosophy may undoubtedly conclude to the idea of a transcendent ground of reality. But even if it attains such an absolute principle, it cannot, on a purely philosophical basis, identify this with what Christians call "God." For many, the very intelligibility of the real has required an absolutely intelligible Logos as its condition. And some, beginning with Plato, have, on various grounds, identified the ultimately intelligible with the ultimately real. Others have wondered with Kant why the real should be ultimately intelligible. That it is not self-explanatory does not necessarily imply that ultimately there must be a transcendent explanation. But, then, what of all the "arguments" for the existence of God presented by such Christian philosophers as St. Anselm and St. Thomas? Their arguments are not religiously neutral, as modern "proofs" for the existence of God claimed to be. They merely showed that the existence of the finite and the contingent requires the presence of an infinite, necessary being. That is difficult enough, and most of the attempts have been subjected to serious criticism. Yet at least they made no pretense of deducing the idea of God out of reason alone. Rather, they conveyed some rational justification to our religious beliefs. Once they established the logical necessity of the infinite and the nec-

---

[3] Henry Duméry, *Le problème de Dieu* (Paris: Desclée, 1957), p. 15.

essary, they identified it with God without further proof, since that was as far as they felt rationally able to go.

The notion of transcendence, if it has any birthright at all in metaphysics, is not philosophically determinable, though it invites further investigation. Only in the actual encounter with religious belief does transcendence acquire a positive content. In dealing with this specifically religious content, philosophy must be satisfied to reflect on a given, nonphilosophical experience or on a positive faith. No reflection on the nature of the real as such will accomplish more, I think. On the other side, the content of a given faith must remain open to a philosophical critique, if it is not to remain philosophically unjustified and, hence, irrational. Thinkers of the High Middle Ages were quite aware of the need to provide a "logic of faith," and most of them embraced a healthy religious rationalism. Philosophical reflection upon the religious act as it is *given* in its manifold expressions should have been the real task of what we later came to call "philosophy of religion." While metaphysics ought to refrain from God-talk in the strict, religious sense, philosophy of religion ought to comprehend the full content of religion. But to include one into the other seems to be both a philosophical and a religious error.

Instead of reflecting on religion as it actually appears, modern philosophy adopted quite a different approach. Either it ignored religion altogether in building a closed intellectual universe without access to any real transcendence or without any direct input of faith, or it incorporated the religious content—most, centrally, the idea of God—as if that content had emerged as an autonomous part of metaphysics. In neither case was there room for a Christian philosophy proper—probably less in the latter than in the former. What in Western thought was responsible for rendering impossible what once seemed to be natural? My thesis is that it was a direct consequence of a fundamental departure from a fully integrated vision of the real. Whereas cosmic, anthropic, and transcendent components once had been integrated with one another, they suddenly became fragmented in a manner that destroyed the ancient harmony. Most important for the problem of Christian philosophy, in late medieval theology and early modern thought, the concept of nature, both human and cosmic, became detached from what once had been the constituent ground of its meaning. All that conveyed a positive content to transcendence became relegated to a detached, "supernatural" realm of being.

The process of separation began in the thirteenth century. When it was completed in the sixteenth, philosophy had no choice left but to turn away from theological issues altogether or to fill the theological vacuum with a "natural" or "philosophical" theology. Of those who chose the latter, some fundamentally revised the relation between divine immanence and transcendence, as Nicholas of Cusa, Giordano Bruno, and Spinoza did in various degrees of orthodoxy. Others construed allegedly pure systems of rationality that ran parallel to at least some of the basic principles of Christian theology, supplying them with arguments for God's existence and justifying the divine attributes—all in the guise of a wholly independent rational enterprise. Later, less disingenuously, this philosophical theology often developed into a deist alternative to Christian philosophy.

Needless to say, the "natural theology" (or "theodicy," as it came to be called in the Scholastic curriculum) followed the philosophical trends in which it articulated its arguments. In the seventeenth century, that trend was basically rationalist. Much of that philosophical rationalism has surprisingly survived in the philosophical theology practiced today by orthodox and even fundamentalist Christians. The original assumption remains: namely, that the entire created order, including revelation itself, constitutes a rationally coherent expression of an intrinsically rational God. This rationalist approach conveys to philosophical theology the spare and bare look as well as the argumentative character that renders it rarely convincing to other believers and never to nonbelievers. The amazing thing about this natural theology is that it was considered "Christian" philosophy and was, for centuries, taught as such in seminaries and Catholic universities.

THE ORIGINS OF THE "SUPERNATURAL"

It was sometime during the thirteenth century that the first signs of an opposition appeared between the natural and the supernatural as two separate domains of reality. The original context had been epistemological. Aristotelian Scholastics considered the order of nature the formal object of a rational investigation in its own right. While Albert and Aquinas had incorporated this semi-independent but abstract field of reflection into the undivided whole of a single theological reality, Averroist Aristotelians began to detach, in various degrees, the study of nature from that of revelation altogether. With the condemnation of the theory of "double truth," the powers of Averroism seemed roundly defeated. Yet the more fundamental problem in combining Aristotle's philosophy with Christian theology remained, rooted as it was in a different concept of nature. In Latin theology the term "nature" had originally referred to human nature in the concrete context of a creation which itself was "gratuitous." Thus, St. Augustine calls the original state of justice "natural." But Christian thinkers who adopted Aristotle's conception of nature found themselves confronted with a teleology of which the end had to be proportionate to the natural means for attaining it. Though he considered the Aristotelian concept of nature too restrictive for expressing the Christian meaning of life in grace, Aquinas conceded that nature contained some immanently human teleology—Aristotle's ideal of virtue and contemplation in the good city—yet this end remained subordinated to the more fundamental one, which was not attainable by human efforts.[4] Clearly, then, the Thomist concept of nature continues to be overdetermined by the category of grace. Independently of grace, nature may be a formal and abstract object of investigation, but it is not a concrete reality in its own right. St. Thomas recognizes a purely philosophical conception of nature, object of a rational reflection independent of revelation. But he recognizes this only as an abstraction. In Aquinas's thought, "nature" refers to human nature as already integrated within the context of grace, though considered independently of revealed doctrine. Viewed from that perspective, nature possesses a transcendent openness to grace and, some Thomists would claim, a *desiderium naturale* toward fulfillment in grace. Before the fall, that nature was harmoniously related to its higher vocation; after the fall, it lost this harmony

---

[4] Thomas Aquinas, *Summa theologiae* I–II, qq. 62–63.

but not its vocation. Even the idea of natural law in St. Thomas is based on the assumption of a theologically concrete—that is, wounded and transformed—nature.

In Aquinas, the term "supernatural" refers not to a new order of *being* added to nature, but to the *means* for attaining the one, final end for which the power of nature alone does not suffice.[5] He calls God himself *agens supernaturalis*, to distinguish the order of the Creator from that of creation (in which nature and grace appear together). Nature thereby becomes the effect of a "supernatural" agent. The term *supernatural* did not begin to refer to a separate order until some sixteenth-century theologians clearly distinguished a "natural" human end from humankind's revealed destiny. Aquinas never conceived of nature as an independent reality endowed with a self-sufficient *finis naturalis*. It must be admitted, however, that one feature of St. Thomas's theological construction could, and eventually did, threaten the balance of its complex unity. I am referring to a particular interpretation of the causal relation between God and creation. For the Greeks as well as for Jews and Christians, some form of causality had always been the principal category for expressing the link between God and the world. Yet a comparison between the modern conception of this causal relation and the classical as well as the medieval conception of it discloses a major difference with respect to the immanence of the cause in the effect.

In Plato's *Parmenides* the psychic cause of motion remains entirely *within* its effect. So do the combined causal principles (the *synaitiai*) of the cosmos in the *Timaeus*. True, Plato adds the efficient causality of the Demiurge. But this mythical figure ought not to be understood so literally as to reverse the theory as presented in all other places. Early Christian theologians, understanding Plato's metaphysical principles as physical entities out of which the Demiurge would have fashioned the world, forcefully stressed that God created *ex nihilo*, a concept unknown in

---

[5] Henri de Lubac, *Surnaturel* (Paris: Aubier, 1946), chap. 5. The classical passage (cited by de Lubac) reads: "Oportet quod homini superaddatur aliqua supernaturalis forma et perfectio, per quam convenienter ordinetur in finem" ("Some supernatural form and perfection must be superadded to man whereby he may be ordered suitably to the aforesaid end") (Thomas Aquinas, *Summa contra Gentiles* III c. 150, §5; see also 152, §3).

ancient and biblical cosmology. In presenting the world as an effect of God's efficient causality, they intended to respond to what they assumed to be implied in Plato's "theory" of the Demiurge. It was, of course, a literalist reply to a mythical story. But never had Christians considered an extrinsic causality sufficient to account for the intimate, permanent presence of God to his creation. Once Aristotle's philosophy became the chief conceptual instrument for articulating Christian theology, the use of efficient causality for defining the entire relation of the Creator to his creation became more exclusive, though it did not yet denote a purely extrinsic relation, as it does in its modern usage.[6] Aquinas hesitated considerably between Plato's participation and Aristotle's efficient causality for conceptualizing the creature's dependence on God.[7] But even within the Aristotelian conceptualization, adopted in his later works, participation continues to balance efficient causality in Thomas's description of God's presence in his creation.

The adoption of Aristotle's philosophy was neither the immediate nor the principal cause that grace and nature became separated into two, quasi-independent orders of reality. As Aquinas had proven, they could be kept in perfect harmony within an Aristotelian synthesis. Moreover, Aristotle's own concept of nature possessed a flexibility and a potential for growth that made it adaptable to Christian theology. Since nature functioned essentially as a matrix of development, not as a fixed entity, it remained at least in principle receptive to the Christian theology of fall and redemption. The disintegration of the synthesis into an order of *pure* nature, separate from one of grace, had been foreshadowed by Averroist philosophers, yet, in the end, was mainly the work of those who had led the resistance against Aristotelianism: namely, the nominalists.

The concept of an unrestricted divine power in the nominalist

---

[6] In a mechanistic system of reality, God could not be truly immanent in the finite without being a part of the system, as Spinoza perceived or, because this would conflict with the definition of an infinite Being, without constituting the totality itself as its originating principle. In Spinoza's terms: *Deus, sive natura,* that is, *natura naturans.*

[7] Cf. Cornelio Fabro, *La nozione metafisica di partecipazione secondo S. Tomasso d'Aquino* (Brescia: Morcelliana, 1939); and L.-B. Geiger, *La participation dans la philosophie de s. Thomas d'Aquin* (Paris: J. Vrin, 1942).

theologies of the fourteenth and fifteenth centuries weakened the intelligibility of the relation between Creator and creature. We know how this unconditioned divine power negatively affected any rational *a priori* for predicting the order of nature. It had an equally unsettling effect on the theology of grace. Granted by an inscrutable divine decree, grace might be randomly dispensed or withheld, regardless of the recipient's moral condition. The nominalists reinterpreted the traditional distinction between God's *potentia absoluta* (his sovereign power over all creation) and his *potentia ordinata* (the manner in which he actually exercises that power). This distinction, dating from the eleventh century, had merely attempted to formulate the unconditional dependence of all created reality on God's sovereign power, in whatever manner he exercises that power. The two had been, not distinct powers but, rather, the same one considered first generally, then specifically. The distinction also indicated how God's omnipotence always exceeds what he actually does.

Nominalist theology transformed the concept of God's *potentia absoluta* in two ways. First, it extended the scope of the *potentia absoluta* beyond its previously assumed moral and rational limits. Thus, God's absolute power came to include all that implies no logical contradiction. A second change occurred when late nominalist theology separated the *potentia absoluta* from the *potentia ordinata*, as if there were two independent and successive moments in God's power rather than two distinct aspects of the one divine sovereignty.[8] According to this interpretation, God at a first time possesses absolute power, which he, in the second, entrusts to secondary causes. Thus, despite an absolute power at any time capable of changing the order of nature, that order is perfectly trustworthy once God has ordained it. His decree to

---

[8] This theory of two distinct powers definitely cannot be attributed to Ockham, who explicitly rejects it in *Quodlibeta Septem* VI, q. 1, in *Opera theologica* IX (St. Bonaventure, N.Y.: St. Bonaventure University, The Franciscan Institute, 1980), pp. 585–86. William Courtenay's substantial study *Capacity and Volition: A History of the Distinction of Absolute and Ordained Power* (Bergamo: Pierluigi Lubrina, 1990), came too late to my attention to profit fully from it. But he convincingly argues the traditionality of Ockham's position. This work will force scholars substantially to revise the traditional presentation of the distinction between *potentia absoluta* and *potentia ordinata* among nominalists. On this issue it clearly removes Ockham from the nominalist flock.

abide by secondary causes is *practically* (though not theoretically) irrevocable. While the extreme voluntarism implicit in this interpretation of God's *potentia absoluta* would seem to undermine the intrinsic coherence of the order of nature, at least in Gabriel Biel, the last nominalist theologian of note, secondary causes obtain practical control, both in the order of nature and in the order of grace.[9] Now, the idea of an independent order of secondary causes gradually led to a conception of nature as fully equipped to act without special divine assistance. If nature was allowed to act through its own powers, what distinguished it in the actual order from an independent entity directed only by its own teleology? Within such a perspective, even the person's elevation to grace had to be regarded as a divine "addition" to the realm of nature. Logic required that theology treat this additional order, in principle independent, separately from that of nature.

When the concept of *pure nature* became widely adopted in the sixteenth century, it may have appeared as a partial recognition of humanist naturalism or as a belated granting of philosophical autonomy. It was, in fact, a concept deeply rooted in late nominalist theology. The Reformers rightly considered it a *theological* mismatch. It might have remained a theological abstraction, however, had Renaissance naturalism not given it an acceptable content and seventeenth-century philosophy a rational justification. An immediate result of the split was the rise of a "natural" or philosophical theology, that is, a science of God based exclusively on rational arguments. If nature could be understood as an independent entity in its own right, that understanding required a *proof* of the existence of its transcendent cause. No doubt, medieval Scholastics, especially Aquinas in the *Summa contra Gentiles*, had granted a relative autonomy to the mind's natural powers for knowing God. Scripture itself supported such a knowledge independently of revelation: "His invisible attributes . . . have been visible, ever since the world began, to the eye of reason, in the things he has made" (Romans

---

[9] Heiko A. Oberman, *The Harvest of Medieval Theology: Gabriel Biel and Late Medieval Nominalism* (Durham, N.C.: Labyrinth Press, 1983), pp. 38–48. Cf. William J. Courtenay, "Nominalism and Late Medieval Religion," in *The Pursuit of Holiness in Late Medieval and Renaissance Religion*, ed. Charles Trinkaus and Heiko A. Oberman (Leiden: E. J. Brill, 1974), pp. 25–59.

1:20). Since the early centuries, Christians had defended their faith against outsiders by universally acceptable arguments based on the course of nature. They had found them in classical sources such as Cicero's *De natura deorum* and Marcus Varro's *Antiquitates rerum divinarum* (reported in Augustine's *City of God*, Books 6, 7, 8). Boethis had been among the first to do so in a systematic way. But neither he nor his medieval successors had started from a religiously neutral position. Boethius's argument *assumes* that God is the ultimate reality. Thomas Aquinas, whose "proofs" were later transformed into the backbone of "natural theology," presupposed the monotheist idea of God to be shared by Moslems, Jews, and Christians. Even in his apologetic *Summa contra Gentiles*, Aquinas devotes little space to the so-called arguments for the existence of God. The knowledge of God *through analogy with nature* had always been "informed" by faith: it served merely as a *preambulum to revelation*.

What distinguishes the "natural theology" that emerged in the sixteenth century is that it brackets all theological and even religious assumptions, and detaches the two realms of nature and of faith from each other. Even those who contested the viability of a natural theology objected, not to the separation of two totally independent realms, but to the capacity of one to support the other. Thus, Bacon writes: "Out of the contemplation of nature, a ground of human knowledges, to induce any verity or persuasion concerning the points of faith . . . is not safe: *Da fidei quae fidei sunt.*"[10]

Under such unpromising conditions, the most one could expect reason to accomplish toward this ambitious purpose consisted in showing that nature, though autonomous, implies a natural transcendence that could be conceived as basically conforming to revealed doctrine. In the event, the new philosophical theology attempted a great deal more. First, it derived the concept of "nature" integrally from ancient authors—mostly Stoic or influenced by Stoicism (as Cicero and Seneca were)—for whom it had been linked to religious conceptions of the cosmos, essentially different from the Christian conception. An idea of nature based on such a theological foundation could hardly be consid-

---

[10] Francis Bacon, *The Advancement of Learning*, II.6.1.

ered philosophically "pure." Second, the conclusions of their arguments for the existence of God claimed to establish a far more specific kind of transcendence than the premisses warranted. The arguments all concluded to the existence of a typically Judaeo-Christian God: one, personal, perfect. Little in this natural theology could be called "natural," in the sense in which philosophers had come to understand "nature."

Natural theology began as an earnest attempt to restore a transcendent orientation to a concept of nature that had, in fact, been severed from it. Its early proponents may also have been motivated by a religious desire to remove the discussion from ever-growing theological polemics concerning the interpretation of Scripture and the authority of ecclesiastical tradition. It failed for a number of reasons, of which the presence of alien theological elements—implied in Stoic, Neoplatonic, and Epicurean philosophies—was only one. The basic problem was that the new natural theology, having defined nature as an independent, self-sufficient entity, continued to argue on the basis of God's immanent presence in nature (both human and cosmic). Already before the end of the sixteenth century, many had lost their optimistic trust in the success of such a dubious enterprise.

That loss of confidence is reflected in the change in Montaigne's attitude toward his own earlier project, the translation of Raymond de Sabonde's *Natural Theology* (1484). The young translator, wary of dogmatic or rational *a prioris*, had welcomed the gigantic effort to establish religion on an empirical foundation on which all religious parties ought to have been able to agree. By the time Montaigne wrote his "Apology," however, Sabonde's argument had thoroughly ceased to convince him. Montaigne's controversial epilogue, though it questioned much of what was held to be accepted doctrine, must be read not as an expression of religious skepticism but, rather, as a defense of a wholly nonfoundational fideism. "It is faith alone that vividly and certainly comprehends the deep mysteries of our religion."[11]

Despite its lack of success, natural theology continued its efforts to provide a "foundation" for faith. The arguments devel-

---

[11] Michel de Montaigne, *Essays*, II, 12, trans. Charles Cotton, Great Books of the Western World XXV (Chicago: Encyclopedia Britannica, 1952), p. 209a.

oped in the seventeenth century by the Jesuits, the Cartesians, and the Jansenists formed the backbone of the theological rationalism of the entire modern age. From Lessius, via Descartes, Leibniz, Clark, and Paley, to the seminary courses in *Theologia naturalis* taught until the middle of the twentieth century, the approaches differed somewhat and the accents were occasionally replaced, but the basic structure remained solidly in place. In this new religious architecture, the upper structure, the so-called supernatural, was assumed to rest on a base of nature, but that base itself was conceived as detached from the superstructure. The relation between nature and grace had ceased to be an organic union. Nature had become independent in the sense in which Spinoza defined substance—namely, as "that which is in itself and is conceived through itself, independently of any other conception" (*Ethics* I, Def. 3)—and the "supernatural" order of grace, detached from its concrete base, was relegated to an airless sphere of abstraction. Not surprisingly, the concept of nature lost its transcendent orientation altogether, and the very assumptions that lay at the basis of natural theology contained the seeds of late-modern atheism.

RELIGIOUS NATURALISM, REFORMATION, AND SPIRITUAL MOVEMENTS

As theologians withdrew from the domain of nature and philosophers from that of the supernatural, a new kind of religious thinker rushed in to bridge the chasm. They attributed to nature itself a divine quality, independent of the supernatural realm that theology had arrogated to itself. Pantheistic and panentheistic mystical philosophies erupted in Renaissance thought. They drew heavily on Neoplatonic and Stoic sources. These sources had never ceased to feed Christian speculation, but in the past they had been constrained by the Christian doctrine of creation. Nature had not *emanated* from God with inner necessity, but had come into being through a free, divine creation. For the Stoics, however, as well as for Plotinus and Proclus, nature itself had been divine. So, when thinkers such as Patrizzi, Bruno, and Telesio turned to them, they found a position that greatly contrasted with the dualist theologies of nature and grace. They differed from previous students of those classical theories in uninhibitedly embracing them without worrying about their implications for the doctrine of creation. Earlier "naturalists," such as the members of the twelfth-century School of Chartres, had occasionally appealed to scriptural or theological support for ascribing a divine quality to nature. For pantheistic and panentheistic philosophers of the Renaissance, that divine quality revealed its own truth independently of any "revealed" authority.

Reflecting on the direction religious thought took toward the end of the Middle Ages, we cannot but wonder whether the extremes of a religious naturalism such as Bruno's, and a supernaturalist philosophy such as that of late Scholasticism, could have been avoided. An affirmative answer confronts us in the towering intellectual figure of Nicholas of Cusa. Recapitulating almost the entire past tradition—the Greek as well as the medieval—he adapted it to the new demands of the emerging humanist and scientific culture of the modern age. In a comprehensive synthesis, the Rhineland cardinal succeeded in bridging the gap that nominalist thought had opened between nature and its transcendent source. Cusanus was probably the last thinker to reunite the theocentric and anthropocentric forces that had begun to pull the medieval synthesis apart. He anticipated and avoided the problems a heliocentric picture was to cause to the traditional religious world view by rethinking the relation between God and nature in such a manner that God is no longer the pinnacle of a cosmic hierarchy but a spiritual center that unfolds itself in the cosmos.

Cusanus's theology presents the last major alternative (before the twentieth century) to the dualist school theologies of the modern age. After him, theologians either accepted the late-Scholastic view of nature and grace as independent entities or they stressed one at the expense of the other. Spiritual theologies alone succeeded in recapturing, in the lived experience of devotional practice, the synthesis that systematic theology had lost in speculation. But they did not change the fact that, by the end of the sixteenth century, theology had lost its hold on Christian thinking. It became reduced to a science among others, with a method and object exclusively its own. Other sciences henceforth could freely ignore it. For the most part, modern thinkders did so, all the more readily as it enabled them to avoid potentially hazardous and always useless theological controversies. The picture I have painted of the relation of philosophy and theology at the beginning of the modern age looks bleak. But it would be even more so if we omitted mention of the serious efforts made by several religious movements to reincorporate the theology of grace within a continuous *ascensus ad Deum*: namely, Christian humanism, the early Reformation, and various spiritual theologies flourishing in the sixteenth and seventeenth centuries. According to humanists such as Ficino and Erasmus, a universal divine attraction calls the entire natural order back to its divine source. Archaic religion, ancient philosophy, Hebrew and Christian revelation—all responded in various degrees of intensity to this universal divine impulse. Unfortunately, the humanists were not philosophers, and refused to address the fundamental predicaments of Scholastic theology. Even Valla and Erasmus, who knew the early Christian tradition so much better than their theological contemporaries and who unambiguously defended it against the "classicists," felt such a deep-rooted aversion for school theology *and* philosophy that they rarely engaged in a serious discussion of it. They and, even more, Ficino presented an alternative, but not an answer, to the questions of nature and grace raised by the Scholastics.

The answer of the Reformation, on the contrary, went to the heart of the religious issue. Luther and Calvin rejected any theologically "neutral" concept of nature, the Scholastic as well as the classical one. They perceived that grace conceived as "addition" to nature would sever thought from revelation. Luther's entire theology aimed at overcoming the split between nature and grace. Yet, in solving the theological problem, Luther rendered the philosophical one insolvable. A nature totally corrupt and hence incapable of any independent attainment of truth stands to philosophy as Renaissance naturalism stands to theology. How much positive content does Luther's concept of nature preserve? The answer is not altogether clear. Despite his fundamental principles of a corrupt nature and an imputed justice, Luther's theology also displays a mystical trait that asserts the real presence of God in the soul, as clearly appears in the medieval text that he reedited twice and that he claimed contained the essential message of the Reformation: namely, the *Theologia Germanica*. This fruit of late medieval piety unambiguously stresses a full sanctification of the soul through God's direct inhabitation. The justifying justice remains God's own, but the justifying God is himself present in the soul. This implies a far more intimate union than is suggested by the term "imputation," commonly interpreted as a merely forensic justification. Elsewhere, however, Luther, under the impact of nominalist theology, insists that God's will is totally sovereign and that natural virtue plays no role in salvation. Indeed, the corruption of human nature vitiates all acts it performs. This conflict of two incompatible positions exacerbates the problems of a Christian philosophy rather than solve them.

Calvin leaves us with a similar ambiguity about the powers of nature. On one hand, he asserts that, after the fall, human nature retains a *residuum* of its divine image that God in the elect restores "to true and perfect integrity" (*Institutes* I.15.4). Divine justification transforms the believer *from within*, granting him or her an actual *experience* of salvation. On the other hand, that nature is so irremediably wounded that the way of truth remains closed to it. God's absolute power overrules the inherent powers of nature. Salvation becomes a matter of election, and that election owes nothing to the natural course of creation. The natural order has entirely been disturbed in the individual, in the cosmos, in society. All natural powers depend directly on God and are at any moment subject to direct divine intervention. The order of nature is now an order of divine decree. Only a positive law remains. The person is both an image of God and a moral degenerate; the cosmos reflects God's greatness and yet is groaning "as if in the pangs of childbirth"; society bears the scars of human sinfulness, yet supports the elect on their way to their divine destination. Nature no longer serves as a reliable guide; the mind must rely on a positive revelation rather than on a natural knowledge.

Obviously, the prospects for a Christian philosophy are far from bright in this perspective. Nor are they much better in the several mystical theologies that were sprouting up everywhere at the time, not only among Catholics but also among Lutherans and even Calvinists. Philosophically, those movements withdrew from the natural order into a direct contact with the God from whom theology and philosophy had severed them. Their attitudes contained the seeds for a new theology that would definitively break with the ontological fragmentation. But they themselves did not yet develop such a theology, and withdrew from philosophy altogether. The question of what a Christian philosophy ought to be after the modern break can be answered, I think, only once Western thought has somehow restored its ontological unity. I suspect that a fundamental rethinking of our philosophical approach may be necessary—a new kind of metaphysics, such as Nicholas of Cusa initiated in the fifteenth century. Such a new search for unity may possibly free us to explore the radical ways opened up by Spinoza and partly Christianized by Schelling. At least they overcame the baneful absolute priority of the subject as sole source of meaning and value.

QUESTIONS AND ANSWERS

Q: You have given us an almost Hesiodic account of a golden age, an age where the divine and the human are reconciled with each other in an Arcadian Nature, and I'm very persuaded by that. But Hesiod is, of course, a good deal before the medieval era, and I'm wondering whether there was not some kind of divorce of nature from the nonnatural and the human in the division between the *mythos* and the *logos* that took place in antiquity?

A: Yes. Exactly. The breakup of the unity was anticipated by the Sophists. That is what Sophism is all about, whereas, previously, nature and selfhood were harmoniously united. With the Sophists we see a break where the question becomes very important: who is in charge here? Is it nature or us? This becomes clear in the question of the attitude toward tradition. Before the Sophists, tradition was the truth; in other words, don't blame tradition—tradition is what people do, and they do these things because it's in the order of nature. This view of tradition is questioned when the Sophists raise doubts about human thinking and willing. They said "Tradition has nothing to do with nature, with the cosmos: *we* make that!" So, you are quite right, but I wouldn't call my picture Arcadian. It's more like the Hell of Dante than the Arcadia of Hesiod, I think.

Q: It seems to me that part of what you're saying is that the theological doctrine of creation, as it was developed in the Middle Ages, underwent a kind of emigration out of theology and into what we now call the New Science. It became a presupposition or kind of paradigm for the New Science. Would not bringing into focus a distinction between the natural and the supernatural have been a very important dynamism for development?

A: Yes, and Professor Gerald Galgan, who just asked this question, has written a beautiful book on some of these problems, *The Logic of Modernity*. I quite agree that, regarding the success of the notion of nature, I pointed out only one aspect, and that is obviously insufficient. What you say complements that. I spoke of the success of the content that was given to that notion of nature by Italian humanism, but there is another story, and perhaps a more important one that you point out here: namely, the success of science. Science was about nature and was done by laws that were clearly defined in the seventeenth century by efficient causality. In the beginning, . . . well, it's a long story. But in any event, nature had something to show for itself. This very emphasis upon the autonomous functioning of nature in science has been a major contribution to the independence of nature, and also to the fact that, at a point, scientists (or philosophers, as they were called) tend to say, "We have enough on our hands without getting involved in things that create nothing but trouble!"

Q: You tend to begin to blame Aristotle for that extrinsic notion of efficient causality, which you mentioned, and you stress beautifully, I think, how St. Thomas and others held together participation and causality. However, St. Thomas used Aristotle to do that. Aristotle has a brilliant metaphysical move where he says of efficient causality "actio est in passione." Where is the action of the agent? It's in the effect! That's brilliant! It's absolutely immanent in the effect, not back in the cause. That was Aristotle who said that. St. Thomas was able to draw together efficient causality and participation because Aristotle had not made the break of immanence yet.

A: Yes, you're absolutely right; I should have mentioned this. I mentioned only Plato as not achieving that break in causality, then I immediately started speaking about St. Thomas and said he kept it together. The reason why Thomas could keep his notion of efficient causality without creating any havoc in that field was precisely, as you said, because the concept of causality that he inherited from Aristotle was open to that and lent itself to that. Thomas in this respect is very much more in the ancient tradition of causality than in the mechanistic one.

Q: When you talk about the separation between nature and God, do you connect that at all with the abandonment of the teleological explanation of nature, or with the change in the account of natural teleology from defining created natures as constituted by imitable relations to God, let's say, as opposed to not being so constituted? Or do you think those kinds of considerations have anything to do with this separation?

A: Yes, they have a lot to do with it. But I was not thinking of the question of teleology in the first place. That is why I zeroed in on the theology, because I think the theology was more directly influential upon later theology than the philosophical issue you bring up was. By that, I mean the theology of the relation between God and the world and, specifically, the definition, or lack thereof, of omnipotence. In other words, the distinction of the *potentia absoluta* and *potentia ordinata* also in theology developed into an abolition of natural teleology, as we see in Calvin. In Calvin, we end up with the natural law being no more than the law that is ordained by God at each single moment. In that context, this question of teleology that you are bringing up would be extremely important in my story, but I was not talking about it. I think it is crucial, and perhaps more important than what I was doing. But I was directing my remarks exclusively to the sovereignty, the absolutely unbounded, unlimited sovereignty, of God, and how it accomplishes a break in rationality between God's reasons and human reasons. Of course, Biales is the epitome of it, but you also find things like that in *D'autre* *coeur Dei* and so on—the sovereignty of God, the distinction, the distinctness, total distinctness.

Now, from your point of view, you could attack my position again in a different way. You can say, "All right. You speak about mystics and spiritual life. When did they come to the fore? What philosophy, if any, and theology did they profess?" And the answer is "Nominalism, of course." All the late medieval mystical movements, even including Erasmus, were influenced by what they called the *Via Moderna*, by nominalism.

So, my point is not that nominalist theology made spiritual life impossible. Quite the opposite. There was nothing else but experience, the direct experience of God. Since all the other ways were closed, the rational ways were closed; there was only the way of experience. And that, I think, was extremely conducive to spiritual life in the late Middle Ages and the early Renaissance. But my point was exclusively directed at Christian philosophy.

4

Original Sin: A Study in the Interaction of Philosophy and Theology*

Robert Merrihew Adams

MUCH THAT HAS BEEN SAID about the relation of Christian theology to other disciplines in a modern (or "postmodern") intellectual environment assumes a deep opposition between Christian traditions and the secular liberalism of the modern West. I have never been able to see an irreconcilable opposition here. For it seems to me that I have lived my whole life as a member of a tradition that fuses versions of Protestantism and modern liberalism—a tradition whose most typical American exemplar, perhaps, is Reinhold Niebuhr. Niebuhr blended those sources with an illuminative power that may have been as effective for his generation as St. Thomas Aquinas's fusion of Aristotelianism and Augustinianism was for his generation.[1] Many American Catholics have a similar experience of a tradition combining liberal and Christian strands, in a Catholic version, with John Courtney Murray, per-

* A version of this essay was presented as a lecture at a National Endowment for the Humanities Institute on Kant's moral philosophy at The Johns Hopkins University in the summer of 1983, and later at Reed College. I am indebted to many, and especially to Marilyn McCord Adams, for helpful comments. It is a pleasure to thank the Center of Theological Inquiry in Princeton for fellowship support during part of the writing, and Princeton Theological Seminary for hospitality and use of its library.
[1] See Alasdair MacIntyre, *Whose Justice? Which Rationality?* (Notre Dame, Ind.: University of Notre Dame Press, 1988), chap. 17 (for a verdict on liberalism quite different from mine); and *Three Rival Versions of Moral Enquiry: Encyclopedia, Genealogy,* and *Tradition* (Notre Dame, Ind.: University of Notre Dame Press, 1990), chap. 7 (on the limited influence of Aquinas in his own time).

haps, playing something like Niebuhr's role; but I will leave it to them to speak for themselves.

Niebuhr's work was at once social criticism, political ethics, and Christian apologetics. Its apologetic force lay in its showing that Christian thought could illuminate contemporary moral situations and depended, therefore, on its having an appeal to experience and to contemporary moral sensibilities that was independent of any appeal to religious authority. This is exemplified in Niebuhr's most famous intellectual project, his exposition and rehabilitation of the doctrine of original sin. While the exposition is rich with biblical and theological allusions, and is clearly inspired by religious sources, Niebuhr's version of the doctrine can easily be read as a mainly empirical thesis.

Behind Niebuhr's treatment of the subject lies Kant's—not in Niebuhr's consciousness,[2] but in the line of historical development. Kant is one of relatively few modern philosophers to pay much attention to questions of sin and forgiveness. What is striking, for our present concern with the relation of Christianity to philosophy, is that Kant sees these topics both as historically Christian and as belonging to the realm of *Religion Within the Limits of Reason Alone*—as topics to be treated by *mere* reason, *bloße Vernunft*. In the present essay I will try to illuminate the relation of Christian theology to philosophy by recounting and reflecting on some of the history of the doctrine of original sin, beginning and ending with Kant.

WHAT LED KANT TO A THEORY OF ORIGINAL SIN?

It may seem strange that Kant should be interested in such a doctrine at all, since it is commonly understood to involve the ascription to us of guilt for the sin of Adam, whereas Kant is committed to ascribing moral merit and demerit only on the basis of the free acts of one's own will. Kant is well aware of this problem, and tries to work out a form of the doctrine that is

---

[2] Niebuhr's acknowledgment of Kant's theory, in a footnote, seems to me to reflect only a superficial engagement with Kant on this point. See Reinhold Niebuhr, *The Nature and Destiny of Man: A Christian Interpretation*. I. *Human Nature* (New York: Scribner's, 1941), p. 120.

compatible with his voluntarism. But why should he take an interest in this subject at all?

It is foreign to much of the current lively interest in Kant's ethics, which has only recently begun to take seriously the difficulty of isolating his permanently interesting ethical theses from his religious views and his metaphysical hypotheses about noumena, or timeless things in themselves. Perhaps, indeed, a fragment of Kant's ethics, consisting chiefly in the Categorical Imperative, can be isolated in this way from his metaphysics and philosophical theology. But there is much more to Kant's moral thought than the Categorical Imperative, and his interest in the problem of original sin[3] arises naturally from something that has a pretty good claim to be regarded as the first principle of his moral philosophy, as it is enunciated in the very first sentence of the body of the *Groundwork of the Metaphysics of Morals*: "Nothing can possibly be conceived in the world, or even out of it, which can be called good without qualification, except a good will."[4]

Of course, in order to understand this principle or interpret it, we have to have some sense of what Kant means by "a good will." What is it to have a good will? What is a good will? A preoccupation with the Categorical Imperative, as a source of ideas for developing criteria for the evaluation of actions, may mislead us here, tempting us to think that for Kant having a good will must be a matter of acting voluntarily in accordance with the moral law, which he calls *pflichtmäßig handeln* (acting in accordance with duty). But that is quite explicitly not what Kant means by "having a good will." Having a good will for Kant is not *pflichtmäßig handeln* but *aus Pflicht handeln*, not acting in accordance with duty, but acting out of duty—in other words, acting from a certain motive.

In support of this view Kant appeals, very plausibly, to ordinary moral judgment. If we think people are acting in accordance with duty only because they fear punishment, or because they hope for some reward from other people, or merely because what

---

[3] The same is true of his interest in the problem of the justification of the sinner, which is also treated in *Religion Within the Limits of Reason Alone.*

[4] Immanuel Kant, *Fundamental Principles of the Metaphysics of Morals*, trans. Thomas K. Abbott (New York: Liberal Arts Press, 1949), p. 11.

they are doing happens to be expedient for purposes that have nothing to do with morality, we do not give them much credit for it. But if they do it because they believe it is right, that seems morally worthy.

Kant makes no appeal to religious authority, and none seems needed to sustain this point. At the same time, it is obvious that his conception of a good will resonates with the emphasis on good motivation in the Bible and in Christian traditions. How much is Kant influenced, and how much is our "ordinary" moral judgment influenced, by that background? It might be hard to say.

Furthermore, Kant understands the good will, not as a particular act, but as something more global. The good will, for Kant, is the moral agent him- or herself being rightly motivated, or something approaching that. This comes out in several ways. For one thing, it is quite clear that the question about the good that grips Kant's interest is not "Was that a good act?" or "Was that an act deserving of reward?" The question that grips his interest is, rather, "Is my will good?" or "Am I a person well pleasing to God?" or "Do I deserve to be happy?"—questions, in other words, about himself as a whole, not about particular acts. He insists also that a good will (or, for that matter, a bad will) is not to be inferred, even with probability, from a single action; rather, such an inference should take into account a course of life continued over some time.[5]

A good will, therefore, is a motivational state, and a very comprehensive one. In saying that nothing is unqualifiedly good except a good will, Kant is proclaiming, first of all, that the value of morality is intrinsic, not merely instrumental; and, second, that moral worth depends on one's motivational state. The first of these convictions grounds Kant's interest in problems of guilt and forgiveness. His theory of original sin is strongly rooted in the second conviction, about the moral value of motivation.

---

[5] Immanuel Kant, *Religion Within the Limits of Reason Alone*, trans. Theodore M. Greene and Hoyt H. Hudson (New York: Harper Torchbooks, 1960), pp. 16, 62ff. Henceforth, I will cite this text by parenthetical page references. I have also used the German text, in the Philosophische Bibliothek series, *Die Religion innerhalb der Grenzen der bloßen Vernunft*, ed. Karl Vorländer, 8th ed. (Hamburg: Felix Meiner, 1978).

We can trace, in Kant's *Religion Within the Limits of Reason Alone*, a rationale for belief in original sin that begins with his conviction that moral worth depends not merely on our action, but chiefly on a disposition (*Gesinnung*) which is, as he puts it in the *Religion*, an "ultimate subjective ground" of choice (p. 20). This disposition consists, I take it, of the most basic maxims or principles of action we adhere to, together with such facts as how strongly or weakly we adhere to them and any motives we may have for our adherence.

The second point in the rationale is that if we consider any act that we perform at any time, we see that this act proceeded from an ethical disposition that we already had. This seems to follow from the very structure of human action. As Kant says, "The ultimate ground of the adoption of our maxims . . . is posited as the ground antecedent to every use of freedom in experience (in earliest youth as far back as birth)" (p. 17). Our actions must, therefore, be traced ultimately to a disposition that we did not adopt by any action that we have performed in time. Kant is prepared to call this original disposition an "inborn natural constitution" (*Beschaffenheit*) (p. 20) precisely and only in the sense that it has not acquired in time. It would seem to follow also that having it is not voluntary, since we have never adopted it.

In the third place, while our original constitution could have been wholly good, Kant believes that experience constrains us to judge that that is not the case, and that in each of us, before we performed any evil act in time, there was a propensity (*Hang*) to evil included in our ethical disposition. For immoral action proceeds from a disposition that is morally flawed. If one did not already have such a corrupt propensity, Kant thinks, one would not do wrong.

It would be consistent with these first three points to maintain that while our original bad disposition preceded any act in time and thus could not have been adopted by such an act, the good or bad disposition that we now have as adults was determined, not by the original disposition, but by our voluntary acts in the past, and can, thus, be regarded as voluntarily adopted. But, in the fourth place, Kant denies that we have that kind of control over our ethical disposition. He says that while "it must be possible to overcome [*überwiegen*] [the propensity to evil] because it is found in man as a being that acts freely," it "cannot be eradicated [*vertilgt*, or (p. 27) *ausgerottet*] because this could happen only through good maxims, which cannot take place when the ultimate subjective ground of maxims is presupposed as corrupt" (p. 32). Thus, our predicament in original sin is serious indeed.

In spite of having said all this, Kant quite explicitly holds that we are to blame for this condition. "We are accountable," he says, "foɪ the propensity to evil . . . despite the fact that this propensity is so deeply rooted in the will that we are forced to say that it is found in man by nature" (p. 30). And he ascribes to us guilt (*Schuld, reatus*) for the propensity to evil (p. 33).[6]

I want next to examine more closely the epistemological status of Kant's theory of original sin, in comparison with traditional Catholic and Protestant views. This will help to prepare us for an historical and comparative consideration of the issue that most interests me in all this, which is the relation between voluntariness and our accountability for motivational states. Finally, I will discuss the treatment of it in Scholastic philosophy, the Protestant Reformers, and Kant.

THE EPISTEMOLOGICAL STATUS OF ORIGINAL SIN

In the rationale that I traced in the previous section, the first point, that moral worth depends on disposition, is integral to Kant's ethical theory; I have already discussed its grounds. The second point, that every act in time proceeds from a disposition that we already have, and the fourth, that a propensity to evil cannot be eradicated by human powers, belong to a clearly philosophical analysis of human action. The crucial third step, that our original disposition includes a propensity to evil, is justified by appeal to experience. Kant says that we are "evil by nature" in the sense that "evil can be predicated of man as a species; not

---

[6] He says here that this guilt is "intentional" (*vorsätzlich*) with respect to wickedness, but "unintentional" with respect to frailty and impurity. I take it that the point is that wickedness involves a full, though conditional and not necessarily conscious, acceptance of violation of the moral law, whereas frailty and impurity do not.

that such a quality can be inferred from the concept of his species (that is, of man in general)—for then it would be necessary; but rather that from what we know of man through experience we cannot judge otherwise of him, or, that we may presuppose evil to be subjectively necessary to every man, even to the best" (p. 27). Thus, Kant presents the claim that we are evil by nature as an empirical thesis about human beings as we now actually find them. The empirical character of his theory of original sin is closely connected with his relation to theological tradition on three different issues.

(1) Kant's theory of original sin is not grounded in any appeal to the authority of the Bible. It does not essentially depend on the story of the Fall of our first ancestors from innocence, narrated in the second and third chapters of Genesis. For Kant denies that the evil in us was caused by their sin. "Of all the explanations of the spread and propagation of this evil through all the members and generations of our race," he says, "surely the most inept is that which describes it as descending to us as an inheritance from our first parents; for one can say of moral evil precisely what the poet said of good: 'race and forebears, and what we have not done ourselves, I hardly count as ours'" (p. 35).[7]

This rejection of the hereditary character of original sin is the chief departure from theological tradition in Kant's views on the subject. He does find a use for the Genesis story of the Fall, but it is merely illustrative. According to him, we have sinned in Adam only in the sense that we have sinned as he did. A line Kant quotes from Horace aptly expresses the religious signifi-cance Kant finds in the story of Adam and Eve: "Mutato nomine de te fabula narratur" (Change but the name, of thee the tale is told) (p. 37). In other words, the point of Genesis 2 and 3, for Kant, is to provide a parable or model for the understanding of our own sin.

It is of interest to note that Kant has largely been followed in this by the most influential Protestant writers on original sin in the nineteenth and twentieth centuries, such as Schleiermacher, Kierkegaard, and Reinhold Niebuhr. Despite various differences

---

[7] I have slightly modified the translation of the German, and translated the quotation from Ovid.

among them, it is true of all these theologians that Adam and Eve play no crucial role in their conception of original sin. The only importance that the Genesis story of the Fall has for any of them is "Of thee the tale is told." Niebuhr is quite explicit about this, declaring: "When the Fall is made an event in history rather than a symbol of an aspect of every historical moment in the life of man, the relation of evil to goodness in that moment is obscured."[8]

(2) It follows that there is room in Kant's theory for only one of the two leading ways of thinking of original sin that are found, often in combination, in the history of the doctrine. The first of these ideas is that guilt is imputed to all of us for Adam's sin, because we all, in some sense, sinned in him, or were in him when he sinned. Here the sin in question, of which Adam and we are guilty, is the sin that he sinned in eating the forbidden fruit. For this idea Kant has no use, because Adam's sin plays no essential part in his theory, and, more fundamentally, because he rejects any ascription to us of guilt or responsibility for another agent's act.

The other way of thinking of original sin is as a morally corrupt condition, a state or disposition, that we all were in at birth. This is not a sin that Adam committed, but a sin that is in us, at birth. To be sure, it was Adam's sin that led to our being in this condition, on the traditional account; but the condition was in us, and we are individually guilty for it, with a guilt that is not merely imputed to us. The corrupt condition is conceived as at least largely a motivational state; in this conception of original sin, therefore, we are held accountable for motivational states.

The first idea, of imputed guilt for Adam's sin, is probably what many people think of first in connection with the doctrine of original sin. But I think, in fact, it is the second idea, of the morally corrupt condition in which we all were born, that has been the more important in the history of the doctrine.[9] To con-

---

[8] Niebuhr, *Nature and Destiny of Man*, p. 269.

[9] Calvin, for instance, who can hardly be accused of not believing in original sin, characterizes it as "a hereditary depravity and corruption of our nature," and declares that "not only has punishment fallen upon us from Adam, but a contagion imparted by him resides in us, which justly deserves punishment. . . . For that reason, even infants themselves, while they carry their condemnation along with them from the mother's womb, are guilty not of another's fault but

ceive of original sin, as Kant does, exclusively in terms of a corrupt condition is, therefore, a less radical departure from theological tradition than his denial that either corruption or guilt is inherited from our first parents.

(3) The treatment of the doctrine of original sin as an empirical thesis about a corrupt condition found in human beings as we observe them is facilitated by another position characteristic of Protestant theology. One of the original topics of controversy between Protestants and Catholics in the sixteenth century was whether original sin remains in those who have been baptized. The Reformers held that it does, whereas the Council of Trent maintained that both the guilt of original sin and any sinful corruption are cleansed away by baptism and that although some consequences of the Fall remain in the baptized, the consequences are not sin. An exploration of some of the ramifications of this dispute will shed light on the epistemological status of claims about original sin and will also provide important background for our subsequent discussion of approaches to the relation between voluntariness and accountability for motivational states.

Underlying the debate about the consequences of baptism is a disagreement about what happened in the Fall. According to the Scholastic theology that is reflected in the thinking of the Council of Trent, the Fall did not corrupt human nature. What happened was, rather, that Adam and Eve lost, and lost not only for themselves but also for their descendants, a gift that they had been given in addition to their nature. This preternatural gift, which was called "original righteousness," or "original justice" (*justitia originalis*), consisted, first of all, in an orientation of the soul toward God, which made the soul able to know and love God more fully than it naturally could. It carried in its train an ordering of the powers of the human soul and body, such that all of them, including all the emotions and desires and all the functions of the body, obeyed the highest part of the soul, the reason, more fully and perfectly than would have been naturally possible.

of their own" (*Institutes of the Christian Religion*, trans. Ford Lewis Battles, ed. John T. McNeill, 2 vols. Library of Christian Classics 20–21 [Philadelphia: Westminster Press, 1960], II.i.8, p. 251).

Original righteousness was lost in the Fall and is not restored completely by baptism. Baptism provides something that is in some respects as good and in some respects even better—a sanctifying grace, which makes it possible again for the soul to know and love God properly if it makes proper use of its freedom. But sanctifying grace does not completely restore the ordering of all the powers of the soul and body. It does not remove the natural independence of the desires and emotions from the reason, which constitutes, so to speak, a natural disorder within us.

This disorder is called "concupiscence." Concupiscence is not nice but, being natural, is not itself sin. It can be called "tinder for sin" in the baptized, the idea being that this lack of natural agreement between the desires and the reason is there waiting to burst into flame if sin comes along to set it off. But it is not ignited unless the soul, by its own free will, sins. Consequently, any sin occurring in someone who has been baptized is not "original" sin, but "actual" sin.

The Reformers held a different view of the matter. According to them, a corruption that is itself sin remains after baptism and even after the fullest regeneration that is possible for us in this world. Regeneration does remove any guilt that may be imputed from Adam's sin. And as long as the Christian is in a state of grace, justified by faith, the corruption that remains is not imputed as liability to punishment. The corruption is in itself sin, however, and the regenerate person is "at once righteous and a sinner" (*simul justus et peccator*), in Luther's famous phrase.

This is connected with the Reformers' view that what was lost in the Fall was not a preternatural gift, but something that belonged to human nature. Our nature itself having been corrupted, the ensuing disorder in us, which the Reformers also called "concupiscence," cannot be excused as natural. Protestants were accordingly prepared to say that concupiscence is in itself sin.

I think it follows from this disagreement that the Catholic and the Protestant doctrines of original sin have rather different subject matters and different epistemological bases. The Protestant doctrine is not primarily about infants. Claims about infants get involved in it, but it starts with a morally corrupt condition discoverable in all of us as adults. Then the observation that this corrupt condition can be traced back before any sinful act of ours yields the conclusion that it was already in us as infants.

The Protestant doctrine of original sin, thus, has a largely empirical basis in our experience of the thinking and behavior of human adults and children. The Genesis narrative of the Fall has undoubtedly played an important part in Protestant theology. But the identification of original sin as a persisting evil, observably at work in baptized adults, has enabled Kant, and leading post-Kantian Protestant theologians, to retain the main substance of the Protestant doctrine without any essential dependence on the story of Adam and Eve.

The Catholic doctrine of original sin, on the other hand, at least in its sixteenth-century context—a society where almost everyone was baptized soon after birth—is mainly about infants and secondarily about members (mostly remote in space or time) of non-Christian societies. It is obviously, I think, much less empirical than the Protestant doctrine. For original sin itself, as opposed to the tinder left behind after it, is something that no one, on the Catholic view, would have experienced in a society where everyone had been baptized as an infant.

MOTIVES AND THE WILL: SCHOLASTICISM

Let us return now to the crucial difficulty about the relation between voluntariness and our responsibility for motivational states. This problem has a long history in the Christian ethical tradition. For it is characteristic of that tradition to see ethical goodness and badness as depending heavily on motivational states and especially on our deepest motivation, on what Kant would call our "ultimate subjective ground" of choice. Among the chief sins are hate and indifference toward God and our neighbors and misdirected or disordered love. I will discuss three different ways in which the idea of voluntariness has historically been related to this conviction of our accountability for motivational states.

The first approach I want to discuss is that which prevailed among Scholastic philosophers and theologians such as St. Thomas Aquinas. They held both that we are directly account-

able for love and hate and certain other motives and that we are
directly accountable only for what is directly voluntary. What
enabled them consistently to hold both these positions is that, on
the Scholastic view, love and hate are acts of the will and, thus,
directly voluntary. They are acts of the will in the sense that they
are the will doing what it is a faculty for doing: namely, being
for and against things.

This is not to say that we are directly accountable for all our
motivational states. Scholastic philosophy does not hold us directly accountable for hunger and thirst, for example. That is
because they are not acts of the will but, rather, acts of another
faculty, the sensory appetite (*appetitus sensitivus*). Thus, the distinction between what is and is not directly voluntary, on the
Scholastic view, is drawn on the basis of a faculty psychology. I
will elaborate on certain important points in this. I want to say,
first, something about the will and about love and hate as acts of
the will; second, something about the sensory appetite; and, finally, something about concupiscence.

First, the will. Aquinas calls the will "the intellectual appetite"
(*appetitus intellectivus*). We are accustomed to use the word "appetite" mainly for desires for physical satisfactions. Obviously,
it has a broader meaning in St. Thomas's term." Any faculty of
going for something or against something is an "appetite," in his
sense. It is interesting, and I suspect significant of the Scholastic
background of eighteenth-century German philosophy, that *appetitus* has a closer translation in Kant's German than in our English; it is precisely a *Begehrungsvermögen*.

More important for our present purpose, the notion of an intellectual appetite, or a will in Aquinas's sense, is broader, in another direction, than the notion that I think most of us usually
have of the will. This appetite or appetitive power is a faculty not
only of controlling actual behavior, but also of intending, desir-
ing, enjoying, and their opposites. This is also quite clearly the
case with the Kantian *Begehrungsvermögen*. It is explicit in
Aquinas. He says of the will,[10] for instance, "The appetitive part
has not only this act, that it seeks [*appetat*] what it does not have,

---

[10] In this passage he speaks specifically of God's will, but I think it clearly
applies to the will generally.

but also that it loves what it has and delights in it."[11] It is a standard Scholastic view that enjoyment (*fruitio*) is an act of the will. The will, of course, is not just any appetite. It is specifically an intellectual appetite, because it is situated in the reason—that is, because it always involves an understanding of its object. As Suárez puts it, "Actus voluntatis non potest ferri in incognitum" (an act of the will cannot be directed to something unknown).[12]

In speaking of the acts of this intellectual or rational appetitive faculty, later Scholastics distinguished two kinds of acts of the will. They distinguished "elicited" from "commanded" acts of the will. The commanded acts of the will are those that consist partly in events other than the operation of the will itself—for example, acts that consist partly in motions of the limbs. The idea that inspires this way of speaking is that, in order to move the limbs, the will has to command another and inferior faculty to move the limbs. The will cannot move them all by itself, and if it were disconnected from the inferior faculty by some paralysis, the will could not move them at all.

The elicited acts of the will, by contrast, are those that consist entirely in the operation of the will itself. In these the will does not depend on any inferior faculty to accomplish the act; and for that reason the elicited acts of the will were regarded as more fully within the will's control than its commanded acts. Motivational states belonging to the will, such as love and hate, being seen as internal to the will, were classified as elicited acts of the will.

The word *act*, of course, is being used here in a broad sense in which being in a motivational state over an indefinitely protracted period of time can count as an act. Any actualization of a power or faculty is an act in this sense; it does not have to happen at an instant or in a minute. The Scholastic notion of "act" is not essentially episodic.

Hunger and thirst, as I have noted, were not viewed in Schol-

---

[11] St. Thomas Aquinas, *Summa Theologiae* (hereafter, ST), I, q. 19, a.1, *ad primum*. Henceforth I will cite this text by parenthetical references.

[12] Francisco Suárez, *De voluntario et involuntario*, VI.iv.2 (*Opera omnia* IV [Paris: Vivès, 1865], p. 245). I am ignoring a distinction between a "higher" and a "lower" reason that figures in some Scholastic discussions of the will.

astic philosophy as acts of the will. They were assigned to a different faculty, called the "sensory appetite" (*appetitus sensitivus*—or, in Kantian German, the *sinnliches Begehrungsvermögen*). Aquinas says that "the sensory appetite is an inclination following a sensory apprehension" (ST, I, q. 81, a. 2). The sensory appetite presupposes a sensory apprehension of its object, as the will (the intellectual appetite) presupposes an intellectual understanding of its object. The desires or cravings that belong to the sensory appetite are not voluntary, because they are responses, not to intellectual apprehension of an object, but only to sensory stimulation. Aquinas holds that the will, and, indeed, the soul, cannot completely control the sensory appetite, because the sensory appetite, unlike the will, "is a power [*virtus*] of a bodily organ" (ST, I–II, q. 17, a. 7).

The notion of concupiscence is closely connected with that of a sensory appetite. The word *concupiscence* (*concupiscentia*) has at least three senses in Saint Thomas. (1) In the first sense, the Latin word *concupiscentia* originally meant desire rather generally. In New Testament contexts, for example, it is a translation of the Greek *epithymia*, which, while it sometimes has a sensual flavor to it, really is a general word for desire. Sometimes Aquinas uses *concupiscence* in this general sense, speaking for example, of a "*concupiscentia sapientiae*" (a concupiscence for wisdom, a desire for wisdom), which is an act of the will, according to Aquinas, because it has a nonsensible object and occurs without passion or excitement of the mind (*animus*) (ST, I, q. 82, a. 5). However, this is not the typical use of *concupiscence* in Aquinas or in other Scholastic sources.

(2) Most commonly, and in the second sense, concupiscence is one of the two main functions of the sensory appetite. The other function is anger, very broadly construed. "The object of the power of concupiscence," Aquinas says, "is sensible good or evil, simply understood, which is the delightful or the painful"; whereas "the object of the power of anger is the same good or evil according as it has the nature of the arduous or difficult" (ST, I–II, q. 23, a. 1).[13] In this sense concupiscence is simply a natural function of our sensory appetite.

---

[13] Somewhat freely translated, for the sake of clarity.

(3) But there is still a third sense. *Concupiscence* can also mean, in Aquinas, the disorder (*inordinatio*) by which other powers of the soul besides the will "are inordinately turned toward a changeable good" (ST, I–II, q. 82, a. 3). On Scholastic and Tridentine views, this disorder is a deplorable but natural result of the natural operation of sensory powers, once original sin removes the restraint of the preternatural gift of original righteousness, which in Adam restrained this disorderly operation.

It is with regard to this third sense, from the Scholastic point of view, that controversy arose with Protestants as to whether concupiscence is sin. Catholic theologians held that concupiscence in this sense, not being a function of the will, and hence not voluntary, cannot be imputed as sin in its own right. They accommodated biblical texts that could be alleged as evidence for an opposing view by saying that concupiscence, as a disorder in the functioning of the nonvoluntary powers of the soul, can be called "matter of original sin" in the unregenerate.[14]

There is, I think, at least one feature of these Scholastic views about sensory concupiscence that will be retained in a plausible account of our responsibility for motivational states. There are desires that seem to be merely natural responses to sensory stimulation, or to something as primitive, cognitively, as sensory stimulation. An example would be the desire for food when one's blood sugar level is low. It would be bizarre to hold us directly accountable for these desires, even if they happen to be desires that, in a particular situation, it would be wrong to act on. Scholasticism seems to be right about that. I will argue that the Reformers, or some of them, also agree with it.

MOTIVES AND THE WILL: THE REFORMERS

The simplest thing to say about how the Reformers deal with the problem of relating our accountability for fundamental motiva-

---

[14] Catholic theology gives a complicated account here because it is recognized that both St. Augustine and St. Paul refer to concupiscence as sin in certain contexts. In order to accommodate Scholastic doctrine to this way of speaking, it is said that concupiscence can be called "sin" because it proceeds from sin and incites to sin. In the unregenerate, moreover, who still have origi-

tional states to considerations of voluntariness is that they deny that we are accountable only for what we freely and voluntarily do. They take the view, in effect, that freedom is not necessary for accountability. This is obviously connected with their doctrines of grace and predestination, and perhaps, indeed, largely motivated by those doctrines. However, it seems to me that we can find, in the Reformers, particularly in Philip Melanchthon, indications of other, more narrowly philosophical objections to the Scholastic solution of the problem; and that is what particularly interests me here.

Melanchthon focuses on an issue about control, which I think will seem obvious to us, once we think about it, but which, rather strikingly, is hardly mentioned in Scholastic discussions of the problem that I have read. Melanchthon acknowledges that our will has a control—a "liberty," as he puts it—over the motions of our limbs; but he denies that the will has that sort of control over our own emotions (*affectus*), such as love and hate. He writes:

> If you estimate the power of the human will as touches its natural capacities according to human reason, it cannot be denied but that there is in it a certain kind of liberty in things external. These are matters which you yourself experience to be within your power, such as to greet or not to greet a man, to put on a certain attire or not to put it on, to eat meat or not to eat it as you will. . . . In truth, however, because God does not look upon external works but upon the inner motions of the heart, Scripture has recorded nothing about such freedom. . . . On the other hand, internal emotions are not within our power. For by experience and practice we have found out that the will of its own accord cannot assume love, hate, or the like emotions, but that one emotion is conquered by another. So much so that, for instance, because you were offended by someone you at one time loved, you now cease to love him; for you love yourself more ardently than you love anyone else.[15]

---

nal sin, concupiscence can be regarded in some sense as the matter of original sin—the form being the lack of original righteousness. In the baptized, as I have noted above, Catholic theology would speak of concupiscence as "tinder for sin." Strictly speaking, however, concupiscence, not being voluntary, cannot be imputed as sin in its own right, according to Catholic theology.

[15] *The Loci Communes of Philip Melanchthon* [1521], trans. Charles Leander Hill (Boston: Meador Publishing Co., 1944), pp. 75f. I have slightly modified the translation.

In Scholastic terms, Melanchthon is claiming here that certain commanded acts of the will are more within the control of the will than such elicited acts as love and hate—which is just the reverse of the Scholastic view that the elicited acts are more within the control of the will than the commanded acts. Why would he think that? Melanchthon argues as follows:

> We learn from experience and practice that we cannot take on or put off the love or hate of any thing. Suppose you love a girl; that you think six hundred times to yourself that from now on you will neglect her—that is a frigid and fictitious thought of the understanding, not a decision of the will. For the heart cannot decide against itself. Suppose you hate an enemy, or that you envy an enemy something; that you think six hundred times that you are going to return to friendship with him is a frigid and fictitious thought, until a stronger emotion conquers this emotion.[16]

Concluding, or deciding, by a conscious decision of the intellect and will that one ought to change one's love or hate, and consciously resolving to do so, will not produce the desired change. Melanchthon claims that that is a fact of experience; and it seems to me that that is true. There is a kind of direct voluntary control that we have over the motions of our limbs in certain circumstances—when we are not paralyzed, for example—and that we do not have over our loves, hates, desires, and many other elicited acts of the will, in the Scholastic sense, though we often wish we did have this power over them.

I believe that, in modern thought, faculty psychology has been discarded in favor of this sort of control as a criterion of the voluntary. Modern thought has predominantly adopted a conception of the voluntary according to which the directly voluntary is only that which is within our control in approximately the way and the degree in which the motions of our limbs normally are. I think we see this change, this shift of focus, taking place in Melanchthon.

It is true that in the 1521 edition of the *Loci Communes* he has not completely made the shift, at least as regards his use of the

---

[16] Philip Melanchthon, *Loci Communes in ihrer Urgestalt*, ed. G. L. Plitt and Th. Kolde (Leipzig, 1900), p. 79. This passage is from the second edition of the *Loci*, published in 1522.

term *will*. For he ascribes emotions to the will, saying, "Nor will I hear the sophists if they deny that the human emotions, such as love, hate, joy, sorrow, envy, ambition, and the like, pertain to the will. For now, nothing is said about hunger or thirst. But what is the will, if not the fountain of the emotions?"[17]

Here we still see something of the Scholastic conception of the will, as a faculty of, among other things, loving and hating. But the question as to what faculty these things are operations of is clearly much less important to Melanchthon than the question of control.

Taking love and hate and the like to be involuntary because they are not controllable in the relevant way is, of course, not to deny that love and hate are operations of the will in the Scholastic sense of "the will." This point has often been acknowledged by Protestant writers—as, for example, in the following statement by the seventeenth-century Reformed theologian François Turretin:

> In the first place, "voluntary" is said either strictly or broadly. In the former sense, it is said for that which happens through the actual motion of the will. In the latter sense, it is said for that which in any way either affects the will or inheres in it or depends on the will. Here, indeed, we are not concerned with the voluntary broadly speaking. For we do not deny that sin is in the will, and can to that extent be called "voluntary," at least with regard to the subject in which it inheres. But we are concerned with the voluntary strictly speaking, which involves an act of choice [*prohaeresis*] and of the will. And in this sense we deny that all sin is *hekousion* [voluntary].[18]

In other words, Turretin would not deny that all sin is voluntary in relation to a criterion of the voluntary drawn in the Scholastic

---

[17] *Loci Communes*, trans. Hill, p. 76; translation modified.

[18] Franciscus Turretinus, *Institutio Theologiae Elencticae*, Part I (New York: Robert Carter, 1847), p. 537 (Locus IX, q. ii). A similar distinction, explicitly aimed, like Turretin's, against the "Papists and Socinians," can be found in Turretin's younger Lutheran contemporary David Hollaz. The explicit Protestant rejection of the doctrine that all sin is voluntary can be found quite clearly as early as Melanchton's 1531 *Apology for the Augsburg Confession*. For references to Melanchthon and Hollaz, see Karl Hase, *Hutterus Redivivus*, 7th ed. (Leipzig: Breitkopf und Hartel, 1848), p. 194n.

manner from faculty psychology, but he does deny it in relation to a criterion based on control.

It is doubtful whether Protestants should grant, as Turretin seems to do here, that all states that are directly and inherently sinful are in the will, even in the Scholastic sense. For some states regarded by Protestants as inherently sinful, such as unbelief, are cognitive states, and it is not clear that they should be regarded as inhering in the will rather than solely in the intellect. But we need not pursue this issue here.[19]

It will be more important to say something about the Protestant treatment of concupiscence as sin. Luther was vehemently attacked for holding that concupiscence is sin. Catholic writers have sometimes accused Protestants of meaning that there is full-fledged sin in the sensory appetite as such. But this seems at least not to have been Melanchthon's meaning, so far as I have read him. It is noteworthy that, in one of the passages I have quoted, Melanchthon says, "Nothing is being said here about hunger or thirst." In excluding hunger and thirst from consideration when he talks about the emotions of the heart that God is concerned with and that we are accountable for, Melanchthon is ruling out precisely the cases where it is most plausible to say, "This is not imputable because it is a natural response to a sensory stimulus."

There was a great deal of talking past one another going on in the dispute about concupiscence. I think that the Protestants, for the most part, were abandoning the Scholastic use of *concupiscence* in favor of a different use based on their exegesis of the Bible. Their use of the word was influenced, for example, by the fact that "Thou shalt not covet," in the Tenth Commandment, was rendered in Latin as *Ne concupisces*, with the verb related to *concupiscentia* (concupiscence) used for "covet." This was important because this is the one of the Ten Commandments in which a motivational state seems to be explicitly forbidden in its own right. Expounding this commandment, Melanchthon says,

> For it does not only condemn here those vicious emotions to which "consent" is given, as they say;[20] it also condemns the wicked

---

[19] I have discussed it elsewhere: see my "The Virtue of Faith," *Faith and Philosophy*, 1 (1984): 3–15, esp. 4–6, and "Involuntary Sins," *The Philosophical Review*, 94 (1985): 3–31, esp. 17–21.

[20] The reference is to a Scholastic notion of "consent."

inclination itself, which is a certain perpetual aversion from God and a stubborn opposition fighting against the law of God, and which begets an infinite confusion of appetitions, even if consent is not always given. . . . And enmity against God is not to be understood as a light evil, for it includes many plagues: doubts about God, aversion from God, grumbling against God when we are punished; also infinite wandering and errant motions against the law of God—namely, confidence of one's own wisdom and powers, contempt of others, envy, ambition, avarice, flames of libido, desire for vengeance.[21]

We see here something interesting about the use of the word *concupiscence* and the conception attached to it. On one hand Melanchthon wants to seize on the commandment "Thou shalt not covet," understood with the use of the word *concupiscence*, to oppose the idea that nothing is inherently sinful except what involves a full, conscious, voluntary consent. On the other hand, if you look at the sorts of things that he brings under this heading of concupiscence (or *Ne concupisces*), it is quite clear that very few of them are matters of natural response to sensory stimulus. Melanchthon just is not interested in connecting concupiscence with sensation. Because it has nothing to do with the use of these terms in Scripture, which is his primary concern, the fact that that connection was crucial in the Scholastic tradition seems to be of no importance to him.

This disregard for Scholastic tradition may be due in part to influences of Renaissance humanism, but Melanchthon is doubtless driven here primarily by his interpretation of the Bible and by Martin Luther's religious experience and religious vision. Behind what Melanchthon says, however, there is also a more narrowly philosophical point of some interest—a point distinct from the one about control that I mentioned before. If we ask ourselves how we should classify such a state as antagonism toward God, or sexual lust for another person, the Scholastic theory offers essentially two alternatives: either a natural response to a sensory stimulus or a conscious consent of the will. To be sure, this dichotomy is modified by a gradation of degrees of consciousness,

---

[21] From the 1543 edition of the *Loci Communes* (*Corpus Reformatorum* XXI, col. 710).

but that seems to be the only sort of modification that fits into the theory. Even with this modification, the dichotomy seems to me—and I think it seemed to Melanchthon—a Procrustean bed; it simply is not all that plausible to try to fit such states as antagonism toward God or sexual lust for another person into that dichotomy, and Melanchthon does not want to do it.

The Protestant reaction to this situation, I take it, was largely to give up faculty psychology as a criterion of ethical accountability. I have a lot of sympathy for that response. Another alternative, however, would be to try to develop a more adequate faculty psychology that could be used to provide a criterion for ethical accountability and to relate accountability for motivational states to considerations of voluntariness; and in a way, that was Kant's approach.

MOTIVES AND THE WILL: KANT

Protestant though his theory of original sin is in other respects, Kant's treatment of moral responsibility has more in common with the Catholic and Aristotelian Scholasticism that was so deeply entrenched in the German universities. In the first place, he was not willing to give up the thesis that we are accountable only for our free and voluntary actions. And, in the second place, like the Scholastics, he finds the criterion of accountability in a distinction between active and passive faculties, and sometimes calls the passive one "sense," and the active one "reason" or "intellect."

We must not suppose, however, that Kant conceives the distinction of faculties just as the Scholastics did. For Kant, a desire or inclination of the sensory faculty need not be in any simple way a response to sensory stimulation. Reason may be very much involved in its formation.[22] What is crucial, for Kant, in the distinction of faculties is that the self is passive in its sensory functioning—that it has no power to determine that functioning by a choice moved only by pure practical reason—whereas it is active

---

[22] See Kant's account of the "predisposition to humanity" in *Religion Within the Limits of Reason Alone*, p. 22.

in the functioning of its rational power of choice. Accordingly, Kant says that sensory pleasure (*Lust*) and displeasure (*Unlust*), or desire and inclination, are given causally prior to any decision of the will, whereas pleasure and displeasure that follow the decision of the will are intellectual.[23]

There is another and even more important difference between the Kantian and the Scholastic distinction of faculties. The Scholastic faculties are part of an essentially empirical psychology. The Kantian faculties are not. For the crucial move in Kant's reconciliation of the doctrine of original sin with his insistence that "nothing is ethically, that is, imputably evil but that which is our own act"[24] is to deny that the relevant act of will is accessible to empirical observation.

Kant holds, as we have seen, that our fundamental ethical disposition and our propensity to evil were not adopted by any act in time. How, then, can they be imputably evil? Kant's answer is that they were adopted by a free and voluntary act, but it was not an act in time. Being outside of time, which is the necessary form of all our experience, this act is also outside our experience. It is neither an empirical nor a temporal event.

It might be thought that, by its very meaning, the word *act* can only signify an event in time. But Kant holds that there are two senses in which the word *act* can be used: in the first, it refers to acts occurring in time, empirical acts; in the second, it applies to something that is not an event in time: namely, to an act of the self as a being that transcends time. The latter, according to Kant, is the sort of act by which we freely and voluntarily adopt our most fundamental maxims, our ethical dispositions. "The propensity to evil, then, is an act in [this] sense, and at the same time the formal ground of every unlawful act in the [other] sense."[25]

This explanation, which Kant gives quite explicitly, is in full agreement with his metaphysics. His talk of timeless acts, with its implication that the choosing self has an existence outside of

---

[23] Immanuel Kant, introduction to *The Metaphysics of Morals* (pp. 211f. in the Prussian Academy edition of the original German); pp. 8f. in Kant, *The Doctrine of Virtue*, trans. Mary J. Gregor (New York: Harper Torchbooks, 1964).

[24] *Reason Within the Limits of Reason Alone*, p. 26.

[25] Ibid., p. 26.

time, is unpalatable to most of us. But Kant is already committed
to a distinction between things as they appear to us ("phenomena") and things as they are in themselves ("noumena"), and to
the thesis that it is only the phenomena that are in time, and the
noumena have no temporal properties or relations. Time and
again, beginning with the Antinomy of the first *Critique*, Kant
appeals to this distinction to resolve a paradox. Here he uses it
to enable us to see the holding of an attitude, the having of a
motive—indeed, the having of a propensity to evil—as a free act,
and thus to see ourselves as free, not only in what we would
ordinarily think of as actions, but also in the having of motivational states. The faculty psychology, therefore, which grounds
Kant's criterion of ethical accountability is a psychology of nou-
menal faculties, a distinction between those things in which we
are active and those in which we are passive, as we are in ourselves, outside of time.

Within the framework of Kant's metaphysics this is not merely
an ingenious but also a reasonable solution of the problem. It is
perfectly intelligible and coherent if Kant's conception of the
phenomenal/noumenal distinction is intelligible and coherent.[26]
This does not necessarily commend his solution to those of us
who are not prepared to accept his phenomena/noumena distinction as it applies to the self. Still, there is something I like about
it. It exemplifies a more general idea, that our ethical motives
and dispositions may be something that we are doing, something
that we ourselves spontaneously produce, even if we do not acquire them by anything that we experience as an act of choosing
them.

This idea is not necessarily tied to the notion of timeless nou-
menal action. The view is gaining currency again that not only
events, but also substances, or, at any rate, persons, can be causes
and that free actions are not caused by preceding events but by
their agents. And if persons can in this way be spontaneous

---

[26] Whether it is consistent with Kant's theology of regeneration is another
question. Philip Quinn argues for a negative answer in his excellent paper
"Original Sin, Radical Evil and Moral Identity," *Faith and Philosophy*, 1
(1984): 188–202; but I am not completely convinced. See also Quinn's later
paper, "Christian Atonement and Kantian Justification," ibid., 3 (1986): 440–
62, esp. 448.

causes of their actions, why can't they also in the same way be spontaneous causes of their motivational states? Why not, indeed?[27]

CONCLUSION

Even if we believe in original sin, few of us would adopt without qualification Aquinas's or Melanchthon's or Kant's theory of the matter. Certainly, I would not. But we can learn from all of them. One thing we can learn is that a theory of original sin will draw on a variety of sources. We should not have expected it to be otherwise. Any such theory will obviously draw inspiration from the Bible and Christian tradition. The thinkers I have discussed differ in the extent to which exegesis of Scripture or other authoritative texts governs their thought on the subject, but they all draw on ideas of the Christian tradition, and they all are giving form to a conviction of the central ethical importance of good motives. This conviction is very deeply rooted in the Christian faith and its primary texts, though (at least in our culture) it can also appeal to moral common sense.

At the same time, it is clear that, on pain of schizophrenia, a theory of original sin will be part of a more comprehensive psychological theory and will draw on materials of psychological theorizing that are not specially Christian. Many of the differences among the historic figures I have examined arise from differences in their nontheological views.

It is hardly imaginable that Kant would have written as he did on this topic if he had not thought a lot about Christianity. His treatment of it demonstrates the depth of his engagement with Christian theology and provides grounds for classifying him as a Christian philosopher, if not an orthodox one. Nonetheless, Kant proposes the possibility of a theory of original sin that makes no essential appeal to religious authority. This possibility is important to the apologetic role of the concept of original sin exemplified in the thought of Reinhold Niebuhr.

---

[27] I have developed this suggestion, without reference to Kant, in "Involuntary Sins," 24–31.

More surprisingly, perhaps, the history we have surveyed suggests ways in which philosophical understanding may depend on an understanding, if not an acceptance, of theology. We have seen that important parts of the development of conceptions of the voluntary and of moral responsibility from the Middle Ages into the early modern period took place in the context of discussions of original sin. It would be fatuous to expect to comprehend the former without some understanding of the latter.

QUESTIONS AND ANSWERS

Q: I very much admired your carefully reasoned exposé of Kant's theory and of what preceded it. I think you indicated quite well how this is a beautiful instance of how theology can directly influence philosophy without killing its autonomy. I have two historical points and one point of exegesis. It is interesting historically that the interpretation of Adam as merely a model is very much present in the earliest Fathers. For example, we find that Irenaeus and also the entire Antiochian school of exegesis had basically that idea, contrary to the Alexandrian school. The other point, where I'm not sure I completely share your interpretation, if I understand it, is on Kierkegaard. It is not the case that Kierkegaard says simply, "Each one is responsible for his own sins and for nothing more." He does say that, but that is not the whole story. There is also this element in Kierkegaard, that the situation, as he says in *The Concept of Dread*, fundamentally changes with the entrance of sinfulness in the human race, and he explicitly appeals to Romans 5:10. He does not want a purely liberal interpretation of that text as a model. He says, "We are a species, and when sinfulness once enters that species, the whole situation of the species changes." And, consequently, there is an accumulation of what he would call then a concupiscence that grows ever more intense as human beings become more sinful.

Finally, the one small question of exegesis. There is one thing I have never understood in Kant's interpretation of original sin, and I am wondering whether you can perhaps enlighten us a bit further than you have done so far on that point. When Kant speaks of "the evil disposition" or the "disposition toward evil" which affects all human beings, he speaks of a free and voluntary act, but not in time. I do not understand how such a thing could be compatible with any kind of responsibility for it, because it seems to me that the notion of voluntariness he invokes here explicitly would require at least consciousness of it, and that for consciousness of that original act in time, it is not sufficient in this case to say, "Well, I'm discussing the matter on a nonempirical level." When it comes to voluntary acts, there is no other level but the empirical, one would think.

A: Those are very good questions. Let me say, first, that I certainly do not disagree with what you have said about the early Fathers. I have not studied the Antiochians on this, but I certainly agree about Irenaeus. In general, I guess, I have found plausible those interpretations which suggest that what we think of as a traditional codifying of the doctrine of original sin is enormously influenced by Augustine, and that things that happened before or independently of Augustine in the Christian tradition show a much greater variety of uses of the Genesis narratives.

With regard to Kierkegaard, it has occurred to me that I might be incautious in what I said about him here, and I want to think more about that, and I thank you for raising the issue.

On the interpretation of Kant, I think I want to stick by what I said. It seems to me that it is clear that he says that the most fundamental maxims are adopted by an act that is not an act in time. It cannot, therefore, be an act of which we have experience in his system. What is our cognitive relation to it? At a minimum, it is an act in which he thinks we have moral grounds for believing. Is it an act of which we have some sort of consciousness, perhaps by reflection? Well, I haven't worked that out. I think that this is a very interesting issue and would relate, specifically, to what view one would take in the rather controversial interpretation of things he says about the fact of reason and, in general, the view one takes of his theory of freedom. So, while I'm not sure that I have an answer to that question you raise, I think it's a very good question.

Q: I was both instructed and persuaded by your reading of the complex passages in Kant.* I would like to hear more, however,

---

*Editor's note: The questioner is David Tracy, one of the symposium speakers.

on your references to Reinhold Niebuhr and to Thomas Aquinas on at least a general way of formulating one of the issues they have both shared in, the move from original sin to personal sin, and the understanding of the responsibility and the freedom that is present in the human situation. Surely, one of the most puzzling concepts in Niebuhr, and one of the controversial and influential, was precisely his insistence that sin is inevitable but not necessary.

There have been, as I'm sure you know, analyses of Thomas Aquinas in a more contemporary setting on this issue. Most famously, Bernard Lonergan's *Grace and Freedom* suggests that Thomas's view is really not confined only to the passage you cite or to the understanding you cite of original sin, but pertains to the movement from original to personal sin. I have always been persuaded by Lonergan's reading, though, as he admitted himself, it's a contemporary reading, as is Niebuhr's of the Protestant tradition. In Lonergan's reading, as I remember it, the question in Thomas Aquinas is how much deliberation do you need for a free act? To use, not Thomas's example but Lonergan's: we eat breakfast everyday, but we very rarely explicitly deliberate about that act of eating breakfast. Nevertheless, if pressed, one would say one freely eats breakfast. Thomas's psychological theory is very much like that, especially in the *Summa*. I think Lonergan is right to read Thomas as positing a difference. It is like Niebuhr's problem with "inevitable" and "necessary." Thomas's problem, as Lonergan reads him— correctly, I think—is distinguishing the difference between classical and statistical necessity. How much deliberation do we need for a particular free act? The movement from original to personal sin is on that model. The movement from "eventually we're going to be tired and exhausted and not able to deliberate; that is the effect of original sin" gives us to an inevitability, but not a necessity, to sin. That can be retranslated into contemporary terms from the philosophy of science of a statistical but not classical necessity. So, I suppose all I am saying is that it would be helpful to hear further your own reflections on Niebuhr and a comparison with Thomas, which has been made by John Courtney Murray, as a matter of fact.

A: Thank you. I have to say I'm not familiar with Lonergan's interpretation of Aquinas and am therefore reluctant to comment on it. The other point you raised, about Niebuhr, is a very good one, and it's well worth comparing Kant with Niebuhr on this. This is a point on which Kant differs, I think, from Niebuhr and, indeed, from most of the other people I was talking about. You are absolutely right about what Niebuhr says, and Kant says nothing of the sort. In fact, one of the most disturbing points in Kant's analysis, from a theoretical point of view, is that he doesn't really say much to account for the universality of original sin; he attests that it's an empirical fact. There's a reason why he doesn't: Kant, in a certain sense, is not about to explain the radical evil in human nature. He is trying to explain *how* it happens, but he is not about to explain *why* it happens.

Now, Niebuhr—and in this I take it he's following Kierkegaard—tries to give an explanation of why it's there. Kant does not want to do that, because to give an explanation of why it's there would be to offer a rationale for it, and, of course, Kant's ethical theory is so profoundly and fundamentally a theory of practical rationality that Kant is totally committed to the view that, at bottom, radical evil is thoroughly irrational. So, we have in Kant no analogue; there is no analogue, I think, to Niebuhr's claim that it's inevitable but not necessary. No, it's not inevitable; it's just a fact, a fact that it's too late for us to change in some way—although there is also the theory of the overcoming of evil by good.

That is a difference between Kant and Niebuhr, and I think a difference profoundly rooted in Kant's ethics.

Q: Like the other speakers, I'd like to thank you for a very informative and illuminating discussion. I'd like to suggest and question a couple of things. One is the idea in itself of calling this "original sin." After all, everyone knows that there is weakness, vice, turmoil, and disorder in the human condition. For people like Aristotle or Plato, it's easier to handle it. It's simply the way things are, then we try to become better through virtue and good actions. Once you put that into a context of creation, you've got to say, "Well, where could this have come from?" And it couldn't have come from God. Therefore, there must have been something that brought it about. I think that kind of negative theology—not about the best but about the worst, in this case—is part of the sense of original sin, and perhaps it has something to do with Kant's appeal to the ultra-noumenal here, some kind of action that we never really experienced as a root, that is the theological source for this. That's one point I'd like to make.

The other is that I really enjoyed your analysis of faculties, issues of guilt, and the shifts that occurred within them. That was extremely illuminating. I wonder if you think the Scholastic and the Reformist traditions had enough of a role for character of the dispositions that are shaped through earlier actions. It seems to me that we're left with a radical difference between a choice and something that's there by nature. In between, there's something that would be *ethos*, the way we are because of the way we've acted or because of a certain endowment at birth. Within that area could there be an element of freedom, but freedom that is not as punctual as a single choice?

A: That was a very interesting question about the role of character—two very interesting questions. Let me start with the second one about the role of character. I'm not sure why it is, but it's clear that the notions of character and of virtue and vice have, in fact, tended to play a smaller role in Protestant ethics than in Catholic ethics. The emphasis in Protestant ethics has fallen more punctually on particular actions and their particular motives. That probably has something to do with the notion of obedience being very central to the Protestant interpretation of biblical ethics. The Protestant emphasis on grace and forgiveness also supports this thinking. Forget about the past; this is what God says to you now—obey now. There's that sort of mood in Protestant ethical thinking which probably has been less conducive to emphasis on the virtues and vices and the ethics of character.

There is perhaps a deeper reason. I'm not very confident about this, but it may be that, even in Scholastic ethics, for all the talk about character, it may not be so natural to plug that right into the issues of accountability, sin, and so forth because of what is clearly recognized in Aristotelian traditions as the social nature of the formation of character. I think there is something in all Western Christian traditions that tends to zero in on the individual when we start thinking about sin, and that may be a mistake in Western Christian traditions.

Q: I agree, and it seems to me it's because you have this eternal destiny there as a kind of ultimate horizon, so that the actual life and the human situation pales in comparison with whether or not you're guilty for eternity.

A: Yes.

Q: I think that is true, that it's downplayed even in the Catholic tradition.

A: Right. I suppose that's also connected with the fact that in the Christian tradition, individuals have an eternal destiny. Communities, except for the Church Universal, don't. And the Church Universal is, I think even in Catholicism, a little bit too ethereal to grip our emotions in the way that the Jewish sense of the Jewish people grips Jewish emotions.

Remind me again of the other point; I thought it was a very interesting one.

Q: The contrast between treating human vice and wickedness and so forth as original sin, as coming from original sin, is related to creation, because where else would it come from, but from within ourselves? Do you agree?

A: Yes. Certainly. To finish with a little note of possible disagreement with the other speaker this morning,* there's a point here at which I suppose I feel a strong resistance to disconnecting the Christian tradition from certain metaphysical drives, although I can also see interesting possibilities in trying to disconnect it. That is, the Christian tradition, at least in the West, has had a strong drive to develop an integrated picture of the world, its history, and its relation to God with God at the absolute origin, and that, of course, creates problems about how evil gets there. And there is, I think, a clear contrast with Judaism on that. The Jewish tradition has been much more relaxed about that. The rabbis talked about the "evil impulse" without worrying how it got there, and as people like John Levinson have been reminding us, the Jewish tradition has been much more relaxed in general about playing around with nonmonistic treatments of the problems of evil. That's true.

---

* Editor's note: John Caputo is being referred to here.

And while I see some attractions in those Jewish alternatives, I must say I find myself very reluctant to give up the traditional Western Christian impulse to try to get the picture whole, which I think does, indeed, account for a lot of what goes on in discussions of original sin, both in the most consciously theological and most consciously orthodox thinkers and also in the most liberal such as Kant, who still, as I argue, is very much a Christian philosopher.

5

The Problem of Christian Philosophy

Adriaan Peperzak*

HISTORY, SOCIOLOGY, AND CULTURAL ANTHROPOLOGY have turned the earth into a museum of cultures. Similarly, the history of philosophy is in danger of transforming its ongoing search for truth into a museum of philosophies, where none are taken very seriously, although most may be deemed interesting enough to be studied with admiration and a kind of detached sympathy. A museum displays many specimens without imposing specific preferences on its visitors. Besides modern, postmodern, classical, and medieval philosophy, we now have Continental, American, French, German, African, feminist, analytic, phenomenological, Jewish, and perhaps even Christian philosophy. Some contemporary professionals of philosophy claim that philosophy is essentially Greek; others admit the possibility of a Jewish, Greek-Jew or Jew-Greek, philosophy, but "Christian philosophy" is mostly seen as a hybrid. Even for Christians who are devoted to philosophy, it is a problematic term. There is a strong suspicion that to be Christian and to be passionately engaged in philosophy are mutually exclusive. Isn't the separation of faith and philosophy one of the most legitimate and well-probed axioms that belong to the legacy of modernity?

On the other hand, it seems odd that Christians who are engaged in philosophy feel greater affinity toward those modern and postmodern philosophers whose commerce with truth seems to be un- or anti-Christian than toward the tradition that extends

* An earlier version of this essay appears in Adriaan T. Peperzak, *Reason in Faith: On the Relevance of Christian Spirituality for Philosophy* (New York and Mahwah, N.J.: Paulist Press, 1999), pp. 105–29.

from Clement to Blondel and Marcel, thinkers who did not hide their attachment to the Christian community. Must philosophy be restricted to questions that are not of ultimate importance? Is philosophy a skill or science like other skills or sciences, or does it involve us in questions of life and death, of nihilism and ultimate meaning? Today it has again become possible to treat the question of Christian philosophy seriously, and we are invited to retrieve a long tradition of Christian thought in a postmodern or post-postmodern way. This enterprise involves the invention of a new relation to modernity and to its axioms about the nature of philosophy.

In this essay I will focus on some thematic aspects of our problem by concentrating on the following three questions:

1. What is philosophy and how do we engage in it?
2. What should we understand by the word *Christian*?
3. How are the philosophical and Christian moments connected in a person who is both a Christian and a philosopher?

The perspective from which I will reflect on these questions is that of one who attempts to be a Catholic and a philosopher at the same time. I am aware that the questions that must be answered have been debated before, particularly in France sixty years ago, but the situation has changed profoundly since the heyday of neo-Thomism. Neoscholasticism has disappeared; exegesis and history have shown how many meanings the word *Christian* has; the modern idea of an autonomous philosophy has made room for conceptions according to which philosophy is always rooted in prephilosophical soil and fed by nonphilosophical moods, mores, and traditions. We must, therefore, redefine the terms of our problem and start from the historical information and the thematic styles of thought that are available today, an enormous task to which I can offer only a modest contribution.

PHILOSOPHY

The contemporary situation of philosophy cannot be understood without a thorough knowledge of modern philosophy, by which I mean those methods and doctrines developed in the period from

Hobbes and Descartes to Hegel and twentieth-century analytic and scientific philosophy. All postmodern philosophies from Feuerbach, Marx, and Nietzsche to Heidegger, Levinas, and Derrida are parasitic on the modern predecessors whom they try to overcome in various critical ways. Most contemporary philosophers know little about the more than two thousand years of thinking that separate modern times from Plato and Aristotle. Nonetheless, they deem their acquaintance with the last four hundred years of thought to be a sufficient basis from which to understand *the* history of philosophy. Fortunately, a host of historical studies has made it impossible to identify philosophy with postmedieval thought. It has become a symptom of ignorance to see antiquity and the Middle Ages as a mere preparation for the scientific projects of our own time. Let us distance ourselves from such crude assumptions and challenge the monopoly of a certain "enlightenment" in setting the stage for philosophizing and the understanding of our history. With a view to the problem of Christian philosophy, at least the following modern assumptions must be made explicit and, perhaps, rejected:

1. The modern subject/object schema is determinative for all scientific thought;
2. Philosophy is synonymous with theory;
3. Philosophy is fundamental and autonomous; as such, it must be clearly separated from any other form of thought and language, such as literature, religion, theology, and spirituality.

A full explanation of these assumptions and their consequences cannot be given here, but since it is crucial to see their importance to our problem and to question their solidity, I must at least briefly summarize the extent to which they have been overcome after a hundred years of phenomenology.

Subject/object

Phenomenology has shown that neither human experience nor being can be understood within the framework of a subject in confrontation with objects. Objectivity is a specific kind of phenomenality; there are many other, and more primordial, modes of being. Since the phenomenality of being, as that which we feel, smell, desire, enjoy, recall, and so forth, each time demands an appropriate response, we cannot characterize the human openness to phenomena as the consciousness of a subject, if "subjectivity" is understood as a correlate of a phenomenon's objectivity. Appearance and openness form a much vaguer, freer, and wider horizon than the narrow, but scientifically more manageable one of the subject/object correlation. The vagueness of the wider horizon invites us to investigate all the possible modes and ways of being and to explore the entire analogy of beingness and perception characteristic of the human universe as such. Husserl, Heidegger, Scheler, Marcel, Merleau-Ponty, Levinas, Ricoeur, Marion, Chrétien, and others have laid much of the groundwork for a new era in philosophy. They have radically transformed the soil of philosophy and thus also altered the possible uses of philosophy in science or theology.

Not only has the analogy of being again become a central issue for thought, but also the givenness of beings in their various modes of being has been discovered—or rediscovered. By making us aware of the ontological difference between Being and beings, Heidegger awakened us to new amazement about the emergence of beings in their being given as such. That there is being at all is the wonder of wonders. The givenness of being in all its diversity is that which most amazes thought and urges it to unfold its questions.

Theory

Modern philosophy is theoretical. *Theoria* was also the ideal for Plato and Aristotle, and even for Thomas Aquinas, who saw perfect theory as the happy fulfillment of our most radical desire; but modern theory has a different character. Its relation to reality, including the objectivity of the outer world and the interiority of human consciousness, is characterized by the search for objective knowledge of the subject's objects, and its own nonsubjectivistic, universally valid, and thus "objective" subjectivity. The theoretical intention does not coincide with the objective or objectifying one, however; theory is wider and permits other forms of being acquainted or being in touch with things. It encompasses many ways of understanding; even the acquaintance with being as such has been thematized as a mainly theoretical—meditative, questioning, or contemplative—way of dealing with our being-in-the-world. Modern theory typically maintains a distance from emotional and practical involvement. It relies on observation and intellect, but is suspicious of emotion and delays praxis (and ethics as the theory of human praxis) until later, when theory is complete. The only exercise it deems necessary is experimental and logical: accurate perception, analysis, and reasoning seem to be the only tools needed for the discovery of nonsubjectivistic, scientific truth. Very different from the Eastern and Western traditions of spirituality, the practice of modern science and philosophy demands no emotional or behavioral preparation; the quality of a human life is irrelevant to theoretical truth and validity. The modern idea of an introduction to philosophy does not involve an ethical preparation of mind and body; without any *psychagogia* the teacher starts directly from the pupil's intelligence and extant knowledge in order to show how this starting point must unfold into deeper and more complex thoughts. Truth is a set of true sentences or theorems—ideally, the totality of all theoretical truths; it can be known indiscriminately by saints and criminals. The only conditions for good philosophy are loyalty to the facts (which are obvious to everyone whose perception is not handicapped) and "faith in reason."[1]

Phenomenology and the human sciences have demystified the mastery of theoretical reason by disclosing its entanglement in the emotional and practical life of individual thinkers, communities, and cultures. Historical studies have revealed how much of Descartes's, Spinoza's, Kant's, and Hegel's ideas are rooted in, suggested by, and even dependent on unproven emotional attachments to certain points of view.[2] Their search for happiness or

---

[1] See Hegel's inaugural lectures at the University of Heidelberg (1916) and the University of Berlin (1818) in *Gesammelte Werke* XVIII (Hamburg: Felix Meiner, 1968–), pp. 6, 18. At p. 6, we read" "Faith in the power of the spirit is the first condition of philosophy."

[2] I have tried to show this for Anselm in "Anselm's Proslogion and Its Hegelian Interpretation," *The St. John's Review*, 42 (1993): 59–77; for Descartes in "Life, Science, and Wisdom According to Descartes," *History of Philosophy Quarterly*, 12 (1995): 133–53; for Leibniz in "Dieu et la souffrance à partir de Leibniz," *Theodicea Oggi? Archivio di Filosofia*, 56 (1988): 51–74; for Hegel

salvation committed them to positions founded on emotion as well as the intellect. Thematic studies, and first among them Heidegger's *Sein und Zeit*, have shown how thinking, in the narrow modern sense of theoretical investigation, is rooted, embedded, oriented, guided, tuned, and enveloped by something much deeper: an acquaintance with world, things, events which lies before or under the differentiation of theory. This acquaintance is neither objective nor subjective,[3] because it is much more radical than such a superficial distinction. The appropriate human response to most phenomena and modes of surprising, touching, impressing, or affecting is affection rather than observation or intellectual grasping. As being in time, this affective acquaintance is not a static fundament or a treasure, once-for-all acquired or acquirable; it is not a set of principles or a toolbox for disclosure. It is desire, drivenness, movement, motion: a passionate involvement that tries to cope with the world, with others, and with the riddles of life itself.

This passion has a history, a history of responding and experimentation. Human life is touched, moved, affected by phenomena that invite appropriate responses. Life itself demands a responsive and responsible self to live it in an appropriate—that is, authentic, correctly corresponding—way. This demand cannot be fulfilled without the trial and error of the self's adjustments to its life-filling task. The experiment of life is the ongoing practice of the self's responsive attempts to cope with the reality of its being on earth. Experience, *empeiria*, is the general name for all the modes of being involved in affections and affective responses by which the self is constantly transformed. If its orientation is good—which presupposes a turn from inauthenticity to authentic responsivity—the transformation makes the self better and wiser. This enables us to feel, behave, and speak well in response to the phenomena of life and world. Speaking to or about them must do

---

in *Le jeune Hegel et la vision morale du monde* (The Hague: Martinus Nijhoff, 1969) and in "Existenz und Denken im werden der Hegelschen Philosophie," *Scholastik*, 38 (1963): 226–38; and for Levinas in "Judaism According to Levinas," in my *Beyond: The Philosophy of Emmanuel Levinas* (Evanston, Ill.: Northwestern University Press, 1997), pp. 18–37.

[3] I presuppose here the phenomenological critique of the subject/object schema: though it has its legitimate use within certain limits for certain domains of knowledge, it is incapable of constituting a universal framework.

justice to their appearance and touch them in what they truly are, even if they blind or paralyze the self's experience. Modern philosophy and science have developed a deep mistrust of such personal involvement. Both warn that the universal validity of the truth should be protected by unemotional objectivity. The subjectivism of emotions and the particularity of individual experience must be corrected by critically distant observation and cold rationality. The correction of the self's modes of coping with reality was sought in an "emendation of the intellect,"[4] not primarily in an adjustment of affective responsibility. Emotional adjustment was seen as a result of conceptual considerations; these could and should dominate and rule the chaotic and irrational mass of unguided pleasures, drives, and inclinations.

The modern exclusion of affectivity from the basic orientation of a life in search of wisdom devalued all those phenomena which cannot be perceived and do not exist unless we accept them as surprising, amazing, moving, wonderful, delightful, happy, terrible, horrible, and so on. Philosophy was thus robbed of all passionate, fascinating, admirable, or simply interesting experiences. Even boredom, the inevitable result of this sort of rationalism and empiricism, was not allowed to have a say in philosophy. Passions and emotions do not allow us to exclude them from philosophy, however. It is, therefore, quite possible to write a history of the unrecognized passions revealed in the systems of Descartes, Spinoza, Leibniz, Kant, et al. Notwithstanding their efforts at objectification and scientification, the texts of these philosophers are still interesting because of the passion that drives them. A fundamental mistake of the modern project is its illusion that passions and emotions can be civilized by anything other than a passionate and emotional purification of these same passions and emotions. The responses demanded and suggested by a beautiful tree, radiant eyes, a deep depression, or similar phenomena are essentially emotional; they cannot be replaced by "objective" observation or theory. Involvement is an unavoid-

---

4 Cf. Spinoza, *Tractatus de intellectus emendatione* and its explanation in Herman de Dijn's *Spinoza: The Way to Wisdom* (West Lafayette, Ind.: Purdue University Press, 1996).

able part of the suggested response. Respect, gratitude, admiration, desire, and the like cannot be replaced by theoretical or practical equivalents.

The remedy to the dangers and distortions of emotional responses must be sought not in conceptuality or in disinterested observation of empirical facts, but in more appropriate responses emerging from a more appropriate, more open and authentic, truthful, and pure affectivity. Purification of the ways in which we let ourselves be affected, and—more primordially—purification of our *being* tuned to the various levels and instances of phenomenality are necessary conditions for thinking in accordance with reality.

To be in tune, such that the correct responses are given, presupposes a turning away from inauthentic positions and movements in which we are immersed. Without conversion, no affective or other purification, and thus no authentic thought, is possible. Perception and thinking start from an urge for authenticity; they represent a specific form of ongoing conversion and catharsis.

If it is true that philosophy can be neither practiced nor understood as a passionless and emotionless exercise in rationality, then it is led by a drive and a passion other than the typically modern preoccupation for scientificity and objective theory. The recognition of its emotional character is not a plea for subjectivism in philosophy, for, with the absolutization of objectivity, the alternative, absolutization of subjectivity, has also come to an end. Life and selfhood themselves, like all other phenomena, call for ongoing experimentation through which the quality of our experiences is at stake. To live philosophically is to exercise responsiveness to, and responsibility for, genuine ways of being touched and moved. If philosophy encompasses a basic responsibility for authentic affectivity, including a constantly adjusted orientation toward that for which a life ultimately is meant, philosophy is a specific form of spirituality. Its specificity lies in the "organ," the logic, and the method through which it is distinguished from other, nonphilosophical forms of practice, speech, meditation, or contemplation. This specificity need not hide its belonging to a long tradition of moral and religious self-transformation, however. Important historical studies by Festugière,

Courcelle, Hadot, and others[5] have laid the ground for the possibility of continuing the premodern traditions of philosophy as a way of life, broken off by modern theory. Theory, in the restricted, modern sense of the word, must again be practiced and understood as only one of the elements of an entire life on the way to its own transformation. The theoretical perspective is merely a part, and often not the most important part, of human responsiveness and thoughtful experience. The language of logic, in the widest sense of this word, must unfold in the closest possible proximity to the language of desire and engagement. The passion of life, in its attempts at authentic purity, must be heard in the fine-tuned analyses and argumentations of a highly sensitive theory. That which is sought most of all is "correspondence": a well-tuned accord between the life of the self and all nodes of being. It encompasses philosophical theory and tests how true it is to the nontheoretical moments of life's experience—some of which are more basic than theory.

Tasks

"The end of philosophy," proclaimed by several thinkers of our century, is in fact the end of *modern* philosophy and the beginning of a new, promising era in which the tasks and promises of philosophy have to be pursued on a new basis. We are not necessarily ungrateful for the lessons of the last four hundred years, if we interpret modern philosophy as an experiment whose discoveries made us forget a wiser tradition of thought. As search for wisdom, philosophy was much more than theory. The Greek enlightenment certainly stressed contemplation (*theoria*) as a most divine possibility of human existence, but it never forgot the vital

---

5 Arthur Darby Nock, *Early Gentile Christianity and Its Background* (New York: Harper & Row, 1964); *Conversion: The Old and the New in Religion from Alexander the Great to Augustine of Hippo* (Oxford: Clarendon Press, 1933); *Essays on Religion and the Ancient World* (Cambridge, Mass.: Harvard University Press, 1972); Pierre Paul Courcelle, *Les lettres grecques en Occident, de Macrobe à Cassiodore* (Paris: E. de Boccard, 1948); *Connais-toi toi-même, de Socrate à Saint Bernard* (Paris: Études Augustiniennes, 1974); Pierre Hadot, *Exercices spirituels et philosophie antique* (Paris: Études Augustiniennes, 1987); *Qu'est-ce que la philosophie antique?* (Paris: Gallimard, 1995).

unity of *theoria* with practical nobility and emotional harmony. With the advent of Christianity, the spiritual orientation changed and the importance of thinking was relativized with respect to religious contemplation; love (*agape*) and grace became more important than *episteme*; still, theory was venerated as a part of the dynamic that belongs to human maturity and perfection.

Many tasks are waiting for Christians who are passionate, skilled, and courageous enough to rethink the basic issues of our existence in history. One of those tasks lies in a new assessment of the relationship between wisdom, life, and theory, and the realization of a phenomenology that does justice to those experiences that have been obscured or distorted by the modern and premodern theory. Two issues especially demand to be treated with greater respect and sensitivity than they have received in the past: human intersubjectivity and our relationship to God.

The work of Emmanuel Levinas has clarified some phenomenological difficulties concerning the appearance of human individuals.[6] As soon as I objectify, thematize, or simply talk *about* an other's face or speech or gesture, the other's otherness, as experienced in my greeting, listening, and looking, disappears. The following problem then arises: how is it possible to philosophize about the other's existence and my relation to the other without distorting the very topic or theme I am trying to bring to light? How can my talking *about* the other remain a part of my listening or talking *with* the other? To "save the phenomenon" of the other, we must invent a language, or, perhaps, more than one language, that overcomes the deficiencies of pure theory. The fact that twenty-five hundred years of Western philosophy has not yet done justice to the otherness of the other is already reason enough to believe that philosophy has not yet reached its end. It has hardly begun. Indeed, "intersubjectivity"—as we say much too easily—is not just one topic among others. The question of "youness" and "mineness" involves us in attempts to

---

[6] I have presented his work in *To the Other: Introduction to the Philosophy of Emmanuel Levinas* (West Lafayette, Ind.: Purdue University Press, 1993) and *Beyond: The Philosophy of Emmanuel Levinas*. For a discussion of his phenomenology of intersubjectivity, see my *To the Other*, pp. 167–84; *Beyond*, pp. 123–29; and *Before Ethics* (Atlantic Highlands, N.J.: Humanities Press, 1997), pp. 47–53, 69–72.

find a radically new interpretation of our relationship to one another and to society, as well as new interpretations of our relationship to God, to whom we refer, again much too easily, as a person. The relationship to God also confronts us with an as-yet-unresolved problem of its own. Doesn't all talk *about* God miss the point, while talking *to* God, as in prayer, is a natural and appropriate response to his being? Isn't adoration, including gratitude, love, and hope, the heart of all responsiveness with respect to God? St. Augustine, St. Anselm, St. Bonaventure, and other Christian philosophers have thought about this question, but their answers are no more than hints.

It is obvious that a more faithful rendering of our relationships to God and other humans would have profound consequences for all other questions in philosophy. Philosophy is not exhausted at all; it is eager to start again. In the meantime, however, I do not want to suggest that the continuation of philosophy depends on the emergence of new problems and tasks. Even if only the same old questions persist, they must be meditated upon again and again. The most important questions of human life probably do not change, but every epoch has its own tasks and possibilities.

Autonomy

I can be brief with regard to the third feature of modern philosophy, its autonomy. All the great thinkers after Hegel have shown to what extent philosophy is rooted in prephilosophical desires, symbols, convictions, and traditions. This fact does not require us to reject the ideal of autonomy proclaimed in modern philosophy: despite the failures of the past, it might still be possible to demonstrate the truth of presupposed convictions on the basis of empirical and logical evidence alone. However, all the holes and unproved assumptions we have discovered in the Herculean works of the last centuries have made us dubious about the feasibility of the autarchic program they wanted to realize. If we connect this doubt with the question of the difference between philosophy as a way of life and philosophy as theory, it becomes more plausible that the idea of rational autonomy is an illusion.

It might still serve as a regulative idea, but as dogmatic affirmation of philosophy's autonomy it has exhausted itself.

If philosophical theory cannot be practiced without a deeply rooted passion, the word *faith* is not too strong to express the involvement of a real philosopher. Notwithstanding its own interpretation of philosophy as objective theory, the adventure of modern philosophy has, in fact, been motivated by a desire for salvation and wisdom.[7] Just as for "the Greeks," so also for most modern thinkers, and even for some scientists, philosophy replaces religion. At the source of all lives there is a sort of wager with ourselves, a lived, preconscious, and certainly pretheoretical affirmation which takes the risk of being oriented in a certain direction and tries to accomplish a certain task as well as possible. Perhaps we might use the word *religion* in a very fundamental sense to stand for the attachment—a kind of Amen—that makes it possible for us to undertake the adventure that constitutes the course of our life. The adventurous history of rational theory and scientificity is supported and motivated by a pretheoretical and subconscious engagement.

The hidden faith that guides a life is expressed in its anticipations and disappointments, its joys and delights, and the stubborn responsibility with which its program is achieved. Moods and emotional dispositions, imaginative associations and conceptual preferences can be interpreted as symptoms of that faith. No artist, scientist, or philosopher is without faith: hence, it is an important question of philosophy to ask how their faith relates to their skills and to the way of life in which those skills play an important role.

CHRISTIANITY

Before we ask whether a particular kind of philosophy or philosophy in general can, or even should be Christian, we must agree

---

[7] For Descartes, see his "Letter of the author to him who translated the book, which letter can here serve as preface" (1647). The entire letter, as also his letter to Princess Elisabeth, which prefaces the Latin edition of the *Principia* of 1644, insists on the meaning of philosophy as the study of *wisdom*. See also note 2 above. With regard to Spinoza (see note 4 above), the title of his *Ethica*

on the meaning of "Christian." While "Christian," "Christianity," and "Christendom" can be used to point at a cultural and historical phenomenon, "faith," in its biblical meaning, is a gift that does not belong to any particular culture. It is peculiar neither to a particular theological or philosophical, dogmatic, or catechetic formulation, nor to a specific ethos. Christian faith certainly demands its concretization in appropriate ethical, communitarian, and cultural traditions and institutions, but the inevitable particularity and historicity of all concretizations suggests a fundamental ambiguity in the word "Christian." Many different communities and practices are Christian, but it is common faith alone that holds them together as varieties in place and time. The Christianity of Western civilization is rather different from the evangelical picture of Jesus's "small herd." Even the oldest documents present various versions of evangelical life. To what extent these versions contain elements of human sinfulness is a question I shall not address here, but it is obvious that, for instance, the Church of the crusades, the Church of the Inquisition, and the Church of absolute monarchism can be called "Christian" only on the condition that we understand it as an indication of our "being just and sinners simultaneously." All this must be said in the name of faith itself, but as soon as we try to formulate this supreme criterion, our formulations and applications are indebted to a particular culture for the concretization of faith and the "purity of the holy Gospel."

"Christian" culture is always a mixture; the lives of Christians are attempts and experiments in appropriating the Spirit's inspiration, despite our unavoidable participation in a particularizing and contaminating world. Christian faith itself remains hidden in a host of historical, situational, and biographical ways of concretization and partial distortion. To be a Christian is to live an adventure, continually searching for the pure source of grace. Without mixture, in its precultural purity, the Trinitarian faith in God and incarnation would not exist at all; its translation into language, behavior, ethos, myths, ideas, arts, and idols is a per-

---

and the prefaces of its last three books already testify to this desire and purpose. It would be easy to show the same for Leibniz, Kant, Fichte, and Hegel, but most moderns see wisdom as very close to knowledge.

sistent battle between contamination and purification. The purity of the Gospel does not consist in an unworldly or supracultural spiritualism; the human body in its world and history is sanctified by grace. What we ambiguously call spirituality aims not at a separation or destruction of the body, as if the body were a corpse, but at total transfiguration. To follow saints and prophets is a sustained search for the authenticity of the appropriate call.

The incarnatory structure of faith has two sides that are not easy to balance, as the history of Christian spirituality shows. On one hand, grace maintains a distance from the world—God is our temple, and in heaven there is neither sacrament nor law—but, on the other hand, the whole of creation is called to union with God's life and has already begun to participate in it. The tension between distance and participation expresses itself in an individual Christian life as the tension between love for *and* detachment from the finite, admiration *and* "contempt for the world,"[8] passion *and* indifference, solidarity *and* patience, even with regard to the most urgent demands.

With regard to the Christian community of faith, a similar tension can be observed. As the "mystical body of Christ," the Christian community is sanctified and guided by the Spirit. The hope that surges from this certitude permits us to be at home in the world. Jesus the Christ is not "Yes" and "No," but only "Yes." It is in him only that we can say *"Amen"* (2 Cor. 1:19–20). In the course of history (*in via*) it is not so easy to identify the community of Jesus Christ, however, and it is even more difficult to determine who truly belongs to it. But even if we are able to do this, it is obvious, and an element of faith itself, that the historical community of Christians also participates in the idols and sins of the world. Among those idols are the various forms of absolutization on all levels of culture, such as the dogmatic fixations of a particular ethos, thought, taste, or government.

---

[8] *Contemptus mundi* is a perversion if it is not motivated by admiration and gratitude toward the Creator whose gifts are good and enjoyable. The negative moment of detachment, sacrifice, and looking down must express the infinite distance between the finite and its infinite source, not declare or treat it as bad or despicable. However, it demands much practice to reach a pure sense of the difference between God and God's imitations (from the most sublime gods to the lowest demons.

Christians who desire to become more authentic cannot go the way of purification unless they first belong to a Christian community from which they hear and learn how to respond to the call of God in Jesus through the Spirit. The education they receive from those who pass on what they received from others is a particular and contaminated translation of grace and faith, but without initiation and catechesis nobody would be able to invent the truth of revelation. A Christian life begins in a mixture of faith, culture, and sin, in which faith is the critical element that rejects sin by forbidding any absolutization of culture. This rejection holds even if faith has become tightly attached to its translation into a particular ethos or doctrine. The faith that breaks all idols has been alive "from Abel on"[9] and will remain alive in many forms inside and outside the communities of those who call themselves Christian.

Faith urges us to progressively overcome our idolatrous attachments to particular forms of human culture. Yet how can one distinguish between the purity of faith and its investment in the variety of "human-all-too-human" concretizations? The "sense of faith" by which to distinguish it from its cultural concretization cannot be learned in a few lessons. We are fortunate when the family or the church in which we are educated has good taste in questions and practices of faith, but even then it takes time to acquire an appreciation for what is and is not essential. It is the living experience and the achievement of Christian life itself which test the quality of this very experience. The Spirit creates receptive hearts through the self-critical experience of Christians. The "discernment of spirits"[10] is not guaranteed by repetition or imitation of words or deeds; a good sense or taste for things of the Spirit is a charism without which purification is impossible. A Christian trusts that God will not deceive anyone to whom he gave a good beginning. Grace procures all that is necessary for an appropriate response; but such a response cannot emerge without passionate concentration on that same grace through gratitude, hope, and adoration.

---

[9] This topos of the patristic literature comments on Heb. 11:4ff.

[10] See "Discernement des esprits," in *Dictionnaire de spiritualité, ascétique, et mystique, doctrine et histoire* III, cols. 1222–91.

At this point we could meditate on the possibilities of the "inner master" of whom St. Augustine and St. Bonaventure speak.[11] If Christians are governed by faith, wouldn't they recognize the voice of the Spirit itself as being radically different from the voices of literature, art, morality, philosophy, and theology? Spirituality is an ongoing experiment in which one experiences, tastes, and tests various stages and levels of experiencing; it is a movement toward greater authenticity. Self-testing is the natural way in which grace produces a more sensitive and refined mind or "heart." Through remembering and recognition, critique and transformation, the hermeneutical praxis of Christianity generates its more or less genuine styles of life.

The means used in this process of authentification are sometimes surprising. If faith in the God of Jesus Christ is not restricted to Christians, as the Letter to the Hebrews declares, the very faith in the triune God has led the saints of all times, from Abel to the end of history.[12] The charismata of God's incarnation have been given to many non-Christians before and after Jesus's life. Examples of such gifts can be found in the modern declarations of human rights and the legal treaties that issued from them. The fact that the popes of the twentieth century support and spread the doctrine of universal human rights is not primarily due to the practice or theory of former popes; it is, rather, the modern ethos of law and morality, as expressed by philosophers and lawyers both without and within the Christian community. The fact that the community of Christians recognizes an extra-Christian development as a welcome translation of its own faith shows that the borderline between Christianity ("faith") and non-Christian elements of faith is not easy to draw. Many who seem to be outside are inside (and many who seem to be inside are outside). While it is true that the meaning of a practice or an idea might change through being integrated into a Christian context, it may emerge outside that context. It makes a difference whether human rights are seen as founded on human autonomy alone, or whether they are recognized as a partial expression of

---

[11] Augustine, *De magistro*, nn. 36–46 (XII–XIV); Bonaventure, *Christus unus omnium magister*, esp. nn. 20–28.

[12] See note 9, above.

God's concern, but this difference does not take a certain affinity away.

Another example is the transformation of Platonic or Neoplatonic thought into elements of Christian theology from Origen to the late Middle Ages. Historical aspects of that transformation have been analyzed by the best scholars in the field. We have thus become aware of our debt to "the Greeks," but are we able to formulate a general theory about the integration of non-Christian philosophy into a Christian life?

CHRISTIAN PHILOSOPHY

Christians who are also philosophers cannot avoid the question of how they can be both. How does philosophy fit into my existence as a member of the Christian community in search of God? How does my being a Christian fit into my philosophical search for truth? Different perspectives and positions can be chosen to answer these questions (or to amend them in order to answer better-targeted questions). In a purely formal way, we can approach them in three ways: (*a*) we can try to integrate philosophy into the experience of Christian life; (*b*) we can try to integrate Christian faith into the philosophical way of life; and (*c*) we can try to show that the Christian way of life and philosophy remain two different and largely separate movements, despite a certain overlap. For a Christian who is involved in philosophy, an absolute separation is excluded from the outset if both philosophy and the Christian way are serious enterprises, for how could such a person otherwise maintain the basic unity of such a life?

Fides quaerens intellectum

If "philosophy" is taken in the restricted sense of a skill with a technique of its own, it would seem easy to solve our problem. "Christian philosophy" would designate a group of Christians who, like anybody else, have learned how to handle the tools of description, definition, analysis, and synthesis developed in the history of logic, ontology, ethics, and so on. Their specificity is that they apply logical, linguistic, imaginative, and rhetorical techniques to the convictions that are proper to their faith, just as Buddhists or Hindus might do. The only difference between Christian and other thinkers would lie in their particular synthesis of various tools with the religious truths that constitute their faith tradition. Their synthesis could then be called "theology," in the sense of a doctrine that appeals explicitly to extra-philosophical truth(s) as a basis for its thinking.

The history of ontology and philosophical theology that stretches from Parmenides to Levinas shows that this view of the relation between Christianity and philosophy is too superficial. Philosophy has never been a merely formal enterprise. Even if philosophy is restricted to theoretical endeavors, it cannot avoid thinking about the conditions of its own possibility, such as the ways in which logical and linguistic skills and strategies are related to the realities to which they are "applied," the modes of appearance and being of those realities, and the wonder of their givenness. Philosophy has always been, in some sense of the word, onto-theo-logy; all classical philosophers were fascinated by Being and by God. Under various names and pseudonyms, God and Being were the focus of their thinking.

The onto-theo-logy developed in philosophy cannot be seen as neutral and undecided with regard to a Christian addition or extension. "The God of the philosophers" is either a rival or a shadow of the God adored in faith and respected in theology, and differences in the understanding of God entail radical differences in ontology. Christian "faith in search of understanding" cannot just adopt a non-Christian philosophy in order to add new truths to it; the Christianity of theology demands a more radical transformation. No philosophy is neutral; every philosophy, Christian or not, even an atheist philosophy, is oriented and ruled by a fundamental affirmation, a "Yes and Amen," that supports and colors all its essential affirmations. The integration of a non-Christian philosophy into a Christian theology demands, therefore, a profound rethinking of its assumptions and arguments. This rethinking must itself be inspired by another Amen: God as revealed in Jesus Christ. The enlightened faith sought by Christian theology regenerates the thoughts it adopts, while producing itself as a "*philosophia*" in the service of Christ.[13] Through the submission of intelligence to the obedience to faith,[14] all phenomena and thoughts change into manifestations of God's glory. Faith in search of philosophical understanding is one of the ways in which the Christian community continues the assumption of the human world, made possible by the Incarnation. In a civilization where philosophy has become an important mode of coping with the drama of human existence, it is a normal kind of search. As the yeast of the world, faith appropriates the key elements of existing civilizations. The field of research that opens at this point invites us to analyze the structure of the conversion and the movement of transfiguration through which intellectual life becomes an element of faith. The patristic and medieval thematizations of the soul's journey, the mystical experiences of the sixteenth century, the Hegelian phenomenology of the Spirit's discoveries, Kierkegaard's stages on the way of life, and so on are highlights of a tradition that must be continued and renewed if we want to understand how philosophy, or thinking in general, can or must play a role in the maturation of faith.

Christian and Philosophical Ways of Life

If philosophy is the engagement in a specific way of life, more radical than any theory, the problem of Christian philosophy is the problem of whether the Christian way can be combined with an authentic involvement in philosophy. Since such an involvement can only be passionate, we must answer the question of whether love of God is compatible with a profound passion for philosophy.

---

[13] I use here the Greek word "philosophia" to indicate a quest for wisdom in the line of philosophers from Plato to Proclus and theologians from Justin to deep into the Middle Ages. See "Philosophie" in *Historisches Wörterbuch der Philosophie* I (Darmstadt: Wissenschaftliche Buchgesellschaft, 1971–), cols. 574–83, 592–99, 616–12, 630–33; Paul Rabbow, *Seelenführung: Methodik der Exerzitien in der Antike* (Munich: Kösel-Verlag, 1954); Hadot, *Exercises spirituels et philosophie antique*; Jean Leclerq, *Études sur le vocabulaire monastique du moyen âge* (Rome: Herder, 1961).

[14] Bonaventure, *Comm. in Sent.*, III, dist. 23, art. 1, qu. 1: "Faith is nothing other than the habit through which our intellect voluntarily is caught in obedience to Christ" (cf. 2 Cor. 10:5).

(*a*) *From the perspective of Christian faith*, philosophy is certainly not a necessary kind of existence. Since all humans are called upon to participate in grace, the ability to philosophize cannot be a condition of its possibility. In a civilization where philosophy has become an essential moment of the prevailing culture, however, engagement in philosophy is one of the charismata through which the Christian community realizes its incarnatory character. At least some of its members must participate in the history of the philosophical search for wisdom and human perfection. Which Christians become philosophers is a question of vocation, just as prophets, priests, and artists are called to their respective kinds of charismatic life.

However, if it is true that the seriousness of authentic philosophy implies a fundamental affirmation or trust, from which it draws courage for its search, how, then, can the Christian faith in the unique Amen of grace be combined with that philosophical affirmation? For a Christian, the passion for a life of thinking and discussion cannot be ultimate, but it can be lived as a possible and enjoyable concretization of the decisive call to love.[15] Yet doesn't this presuppose an "imprisonment" of philosophical autarchy to "the obedience of faith"?[16] Can involvement in philosophy be converted into a specific mode of the Christian way, or can it only be enacted as a not-quite-serious game?

It is important to note that the question I am asking here does not set two different doctrines or practices in opposition. Faith establishes the Christian community in the truth of revelation, which, in some way, embraces and supports all possible truths discoverable by human reason, while the philosophical search is a meditative way of living out the answers it finds *and the questions* it asks such that they are felt, understood, and incorporated in growing wisdom; it is a gradual, not only theoretical but also emotional and practical transformation of the philosopher. A Christian who engages in philosophy lives his faith in the contingent and historical form of a contemplation that was invented by

---

[15] Deut. 6:5 and Matt. 22:37: "You shall love the Lord your God with all your heart, and with all your soul, and with all your mind."

[16] See note 14, above, and Bonaventure, *Comm. in Sent.*, III, dist. 23, art. 1, qu. 2, obj. 5 and corpus: "Fides habitus est per quem intellectus captivatur in obsequium Christi et innititur primae veritati propter se."

the Greeks but transformed by the Christians with the help of Romans, Jews, Muslims, and modern thinkers, including agnostics and atheists.

Because Christian appropriation includes conversion and transfiguration, it is possible to recognize the philosophies of non-Christian origin with which various groups of Christians have been involved. Thus we can discern Christian forms of Platonism, Stoicism, Aristotelianism, Kantianism, Hegelianism, and so forth. In all such varieties, however, the symbiosis of faith and philosophy is experienced in the mode of the "as if not" which, according to Paul's First Letter to the Corinthians, characterizes the transitoriness of this world's "*schema*" or "*figura*" (1 Cor. 7:29–31). The distance between grace and culture does not exclude their intimate synthesis, but this synthesis is not a necessary one; all attempts at translating into philosophy are tentative and provisional. The passion of philosophy and its Amen cannot replace or conquer the Amen of grace. Compassion is better than insight, but it does not dishonor or despise it.

Philosophy itself has discovered that it is not radically autonomous; contemporary relativism must be understood as an expression of its need for another, more radical Amen than the purely philosophical one. The search for wisdom is a search for the true name of the Yes that is somehow present in the trust and the courage without which the very search would be impossible. Revelation and faith do offer the primordial affirmation, but they do not abolish the philosophical search, its questions, and its radical trust; these are relativized, however, and made provisional, by the grace of a compassion that does not need philosophy but frees it for the contemplation of delightful possibilities and limitations.

The freedom of grace realizes itself in the union of an absolute love for God's compassion and an authentic but mortal and controlled passion for a philosophical kind of life. Using logical and linguistic tools, and experimenting with various modes of understanding, a Christian philosopher is engaged in a history of meditation and discussion, while remaining well aware of their provisionality.

The provisional character of all philosophies within the Christian context is one aspect of its phenomenality. The wider question must be asked of how faith becomes phenomenal in the philosophies of authentic Christians who are passionately involved in it, and how these philosophies differ from other, non-Christian philosophies. A theological phenomenology of historical philosophies is necessary to prepare a thematic answer to that question. Paul's "as if not" can guide us, if we do not mistake it for an exhortation to divorce or contempt.

(b) *From the point of view of philosophy*, we must ask whether a Christian engaged in a philosophical discussion can be taken seriously enough to be accepted as an interlocutor.

Since the modern ideal of philosophical autarchy has been abandoned, it is not easy to define or defend the universality of philosophy. Insofar as it maintains essential relations with particular religions and cultures, philosophy seems to be radically fragmented. However, if it did not at least try to speak a language and to think thoughts that are comprehensible to every human being, philosophy would die. Somehow its universality must be saved. Mathematics, the sciences, logic, technology, economics, and utilitarianism have become universal languages, but it would be disastrous if they constituted the only possibility for humankind's communication and wisdom.

To be involved in the search for wisdom is certainly an impassioned affair, but can we count on Christians to participate in it? Don't they feel superior by having the right answers? Don't they act like pastors or missionaries rather than companions in the search?

As I have said, the answers of faith cannot replace the answers hoped for in philosophy. Even if I believe in God as the source of my salvation, I do not thereby have a philosophical concept of God; nor do I necessarily have insight into the structure of salvation, its relation to culture, my desire for salvation, my individual and unique destiny, and so on. All these questions concern also my non-Christian colleagues in philosophy, even if they do not pay attention to them. They, too, start from particular and personal assumptions and aspirations when they ponder them. We share a collection of opinions, hopes, and orientations which belong to the historical period and situation in which we live. That we are philosophers testifies to a common trust in the possibility of approaching truth. Our interpretation of the primordial Amen might differ, but it creates a fundamental affinity. Might we not surmise that for each of us the Amen hides the universal guidance of a God whom we confess without clear knowledge of what and how he is or how he guides? While a faith that identifies itself with a particular philosophical or theological doctrine is dogmatic and idolatrous in neglecting the distance between faith itself and the translation of faith into thought, a philosophy that despises the possibilities of faith, believes in its own superiority: it has its own faith. Philosophical discussions are not possible unless the participants share common questions and contexts, but their profoundest convictions need not be the same. Philosophy does not come into being *ex nihilo*; it begins when someone, in the midst of a full life, tries to restructure through thinking that same life with all its opinions, convictions, practices, and feelings. A philosophizing Christian experiences participation in the philosophical debate as an involvement which, though seriously concerned with God, humankind, world, salvation, truth, and wisdom, cannot decide the ultimate meaning of human destiny. A Christian is not alone in this: in everyone's life there is a distinction between belief (or religion) and reason. As a way of life, the philosophical experience is close to the Amen of religion and faith; if its trust is ultimately motivated by God, it coincides fundamentally with the Amen of Christian faith; if not, it is idolatrous or a provisional stage of the search for Meaning. In the first case, philosophy might help to disclose the convergence of positions that seem to differ radically.

The *gnosis* (1 Cor. 1:20–31; Eph. 3:14–19) of faith has a different character than philosophical knowledge does. Committed Christians are on the way to a better understanding of the revealed truth about the human universe, but this does not necessarily mean that they grow in conceptual possession or mastery. What we heard about God who shows his love in Passion and Resurrection frames an endless program for growth in the wisdom of love. Such a *gnosis* does not entail a phenomenological description or a conceptual analysis of what it means to be a Christian, although philosophical descriptions and analyses play a role in spiritual growth. As an enlightened kind of advancement, such techniques can serve to respond to the Spirit that moves beyond all knowledge. Neither theory nor a virtuous way of life can replace the adoration from which authentic *gnosis* springs. But a well-ordered life and even, to some extent, good theories, are nonetheless welcome as possible "*schemata*" or "*figurae*" of God's embodiment (1 Cor. 7:31).

(*c*) *The philosophical perspective is a desirable moment of the perspective of faith itself.* Not only do philosophizing Christians participate in the discussions of humankind, but their philosophical engagement is also a necessary moment of their own theological self-reflection and that of the Christian community to which they belong. A philosopher cannot avoid meditation on the question: Who, how, why am I? In Christians, such meditations are characterized by gratitude, hope, patience, and adoration. Although a neutral mode of philosophy might not permit an accurate phenomenology of the Christian mode of existence in faith, it is a valuable way of discovering the difference between faith itself and its translation into cultural or biographical expressions. By participating in the practices, languages, theories, and emotional patterns of non-Christian philosophers, without appealing to the specificity of Christian faith, we accomplish an *epoche* which might enable us to discover the limits of our understanding and the infinity that lies beyond it. The overwhelming message of a loving and suffering God reveals its incredible grandeur when we have measured the totality of dimensions and possibilities that can be explored philosophically. Seriously oriented lives in the style of Plato and Spinoza, compared with those of, for instance, Francis of Assisi and Charles de Foucauld, demonstrate the distance between philosophers and saints, although a sort of unrecognized sainthood might also hide in some philosophical lives. The distinction between Christian theology and non-Christian philosophy must be maintained in order that the latter's tendency to idolatry and the former's tendency to dogmatism do not dominate the discussion. Theology , too, is threatened by idolatry, and one of the weapons we can use to overcome this danger is precisely a certain way of practicing philosophy. In order to grow in wisdom, both philosophy and theology must spring from patient receptivity and avoid arrogance. Sincere philosophy helps theology to discover how much it has borrowed from the non-Christian wisdom found in secular science, ethos, politics, literature, rhetoric, and philosophy. This discovery does not *per se* exclude these borrowings from the patrimony of faith; on the contrary, it allows us to question the extent to which such concretizations must be accepted as appropriate to the historical situation and period of the Christian community and how much they ought to be retained once that situation has changed. Thus, participation in the extra-Christian practice of philosophy can become part of the ongoing fight against fossilization and superstition within the Church, and so in its ongoing purification.

Many thinkers who have opposed Christianity have, in fact, offered helpful criticisms against the lies and the violence, the resentments and the hypocrisy that have been perpetuated by Christians. Often, their target was a caricature of Christianity, but the words and the deeds of many Christians seemed to justify such caricatures. It is a healthy, though painful, exercise to look with un-Christian eyes at philosophical parodies of the Christian community in different periods of its history and to notice their partial accuracy. It should spur us to do penance for many infantile and morbid, superficial and unjust, arrogant and idolatrous distortions of grace. Although these distortions have not destroyed the fundamental Amen on which the Church is built, they do testify to its contamination by human-all-too-human corruptibility. In no way, however, should the recognition of this contamination override the joyful gratitude of Christian philosophers for the spirit of grace which freed them for something better than absolute knowledge.

Christians who exclude their being what they are from philosophical discussions will not be genuine; they are, at best, pale images of the best non-Christian philosophers. Imitation of modern and postmodern attempts at philosophical autarchy has damaged the authenticity of Christian thought, no less than the church's condemnations of important developments in art, science, politics, law, and philosophy. A post-postmodern renaissance of Christian spirituality in philosophy is necessary.

QUESTIONS AND ANSWERS

Q: Perhaps a philosopher's reservations regarding a *conjunctio* with Christian faith might arise not so much out of what happens when they first get together as from how far they end up going with one another; objections can arise from either side. Christians might get a little exercised when, for instance, Hegel remarks that in Christianity you actually know God. He seems to assert, in *Lectures on the Philosophy of Religion*, that the Christian life consists in knowing God. On the other hand, philosophers may raise concerns about religious believers' unquestioning acceptance of certain doctrines and their claims that these doctrines are to be accepted and not be inquired into further. While I agree with your sentiment that philosophy and theology have a great deal to do with each other in the Christian context, how far can that engagement be permitted to go? Are there limits? Can you speak about the limits of this engagement?

A: Well, I think that was my question, but perhaps, in fact, you are asking what the difference is, then, between philosophy and theology and if this view can be defended. Briefly, I would answer there is no difference between philosophy and theology. As soon as you are a real philosopher and you are a Christian, you become a theologian. There are moments when, for instance, you may be analyzing some subject matter and, at a certain moment of your analysis, you are explicitly aware of your faith; but implicitly it is always operative and effective. I tried to say something about how, subconsciously, one is always effectively Christian. There is always this awareness, and if it's a fundamental awareness, it is always involved.

What I said is, of course, very vague, as it must be, to the degree that one is authentically Christian: we continually have to develop concepts like inspiration, the Spirit, the *anima*—all of which precede cognitive awareness. Hegel and Fichte, for example, have done a lot of work on such issues as the presupposition of an autonomous philosophy in which there is a sort of transcendental ego that justifies itself and can be brought to light in an explicit conceptual knowledge of what happens to us.

Now, a Christian cannot go along with them in this, because that would be to deny that grace is the first principle. You can speak of love, but we do not know what such love means. We may discover it has a meaning, but one discovers it only in the experience of life, if at all. Neither can it be established philosophically that the Holy Spirit is more primordial—"pre-original," as Levinas would say—than every possible assumption that can be explicated in philosophy. So, we start already with a distinction between what can be made explicit in a conceptual analytic or phenomenological language and what must be affirmed without any possibility of understanding it in such a way. But a Christian philosopher cannot finish with that; he or she must start with that. So, one could say it is always theology, but the fact is that theology emerges only at a certain moment. The implication, however, is that it is not all over at the beginning with a sort of neutral *cogito*. That's what I tried to show: that in Christian philosophy the neutral *cogito* always masks a hidden Christian *cogito*, if you know what it is to be Christian. That knowing must be purified, as I said, and that is a long work for the community and the individual. The mystics give us an example of how difficult it is to know what it is to be Christian, and even they don't know it in the way a theologian knows it.

We are guided by what we try to discover at the end, and yet the end is not given explicitly there in the beginning, because it is provisional and mortal. So all theology and all dogma is as mortal and as provisional as any philosophy, perhaps more so, because they are, in fact, a mixture of philosophy, of a period of philosophy, with this presupposed, pre-conceptual affirmation for which I use the word "Amen."

Q: There seems to be a very interesting development in this whole conference, a development that, instread of sharpening the difference between philosophy and theology, is, rather, drawing the two together. As you said clearly, you think a philosopher who is a Christian and is inspired by his Christian thinking is doing theology. So there is a remarkable drift, it seems to me, toward breaking down what used to be, in the medieval period, a sharper distinction between philosophy and theology by bringing out the deep, hidden suppositions that lie between the two, so that what really emerges is a kind of Christian wisdom. That is very interesting. There seems to be a definite trend in many of

the speakers toward breaking down any sharp distinction between theology and philosophy. I know you feel that this trend
is specifically contemporary and that all our contemporary philosophy has led us away from making any kind of sharp distinction and toward something new, which is a kind of Christian
wisdom. Could you comment on that?

A: Yes, thank you for your question. I might say—at the risk
of caricature, probably—that I have the impression that sixty
years ago, when this whole debate was going on in France, Catholic philosophers felt the need to defend themselves precisely as
being really serious philosophers. They felt, I think probably
quite rightly, that everybody was suspicious about what they
said, assuming that there was something unspoken behind it. And
so they said, "We're not theologians; we are philosophers!" So,
the debate was very much dominated by the difference between
theology and philosophy, and one had to plead to be taken as a
serious, authentic philosopher and not as a theologian. Today, I
do not think that this is such a problem, as you say. Because how
can we define the method of Theology? When I read definitions
of theology, I always have the impression that this is the way
philosophy is done everywhere today, because we cannot say
anymore that philosophy does not have authorities and that theology does. We cannot say anymore that philosophy does not live
from a tradition and that theology does, because the philosophers
of today quote such poets as Hölderlin and Hesiod or scientists
as authorities, and then afterward try to make it plausible that
you can say such things meaningfully and truly. But authority is
always authority, even if you claim it is divinely inspired. And
so, if you do historical studies, how much authority is there in
Descartes, in Kant, in Hegel? We can always identify the point
beyond which they cannot prove anything anymore, where there
is just a big hole and then they bring in a nonsystematic starting
point. My personal opinion about the concept of originary sin in
Kant is that here, for example, is a very clear case of a concept
borrowed from theology, which is an absolute given, because it
is an absolutely unempirical concept. Kant cannot justify even
that we would have an experience of that—it is all against his
own epistemology—but he says it's a fact. That is the way he
starts. I think everybody talks in some such way. We have Greek

philosophy, Jewish philosophy, and everybody speaks as if philosophy were a school with a certain loyalty to sources that do not have to be justified but simply brought in to clarify and understand why people say these strange, amazing, surprising, beautiful, splendid, or insightful things.

So, I do not see the distinction very well, but I hope someone will convince me that I am wrong, because then I have learned a lot. The question nowadays is not so much how we can relate philosophy and theology. I think there is no good theologian who is not a good philosopher. So, too, I think there is no good Christian philosopher who is not a theologian. That is the consequence if I am right. The real problem is, how does the intellectual and conceptual way of experiencing Christianity relate to being a Christian? What I suggested in response to that question was that between faith and theology or philosophy there is spirituality, and spirituality is the source of life, the source of authenticity for all philosophy, as it is for all theology. My authority to say this is not only Plato, but also eight hundred years of Greek philosophy, which had a totally different conception of philosophy from these futile four hundred years of modern philosophy, despite great modern heroes. For eight centuries, Greek philosophy saw philosophy as religion.

Q: That's a very attractive perspective, and I'm not entirely sure of where I would go from there, but could we just hold on to this: when you are in the philosophical moment you are using different kind of evidence. You are trying to use evidence that is accessible to all, without appealing to any authority. There is a distinct philosophical moment based on the kind of evidence that you are using and the kind of arguments. Even though it is inspired by other philosophers—"authorities," as you say—still, in the philosophical moment, you are using evidence that you can lay out before everybody and show how it should follow from ordinary experience. Therefore, there is a distinction between the philosophical moment and the theological: namely, theology appeals to faith, whereas philosophy, even though it is "inspired," does not.

A: Yes. That's difficult. First of all, I don't think that anything is evident for everybody. Even the simplest empirical statement means something that could be clarified only if we get a sort of constellation in which that sentence can function. But what is the constellation? I'm obsessed with Hegel, of course. That only constellation that decides meaning is the totality of all truth. Now, we never have that totality of all truth, of course, so I tried to explain that in order to think there must always be a sort of fundamental affirmation. Consequently, although these things cannot be proven, perhaps they may, indeed, be shown. I'm convinced, and I would like to show that all serious philosophers, all seriously engaged philosophical lives, thrive on and are fed by such a "Yes" or "Amen." Then the question is, how does the meaning that is nurtured in such a life come to the fore? How is it expressed? How is it explained, how is it lived, how is it said?

Q: First, let me say that I, as a theologian, can very warmly receive the proposal you make as a philosopher. I think it gives us something to share.

A: Theology is wider, so philosophy is a part of it.

Q: Yes. But your proposal doesn't make you feel that theology can be in some way so domineering. There are proposals of making a distinction between theology and philosophy such that one would want to assert a certain superiority over the other. I don't think that's useful, and I don't think your proposal does that, and that's why I can receive it warmly.

If I understand you correctly, maybe the simplest way to see the commonality of theology and philosophy is in the spirituality, to see that they both meet there. That is a spirituality that is not an enthusiasm but one of maturity and growth. I believe you offered, as a proposal or an invitation, a phenomenology of Spirit both from philosophy and from theology together, yes? Since you have thought about this and made an invitation, I want to invite you simply to tell us more about the thinking that you've done on it.

A: Thank you very much. Let me say first, regarding phenomenology of the Spirit, yes, that sounds very appetizing. However, the Spirit, of course, is not simply a phenomenon, but the fruits of the Spirit are phenomena. The way, the tune, the mood, the splendor of St. Francis, for instance, is a phenomenon of the Spirit. But how can I describe that in such a way that it not only is a translation of the Spirit but also, at the same time, brings the Spirit in a contingent and historical form that is not essential to the grace of the Spirit (because it can be also manifested in another form—in St. Ignatius, for example, or even perhaps in St. Jerome, although it's not so apparent, I think)? Anyway, you have to scratch a little bit. It would be great if we could do that together, and I hope that direction will be taken by many people.

6

A Theological View of Philosophy: Revelation and Reason

David Tracy

Introduction: Revelation and Philosophy—Ideal Types

In the history of Christian theology, philosophy has played many roles. The crucial factor, from the theological side, is some notion of revelation, as well as the divinely engifted reception of that revelation called faith—a knowledge born of revelation. A theological position is this: if there is divine self-revelation and if there is a form of human knowledge constituted by that revelation, then theology can neither ignore nor be sublated by philosophy. Many modern philosophies focus on the category "religion," and any claims to divine self-revelation will be philosophically interpreted under a philosophical construal of religion. Indeed, that peculiarly modern discipline, philosophy of religion, is a discipline invented by modern thinkers. Its most characteristic moves are twofold: first, to religionize the traditional question of God and revelation and thereby any understanding of divine self-revelation; second, to render philosophically intelligible the cultural and empirical category of religion. Philosophy of religion is the discipline most clearly allied to theology in modernity. And yet the two disciplines are constituted entirely differently. Philosophy of religion must clarify the category "religion" and, through that strictly philosophical clarification, any further philosophical notion of "revelation" or even "God." Theology must clarify the strictly theological category "revelation" and, through that clarification, any theological claim to a form of knowledge ("faith") constituted by a divine self-disclosure. Only after a self-clarification of their distinct subject matters (and, therefore, methods) can a philosophy of religion and a theology of revelation clarify their further relationships to each other. Such, at least, is my basic hypothesis. Since I have elsewhere written on the "origins" of modern philosophy of religion and how the category "religion" (not God or revelation) began to play the major philosophical role in Hume, Kant, and Hegel, I will here turn to the second discipline in conversation, Christian theology. My hope is to clarify one way in which a theology grounded not in religion but in revelation may nonetheless relate in significant ways to philosophy—indeed, must relate to philosophy insofar as a revelation-constituted understanding of faith as knowledge is a meaningful cognitive claim.

First, however, it is important to eliminate two often-employed models as not useful for understanding, much less assessing, the relationship of philosophy and theology. These models are fideism and rationalism. These models are almost never used by a thinker for a self-description but are often used by other thinkers in describing what is judged to be an inadequate alternative. But since such ideal types are used so widely in both philosophical and theological forms, it is well to eliminate, at the very beginning, at least the "vulgar" (both as intellectually unsophisticated and, alas, also as popular, especially in the textbooks) understanding of these two much-used and much-abused terms.

I admit that just as Leslek Kolakowski claims that what is often called vulgar Marxism is, in fact, Marxism (however unhappy that thought may be to revisionary Marxists), so, too, what I am here naming "vulgar fideism" and "vulgar rationalism" may actually prove, in some rare individual cases, to be fideism and rationalism. Even if that proves to be one case, it would not remove the need to develop some further distinction for the large majority of theological options between something like the vulgar and the revisionary forms of each option. Indeed, when one observes the fuller complexity of a position like Karl Barth's, on one hand, or Schubert Ogden's on the other, the labels "fideism" (Barth) and "rationalism" (Ogden) begin to seem entirely inappropriate.[1]

---

[1] On Barth, for some recent assessments, see H. Martin Rumscheidt, ed., *Karl Barth in Re-View* (Pittsburgh: Pickwick Press, 1981); for Ogden, see Schubert M. Ogden, *On Theology* (San Francisco: Harper & Row, 1986). For a helpful

Strictly speaking, a fideist position insists that faith is the only relevant form of knowledge on matters of revelation. Philosophy, therefore, may be useful on other topics such as science (or even religion!), but it is irrelevant for understanding faith (except in relatively trivial ways). It is difficult to find a pure form of fideism (hence, its ideal-type status), for even fundamentalists usually admit that every believing theologian uses some philosophical categories at least for the expression of his or her understanding of faith. Therefore, at the very least, philosophy as clarificatory conceptual analysis of some categories inevitably used by theologians (for example, causality) is necessary even for a fideist perspective. But this "conceptual analysis" position, on strictly fideist grounds, cannot play the more ambitious (if still philosophically modest) role that several analytical "Christian philosophers" accord their philosophy of understanding Christian faith as knowledge. For these Christian philosophies, after all, include both defensive moves against philosophical critiques of faith and constructive (or better, reconstructive) moves to clarify and sometimes even to develop the understanding and, thus, intelligibility of Christian beliefs as forms of knowledge. The better position (like its theological counterpart Karl Barth) is far more complex than the usual meaning of "fideism" allows.

The same kind of intellectual difficulty holds for the category "rationalism." Strictly speaking, a rationalist position holds that only reason is relevant for understanding and judging any cognitive claims implicit in Christian faith. Just as there are some strict fideists, so, too, there are some strict rationalists. However, the very turn to religion as the central category needing analysis in modern philosophies of religion has occasioned a hesitation in assuming that religion can be adequately interpreted and thereby assessed or judged by reason. This move to the acknowledgment of the complexity of the religious phenomenon as nonreducible to other phenomena, even as understood by Kant in *Religion Within the Limits of Reason*, is, in various forms, a now-familiar position in modern philosophies of religion. No more than Kant can be considered a strict rationalist in relationship to religion (as

study of these issues, see Ingolf V. Dalforth, *Theology and Philosophy* (Oxford: Basil Blackwell, 1988).

D'Holbach or Brand Blanshard can be) can most philosophers of religion, and most liberal or revisionary theologians employing some philosophical analysis of "religion" (beginning with Schleiermacher), be construed as rationalist. Something more complex is at stake in positions often named "fideism" by opponents or "rationalism" by adversaries. This complexity can be viewed by observing two familiar theological candidates for these labels: Karl Barth (often called a fideist) and Schubert Ogden (often called a rationalist). Karl Barth's position is well known: Christian theology must be based in God's self-revelation and should not search, via philosophy or any other discipline, for any point of contact between human experience and knowledge and that revelation. At the same time, Barth insists that reason and all human culture should be reconstructed from the viewpoint of the new knowledge gained through the gift of faith. In short, faith as knowledge clarified through the discipline of theology precisely as *theological* knowledge can reconstruct philosophical knowledge in such a manner that philosophy, too, can acknowledge the reasonableness (although not the truth— that is constituted by faith alone) of the knowledge constituted as faith by revelation.

At the other end of the spectrum, Schubert Ogden insists, from his work on Bultmann to the present constructive work in the Hartshornian tradition, that theology is accountable to the "right [correct] philosophy" in order to develop criteria of credibility or intelligibility for assessing the cognitive claims of Christian faith. However, the strictly existential character of Christian faith, in Ogden's view, does not allow faith to be existentially reducible to philosophy. Philosophy, on this view, provides a metaphysics for understanding and assessing all relevant cognitive claims. God, existentially, however—the God of Christian faith—is the God experienced through Jesus Christ as revelatory and salvific *pro me*. To understand and assess this existential relationship to God, therefore, demands explicitly theological criteria, including criteria of appropriateness to Scripture, including a Christology, as well as criteria of existential meaningfulness. The latter criteria must include, but are not existentially exhausted by, an understanding of "religion" as a category for human wholeness.

There can be little doubt that Karl Barth inclines to fideism but opens up to a reconstruction of philosophy by theology in such manner that "Christian philosophers" can employ his work for their own, strictly philosophical purposes. At the same time, Schubert Ogden's theology, however dependent on and, indeed, philosophically creative in his use of and development of philosophy, may incline to classical Enlightenment rationalism but is distinct from such rationalism by his strictly Christological (and thereby strictly theological) interpretation of his position on the full use of philosophy in theology. Strict Enlightenment rationalisms, when interpreting and assessing Christian faith, needed something like a theory of religion (or "natural religion") but surely no Christology!

My point in recalling so briefly the main outlines of the complex positions of Barth and Ogden is to suggest, not that there do not exist fideists or rationalists on the issue of the relationship of philosophy and theology (clearly, they do exist), but that the more interesting and influential theological positions—complex positions such as Barth's or Ogden's—are, I believe, too complex and too nuanced to lend themselves to so wooden a designation as fideism or rationalism.

This is even more the case for the mediating positions on the theological spectrum, especially (but not solely) the Roman Catholic and Anglican positions. There are real differences—for example, between Karl Rahner and Hans Urs von Balthasar—on the relationship of theology and philosophy.[2] But those real differences are not clarified, despite the claims of some of their followers, by such terms as fideist or rationalist. Indeed, von Balthasar is even more open to the reconstructive task of philosophy's use in theology than Barth is. This is dependent in part on von Balthasar's use of the Catholic model of grace and nature as distinct from Barth's understanding of grace as power and his Reformation model of grace–sin and gospel–law. There should be little surprise that von Balthasar remains analogical in language and in his construal of basic continuities involved in the relationship of philosophy and theology, whereas Barth, even

---

[2] For a good study, see Rowan Williams, "Balthasar and Rahner," in *The Analogy of Beauty*, ed. John Riches (Edinburgh: T. & T. Clark, 1986).

after his book on Romans, remains dialectical in his analysis of that relationship, even after developing his "analogy" of faith positions. Those classical nature–grace (Catholic) and grace–sin (Reformed) differences remain real and deeply influential on the use of philosophy by a particular theology.

Moreover, Karl Rahner's transcendental reformulation of both philosophy and theology does insist that philosophy can show that the condition of possibility of human being is that we are none other than continent, temporal, and historical hearers of a possible word of revelation. But that Word comes to us as pure gift, sheer grace, categorical revelation which correlates to but is not equivalent to transcendental revelation. This transcendental position frees Rahner for a greater intrinsic use of philosophy in his theology than it does von Balthasar. But both work within the same grace–nature Catholic model, so that the differences, although real, are not mutually exclusive.

REVELATION AND THE KNOWLEDGE OF FAITH

The first need, from the viewpoint of theology, is to clarify the category "revelation," not religion. Theologically construed, revelation is an event of divine self-manifestation in the event and person of Jesus the Christ.[3] Each of these categories demands clarification:

(1) Event—"Event" language in contemporary theology is indicative of the gratuitous or gracious character of divine revelation. The very fact that God reveals Godself *is* grace, event, happening. Theologically, revelation is never a human achievement, work, or necessity; revelation must be understood as event, happening, gratuity, grace. Hermeneutically, the category "event" (*Ereignis*) is applicable even to word as Word-event (*Sprach-Ereignis*) as a happening of language itself and as, therefore, not under the control of the modern subject.

(2) "The event of divine self-manifestation"—The language

---

[3] For an expanded version of my hermeneutical analysis here, see my paper at an earlier conference on "Word, Language, and Religion," in *Religione, Parola, Scrittura*, ed. Marco Olivetti (Rome: Archivio de Filosofia, 1992).

of divine self-manifestation indicates, theologically, that revelation is not construed primarily (as in the older manual Scholastic traditions) as propositional truths that would otherwise be unknown (that is, "supernatural or revealed" truths). Rather, in modern theologies, revelation is construed primarily on an interpersonal or encounter model as an event of divine self-manifestation to humanity. This interpersonal model of revelation further assumes that some person-like characteristics (namely, intelligence and love) must be employed to understand the reality of God as God manifests God's self as Wisdom and Love even if they also employ impersonal models for the Divine Mystery. The dangers of anthropomorphism here are real but finally unavoidable (as Buber insisted in his critique of Spinoza and his insistence on the biblical God as Thou). Indeed, despite some strong qualifications on the use of personal language for God (for example, Schleiermacher), all modern theologians who employ the category "revelation" as divine self-manifestation must, if they wish to be hermeneutically faithful to Scripture, at some point also employ (biblical) personal language and thereby interpersonal models for God as Wisdom and Love.

Hermeneutically, this use of the category "manifestation" is also, as we shall see below, suggestive of the hermeneutical notion of truth as primordially an event of manifestation (or disclosure–concealment). The subjective correlate to the objectivity of manifestation is "recognition." In an analogous manner, the theological counterpart to the event–gift–grace of revelation as divine self-manifestation is the gift, grace, happening (never "work" or personal achievement) of faith as reorientation of trust in and loyalty to the God disclosing Godself in the Word, Jesus Christ.

(3) "Event of divine self-manifestation in the Word, Jesus Christ"—The decisive event of God's self-manifestation is, as Karl Barth insisted, not merely an event but a person: namely, the person of Jesus of Nazareth proclaimed and manifested as the Christ and thereby as the decisive Word-event of divine self-manifestation. In and through this Jesus Christ, the Christian learns the identity of the God disclosing Godself in Jesus Christ. Here one can find, not strict hermeneutical correlate, but, rather, the possibility of hermeneutically clarifying the nature of Word

as Divine Self-Expression. In Christian theism, the ultimate understanding of the Word is as the Second Person of the Trinity. Any full Christian theological understanding of God would need that further Trinitarian clarification in order to understand both the intrinsically relational character of the doctrine or symbol of revelation and the intrinsically relational (that is, explicitly Trinitarian) reality of the Christian understanding of God.

For present purposes these further important questions on the Trinitarian nature of God as clarified by the Christian understanding of revelation in the Word Jesus Christ need not be pursued further here. Rather, there is a prior need to clarify how Word enters the Christian understanding of revelation as an entirely dialectical reality that determines the Christian understanding of Word.

The dialectic of the Word in Christian theological self-understanding begins with the hermeneutical insight that Word may take the form of either Logos or Kerygma. Hermeneutically, therefore, word is both disclosure-manifestation (Word in the Form of Logos) and proclamation-disruption (Word in the form of Kerygma). In history-of-religion terms, Logos becomes "religion as manifestation," especially the manifestation of primordial correspondences obtaining throughout all reality. The archaic, meditative, and mystical traditions analyzed by Mircea Eliade and others are the clearest illustrations of these "Logos" traditions, just as sacrament, nature, creation, cosmos, and analogical correspondences are the clearest Christian analogies of Word in the form of Logos manifesting all reality (God–cosmos–history–the self) as a vast system of disclosive and participating, analogical correspondences. The reality of participating symbol (sacrament) is crucial for the Word as Logos

In history-of-religion terms, Word in the form of Kerygma or proclamation also becomes word as interruption, disruption, that is, word as a distancing from a sense of manifestory participation. Where Word as Logos discloses a vast system of participatory and analogical correspondences, Word as proclamation both discloses and conceals Word as proclamatory interruption of all senses of continuity, participation, and rootedness (all now labeled "paganism"). When Johann Baptist Metz (here, following Walter Benjamin) describes religion with the one word "interruption," he describes well this classical trajectory of the prophetic, apocalyptic proclamatory Word in Judaism and Christianity.

In Christian theology, the dialectic of Word in the form of Logos and Word in the form of Interruptive Kerygma can be found in all the classic dichotomies become dialectical antinomies of Christian theological self-understanding. Consider the contrast between Logos Christologies beginning with the disclosive manifestory Gospel of John and apocalyptic Christologies like Mark's or proclamatory and disruptive Christologies of the Cross like Paul's Christology of Christ crucified. Or consider the contrast in Christian theologies between the Comprehensible–Incomprehensible Logos tradition's understanding of God in Aquinas and Rahner and the Hidden–Revealed proclamatory God of Luther and Calvin. Recall Tillich's formulation of the dialectic of Protestant principle (word as disruptive, critical, suspicious proclamation) and Catholic substance (word as participatory logos). Or recall, in conceptual terms, the differences between the analogical languages of classical Orthodox, Anglican, and Roman Catholic theologies and the negative dialectical theologies of classical Protestant theologies.

Even in terms of the symbols of incarnation–cross–resurrection, Word as Logos instinctively appeals to the symbol of incarnation, whereas Word as Kerygma instinctively appeals to cross. Both find the need for each other in their distinct appeals to the symbol of resurrection to complete the dialectic of Christian symbols. Only the fuller symbol system of incarnation–cross–resurrection clarifies the dialectic of Jesus the Christ as the Word—that is, as both Logos and Kerygma, both John's Word of Glory and Paul's Crucified Christ, both Mark's word of the cross and Luke's word of resurrection–ascension.

It would be possible to clarify further the Christian understanding of Word through a further exposition of one or another of the classical dialectics noted above (incarnation–cross; sacrament–word; cosmos–history; symbol–allegory; icon–idol; analogy–dialectic; Comprehensible–Incomprehensible God or Hidden–Revealed God; creation–redemption; nature–grace or grace–sin; love–justice; participation–distance; continuity–discontinuity; continuity–interruption). Pervading all these dialectics is the originating Christian dialectic of revelation as Word:

Jesus the Christ as Word—Word in the form of Logos and Word in the form of Proclamation. It would also be possible to see this same dialectic continued in the two distinct readings of the tradition: either the prophetic-apocalyptic reading of the Word-as-proclamation tradition, beginning with Mark and Paul, or the meditative tradition which yields wisdom, mystical, and archaic (cosmic) reading of Word as disclosive Logos, beginning with John.

As anyone familiar with the history of Christian theological reflection can readily see, all these formulations of the Christian dialectic of Word have been tried and reformulated many times in the history of Christian reflection in both philosophy and theology. Each of them has yielded genuine fruit. However, too many of those theological formulations of the dialectic of the Christian revelation as Word have ignored the fact that Jesus Christ as Word *is* both disclosive Logos and disruptive Proclamation of God and humanity, of cosmos and history. Word, therefore, manifests both nearness and distance, both participation and interruption.

To ignore this dual function of Jesus as the Christ is to ignore the fact that the Word, Jesus Christ, is testified to and, indeed, rendered in written words and written forms like narratives in Scripture. This singular fact of revelation as written and, therefore, in-formed by the forms of Scripture cannot be hermeneutically and theologically irrelevant. The fuller Christian description of revelation, in the event of divine self-manifestation in the Word, Jesus the Christ, is testified to and witnessed to in the written words of the scriptures. Christianity must affirm its self-understanding in its scriptural-biblical base and its Jewish, not Greek, roots. Christian theology, moreover, must leave behind both naïve and Gnostic notions of the Letter and the Spirit in order to understand the place of written Scripture in Christian self-understanding. Only by a focus on Scripture as written word can any adequate hermeneutics of the Christian understanding of revelation through Word in writing occur.

For Christianity, the New Testament and the Christian Old Testament are Scripture: the written original witness to the revelation. The decisive revelation for the Christian occurs in the event and person of Jesus Christ as true Word of God. The Word, Jesus

Christ, is affirmed as present to the community and the individual Christian in two principal forms: word (proclamation) and sacrament (those disclosive signs which render present what they signify). Even the common confession of the principal Christian churches—"We believe *in* Jesus Christ *with* the apostles"—is dependent on this notion of the Word's presence to the community. The rule for the *lex credendi* is the *lex orandi*. The present worshiping community renders present the same Jesus Christ in word and sacrament to all Christian believers. The Scripture remains the authoritative *normans non normata*. The written texts called "Scripture" assures that the Christ of the present Christian community is the same Christ witnessed to and testified to by the apostolic witnesses as the decisive self-manifestation of God and humanity. Neither "Scripture alone" nor "Scripture and tradition" clarifies this important hermeneutical role of Scripture for the Christian. Rather, one may speak of Scripture-in-tradition, that is, the rendering present in word and sacrament of the Word witnessed to in the scriptures as decisively present in Jesus Christ.

The recent recovery of the import of the genre "gospel" as a proclamatory narrative has clarified this peculiar, indeed unique, role of form as indispensable in the written narrative and confessional scriptural texts for Christian self-understanding. If gospel is both proclamation and narrative, gospel is both a proclamatory confession of faith and a disclosive narration of the identity of this Jesus as the Christ and of Jesus Christ and thereby ultimately of God. *Lex credendi* is based on the presence of the Word as Logos and Kerygma to the worshiping community (*lex orandi*). Both are held together by what may be named the peculiar role of narrative writing as rendering present what is absent, the identity of the God manifesting Godself in Jesus Christ.

FAITH AS KNOWLEDGE:
EVENT, MANIFESTATION, POSSIBILITY, EXERCISE

In Christian self-understanding, faith is a gift. Faith is the gift-grace for the reception of revelation. Faith is constituted by God's own self-manifestation. In and through the Spirit, Jesus is recognized in faith as the very Christ of God. Jesus Christ is acknowledged as God's own self-manifestation. Who God is— Love (1 John 4:16)—is known to faith in and through knowing God's identity as that identity is manifested primarily in the form of the passion narrative of Jesus Christ. Who Christians may become—those commanded and empowered to love—is known by Christians in and through their faith in Jesus Christ. Bernard Lonergan's understanding of faith as "a knowledge born of love" is surely a correct, if somewhat cryptic, description of the kind of knowledge Christian faith is.[4] For faith is a knowledge born of revelation, and what revelation in Jesus Christ manifests to those engifted by the Spirit to that faith is Love: God is love, and human beings are loved and, therefore, commanded and empowered to love in their turn. Indeed, all Being is now known as gracious. Here, as Lonergan suggests, is the one great exception to the dictum *non amatum nisi cognitum.*

What knowledge is this knowledge of faith? Here the traditional analogy of love seems entirely appropriate. What love fundamentally gives is a new understanding of possibility. What once seemed "reality" (more exactly "actuality") now seems, in the light of love's new understanding, relatively narrow in scope and small in spirit. The new knowledge born of all human love is the knowledge, above all, of new possibility. The knowledge born of Christian revelation—the knowledge of God as Loving Father and Mother, a knowledge obtained through Jesus Christ in the Spirit—is a knowledge in and through the manifold forms of revelation, beginning with and grounded in the form of the passion narrative, which identifies who this Jesus is and thereby who Christ is. In identifying Jesus as the Christ, the narrative also identifies the God manifesting Godself in Jesus Christ as none other than Pure Unbounded Love.

The knowledge born of that revelation of God as Love is the new knowledge of faith—the gift/power/grace of faith. Such faith-ful knowledge disrupts (knowledge as disruptive proclamation) our sinful, self-deluding grasp of what we consider "reality" and "realistic" knowledge. The new knowledge of faith also

---

[4] For Bernard Lonergan, see *Method in Theology* (Philadelphia: Westminster, 1982).

gives the gift of Love, now understood to be pervasive of all reality within which we, as thus engifted to love, now understand the possibility to love beyond even our best actualities. The further development of such knowledge—the knowledge born of revelation now become the new knowledge of new possibility (faith, hope, and love)—also demands, as the ancient philosophers knew, the discernment and development of what Pierre Hadot nicely names "spiritual exercises" (of which more below). It is little wonder that so many ancient Christian thinkers found Platonism in its many forms so natural a philosophical ally to the new knowledge of the revelation of Jesus Christ. For Platonism, in its many forms, does live in and by a sense of sheer wonder at the engifted, gracious possibilities within which we live and move and have our being. From Plato's own vision of Beauty occurring "suddenly" (as event, happening) in the *Symposium* to his "Good beyond Being" (and beyond the achievements even of dialectic) in the *Republic* to his final mythic-philosophical vision of all reality in the *Timaeus*, one cannot but sense in Plato, as in his Platonist successors, a sense of the sheer wonder of existence as a feeling of genuine participation in the possibilities opened by Beauty, by the Good, by the One, by Intelligence, and by all the Forms.

The Christian Platonists, moreover, sensed this wondrous, participatory reality in Plato and the Platonists. The Christian thinkers did not hesitate to transform the forms of Platonism, when necessary, to cohere with *the* form of God, the Form where God is manifested in and through Form, Jesus the Christ. This incarnational Christology freed Dante to understand the necessity for the particularity of Beatrice—that is, the necessary particular form in and through which essence manifests itself and without which the manifestation could occur. Thus can a new ethic of the Good be worked out through manifold forms in the theology of Augustine. Thus could a new understanding of truth itself as manifestation in and through Christological form occur for Christian thinkers from Bonaventure to von Balthasar. Plato and Platonism, once reconstructed or transformed through the possibilities disclosed by a new form of forms, Jesus Christ as proclamatory and manifesting word, were far more religiously available to Christians that either Aristotle or Stoicism was.

And so today, in the twilight of Platonism, other philosophies may seem more appropriate to the Christian insight into faith as knowledge of possibility born of that love empowered by the revelation of Christ in the Spirit. Among contemporary philosophies, I continue to believe that hermeneutical philosophy provides the kind of contemporary philosophy needed by a revelational theology.[5] Although I have argued the case elsewhere, for the present purposes, the following summary statement of why hermeneutics aids theology in its understanding of revelation can be stated as follows:

(1) Hermeneutics, philosophically, accords a priority to "possibility" over "actuality" analogous to revelation's disclosure of new divine possibility over present actuality.

(2) Hermeneutics (unlike Platonism) takes history and historicity with full philosophical seriousness. For Judaism and Christianity, with their revelation on and through historical event, this is crucial.

(3) As Paul Ricoeur argues, truth is primordially, on the hermeneutical vision, an event of manifestation (Ricoeur) or disclosure (Gadamer) or disclosure–concealment (Heidegger). This defense of how manifestation (not correspondence or coherence) is the primary, indeed primordial, notion of truth in hermeneutics is clearly fruitful for a philosophical clarification of the meaning of revelation as the self-manifestation of God in and through form as event.

(4) Hermeneutics, by its concentration on text (or even on action as text), provides philosophical clarification of how essential form is for rendering manifestation. Form is not dispensable but crucial for understanding the manifested essence. Moreover, precisely the interest in the in-form-ing of text by such strategies of form as composition, genre, and style (Ricoeur) opens to exactly what a theology or revelation needs: an understanding of the text disclosing in and through form (*Dar-stellung*) a *possible* mode of being in the world. Philosophically, the hermeneutical world

---

[5] Inter alia, see Hans-Georg Gadamer, *Wahreit und Methode* (Tübingen: J. C. B. Mohr, 1965); Martin Heidegger, *Zur Sache des Denkens* (Tübingen: Max Niemeyer Verlag, 1969); Paul Ricoeur, *Hermeneutics and the Human Sciences* (Cambridge: Cambridge University Press, 1981).

of possibility[6] is an appeal to the productive imagination. Theologically, it is persuasive, not argumentatively coercive, as a Christian revelation's appeal to new possibility—the self-manifestation of this hermeneutical understanding of imagination is analogous to God in and through the indispensable and unsubstitutable Form of Jesus Christ as witnessed to in all the scriptural forms, especially the passion narratives which render that self into three identities: Jesus, Christ, and God.

(5) Hermeneutics, through its dialogical model for understanding, encourages the philosopher, in my judgment, to develop an ethics of the Good as the Good transforms reality by theologically understanding all Being as gracious.

All these moves suggest that philosophy (here hermeneutical philosophy) has two central roles in a theology grounded in revelation. The first is to reconstruct the hermeneutical categories (possibility, event, historicity, manifestation, form, dialogue) in accordance with the Form of Christian revelation in and through Jesus Christ. This theological reconstruction, moreover, will itself be informed by hermeneutical philosophy by finding categories (via hermeneutics) that genuinely clarify and develop the meaning of revelation itself. The second role of hermeneutical philosophy—especially through its development of the notion of the productive imagination in and through forms—is to provide a new way to clarify, and, when necessary, challenge and correct theology's own self-understanding of revelation as manifestation of *reasonable*, even if formerly unimagined, possibility. Whether such correlation occurs in an ad hoc or more general (inevitably transcendental) way is a further question that demands both further philosophical and further theological analysis. For the moment, it is enough to see that a correlation can and does occur between revelational theology and hermeneutical philosophy even without prior decisions on the general or ad hoc question.

Like Platonism before it, contemporary hermeneutical philosophy keeps alive the sense of wonder and participation crucial to revelation and philosophy alike. Unlike Platonism, moreover,

---

[6] For the spectrum of reception of this possibility, see Hans Robert Jauss, *Toward an Aesthetics of Reception* (Minneapolis: University of Minnesota Press, 1982).

hermeneutical philosophy can open philosophy itself to its ancient heritage by uniting theory to the praxis of spiritual exercises. As theology struggles to undo the nearly fatal separation of (not distinction between) theology and spirituality, perhaps theology may also suggest new ways for philosophy itself (including hermeneutical philosophy) to abandon all modern separations of theory and practice and retrieve the ancient philosophers' understanding of the role of spiritual exercises in and for theory itself. As Pierre Hadot's work has shown,[7] the ancients—whether in the schools of Stoics, Epicureans, Aristotelians, or Platonists or in the non-institutionalized movements of skepticism and cynicism—all insisted on philosophy as a way of life. As a way of life, philosophy united theory to praxis (and vice versa) partly by means of the regular, systematic use of spiritual exercises (for example, exercises of a tensive attentiveness to the Logos for the Stoic; exercises for a letting-go for the Epicureans). The loss of such exercises—even the classical use of mathematics for understanding pure intelligibility in Pythagoras and Plato, much less the exercise of ancient dialectic and the Hellenistic spiritual exercises of the Platonists—is peculiar to modern Western philosophy and theology. As our Western philosophy and theology learn to acknowledge the cognitive point of such exercises in, for example, Buddhist philosophies, perhaps at least "Christian philosophers" might join their theological colleagues in new, if tentative, attempts to recover what was once held together in both our disciplines: spiritual practice and theory, theory and a way of life. The new, global, cross-cultural understanding of both disciplines can encourage all responsible thinkers to take that new intellectual journey back to the future of both theology and philosophy as thought-ful ways of life.

QUESTIONS AND ANSWERS

Q: I was especially struck by your notion of the reunion of spiritual praxis and theory; I think that is very important. Now, the

---

[7] See Pierre Hadot, *Exercices spirituels et philosophie antique* (Paris: Études Augustiniennes, 1987).

deconstructionists have tried to do this in a very negative way, but this is a more positive way of getting them together. Could you comment a little more about the role of creative imagination in this process?

A: Thank you. Before responding directly to the question. I should say that elsewhere I have suggested that deconstruction, among other so-called postmodern movements, is responsible for this kind of recovery, and not only negatively, in fact. I've persuaded myself, and a few others, that part of the reason for the recovery of the mystical traditions—including by such highly secular thinkers as Derrida, Kristeva, and others, as well as Christian thinkers like Louis Dupré and many others—is that, as in the deconstructive case, these movements are not purely negative. The approach in these movements, to be sure, is to the traditions of love as radical excess and transgression. That is what fascinates me in them. You notice that, in the Christian tradition, the appeal is always the unity of intelligence and love. How do you relate these two approaches? Love in postmodernity tends to use categories like excess or transgression. This is analogous, on the side of what I called "proclamation tradition," to the attempt to provide, even within postmodernism, an ethic that is largely an ethic of resistance, as far as I can see. It was not surprising to me that John Caputo goes to Mark's Gospel for a reading in the Christian tradition of something like an ethics of difference and resistance. Now, these seem to me quite positive moves.

With regard to your specific question about imagination, I am thinking, of course, of Ricoeur's work under the rubric of productive imagination. I think Ricoeur's work is very important for my understanding of Christian theology, because it is an attempt at a theory of productive imagination. Everyone keeps saying to him, "Well, where is the poetics of the will that you promised us thirty years ago?" Well, maybe it exists. It is not just that he had to take his famous detours, that he had to actually investigate the different forms of imagination, both metaphor and narrative. He had also to rethink the relationship, for example, of sense and reference and how referent produced through sense became hermeneutically a notion of productive imagination that will allow a proper understanding of the relationship of composition, genre, and style. Style is that which individuates to produce the possible mode of being in the world. So, insofar as faith is this knowledge born of revelation that provides new possibilities, including, as Marion's work and others' have so fruitfully shown, the understanding of gift as a new possibility beyond actuality, the next step philosophically, in my opinion, is to show how that is a possibility in the sense of an appeal to the imagination. So when one says "productive imagination," Ricoeur says it means how the possible mode of being in the world, the referent, is produced in and through the different genres, the different forms. What strikes me as promising, for a theologian at least, about hermeneutics as a kind of successor to Platonism is that it provides a new, more sophisticated way of analyzing form and the relationship to imagination. Of course, it is not reproductive imagination—not just rendering present what is thought to be absent—and it's not romantic notions of creative imagination; it literally has to be productive imagination to be fruitful for an understanding of revelation, I think.

Q: You spoke of hermeneutical philosophy as being valuable in assisting a theology of revelation. I'm interested in hearing your thoughts on the value of hermeneutical philosophy in a theology of social change.

A: That's a very important question. There is no disclosure without some transformation, and that transformation is not only individual or personal, but also social and political. Therefore, it seems to me that if I expanded on what I have said here, I would try to show how what I called the "initial logos and kerygma distinction" is alive today in terms of those forms of theology, including those influenced by hermeneutics, that emphasize transformation, both personal and sociopolitical—that is to say, political theologies, liberation theologies, feminist theologies— but without a loss of the connection, and thus the need for hermeneutics, of that transformation to disclosure. I think I could show this in most of those forms of theology as they currently exist. Just as in the hermeneutical theologies, or transcendental theologies as well, there is no disclosure without a transformation, it may be that the transformation needs to be worked out more explicitly, just as Metz may have had to work out the political theology side of Karl Rahner's position. But if I understood rightly, I fully agree that it would be theologically adequate only if it could relate to both logos and kerygma—that is to say, not only to disclosure but also to disclosure that is also transformation.

Q: You referred many times to the question of gift. I was profoundly interested in that.* Could you explain more clearly what you intend by that? Is it a phenomenological theme, a theological theme? Is it directly connected with the identification of God, the hermeneutic of God, of Jesus Christ as love, or both?

A: I would say, as a matter of fact, both. What I did not spell out here is that it's a very important category for understanding the Christian tradition. I hardly need tell you the description of Pascal's Order of Charity, of Grace. But, it seems to me, grace is understood in two principal ways in the Christian tradition— again, through the logos and kerygma distinction. One is as disruptive power, and the other is principally as disclosive gift. Now, the orthodox Anglican and Roman Catholic traditions tend to employ a grace–nature model, and, therefore, a philosophical category like gift is both possible and necessary. In your work, the phenomenology of gift becomes crucial for clarifying what it means to say grace as gift of disclosure. That's all I was claiming for it. It would be less helpful in clarifying and understanding grace as disruptive power.

Q: I think that there has been a kind of drift in the discussion in this conference toward a notion of convergence of theology and philosophy. Let me propose something that might perhaps cut against the grain of that and say that we could think of the relationship of theology and philosophy as more like Rilke's "Two Solitudes" who meet, and touch, and greet each other. My instinct is to accord philosophy its own right or status as a *modus vivendi*, or *cognoscendi* independent of that of theology. As a Christian philosopher (whatever that is), I have no trouble thinking of philosophy as *ancilla Domini*, but I have anxiety about thinking of it as *ancilla theologiae*, to say nothing of its being the *ancilla* of Christian theology.

---

* Editor's note: The questioner is Jean-Luc Marion.

I respect the attempt of someone like Heidegger to secure an autonomous set of experiences which are purely philosophical, even though I share Professor Peperzak's misgivings about appealing to Aeschylus, and Hölderlin, and the like, as if they were some sort of authority.

Let me give you an example. Some years ago, having been provoked by some English translation of the Talmud, I undertook to learn Hebrew and Aramaic so that I could begin to read the Talmud as it should be read. The event was quite astonishing to me. What was opened up to me was an entirely new way of thinking, reading, interpreting, and expounding what had previously been, literally, a closed book to me. I then began to read deconstruction, and I discovered that I was lucky to have done it in that order because if I had not read the Talmud and had read deconstruction first, I would never have been able to get at the Talmud, so far as I've been able to get at it. And if I had not read the Talmud, I do not think I would ever have caught on to deconstruction even as well as I flatter myself that I might understand it.

But I do not think that it is a case of philosophical content being poured into a theological mold, or theological content being poured into a philosophical mold. I'm a long way from resolving in my mind what the relationship is between philosophy and theology in this sense, but I wonder if you could speak to that. As a theologian, do you see philosophy as an *ancilla theologiae*, as autonomous, or do you see the connection between the two modes of living and knowing as being a little bit more problematic?

A: Correct me if I misunderstood you. It was a complex question and statement, I think. I do not like expressions such as *ancilla theologiae*, or *ancilla philosophiae*, for that matter, but your example on the Talmud and deconstruction is a very interesting one.

As you know, there is good reason to believe that there is a real relationship between typically Talmudic ways of reading text and certain Derridean and other ways of reading text. But what would you call that? It seems to me you call that something like—I steal from Max Weber—a kind of "elective affinity," right? You do not have to use stronger language like influence or *ancilla,* etc. I was suggesting that I agree with von Balthasar: there was a real elective affinity between Platonism and Christianity that allowed for the developments that occurred so fruitfully in Christianity, especially of a logos-oriented sort. However, it seems to me one can say more than that, still without using that traditional vocabulary, and the more that I was trying to say was that if faith, this knowledge born of revelation, can also be retranslated more cryptically as Lonergan's knowledge born of love or *caritas—agape* transforming *eros/caritas—* you then have new possibilities, so that possibility itself becomes a central category. That is why possibility becomes such a central category for a theology.

Now, possibility is a very interesting category, because it both lends itself to reflecting on further notions like gift, as well as, in my judgment, reflecting on other theologians like Rahner: namely, how are we capable as human beings of actually appreciating, understanding, appropriating this new knowledge born of revelation?

Now, that's certainly beyond the initial example, either yours or von Balthasar's, of elective affinities, but it is not an example that sets up a hierarchy, which it seems to me the other language does. Christianity is going to be looking for new ways of clarifying that relationship. That is why I spent the time on what my theological view of revelation is and what faith is. Moreover, if we are fortunate, someone might also be able to do a sort of Rahnerian enterprise. If you can't do either, then I think one goes back to the elective affinities, and then it is a matter something like what Paul Tillich said of existentialism. Paul Tillich in Volume I of *Systematic Theology* says existentialism is "the good luck of Christian anthropology," because it was effectively describing the human situation. It was describing the human situation in such a manner that not only Christians but others as well could also understand it and find it, if I may use my own language, disclosive and transformative. That's all I'm claiming.

III
Of What Avail?

7

Lonergan and the Measures of God

Patrick A. Heelan, S.J.

BERNARD LONERGAN is one of the few philosopher/theologians of
our time who by his genius has contributed greatly to the resolution of the question of whether one can arrive at the God of the
New and the Old Testaments through natural science. In *Insight*
he failed, like Aquinas, to resolve the question. He had the good
fortune, however, of living longer than Aquinas. In *Method in
Theology* and other works he came to address the elements missing from *Insight*. But had he by that time lost interest in the
original question or did he think that he had resolved the original
question in *Insight*? What I propose to do is show that if the
apparatus of *Method in Theology* is applied to the original question, one has, on the one hand, a truly sophisticated philosophy
of natural science and, on the other. a method in theology that
embraces both the natural sciences and theology.

The genius of Aquinas is often said to lie in his embrace of
Aristotelian natural science as an independent source of knowledge of the divine and in his grand attempt to reconcile natural
science—Aristotelian natural science—and theology in the two
Summae. This he did, despite the opposition of theologians who
feared that an independent natural science would lead to a double
truth, a truth by the light of natural reason and a truth by the
light of revelation, which could under unfavorable circumstances
stand in rivalry to each other, unreconciled, and mutually opposed. In the last year of his life, Aquinas gave up his monumen-
tal task, declaring his work to be "*sicut palia*," as "straw" or
"dirty straw" (depending on how one translates the phrase) and
giving himself to mystical prayer and sacred poetry. Whether
he acted because of a higher mystical calling or because of his
perception of the impotence of reason in the face of, say, the

politics of power, we do not know. For the purpose of my argument, I take it that he came to distrust the conclusiveness of his own project.

The intellectual tradition of reconciling natural science and theology did not die with Aquinas (although it was briefly condemned in 1277 after his death) but continued in the centers of learning, Oxford, Paris, Cologne, where a mathematical Aristotle was being evolved that gave legitimacy to a mathematical science of Nature. This new reading of Aristotle was used to give scientific legitimacy to the linking of mathematics to experimental contrivances. It gained theological legitimacy by being declared a reading of God's other book, the Book of Nature. The theological nature of the new natural philosophy, then, was evident from the start. The precise terms under which the new philosophy was added to the number of the Aristotelian sciences and given a divine legitimacy were much argued in the seventeenth century by both Catholic and Protestant parties, and ironically it was philosophers and mathematicians in the Jesuit colleges who shaped the ensuing consensus of those times.[1] The centerpiece of that philosophical consensus was to become the principal critical target of Lonergan's *Insight*; it was what he called the false assumption of an "already-out-there-now-real," or what philosophers today simply call "objectivism" or "realism."

The new natural philosophy was from the first pursued under Christian theological auspices, though it was also in open rebellion against the hegemony of traditional theologians who relied strictly on Aristotelian and theological sources. From Descartes to Newton, history attests that the theological categories of orthodoxy, heterodoxy, and heresy were applied equally to science and to theology, for the cultural goals of science, philosophy,

---

[1] See A. C. Crombie, *Styles of Scientific Thinking in the European Tradition: The History of Argument and Explanation Especially in the Mathematical and Biomedical Sciences and Arts*, vols. I–III (London: Gerald Duckworth and Co., 1994), Peter Dear, *Discipline and Experience: The Mathematical Way in the Scientific Revolution*, Science and Its Conceptual Foundations Series (Chicago: The University of Chicago Press, 1995); and Stephen Shapin, *A Social History of Truth: Civility and Science in Seventeenth-Century England* (Chicago: The University of Chicago Press, 1994) and *The Scientific Revolution* (Chicago: The University of Chicago Press, 1995); see, in particular, Dear's *Discipline and Experience*.

and theology were the same, theological goals.[2] Until well into the nineteenth century, natural science or natural philosophy was explicitly an alternative theology, a natural theology, sometimes Christian but often and increasingly heterodoxly so and on its way to becoming a form of theology independent from and incompatible with the Christian tradition. For the new intellectual leaders of an enlightened age, the Book of Nature came to supplant the Book of Scripture as the source of divine revelation about God and Nature; human reason in its scientific form became its interpreter, and God emerged from this process as Nature's engineer, distant and personally detached or, perhaps, as the Divine Spirit of Scientific Reason, or simply as Nature Itself, unique and divine and accessible to the modern scientific spirit.

What was common to natural science and to theology during these centuries was the belief that both were seeking the same truth to be expressed in the same terms, and that such a truth was one, universal, and timeless—and "already out there" and "real" and "objective" for all truly philosophical inquirers to find. These background assumptions were classical: they stemmed from Hellenistic philosophy, were handed down through the Middle Ages, and were reinterpreted by the seventeenth century according to the spirit of that age. They permeated Christian theology as much as natural science, and they set the stage for the later play of dramatic conflicts that continue today between two forms of inquiry—modern science and traditional theology— each declaring its own truth in more or less open conflict and certain disagreement over God's nature and existence, over morality and the rule of law, and God's relationship to suffering, evil, and the meaning of human life.

In *Insight* Lonergan addressed method in science, attacking— through the notion of the "virtually unconditioned" judgment— the classical assumption of the "already-out-there-now-real" that was the historically negotiated underpinning of modern science. In *Method in Theology* he did the same for theology. From *Insight*, we learn how to appropriate the process of scientific inquiry and, in so doing, how to unlearn the classical assumptions

---

[2] See David C. Lindberg and Ronald Numbers, eds., *God and Nature* (Berkeley: University of California Press, 1986).

of the historical tradition of science. Science, says Lonergan, is thing-to-thing knowledge—it is explanatory by relating things to relevant factors in the environment. It can be distinguished from common sense, which is thing-to-us knowledge—relating things to our needs and behaviors. If a wheel is round, it is because its roundness serves the purpose of transportation. You ask: what makes it of a roundness-suitable-for-transportation? You answer: it is circular, that is, its spokes "are" the radii of a circle with the center at the hub.

To be "circular," then, is a scientific explanation of the "roundness-suitable-for-transportation" of a wheel. Circles are geometrical objects, abstract, timeless, necessary, imperceptible, structured forms, differentiated only by location in a background space that is invisible and empty of everyday sensible things. Wheels, however, have none of these characteristics. You cannot ride a bicycle on two circles. Real wheels are contingent, perceptible, made of matter, always in a place with people and serving a human purpose in historical time. These are not the properties of mathematical objects. What joins the two is *measurement*, and the process of measurement constitutes an *experiment*. Measuring is the experimental process that enables the measurer in the course of a specific experiment to put numbers on things by physically comparing them with a standard—for example, for length, with marks on a rigid ruler. An experiment is a public event. How is it done? With what range of precision is it done? When does the experiment—a measurement—"end"? The "ending" of an experiment, as Peter Galison and others point out, is socially and historically underdetermined.[3] Circularity, then, is the scientific explanation of the wheel, because it defines a mathematical model or theory that serves as an ideal infrastructure or template to which a good wheel will conform according to local historical standards.

---

[3] See Peter Galison, *How Experiments End* (Chicago: The University of Chicago Press, 1987); as well as Pierre Duhem, *Aim and Structure of Physical Theory* (1914; Princeton, N.J.: Princeton University Press, 1954); Ludwig Fleck, *The Genesis and Development of a Scientific Fact*, trans. F. Bradley and T. Trenn (1935; Chicago: The University of Chicago Press, 1979), and Stephen Hawking, *The Illustrated A Brief History of Time* (New York: Bantam Books, 1996).

All answers, then, are historically or socially conditioned. However, this does not reach the philosophical core of inquiry, whether scientific or non-scientific. How do inquirers recognize for themselves, apart from external criteria such as convention or authority, when a sought-for answer has been found and presents itself to the inquirers within the context of their inquiry? This is the truly philosophical question whose answer must come from a philosophical study of the questioning of experience. This is where *Insight* is at its best.

The title *Insight* refers to the phenomenology of coming to recognize that an answer to an experimental question is being offered in some theory or hypothesis. The theory that is at first offered need not, however, be accepted. It may fail the test of rational criticism as imposed by a particular historical cultural community; it may turn out to be for this community no more than an illusory answer to the original question, or it may turn out to be the answer to another question that the community now begins to entertain as more significant than the first. The proferred answer could also be shunted aside because of the entrenched bias of this community. Self-appropriation of the process of inquiry means for Lonergan coming to recognize the phenomenology of insight and how it functions in intellectual inquiry as a universal dynamic structure of knowing. It emerges at an historical time and place from a questioning of experience, and it offers answers that call for rational assessment relative to the original question or to a possible shift in the question itself. Insight is a phase of the intellectual pursuit of understanding— the theory-making phase. A theory may answer the original question, may change the original question, or may be shunned as an enemy of entrenched background values. While a theory is always an abstract, general, timeless, differentiated structure of logical or mathematical parts, a theory's acceptance or rejection is always an historical social cultural event, conditioned by the local background of the community's interests and the material standards or measures in which these are expressed.[4]

---

[4] Cf. Patrick Heelan, "Hermeneutics of Experimental Science in the Context of the Life-World," in *Interdisciplinary Phenomenology*, ed. D. Ihde and R. Zaner (The Hague: Martinus Nijhoff, 1975), pp. 7–50; and "After Experiment: Research and Reality," *American Philosophical Quarterly*, 26 (1989): 297–308.

Insight's account then assumes that the cultural meaning of a theory and its validation are an expression of a common horizon shared by the communities that use them. The kind of knowledge so generated has a kind of social ecological character. Two nagging questions press for answers: (*a*) can it be appropriated by groups other than those that share the original horizon? and (*b*) can all historical, particular, and local ties be removed? As to the first question, I have argued elsewhere that scientific theories always have a cultural as well as an explanatory dimension and that, given the constancy of the explanatory dimension of a scientific theory, its cultural dimension can expand into the culture via new technological designs stemming from creative applications of the explanatory theory.[5] Telephones and television are cultural spin-offs of electron and electromagnetic theory. As to the second question, what would such culture-free, history-free knowledge look like? It would be knowledge permeated with the classical values that historically were sought by natural science, and it is precisely these values that *Insight* brings into question, not just for natural science but for all theoretical knowledge.

At this point, *Insight* might have taken a different direction from the one Lonergan chose. The logic of the first half of the book suggests the possibility of a Heideggerian turn toward fundamental ontology or hermeneutic phenomenology, but that was not the path he chose. He chose to follow Aquinas along the metaphysical route, the one that Aquinas, we recall, finally abandoned as "*palia*" or "straw" for reasons, whether personal or theological, we do not know.

But the metaphysical route to God is incoherent with the doctrine of *Insight*, since insofar as metaphysics itself functions as a theory—and that is arguably the way it functions in Lonergan as in Aquinas—it needs to be situated in a normative historical and social community where it is experimentally validated. Perhaps Lonergan meant us to assume that theologians understand their theories against the background of their pastoral experience, using this in the critical assessment of theological frameworks.

---

[5] See Patrick Heelan, "Why a Hermeneutical Philosophy of the Natural Sciences?" *Man and World*, 30 (1997): 217–98; and "Scope of Hermeneutics in Natural Science," *Studies in the History and Philosophy of Science*, 29 (1998): 273–98.

However, it has been felt that the Catholic theological enterprise has been remote from the normative role of spiritual experience or religious life. Certainly, the Reformation and post-Reformation controversies surrounding "religious enthusiasm" generated a deep reluctance among Catholic theologians to connect their scholarship with the experience of spiritual people. The traditional term *sanctifying grace*, used, for example, as part of the theoretical explanation of the salvific faith of Christians, would be called a "theoretical entity" in the terminology of the philosophy of science. On the principles enuntiated in *Insight*, such a theoretical entity must get its cultural meaning from an empirical *explanandum* for which this entity is the *explanans*. What is this *explananum* but the phenomena of Christian faith, hope, and charity? Should these then constitute, as it were, the context for an experiential "measure" of grace? Lonergan is silent on this topic in the chapter on "God" in *Insight*.

In *Method in Theology*, however, he makes the expected turn toward a hermeneutic phenomenology based on "conversion," "horizon," "history," and the structure of "belief." These terms, which Lonergan treats as "methodological" in *Method*, become philosophical to the degree that they apply to science as well as theology. Let us look, then, for a philosophy of science that, like a philosophy of theology, is marked by conversions, horizons, history, and systematic beliefs. This is my next topic.

That part of the philosophy of science that is relevant to the "Received View" (a common term for Logical Empiricism) is structured by insight; it is theory-centered. Let us consider a more comprehensive philosophy of science with a focus on measurement and experiment. This focus is situated in the social and historical world where in the performance of (laboratory) experiments the entities of science make their worldly appearances. For this focus, we turn to the appropriate structures, *conversion*, *horizon*, *history*, and *belief*.[6]

"By *conversion* is understood a transformation of the subject and his world. . . . it is as if one's eyes were opened and one's

---

[6] I have developed a philosophy of natural science that incorporates the methodology of *Method* with that of *Insight*; see, for example, my "Space as God's Presence," *Dharma*, 8 (1983): 63–86; "Why a Hermeneutical Philosophy of the Natural Sciences?" and "Scope of Hermeneutics in Natural Science."

former world faded or fell away" (*Method* 130). While intensely personal, it is also communal and can be handed on within an historical community. Conversion so communicated is, says Lonergan, the foundation for theology. Is it not also the foundation for science, giving rise to *horizons* within which the meaning of doctrines or theories can be apprehended? An horizon is the structured resultant of the combination of a theoretical viewpoint embodied in communal procedures that reveal a perspective on the world. That moment of conversion, for example, in Galileo's life was his telescopic discovery of the phases of Venus. Then he knew that the universe was Copernican, and in his private notes on that evening he changed from Italian, the local language, to Latin, the universal language of science.[7] Speaking to all the world, Galileo wrote that Nature is a Book written in the language of geometry and that the horizons of nature are structured by the geometry of the Copernican system.[8] Other natural philosophers continued to consider astronomy as merely a saving of the celestial appearances, but for Galileo astronomy, mechanics, and the whole of natural science was a divine revelation about Nature expressed in God's own language of mathematics. This conversion experience changed the direction of Galileo's scientific inquiry in a fundamental way; what formerly was experienced one way came to be experienced differently, giving witness to its being a form of existential or practical interpretation. What formerly, for example, was experienced as a stone falling in a straight vertical line toward its natural place at the center of an earth-centered cosmology came to be experienced, after his conversion, as a stone following a parabolic trajectory above the surface of a turning earth in a sun-centered cosmology.[9] The old facts dissolved with the old perspective; they became philosophically and cosmologically irrelevant and gave way to new facts generated by the new perspective. The relevant philosophical and cosmological perspective changed, and the horizons of philosophical and cosmological re-

---

[7] I thank Owen Gingrich for this information.

[8] Galileo in *The Assayer*, in *Discoveries and Opinions of Galileo*, trans. Stillman Drake (Garden City, N.Y.: Doubleday, 1957), pp. 237–38.

[9] Cf. Paul K. Feyerabend, *Against Method* (London: NLB/Verso, 1978), chap. 7.

ality changed, leaving the old ones beached as it were like a ship-wrecked hulk.

History, says Lonergan in *Method*, is not just the unfolding of events in physical or cosmological time. It is

concerned with the drama of life, with what results through the characters, their decisions, their actions, and not only because of them but also because of their defects, their oversights, their failures to act. . . . it does not predict what will happen but reaches its conclusions from what has happened. . . . history is concerned to determine what, in most cases, contemporaries do not know. For in most cases, contemporaries do not know what is going forward . . . in particular groups at particular places and times [178–79].

Lonergan tries to separate the objects of historical study from the objects of natural science.

1. The objects of historical study are constituted by acts of meaning, he says; the objects of natural science are not.

2. The objects of historical study are explained by narratives about particular persons and places that do not claim universality; the objects of natural science, to the contrary, claim universality and can be overthrown by a single counterexample.

3. Historical claims are not verifiable in the fashion of the natural sciences by data but only through interpretation.

While all these dualistic distinctions hold for theory-centered accounts of natural science, they break down as soon as the focus on scientific inquiry is formation of *beliefs* on the basis of measurement and experiment.[10]

1. Galileo's "falling body" is as much the creation of an act of meaning as the battle of Gettysburg is. In "normal science" (to use a Kuhnian phrase), radical reinterpretations do not take place, and so meanings or meaning-shifts can generally be assumed to be irrelevant. Although attention to meaning-creation, -transformation, and -transmission is rarely relevant to the ordinary practice of science, it is nevertheless essential to science in its history. Indeed, in its outer reaches (say, in cosmological or quantum theoretical speculation), and for a philosophical account of science, it has to be included. In fact, it is so important for the

---

[10] See my "Why a Hermeneutical Philosophy of the Natural Sciences?" and "Scope of Hermeneutics in Natural Science."

history and philosophy of science that it has to be brought to center-stage.
2. The outcome of a scientific inquiry is presented in terms of a universal theory, where the narrative of origins is considered irrelevant to the scientific meaning of the theory. But is the narrative of origins really irrelevant? Consider, for example, Newtonian physics. The meaningful content of Newtonian physics—what it is taken to say about the world—differs significantly today from what can be inferred from Newton's own writings and diaries. Were Newton to return today with all his faculties, he would not understand nor, if he were to understand, would he approve of what is currently attributed to him; among many things, he would complain that natural philosophy has lost its theological bearings with the loss of Absolute Space and Time. Or consider William Thompson, the discoverer of the electron: would he recognize in the electron's present-day leptonic description the "currant-bun" electron that he discovered? Or quantum physics: how differently it is taken today from the way Bohr, Heisenberg, and Schrödinger—the founders—took it to be, a microphysics rather than a universal physics. If John von Neumann and others had not tried to make it into a universal physics and successor to Newtonian physics, might physics or at least the philosophy of science not be different today?[11] It appears that what is remembered in natural science and passed on in textbooks is not what the founders thought they had discovered but the product of something that was going forward over their heads and of which they were not aware, and which it is the task of history to uncover often to the discomfort of the scientific community.[12] From this perspective natural science is a sedimented history without the history part, and therefore, unfortunately, without the historian's admonitions. Among these is Lonergan's own admonition that "history does not predict what will happen," namely, "what the future of science will be like," but "it reaches its conclusions from what has happened," that is, "not

---

[11] See Patrick Heelan, *Quantum Mechanics and Objectivity: The Physical Philosophy of Werner Heisenberg* (The Hague: Martinus Nijhoff, 1965).
[12] See Thomas Nickles, "Philosophy of Science and History of Science," in Constructing Knowledge in the History of Science," *Osiris*, 10 (1995): 139–63.

only from what people intend but also from their oversights, mistakes, failures to act," and so forth (*Method* 179).

Again, and from another angle, theories are "confirmed" and become *systematic beliefs* by original credit-generating experiments that, like battles, are particular events and are permeated with a certain prior indeterminacy that is overcome by personal "negotiation" as to how the outcome is to be described. Experimental results or data rarely mention the accrediting procedures or negotiations, for example, about how measurements are standardized, and how the prior indeterminacy of results is converted into scientific data, and always into data suitable for local and temporal purposes of an historical scientific community.[13] Why, for example, given the selectivity Milliken imposed on his data, were Milliken's data nevertheless more credible than Ehrenhaft's?[14] When the full story is told of how experiments "end" or come to be credited with significance, it will appear that much was going on in the world of physics above the heads of the participants and unknown to them. Why, for example, was Michelson's measure of the speed of light accredited but not Miller's?[15] In the history of quantum mechanics, why did Heisenberg's explanation prevail but not Schrödinger's? Why Bohr's account but not Einstein's? Why von Neumann's account but not Bohr's? Why the later Heisenberg's but not the early Heisenberg?[16] In each of these cases, what are credited to be the scientific solution was influenced by what was going on over the heads of the participants and unknown to them. In contrast, what is affirmed by the canonical record—for example, that we inherit the scientific vision of Galileo, Newton, Bohr, and Heisenberg—is attributed to the founders as if they consciously and de-

---

[13] See my "After Experiment: Research and Reality." This warning is particularly necessary in the psychosocial sciences which have too often modeled themselves on a positivistic version of the natural sciences. Looking, for example, at C. L. Hardin's critique of current nativist views of color or the critique of innate deep structure theories of language by J. J. Gumperz and S. C. Levinton, we see that overlooked data point both to the cultural content of the data and to the influence of cultural presuppositions on the conduct of scientific research.
[14] See Gerald Holton, *Thematic Origins of Modern Science* (Cambridge, Mass.: Harvard University Press, 1973).
[15] Ibid.
[16] See my *Quantum Mechanics and Objectivity*.

liberately set the parameters of the present-day account, which, of course, is not true.[17]

3. Scientific data, as I have said, are the sedimented outcome of an historical process, and this process has a narrative that needs to be written by an historian. Natural science, assuming the validity of the classical philosophical dualisms of subject/ object, perception/understanding, thing/environment, particulars/ essences, facts/values, also assumes that the narrative is unimportant. The historical narratives that explain contemporary science may be important, even to physicists, to the extent that they may bring to light what resulted "not only from what people [intended] but also from their oversights, mistakes, failures to act" (*Method* 179); what was the outcome of innocent mistakes, ignorance or inadvertence; and what from less innocent causes, such as power plays, social values, religious views, national goals, gender preferences, funding needs, and a host of other factors discoverable only by historians of science who treat their subject matter with the attitude of historians inquiring into ordinary human events and writing a narrative about important scientific events as if these were ordinary human events.

Scientists are thought to *know*, while theologians are thought just to *believe*. It should be clear from what has been said about the way scientific theories and scientific data are accredited that the intellectual environment of science, like the intellectual environment of theology, is full of local historical background, some of which masquerades as universal knowledge. More precisely, much of what is called scientific knowledge is not what it (usually) purports to be—universal, transcultural, and transtemporal—but the admittedly expert beliefs of an historical scientific community.

Finally, just as a good philosophy of natural science needs Lonergan's *Method in Theology*, so a good theology needs to reflect more the scientific or intellectual structures studied in *Insight*. I shall try to make plausible the claim that the foundations of theology in conversion, horizons, history, and systematic be-

---

[17] See my "Hermeneutical Phenomenology and the History of Science," in *Nature and Scientific Method: William A. Wallace Festschrift*, ed. Daniel Dahlstrom (Washington, D.C.: Catholic University of America press, 1991), pp. 23–26.

liefs must have their own analogue of an experimental laboratory to complement the consecrated words of tradition. New theological insight is not limited to pure theoretical speculation or the purely hermeneutical study of literary texts steeped in the writings of dead theologians, but also comes from the study of current religious witness, a laboratory where theological insights and theories are tested in turn by expert actors and witnesses.

Such a claim may be unsettling in the Catholic theological context because, among other reasons, it raises the specter of enthusiasm, old and new, from the Quakers and Quietists of the seventeenth century to the present-day Pentecostalists, and the threat enthusiasm once and always poses to academic theologians and hierarchical institutions. Theologians and institutions have enormous reluctance to use their theological theories or theory-laden canons to "measure" and pass judgment on local empirical events of a religious character. I stress the context of "measurement," which is done individual case by individual case, each constrained by place, community, and history. In "Belief: Today's Issue," a paper he read to *Pax Romana* in 1968,[18] Lonergan gave among his own reasons for this reluctance: God is not an entity within this world and so cannot become known by experience; no one knows God face-to-face in this life and so no one can look for confirmation of theological theories in human religious experience. In 1968 Lonergan took the position that there was no quasi-laboratory that could provide, as it were, public ecclesial "measures" of religious experience—or at least speaking to *Pax Romana*, he was unwilling to defend such a position. Whatever one might say in defense of the influence of Dionysos on the Platonic tradition, at least within the context of Apollonian classical thinking in theology, there is indeed no other conclusion.

Four years later, in *Method*, and to a different audience, he makes a stunningly different claim: theology in relation to religious experience is like economics in relation to business. Religious life can flourish without theology, just as business can flourish without economics, but just as economics results from intellectual inquiry into business, so theology results—or should

---

[18] See B. F. Lonergan, "Belief: Today's Issue," *Pax Romana*, March 16, 1968.

result, he says—from intellectual inquiry into religious life.[19] Lonergan gives the old word *faith* a new meaning. "Faith," he says, "is the knowledge born of religious love" (115). It is the *cognitive intentional counterpart* of that ontological change wrought by *sanctifying grace.* Faith makes possible a *conversion* that opens *horizons* of *religious experience.* Faith is distinguished from *religious belief,* which is the readiness to accept the historically sedimented pattern of communal understanding that people living within a religious tradition have, based on the totality of their religious culture, comprising sacred books, rituals, accepted teachings, and other cultural traditions of use in daily life. In contrast with religious belief, faith, being the knowledge born of love, expresses its *interiority* in four stages: religious experience; insight or theory-making; judgment or theory-accepting or -rejecting; and responsible *decision,* which is the self-transcendent outcome of the loving part of faith's interior intention.

By the time *Method* appeared in 1972, Lonergan was ready to accept the fact and necessity of a quasi-laboratory[20] of faith, a community practice able to provide the experts with, as it were, public "measures" of the life of faith.

Turning now specifically to Christianity and taking it for the purpose of this essay to be a community defined by faith in a God, Creator of the Cosmos but not a part of it, who has made an historic covenant with a free human community offering individual, social, and perhaps even cosmic redemption through the incarnation, death, and resurrection of his Son, Jesus Christ, in the Church that he founded: the Christian question would be whether faith in such a God, articulated by theologians and administered by the institutional Church, can be referred to a particular historical quasi-laboratory of religious experience, in which theological statements about living "in the spirit of faith"

---

[19] Lonergan is speaking of the scholarly study of religious experience in any religious, not just a Christian, setting.

[20] By a quasi-laboratory, I mean a domain for empirical investigation to set off by common background and context that relevant data can be harvested with security in terms of some antecedent theoretical—here, theological—model. A laboratory in the natural sciences is such a domain where relevant physical phenomena can make their appearance under physical conditions controlled by a theoretical model.

can be "measured" or "tested" by experiential signs interpreted as marked with a divine approval. Such a question may sound strange, perhaps very strange indeed, coming from a practicing Catholic. Beyond the Catholic community, however, there is no such reluctance; one finds today a plethora of religious theologies stemming, for example, from interpretations of contemporary evolutionary and cosmological science.[21] One of the reasons for the widespread appeal of Stephen Hawking's *A Brief History of Time* is his argument that astrophysical theories can lead the religious inquirer to the "Mind of God."[22] Since all scientific theories aim at prediction and control, this kind of argument deeply undercuts our image of human life, for it presupposes a metaphysics in which human freedom is absent and human decisions are preordained by neurological circuits. Existence in this story is determined by cosmological "crunches" and "rebirths" which, though bearing some reminiscence of the mythic cosmological cycles of the Great Year of Stoic or Hindu cosmology with their "eternal return of the Same," are nevertheless of an entirely different genre, secular predictions, not sacred. By contrast, what is characteristic at least of Christianity is the drama of the biblical narratives that underline *human freedom* in making history in this world in which we live. Instead of looking to cosmological models, should we not, following Lonergan, look for a quasi-laboratory of religious experience where human freedom is respected and history retains its edge of uncertainty? Such is more likely to be a faith community of people productive, as Lonergan has said, of "works of self-transcendent love animated by faith"—among whom some are expert in interpreting theologically the horizons of critical religious experience.

---

[21] I refer not just to Einstein's view of a divine Cosmos, but to the writings of John Barrow, Paul Davies, Richard Dawkins, William Day, Jonathan Glover, Stephen Hawking, B. F. Skinner, Frank Tipler, and others who purport to discover in science theological hopes that rival the imaginations of medieval mystics. Typical contemporary approaches of this kind are Barrow and Tipler's *The Anthropic Cosmological Principle* (Oxford: Oxford University Press, 1988), Hawking's *Illustrated A Brief History of Time*, Davies's *The Mind of God* (New York: Simon & Schuster, 1991), and Dawkins's *The Selfish Gene* (London: Oxford University Press, 1976).

[22] Hawking, *Illustrated A Brief History of Time*, p. 233; see also Davies, *Mind of God*.

In such a quasi-laboratory community, what would be the "measures"? One suggestion is criteria afforded, for instance, by techniques of "spiritual discernment." By "spiritual discernment," I mean, prayerful techniques suitable for the members of this community equipped with theological language, who are responsive, say, to what the Christian tradition calls the "spiritual senses" which serve to "measure" divine presence and action in a community. Such historical practices of spiritual discernment were taught throughout the history of the Church and have been an essential part of good or "perfect" Christian living for two thousand years. Borrowed from the Stoics and other pre-Christian sources, they were adapted for Christianity by the desert fathers and monks and they are still taught and practiced and monitored by spiritual directors today. Such Christian spiritual exercises introduce the better prepared and motivated to a religious path where decisions are prompted by a combination of human reason, traditional beliefs, community rituals, and the spiritual discernment of empirical signs of divine communication. Nancey Murphy's *Theology in the Age of Scientific Reasoning* is one of the few books devoted to the history of European and American religious communities founded on such a notion of spiritual discernment.

One such practice, for example, is the exercise of spiritual discernment taught by St. Ignatius Loyola in his *Spiritual Exercises.* Such spiritual exercises, as Hadot has shown,[23] have their roots in ancient philosophy, in Socrates, the Stoics, and Epicurus, for whom wisdom was a form of practical reason focused on the divine. The exercises of St. Ignatius lead participants to enter the narratives of the Gospels as actors in the Gospel story, representing themselves as disciples eager to share the life of the faith community of Jesus and willing to orient their lives according to the spirit of that community. St. Ignatius and other spiritual writers speak of the experience of "spiritual senses." These bear an analogy to the physical senses: of the "eyes" of faith, the "bitterness" of remorse, the "sweetness" of charity, the "tears" of divine love and sorrow, or, more generally, of "spiritual touches," "consolation," and "desolation." All such information is struc-

---

[23] Cf. Pierre Hadot, *Philosophy as a Way of Life* (Oxford: Blackwell, 1995).

tured a priori by theological language in some way analogous to the way laboratory information is structured by scientific theory. With the scientific analogy in mind, can we then speak of such spiritual exercises as constituting a quasi-laboratory of religious experience?

Laboratory experimentation and its protocols are properly described in narrative form, because every experiment is particular, involving actions of particular people in a definite place and time, motivated by a common purpose, equipped with an explanatory theory, and brought to the bar of experience as subject to a jury of experts. So, too, would religious experience in the quasi-laboratory of spiritual exercises be presented in narrative form under explanatory theological categories.

I have argued that both science and theology should exhibit the range of structures that Lonergan describes in *Method* and *Insight*. Such a conclusion does not guarantee that the natural sciences reveal the God of the Bible. What it shows is merely that there is a common philosophically understood method underlying theology and natural science, and that using that method within the established traditions of Christian life and practice, scientists who are Christian and theologians who respect the processes of natural science should be able to gain reliable experiential, intellectual, and rational knowledge both of Nature, the subject matter of the natural sciences, and of the Christian Trinitarian God, the subject matter of the Christian religion.

QUESTIONS AND ANSWERS

Q: It seems to me that you are answering the question of whether there is a difference between philosophy and theology by saying that what the philosopher does is try to lay down certain generally acceptable truths and then establish conclusions on that basis, whereas theology starts from certain truths accepted by faith that would not necessarily be otherwise generally acceptable and proceeds from there.

What I think was interesting about what you had to say was that this particular distinction does not hold, because theology uses, or can use, the method of science, which is the very method of laying out certain truths—or certain bases, certain evidence, that it believes should be generally accepted—from which to derive its conclusions. So, the scientific method is like the philosophical method, on one hand; it's also like the theological method, on the other. You have an evidential basis that everybody should accept; its experiential nature makes theology like science. In the scientific case, you've got the evidence of the senses, presumably gotten from normal experiments; in the theological case, you get the evidence from religious experience. So, that is the way I see you as answering the standard question of this conference which, I think, is an intriguing response.

So, my first question would be, taking both Adriaan Peperzak's line and Marilyn Adams's, whether on the side of the religious experience there is not this key difference—one that would be a lot easier to see if we did not have a room full of Christians— namely, that the religious experience of diverse faiths is very different, and the religious theories constructed on the basis of that experience are not only different, but also profoundly incompatible. Moreover, the further gathering of the evidence of religious experience does not seem to lead to any kind of Peircean approach to the asymptote of truth in the way that it might be viewed as doing in science. Even though there are always differences, scientists gather further data, these differences are minimized, and there is some sign that in the limit they will disappear. So, that would then be the critical difference. Is there really this kind of objective religious experience that is universally acceptable when, in fact, you gather it leads to seemingly ineradicable conflicts?

A: There certainly are differences among religious faiths, each of which would have communities who experience the religious dimension of existence differently. There are a few religions— Christianity, Judaism, Islam—that are monotheistic religions. They work together to some significant extent. Most other world religions do not have a word for "God." Buddhism doesn't have a word for "God." Taoism and Confucianism are not religions, in the sense that they are articulated in theological terms. So, one would need to consider that their religious laboratories, as it were, would be shaped in terms of the language that they use. Whether one could insert Christian religious language into that laboratory, one can by analogy say, "Should one insert quantum mechanics into a laboratory designed for engineering, or for classical physics, or elasticity physics?" In other words, one brings into the laboratory only an appropriate set of theoretical concerns. So, to bring the Christian God into a Buddhist religious lab might be quite inappropriate.

Now, how one would span the hermeneutic of these two different communities is, of course, an open question. One could speculate on there being Christians who are also Buddhists, Buddhists who are also Christians; perhaps they could converse with one another. To understand how to communicate with religions other than Christianity, we may need to have people who are committed members of both communities and who can interpret on the basis of a shared experience. But, certainly, to interpret Buddhism on the basis of Christian theology would be a very hazardous enterprise. I wouldn't have an awful lot of confidence in it. It's done all the time, nevertheless. It's no worse than the metaphors Steven Hawking uses in his book on cosmology. Just as false, just as true. Do they serve a purpose? Well, they make you feel good at the end of it and give you some sense that one is talking to a great intellect who somehow has penetrated the mysteries of cosmology. But as far as true information goes, the measure of that is close to zero.

Q: How about within the Christian tradition, say, the difference between whether or not there is a Trinity; whether or not God is eternal, meaning everlasting in time, or whether or not God is eternal, meaning completely outside of time? Do you think there is an evidential basis in religious experience or anything like sensory experience that is commonly enough shared among the participants, even among the various religious traditions, that would enable people to settle these profound theological issues?

A: Well, clearly, there's no experiment for God's eternity; nevertheless, there are some possibilities for shared experience, as I see it. For example, in the *Spiritual Exercises* of St. Ignatius of Loyola, the outcome sought is decision-making, and decision-making could well be decision-making about the further research on a theological proposition. In other words, God's eternity and omnipotence would be part of the background of a theory from which then evolve certain elements that do have descriptive value in the world, and it is only those phenomena that would be appropriate to the laboratory situation.

In physics, likewise, there are entities that are not observable, yet are part of a theory that everyone believes in, so they are accepted because, though not observed, they are necessary for the coherence of the theory. There are many elements of that kind in science, at least at any particular point of development of a scientific theory. Not every element of the theory can be verified directly; quarks have not been observed, and yet they are fundamental to elementary-particle theory today. So, it is not that everything needs to be measurable, but that there are measures that certain interpretations hold up and are good for the making of decisions. For example, if you build a superconducting supercollider, you will build it on the theory of quarks and leptons, and because of the enormous investment, you had better be 90 percent sure that these entities exist, or maybe 95 percent close to sure that spending $50 billion of public money is going to bring you something. It is a form of Pascal's wager. You must be pretty damned sure of an eternal life if you're going to make the sacrifices for Christianity that people sometimes make. You have no certainty about it, or do you?

Q: I would like to return a moment to your conversation about Bernard Lonergan. Even though you endorse his work, I seem to sense that we have lost the teeth of his contribution to philosophy: namely, the structure of his general empirical method, which brings the methods of science to the structures of the mind, or at least applies the methods of science to the structures of the mind, thereby generalizing the method from scientific data to the science of the mind.

This, to me, is what this conference is about: that all theologians have minds, and that those structures are operative when we're doing theology and/or we are doing philosophy. Lonergan's great contribution, I think, is setting out those universal structures of mind in language that a scientist can understand. In his book, Lonergan develops the notion of the self-appropriation of the knower as a way to bring the scientist into an understanding of himself as a philosopher and as a thinking person, trying to wrench people away from the conceptualism of the times.

I think that this contribution is the thing that both rightly distinguishes philosophy from theology and forges that distinction which must be made and kept, I think, on most levels, but at the same time the glue that puts the two things back together, which is what I think this conference is about. It allows one to be able to relate the two, while still maintaining the necessary distinctions between them.

A: I agree with those comments. Naturally, I am taking a select element out of Lonergan that is relevant to this discussion. In picking that out, however, I discovered for the first time the contradictions in Lonergan; that in *Method in Theology* he has a very naïve view of what natural science is, compared to what *Insight* presents. He should have read his own book, you know. Now, I think Lonergan is a great figure. He is a great philosopher who has appropriated the natural sciences and has appropriated self-reflective method in theology, too. I don't want the fact that I am picky about certain things in any way to indicate that I think that his achievement is less. It is when you look at it from a certain point of view, the point of view of this symposium, that I find some small problem.

I also want to say that I do not think Lonergan is the only person whose thinking can serve the purpose, the very purposes that I have pointed out. There are ways of using other philosophers of the European tradition in this way. There is a lot in Lonergan that addresses an English-speaking audience, and, to some extent, addressing the English-speaking audience shaped *Insight*. I have seen other versions of *Method in Theology*—that is, texts of his lectures in Rome—that I found much more interesting than the one that was published in English here. So, all kinds of things intervene that present a writer or a thinker to the world under one guise or another. I am presenting him here under a guise that he probably never thought about but that I think is useful for our present discussion.

I do think he is a great philosopher, a great epistemologist. I would also say, since I rarely use Lonergan myself in my own work, that, in my view, he's not the only one to use. I use Husserl and Heidegger, and I can read in them more or less similar con-

structions to the ones that I have spoken about as coming from
Lonergan.

Q: I was intrigued by the first questioner's point that there
might be a problem with your analogy between theology and
science, because in theology religious experience and the attempt
to articulate it does not tend to lead toward agreement.* That, of
course, is true in some sense, some profound sense, and it is
always a problem for arguments from religious experience and
so on. But it just struck me that one sort of possible line of reply
that sustains the analogy, at least for a time, might be this. If a
subject is extremely difficult, part of our problem as investigators
is that we do not know from which angle to attack it, so to speak.
Even in science, so far as I know, they try different angles of
attack, not randomly, but also not quite deductively. So, if the
topic is sufficiently difficult, the best way to make progress might
not be to try to come to a quick agreement, but for each group to
keep on pursuing its own line of investigation. And one might
have to continue that for quite some time before one could either
decide that one approach was fruitless and off-base, and decide
in favor of another one, or decide that they were all not such
good angles. Now that you've tried them out for quite some time,
you might be able to come up with yet a different one that would
somehow benefit from the research programs in both groups.

It seems to me that when one does look within great religious
traditions, one can see development (I wouldn't want to say *linear* development) and progress, and enrichment, and so forth.
You might think of the so-called great religions as somehow pursuing research programs in the sense of attempting to articulate
their experience of the divine. And one might think that, because
God is such a tough subject for human beings to tackle, the best
way to pursue things is still, after centuries, to keep on with our
individual angles until we can see better.

But then I would just add that it does not have to be God to get
such a hard topic, because it seems to me that in the mind/body
question we also see development in the various different schools

---

* Editor's note: The question here is Marilyn McCord Adams.

of accounts of mind/body relations—dualism, idealism, materialism, and others—but we do not see any convergence and agreement. But we keep on working on our projects, and sometimes people come along and say, "Hey, all of these projects are coming at it from the wrong angle. Come look at it this completely different way. There was an underlying assumption for these research programs that was confusing everyone, and now if you would only look at it from my point of view, you would see that this was not helpful." Some people agree with this, and some people do not. But, while I agree that the model of inquiry has as its aim this sort of asymptotic approach to truth, the fact that we do not see it doesn't automatically vitiate the analogy. I don't know what you would think about that.

A: That is very helpful. First of all, do not think that science is one straight line. Science is full of infighting and differences. Scientific training proceeds on the model of apprenticeships; members of a group agree because they are chosen, the communities are tailored to agree, and there is very much to be said for this notion of discipleship. Fellows who study quantum mechanics are not able to talk to the ones who study relativity. They socialize with them, and they exchange gossip, but their thinking processes are different, literally, absolutely different. And yet they are physicists, and we think of physics as being one thing. You think they all sort of understand what they are saying to one another; yet they do not all understand what they're saying to one another. So, that is just one point. Rest assured that science itself is composed of communities that rarely communicate, but they do have trust in one another because they understand, if you like, the methodological presupposition that each is acting according to a certain discipline that is credible and, of course, has an important person directing it.

With respect to differences among religions, clearly, God chose to send his only begotten son to Palestine and to make disciples. He didn't have to do that, because communications with other peoples could be communications of a different sort, not to make Christian-type disciples, but to do something else. Eventually, one would suppose that this doing something else is not in contradiction with what else he did. You get the direction of that kind of answer? So, God is not like a quark; God is a person whom we know makes choices. And it would be like saying that everyone who knows you somehow gets to see the same person, that you could not have two very close friends who don't know one another, and who, upon meeting, talk about you, in quite different terms.

I was invited to India for a congress on phenomenology, and it was mostly dominated by the Hindu philosophers there. But the general sense of a community of common value orientation was quite noticeable. I mean, there was enormous respect developed between the two groups, and so I would think that further experience of insight would not destroy that, but, rather, would tend to push it in the direction of greater understanding. But once again, it's only a wish, or perhaps a hope.

8

Metanoetics: Elements of a Postmodern Christian Philosophy

John D. Caputo

CHRISTIANITY AND POSTMODERNITY:
TOWARD A HERMENEUTICS OF THE KINGDOM

CHRISTIAN PHILOSOPHY? That sounds like a return to a time long gone when philosophy was Christian because Europe was Christian, or like the world of pre–Vatican II, like the famous debate between Maritain and Gilson in the golden era of Neoscholasticism in the 1940s and 1950s. There was then an overarching Christian—which meant then a Thomistic and neo-Thomistic—philosophy, because there was a more culturally monochromatic, homogeneous, insular Catholicism. (Yet, even then, Catholicism was inwardly disturbed by the forces that eventuated in Vatican II and that continue to disturb it today.)

Christian philosophy *today*? Is that not an anachronism? Does it not ask for a philosophy that is Christian in a world that is not, in a Catholicism that is more pluriform and disseminated? Am I mistaken to think this title is even a little skeptical? Is it possible to think, philosophically, today, in a way that both reflects and arises from a framework of Christian faith? Who would dare? Not today! "The possibility of Christian philosophy today"— does that not mean, in short, that it's not possible?

I agree, it is not possible, if by "possibility" we mean wearily to stage one more revival, yet again, of one more Scholasticism, one more new Scholasticism or Neoscholasticism, an even newer neo-Neoscholasticism. Not now, not *today*. Scholasticism is a movement that has run its course, that has become a permanent part of our intellectual heritage, a part of our tradition not to be forgotten. We should be grateful to the Neoscholastic movement, but in the mode of being ungrateful, by moving on.

So, I begin, not with the Scholastic Middle Ages or its revival but with *today*, not because I understand this word any better than the other three, equally formidable words—*philosophy*, *Christianity*, *possibility*—but because, when I do not know where to begin, I begin where I am.[1] "Today," we are told, is, for better or worse, a "postmodern" day, a day of very late modernity—and capitalism—so late, indeed, that we have, to a certain extent moved on not only beyond the Middle Ages but also beyond modernity itself, though always and necessarily *through* modernity, for "postmodern" does not mean "anti-modern" or "premodern." Postmodernity is the continuation of modernity by another means, a kind of hyperbolic modernity or hypermodernity, a way of being grateful to modernity in the mode of being ungrateful, a way of moving on with modernity. Postmodernity is a reconfiguration of modernity that refines and redefines modernity, that breaks with and is suspicious of modernity in important and decisive ways, but still not in such a way as to become premodern. Rather, postmodernity seizes upon certain modernist ideas while clearly rejecting others. It pursues a great deal of what is meant by liberal, egalitarian democracy, for example, which is very modernist and very post-medieval, while rejecting the ideal of an autonomous Cartesian subject. If modernity is defined by its breach with the medieval worldview, postmodernity maintains and even widens that breach. Postmodernity is even more postmedieval than modernity, and so its break with modernity, its critique of Cartesianism and the Enlightenment, does not offer a surreptitious comfort to medievalists, does not promise or intimate a circuitous route back, a crypto-return to the Middle Ages, when philosophy was Christian.[2]

---

[1] Jacques Derrida, *Of Grammatology*, trans. G. Spivak (Baltimore: The Johns Hopkins University Press, 1974), p. 162.

[2] The by now "standard" presentation of this notion of postmodernity is Jean-François Lyotard, *The Postmodern Condition*, trans. Geoffrey Bennington and Brian Massumi (Minneapolis: University of Minnesota Press, 1984).

But if postmodernity (if that is, indeed, what we mean by "today") does not hold out the promise of a new medievalism, that does not mean that it holds no promise for Christianity, for Christian philosophy, for its possibility, today.

By "Christian philosophy," let me say at the outset, I mean, at least minimally, thinking philosophically within the context and the framework of the New Testament. In Christian *philosophy*, as I approach it, one takes the New Testament as a form of life, as a way to be, as a mode of being-in-the-world, as a certain body of literature, even a certain poetics, whose categories we philosophers need and want to understand. By taking the New Testament as a form of life, "Christian philosophy" pays no heed to the traditional boundary disputes—between faith and reason, human reason and divine revelation—that have preoccupied philosophical theology in the past. I suggest we hear the expression "Christian philosophy" the way we hear expressions like "Greek philosophy" or "French philosophy," as indicative of a certain style, a certain idiom, a certain characteristic historical relationship to the world, to one another, and to God; one that repays our attention, one that we want to bring to the attention of everyone else, Christian or not. Such a philosophical approach need not prescind from the miracle stories or the Easter narratives on the grounds that these are matters of "faith," not reason. Rather, it looks for the characteristic mode of being-in-the world that these narratives imply, the understanding of being and time that they presume. I take the expression "Christian philosophy" laterally, as signifying something different, not vertically or hierarchically, as something that, aided by revelation, stands on higher ground than anything accessible to mere mortal reason. Suspending and suspecting that hierarchical way of thinking, neutralizing the faith/reason distinction, represents a certain hermeneutical *epoche* that opens the doors to thinking through, hermeneutically, the categories of Christian existence. I take "Christian philosophy" to mean the philosophical hermeneutics of Christian existence, let us say a certain hermeneutics of the kingdom. I say "hermeneutics," but, as a thinking that is exposed to certain postmodern styles—deconstruction,[3] for instance—I should rather speak more precisely of a *radical* hermeneutics.[4]

Now, if by "Christian philosophy" we do not mean the Greco-onto-theo-logical tradition of medieval and mainstream modern metaphysics, which cuts a very wide sweep in the Christian tradition—about which Jesus and the early Christian communities would have understood nothing—but, rather, mean the hermeneutic explication of the form of life embedded in the New Testament, then I propose that postmodern thinking interacts in the most striking way with Christian philosophy. The New Testament has a certain categorial structure that converges philosophically with important postmodern categories and allows for the most interesting cross-fertilization with postmodern thought. Postmodern thinkers have certain things to say about time, ethics, justice, judgment, and the individual, all quite classical themes in philosophy, which illuminate and intersect the world of the New Testament, which is, we can all agree, paradigmatically Christian. If the hermeneutic explication of the categorial structure of the Christian world, a hermeneutics of the Kingdom, is what we mean by Christian philosophy, then it is quite striking to see what postmodernism can do for us, for Christian philosophy, and its possibility today.

This is not unheard-of; we have heard something like it before, under the name of the de-Hellenization of Christianity.[5] If the

---

[3] Deconstruction, which is a famous, even an infamous, form of postmodernism, is famous for its love of texts and textuality, while the New Testament is a very famous text, a wonderful text that repays constant revisitation. It is full of powerful rhetoric, classical tropes, gripping narratives, a number of well-known letters, which function like a *carte postale* to the tradition, problems of canonicity, and even a powerful pun on the word *petrus*. It is laced with layers of authorship and conflicting messages to different audiences, so that at certain points we are not sure who is saying what to whom. The New Testament is, in short, just about everything Derrida predicts a "text" ought to be; it is thoroughly textual, textualized through and through—which is perhaps why Derrida has paid it a certain amount of attention. See Jacques Derrida, "Of an Apocalyptic Tone Newly Adopted in Philosophy," in *Derrida and Negative Theology*, ed. Harold G. Coward and Toby Foshay (Albany: State University of New York Press, 1992), pp. 25–72.

[4] See John D. Caputo, *Radical Hermeneutics: Repetition, Deconstruction, and the Hermeneutic Project* (Bloomington: Indiana University Press, 1987).

[5] For an older version of de-Hellenization, see Leslie Dewart, *The Future of Belief* (New York: Herder and Herder, 1966); for a more recent, more Derridean

theological tradition has always kept company with philosophy, there has always been a countertradition that has been suspicious of the company theologians keep, a countertradition that, in fact, goes back to Paul's First Letter to the Corinthians and that is alive and well in Pascal, Luther, and Kierkegaard (which means that the distinction between the tradition and the countertradition is perhaps not so clear). In a passage (1:26–28) of which Professor Jean-Luc Marion has given us a very beautiful analysis, Paul told the Corinthians to give up the categories of power (*dynatoi*), for God has sided with those who are out of power, with the weak things (*asthena*) of the world, in order to confound the strong.[6] Paul told them to give up the categories of being, of ontology, for God has chosen the nonbeings (*ta me onta*) of the world to confound the things that are (*ta onta*). According to Paul, it is not the prestige and power of being that has weight with God, but the ignominy, the foolishness, and the lowliness of nonbeing. It is, not the beauty of being and the being of beauty that counts with God, but lowliness and nullity.

Shall we say that Paul, in this remarkable passage, undertakes a delimitation of philosophical conceptuality, something on the order of what is *today* variously called the *"Destruktion* of the history of ontology," the "deconstruction" of the "metaphysics of presence," the "end of philosophy"? In fact, the postmodern deconstruction of ontotheologic is a de-Hellenization project of its own, a hypervigilance about an inherited ontological and theological conceptuality, that runs a parallel course to the de-Hellenization of Christianity in theology. Seen from a postmodern perspective, Paul is looking for something like what Levinas, whose point of departure is deeply biblical, calls "autrement qu'être, ou au déla l'essence,"[7] what is otherwise than being or beyond being, *epekeina tes ousias*, as opposed to what is simply not being, or nothing at all. Levinas is trying to do two things at

---

version, see Joseph O'Leary, *Questioning Back: The Overcoming of Metaphysics in Christian Tradition* (Minneapolis: Winston-Seabury, 1985).

[6] Jean-Luc Marion, *God Without Being*, trans. Thomas Carlson (Chicago: The University of Chicago Press, 1991), pp. 89–95.

[7] Emmanuel Levinas, *Autrement qu'être, ou au déla l'essence* (The Hague: Martinus Nijhoff, 1974); published in English as *Otherwise than Being, or Beyond Essence*, trans. Alphonso Lingis (The Hague: Martinus Nijhoff, 1981).

once: first, to be a philosopher, to be Greek, and to deploy the
classical conceptuality—*l'être*, *l'essence*, *ousia*, and so on; and,
second, to do this in just such a way as to disrupt what is Greek
by picking up what philosophy systematically erases or excludes,
to think against the grain of Greek philosophy, to break with its
assumptions about the freedom and autonomy of the subject and
about the being and phenomenality of the object.

This is all strikingly similar to the young Heidegger's project
in the first Freiburg lectures (1919–23), in which Heidegger took
his first steps in the *Destruktion* of the history of ontology, under
the title of a "hermeneutics of facticity." The breakthrough in
Heidegger's youthful work occurred when he undertook to break
through the Aristotelico-Scholastic conceptuality that had cov-
ered over the original Christian experience of life embedded in
the New Testament, a project first found in Luther, Schleiermacher, and Kierkegaard. The very word *Destruktion*, it has recently been shown, was a transcription of Luther's call in the
1518 *Heidelberg Disputation* for a *destructio* of Aristotelian
metaphysics and the *theologia gloriae*; it even resonates with 1
Corinthians 1:19, "I will destroy [*apolo*] the wisdom [*sophian*]
of the wise"—I will deconstruct philosophy, saith the Lord.[8]

Hence, the critical renewal and deconstructive reinscription of
the classical metaphysical conceptuality undertaken in postmodern writers goes back, in part, to originally philosophico-religious projects that are motivated by a reading of biblical sources:
to Levinas's sensitivity to the Hebrew scriptures, on one hand,
and to the young Heidegger's reading of the Christian scriptures,
on the other. The convergence of theological de-Hellenization
projects with postmodern investigations is not merely accidental
or purely formal and structural. Religious projects are found at
the very outset of the critiques of ontotheology, and they enter
into its substance. There are, of course, many other sources of
postmodernity—Nietzsche and post-Saussurean semiotics; the
suspicion of philosophy "after Auschwitz" (which would then
pit the Hebrew against the Greco-Christian, thus splitting off the

---

[8] See John Van Buren, *The Young Heidegger* (Bloomington: Indiana University Press, 1994); Theodore Kisiel, *The Genesis of "Being and Time"* (Berkeley: University of California Press, 1993); John D. Caputo, *Demythologizing
Heidegger* (Bloomington: Indiana University Press, 1993).

"Judeo-" in "Judeo-Christian," as in Lyotard and Levinas); the decline of the Marxist states, the expansion of communications technology, and the hegemony of popular culture. There is nothing to be gained from exaggerating the religious impulse in postmodernism; it is enough to show that postmodernity springs, in part, from interestingly religious impulses.

I have no interest in leaving philosophy behind, in taking up residence in a never-never land of pure experience, in a purely Hebraic or a purely early Christian experience, outside or beyond the influence of our inherited Greek conceptuality, which, as Heidegger has shown, runs the length and breadth of the Western intellectual landscape. My aim is, in fact, explicitly philosophical, Christian-philosophical: to produce a certain Jew-Greek effect, to inhabit the space between Jew and Greek, to let philosophy be disturbed by the shock of the Jew, to live with the tension between them, to bring the shock of the Hebraic—for Jesus was a Jew—to the level of philosophical concepts. That is how a Christian philosophy is or would be possible for me. Today.

We make the modest assumption that Christian philosophy has something to do with Jesus—with the style of his life, with his historical singularity and particularity, with the New Testament narratives, with the stories and the images of what he said and did. We are breaking with the assumption, born of a rationalist dichotomy between faith and reason, that Christian *philosophy* must, in fact, abstract from the historical figure of Jesus, who would be a matter of faith and revelation. We lay aside the Enlightenment-inspired conception that a truly Christian *philosophy* must turn its attention to the universal, ahistorical, commonly shared *preambulae fidei*, the preambles of faith that are demonstrable by reason, shared by all people. That would reduce "Christian philosophy" to the "philosophy of religion," to abstract and almost universally ignored arguments about the existence and nature of God, the problem of evil, and the immortality of the soul. That would be, on my telling, precisely to swerve away from Christian philosophy and to embrace a universalistic *ratio*. Further, such a *ratio* is not what it says it is: namely, something universal and common, but precisely a Greek and onto-theo-logical construction, datable and locatable in the very Hellenization that I eschew. On the version of Christian philosophy put forth here, everything turns on the textuality of the New Testament, on a hermeneutic fidelity to the historicality and singularity of the figure of Jesus, and on a sensitivity to the historical form of life embodied in the scriptures. Rather than thinking in terms of a revelation that exceeds reason, I view the scriptures as offering an alternate categoriality in which the categories of ontotheology are simply not in play.

The result of such an approach, I will argue, is precisely to disclose a world of the most marvelous metamorphoses, a world of metamorphosis itself, which is of a rather different sort from the stable *ousia* of Greek philosophy, where every effort is taken to contain change within the tolerances of the reigning ousiology. I will describe this world in terms of a "generalized metanoetics," a world in which being and time are subjected to the most astonishing upheavals, to things undreamt-of in our ontotheologies.

I will address this issue in three steps: (*a*) a generalized metanoetics; (*b*) the kingdom of anarchy; and (*c*) being and time in the kingdom.

Toward a Generalized Metanoetics

Toward the beginning of the Gospel of Matthew (4:23–25), shortly after the baptism of Jesus, when Jesus is just beginning his ministry, Matthew says he went about Galilee teaching (*didaskon*) and preaching (*kai kerysoon*) the good news and healing (*kai therapeuon*) the sick. He begins his work by preaching the word that will change men's hearts and transform their minds (*metanoein*) and also, at the same time, not as an afterthought or merely as a secondary or symbolic operation, heal their bodies. The two things together: both teaching and healing, both didactics or kerygmatics and therapeutics. Word about such a remarkable man spread quickly, and soon they started bringing people to him from all around, people who needed help: all those who were ill (*kakos*), afflicted with various diseases (*nosois*) and pains (*basanois*), those possessed by demons, epileptics (*seleniaxomenous*), paralytics—"and he healed them" (*kai etherapeusen*).

In the subsequent chapters of Matthew, one meets with a succession of similarly afflicted and unfortunate people: the needy, a leper, the centurion's paralyzed servant, Peter's feverish mother-in-law, two men possessed by demons, several more paralytics, a dead girl, the blind and mute, the poor, sinners, and, let us not forget to mention, the tax collectors (the ugliness of whose profession has secured them a place on such lists from time immemorial). All these men and women and children are fit—indeed, privileged—subjects in the kingdom where metamorphosis is the rule.

There are several things about this passage, which is but one among many similar texts in the New Testament, that deserve our attention—philosophically. The kingdom (*basileia*), much as Nietzsche says, albeit very much to Nietzsche's disgust, is swarming with the most singularly afflicted people. There is, indeed, a pervasive preoccupation with bodies in the New Testament, which amounts to what Levinas and Adorno do not hesitate to call a "materialism," although they are speaking of the Hebrew scriptures.[9] This situation is quite unlike the *Phaedo*, which begins with the body just in order to tell us to quit material matters, to leave off a concern with sensation and feeling, and to take up the practice of death, of dying to the body. It is quite unlike the *Critique of Practical Reason*, where the essence of the ethical lay in the triumph over what Kant called the "pathological," the sphere of sensibility and passion, in favor of pure practical reason. In the New Testament, the kingdom is a kingdom of bodies, a realm or sphere of everything fleshlike and corporeal; the body is very much the business of the kingdom, its *Sache*, and a concern with the body goes hand in hand, if I may say so, with *kerygma* and *didaktike*. The two together, teaching and healing, as two transformative powers, belong coequally to the kingdom.

The bodies we meet with in the kingdom are bodies laid low, afflicted with disease, bent by paralysis, racked with fever, withering away with leprosy, struck blind and dumb or even lifeless. These are certainly not the bodies of Greek philosophy or exis-

---

[9] Emmanuel Levinas, *Difficult Freedom*, trans. Sean Hand (Baltimore: The Johns Hopkins University Press, 1990), p. xiv; Theodor Adorno, *Negative Dialectics*, trans. E. B. Ashton (New York: Continuum, 1983), p. 207.

tential phenomenology, which are hale and hardy bodies, upright, agile, agent bodies that move with alacrity through the *Lebenswelt*, sure-handed, quick-footed bodily intentionalities or bodily being-in-the-world. Philosophy's bodies are active and well, a *corpus sanum* cut to fit a *mens sana*, a fit organ of the soul or seat of intentionality. Let us, by way of a certain shorthand, call this New Testament body not a body but "flesh,"and by "flesh" let us signify everything that is vulnerable, that is able to be wounded, which means bent, cut, lacerated, ulcerated, withered, or, finally, killed. These bodies of flesh seek out Jesus, and he seems literally to be swarmed by them; they brought to him everybody like that (*kai prosenengkan auto panas tous kakos*), "[A]nd he healed them." He transformed their flesh, metamorphosized their bodies, just as he meant to change their hearts, *metanoein*. The kingdom (*basileia*) is a kingdom of metamorphosis, or *metanoein* and *therapeuein*. This flesh that is defined by its vulnerability is also healable, transformable, and Jesus is the agent, or perhaps the place, of that transformation, a charismatic place of metamorphosis. If flesh means everything that is laid low and vulnerable, it also means, by the same token, inseparably and correlatively, everything that can be healed. The "miracle" (*mirandum*), the wonder (*thaumazo*), in which Christian philosophy begins is the wondrous transformation that takes place in a kingdom of transformability, reformability, metamorphosis. The kingdom is a land of wondrous change, a kind of marvelous *kinesis* not dreamt-of in our ontotheologies.

The work of bodily metamorphosis is juxtaposed in Matthew and the synoptics with *metanoia*, which is the message of the Baptist, *metanoeite*, for the kingdom is coming near, which is mentioned two chapters earlier. In Mark, who knows nothing of the infancy narratives, the Gospel starts out abruptly with the shock of *metanoia*, even as it ends abruptly with the empty tomb. Jesus takes over John's withering, wilderness message of *metanoia* but not without first submitting it to a crucial reorchestration from a dirge to a dance; the Baptist wails but they do not mourn, and Jesus pipes but they do not dance. Jesus changes John's prophetic tune of *metanoia*; he wants us to retune, to undergo a change of tuning, of *nous* or *Stimmung*. *Metanoeite*: change your tune, adjust your tuning, change your mind and heart, transform your whole disposition, your *Stimmung*, your moodedness, your whole way of being in the world and being with one another. Immerse (*baptizein*) your old heart, your old mind, and wash away the meanness that is centered solely on itself so that you can be transformed. *Baptizein*: that represents a quite literal confluence, a flowing together, of *metanoia* and *therapeia*, of changing one's heart and healing one's flesh, a rushing together of the waters that cleanse the heart and wash and heal the flesh. In this kingdom all things flow, as Heraclitus said, but this flow has a different, not quite Heraclitean drift: all things are transformed and washed clean in mighty waters that flush away the old, in rushing waters that let something new and clean come to be, so that all things are not the same, *pace* Parmenides (and Heraclitus). In the kingdom, being and time take a different drift than in Greek philosophy, which is a point to which I shall return in the third and final section of this essay.

AN ANARCHIC KINGDOM

These Christian waters are not quite Heraclitean on another count: they are not the waters of an elitist old Greek who, like Parmenides and Plato, looked with disdain upon the many, *hoi polloi*. On the contrary, they are waters that are especially reserved for the great unwashed, that is, for precisely the ones who need water. The kingdom belongs to the unwashed, not to aristocratic Greeks or to the healthy, well-fed bourgeoisie of modern Christianity, those mainstream Christians whom Kierkegaard mercilessly attacked under the name of "Christendom." The cast of characters in the kingdom is a cast of outsiders, a cast of outcasts: sinners, lost sheep, prodigal sons, tax collectors, Samaritans, lepers, the lame, the possessed—everyone who is out of sight, outside, outlawed, outclassed, and, in short, everyone who is just plain out. These are the very ones whom Paul called the *me onta* of the world, the nobodies, the nullities, the nothings. They are the ones with whom God has sided, the ones to whom the kingdom belongs, the poor ones who enjoy God's special favor.

If we, good philosophers that we are, think the New Testament is an "ethics" book, then I suggest that it represents a very different ethics, one organized around the "principle" of difference, the *arche* that values the anarchic, the *principium* that takes up with what is very unprincely, which is only a "kingdom" *ironice*, one in which royalty is at a disadvantage. It is an ethics that valorizes difference, alterity, being-out, being nothing in the eyes of the world, being of no account whatsoever. You get nowhere in the kingdom by being well born, well bred, and well-to-do. You get nowhere by loving your friends and family, those with whom you share kin and kind, those who are like you, of like kind. Such people already have their reward, Matthew has Jesus say. The only true reward comes of loving your enemies, those who are quite *unlike* you and who rather *dislike* you, and hating your kindred kind, your father and mother, brother and sister, hating those who love you. "Family values" in the kingdom, much to the chagrin of the Christian right today, are quite anarchic. Anybody can love the same; even the Pharisees—or, for that matter, the Mafia—have those "family values." It is hating the same and loving difference that counts in the kingdom. Who would not want to be a friend of the rich and famous? But standing by the least among us, the little ones, the powerless, is what counts with God. One gets nowhere in the kingdom by gaining the favor of the powers that be (*dynatoi*). The idea behind the kingdom, its an-archic *arche*, is to take the side of everyone who is out of power, the *asthena*, and to denounce the powers that be as vipers and whitewashed tombs whose fathers have killed the prophets. From the point of view of a worldly advancement, that is a recipe for disaster.

The whole of the "ethics" of the kingdom seems to be organized around what is *today* called "difference" or "alterity"; if there is an ethics here, it is an ethics of difference, of alterity. That is just the sort of ethics one finds among the postmodernists, particularly those who, like Derrida and Lyotard, have in differing ways come under the sway of Levinas. Levinas himself is a kind of postmodern prophet, a certain Hosea of the *rive gauche*, who desires not sacrifice but justice, not ontology but ethics, not identity but alterity. So, if there is a Christian philosophy today, perhaps an important element of it is to be found among these mostly Jewish and Parisian postmodernists. Given the Jewishness of Jesus, given the deeply Hebraic roots of his *abba* spirituality, this is not an outlandish result. As a Jew who made war on the authorities at Jerusalem, Jesus is a little un-Jewish, something of a "marginal Jew,"[10] but having never heard of Christianity, and having never had it in mind, he is also not quite Christian. He is in-between, on the slash of undecidability between Jewish and Christian, which is the place upon whose resources I would draw in order to nourish a Christian philosophy today.

The postmodern ethics of alterity, which, I claim, articulates the ethical categories of the kingdom, is likewise an ethics of "responsibility." In such a view, one takes oneself to be always already on the receiving end of the call of the other, always already solicited by the one who comes to me from on high just because she is laid low, like the man lying in the road whom the Samaritan encounters. That is what "alterity" means in postmodernism. Alterity is not a purely formal or merely numerical conception that abstracts from substantive considerations of who or what is different; ruthless billionaires and homicidal rapists are numerical minorities who are different from the rest of us, but they are not the "others" whose alterity lays claim to us. The postmodern notion of "alterity" refers to the out-of-power, out-of-luck, the dispossessed and unfortunate, to the *me onta* who suffer from their otherness, who are diminished by exclusion and apartness (apartheid), to the victims, not the victimizers. Responsibility in this postmodern sense means to be always already claimed by this apartness, always already responsible for such otherness. It is just such farness that defines nearness, neighborliness; my neighbor is not my own kind but the other one, the one lying on the road. Is this not, then, a very biblical sort of neighborliness that is currently sweeping left-bank postmodernists?

As an ethics of responsibility, postmodernism is an ethics of heteronomy, not autonomy; of being held captive by the other, not freedom. Autonomy and freedom belong to the most classical assumptions of Greco-philosophical ethics, of onto-theo-logical ethics. In an ethics of alterity, my freedom and autonomy are

---

[10] John P. Meier, *Jesus, a Marginal Jew: Rethinking the Historical Jesus* (Garden City, N.Y.: Doubleday, 1991).

taken to be the very danger that is posed to the other, to those who are out; for it is my freedom that keeps them out, that keeps them down, that kills them. In Levinas this theme of responsibility is organized around Abraham's "Here I am," *me voici*, which is a particularly felicitous translation of the Hebrew *hinneni* (see me here).[11] Me, in the accusative, standing under accusation, accused and responsible for the address that comes to me from on high, like the voice that overtook Abraham and called him out to Moriah. If the postmodernists have undertaken a systematic critique of the Cartesian subject, of the *ego cogito* and *ego volo* of modernity, they have not dismissed the subject in every sense; on the contrary, they turn to the subject in the accusative, the "me," not the "I," the subject that is responsible for the other, for the neighbor.

The *arche* that rules in this anarchic ethics, the first rule in this anarchic kingdom, is to watch out for rules, to watch out for the killing power of the law, to keep watch for everything that is ground under by the law. One day the people brought a man with a withered hand to Jesus, and the Pharisees watched him carefully to see if he would heal the man, because that day happened to be the Sabbath (Mark 3:1–6). The Pharisees wanted to see whether the work of healing, *therapeuein*, would triumph over the law of the Sabbath, whether healing or the law held sway in this kingdom. Suspecting a trap, Jesus turned the tables on the Pharisees by asking them whether the Sabbath was for doing good or doing evil, for saving life or killing. Whatever their other shortcomings, the Pharisees were not foolish enough to answer that question, but their silence was even more damning. So Jesus, who was grieved by their hardness of heart, lifted the law of the Sabbath from the man with a withered hand, suspending the law, and thereby giving the man a lift. For the Sabbath was made for the man, not the man for the Sabbath.

Thus it was that the law of the Sabbath was deconstructed in the name of justice. With this remark, you will notice, I have slightly recast a familiar biblical story, added a new, postmodern element.[12] But the cast fits, for the transgressiveness of Jesus,

---

[11] See Levinas, *Otherwise than Being*, pp. 114, 142–46, 149–52, 185.

[12] For a more elaborate attempt to work out a deconstructionist concept of obligation in dialogue with the categoriality of the kingdom, see John D. Ca-

his reputation for being an outlaw, a lawbreaker, is once again something that is articulated by a postmodern understanding of justice, law, and judgment, by postmodernism's affection for transgression. For the story corresponds quite nicely to a principle, or quasi-principle, or un-principle, that Derrida enunciated about the relationship between justice and the law. The law, Derrida has written, is deconstructible, but justice in itself, if there is such a thing, is not deconstructible. The law is something written, a bit of *écriture*, a sociohistorical construction which, if it is not revisable, reformable, rewritable, or amendable—that is, deconstructible—would represent the worst form of terror. The justice that the law delivers always limps, is always, to a certain extent, wooden and imperfect.[13]

Justice in itself, on the other hand, is the unique and particular justice that is cut to fit the particular needs of the individual, that is subtly suited to each individual in all that individual's most secret singularity. With justice, every hair on our head is numbered, every tear is counted, and so every secret, most singular need is respected. Singularity is nothing to deconstruct; singularity is that in virtue of which there is deconstruction, if there is such a thing.[14] But the law, which must be impartial, is universal; it must in principle blind itself to singularity. Still, the law should be just; the law is meant to deliver justice, even as justice in itself, if there is such a thing, needs laws if it is to be effective. Deconstruction occupies the space between justice and the law, the irreducible gap or distance that opens up because it is impossible always to make justice and the law converge. Deconstruction keeps watch over the singularities lest they be ground under

---

puto, *Against Ethics: Contributions to a Poetics of Obligation with Constant Reference to Deconstruction* (Bloomington: Indiana University Press, 1993); for a very Levinasian version of a biblical postmodernism, see Edith Wyschogrod, *Saints and Postmodernism: Revisioning Moral Philosophy* (Chicago: The University of Chicago Press, 1990). To be sure, the "Pharisees" in Mark 3:1–6 are the objects of Christian polemics rather than the historical Pharisees.

[13] See Jacques Derrida, "Force of Law: The 'Mystical Foundation of Authority,'" in *Deconstruction and the Possibility of Justice*, ed. Drucilla Cornell et al. (New York: Routledge, 1992), pp. 3–67, esp. pp. 14–15.

[14] Derrida in recent years has been doing a lot of work with the "secret" of "singularity," including a treatment of Kierkegaard's *Fear and Trembling* in "*Donner la Mort*" in *L'éthique du don* (Paris: Métailié, 1992), pp. 11–108; and *Passions* (Paris: Galilée, 1993); *Sauf le nom* (Paris: Galilée, 1993).

by the law, and it calls for lifting the law in order to heal on the Sabbath. The act of healing a man with a withered hand on the Sabbath is an act of deconstruction. There is, of course, a price to be paid for deconstructing the law. The word goes forth that such men are dangerous, that they are the enemies of the law, that they mean to destroy the law and raze the temple (or the core curriculum). That is, of course, a bad rap, a misunderstanding, a slightly panicked reaction to a certain kind of ethics, an ethics that puts singularity first, that subordinates the law to the singular, an ethics that has a heart, an ever so slightly anarchic ethics.

The biblical story says that Jesus grieved over their hardness of heart. He did not disagree with their argument and come back with a counterexample. He did not think that this was a dispute to be settled by the weight of "good reasons" one way or the other. He did not think it was a matter of reason, of *logos* or *nous*, at all, but of the heart: that it came down to whether or not one is hard of heart. *Kardia* is not practical reason, and the *nous* in *metanoia* is not Aristotelian *nous*. Metanoetics is a matter of *kardia*, not *nous*, or of *nous* as *kardia*, not a primarily noetic and cognitive *nous*.

Among the philosophers, it is Aristotle who has seen the most clearly that "judgment" must be addressed to the needs of the particular situation, to the demands of singularity, and that is the essence of what he meant by *phronesis*. *Phronesis* is a certain ethical adroitness that sees into the complexities of the situation, that changes with the changing, for ethics has to do with changing things, with the continually shifting sands of circumstances. *Phronesis* is the capacity to see how the general schema can be brought to bear upon the singular situation. *Phronesis* does not mean a descent down into particulars but an ascent to singularity; it is not a loss or fall but an enriching. *Phronesis* refers to the way the empty and schematic knowledge of the ethical universal can be raised up to the reality of concrete knowledge, of what is to be done, here and now.

But *phronesis* is not *kardia*. *Phronesis* is a kind of *nous*, a practical *nous*, a matter of insight and seeing. It is the acquisition of training, experience, time, a certain expertise; it is in some ways comparable to craftsmanship, to the skill acquired by the craftsman who has completed an apprenticeship (*techne*). *Phronesis* and *techne* are forms of practical *nous*, and the opposite of this *nous* is stupidity, inflexibility, wooden and mindless application of rules. But *kardia* is not insight or the agility of practical knowledge; it is not application or the skill of seeing how the general schema can be fleshed out in the concrete situation. The opposite of *kardia* is not stupidity but hardness of heart, the inflexibility not of mindlessness but of uncaring indifference. *Kardia* represents a certain succumbing to the claims of singularity, a melting down, a surrender to what this other—this poor one, this lame or leper, this withered hand, this justice—needs, over and against and even in opposition to what the law, which is universal, requires.

When Jesus heals the man with the withered hand, he does not bring the universal schema to bear upon the particular situation, but he lifts or suspends the universal in the face of the demands of the singularity before him. The weight, the demand, the claim, the call of the singular one outweighs and trumps the requirements of the law. This is suspension, not application; mercifulness, not *nous*. In metanoetics, the rule of a strictly cognitive *nous* is broken and replaced by a heart-based *nous*, a *nous* that would, in terms of the old physiology, have its seat not in the head but in the breast, for, indeed, the word *phronesis* itself refers to the *phren*, the chest and heart.

Metanoia thus tells us to change our heart, to become merciful to a fault, to lift the strictures of the law and to let ourselves be laid claim to, to be besieged by the other one, by the others who suffer from their alterity. *Metanoia* means to grieve over mercilessness and to succumb to the demands of mercy, to let oneself be touched, be affected by the claims of flesh laid low. *Metanoia* means to be vulnerable to the vulnerability of the other, to be wounded by his wounds, to be affected by her affliction. It is not insight in the manner of Aristotle's practical reason; still less does it have anything to do with the purity of Kant's pure practical reason that triumphs over the pathological impulses of sensibility. On the contrary, *kardia* is precisely sensibility, a sensibility that triumphs over the universalizing impulses of reason, a matter of sensibility in the Levinasian sense, which is a deep and sensitive *pathos* that suffers with the suffering of the other, that enters into a community and communication of suffering, the paradigm of which—if I may miscegenize Levinas and the New Testament—is the communication of withered hands and healing hands.[15] *Metanoia* is likewise always and already implicated in forgiveness. Not only is the other one someone who lays claim to me from on high, who needs me, but he is also the one who offends me and then claims my forgiveness. If the other one goes wrong—and who does not? Such things are bound to happen—indeed, if the other man is your brother, and if he offends you, but then has a change of heart (*kai ean metanoese*), then you should forgive him (*aphes auto*). If this happens seven times over, then you should forgive him seven times over. Luke 17:1–4 puts this in terms that Levinas would appreciate. After offending you seven times in the course of one day, "he turns to you" (*epistrepse pros se*). The phrase suggests that the offense was perhaps done behind your back, but now the other is face to face. He turns to you, Luke says, speaking (*logon*): that is what Levinas would call the mode of *le dire*, of saying, of the human contact between speakers.[16] Now, the man, your brother, turns to you and looks you in the eye, and speaks to you. This transaction does not take place in the sphere of *le dit*, where the point is the content of what is said. The man does not bring up the nature of the offense, the circumstances, the mitigating considerations, or the witnesses, if any. In the kingdom, that is not what matters. The language of the kingdom is not the language of the said, of contents, reasons, justifications, rationalizations, but a language of saying. The kingdom is a kingdom of saying (*logon*).

The man who has turned to you, saying, simply says, "*Metanoo*": "I have had a change of heart." "*Metanoo*": "I have been transformed; my heart has been made over; I am of a new mind and heart; my whole disposition and attunement [*Stimmung*] has undergone a change; I am now playing a new tune." It is very unfortunate that we have chosen to translate this very beautiful word with "I repent," which means "I visit pain [*poena*] on myself, again [*re*]." That is, at best, a Baptist translation, John the

---

[15] For more on the distinction between *kardia* and *phronesis*, see Caputo, *Against Ethics*, pp. 99–103, 113–17, and *Demythologizing Heidegger*, chap. 3.
[16] Levinas, *Otherwise than Being*, pp. 37–38, 45–51.

Baptist. "Repent" is the wrong tune; it is the Baptist's tune; it is the dirge. That is not a very Christian translation; it is still pre-Christian, at best, preparing the way for the kingdom, but not quite the language of the kingdom; it is the wrong talk and the wrong tune. "I have a new heart"—that is the Christian translation, Jesus's tune, the dance, not the dirge.[17] The man turns to you, saying "I am ready to dance, my heart is light, I have a new *nous*." You notice that he does not make an excuse, give a *logos*, an *apologia*, of himself, because in the kingdom it is not the *logos* but the *legein*, the pure *saying* that counts. He does not give an account, or get mixed up with the *ratio reddenda*,[18] offering reasons and explanations that should compel you to conclude that he reasonably warrants forgiveness; he does not get into a rational settling of accounts (*le dit*). On the contrary, the other man has done you in seven times today, and he is your brother, and the day is not over yet. So, if you follow the dictates of reason, reason will point you elsewhere. He just turns to you, face to face, saying *metanoo*: I have been transformed. He does not go into the particulars; this is case of pure *dire*. And you, we, what are we to do? We should melt, change our heart, be transformed; you, we, should just have a heart and forgive him (*apheseis auto*). As beings of *kardia*, we are vulnerable, sensitive, sensible of and to the other, responsive to the heart of the other, and our hearts should be changed by the change of heart of the other. So, Jesus says, Just forget it, let it go, let the past be, let it go by, and wipe it away. Be of a new mind yourself; change your tune. Do not, as Nietzsche would have said, bear any ill will to the past (sometimes Nietzsche was, despite his best efforts, very Christian).

BEING AND TIME IN THE KINGDOM

As a philosopher, I am interested in the time of forgiveness, both in the sense of the moment, the now, in which one is transformed

---

[17] For a beautiful commentary on forgiveness and *metanoia*, see Hannah Arendt, *The Human Condition* (Chicago: The University of Chicago Press, 1958), pp. 236–40.

[18] One could thus rewrite Heidegger's analysis of the principle "Nothing is without a reason" in terms of forgiveness; see Heidegger, *The Principle of Reason*, trans. Reginald Lilly (Bloomington: Indiana University Press, 1991).

by the transformation in the other, and in the structure of the temporality of forgiveness. Forgiveness is a readiness to wipe away the past. The time of forgiveness is a kind of double time, of a past that, having existed for a while, during the *skandala*, the time of the offense and the sin (*amarte*), is now wiped away. The "past" of forgiveness is not merely time gone by, something over, while remaining in the past, for such a past is "retained," as Husserl would say, held on to, and so it can always be recalled. You and I always know it is there. I may not mention it or ever advert to it, but we both know that this is something that I hold over you, that I can call back, if I want. But in forgiveness, I abdicate that power. I give up the advantage I have over you. I wipe the ledger clean, so that the offense is gone, forgotten actively, wiped away, wiped out. The wonder here is that what is in the past is transformed, in the moment of forgiveness, into something that is *not* in the past, not anymore. So, if a man turns to you saying "*Metanoo*," you should say to him that—now that he is forgiven—that there is nothing to forgive, not anymore, forget it!

The kingdom thus runs on an odd time, a non-standard time, a metanoetic time that baffles our philosophers and philosophies. One of the more interesting, if lesser known, attempts of the philosophers to come to grips with the time of the kingdom is to be found in the question raised by Peter Damian about whether God can change past time.[19] This is a wonderful little *disputatio* that illustrates quite exquisitely how medieval onto-theo-logic remained, to its credit, quite inwardly disturbed by its biblical sources. This is exactly the opposite question to the puzzle that the past posed to the Greeks who, onto-theo-logical to the core, were moved to ask whether, once a thing was past, it did not become necessary, even though it may have been contingent at the time that it happened. The past, by its very nature, seemed to the Greeks to suffer from a kind of *sclerosis*; that is, the longer an event sits on the shelf of the past, the more it seemed to them to harden over into necessity. But the Christians were provoked by exactly the opposite consideration. They looked upon things

---

[19] For a good commentary, see Robert McArthur and Michael Slattery, "Peter Damian and Undoing the Past," *Philosophical Studies*, 25 (1974): 137–41.

not in a sclerotic but in a metanoetic way; they sought to avoid letting things harden over, to avoid the hardness of heart (*sclerosis tes kardias*) that turned things to stone, that petrified and froze them over. As Hannah Arendt says, resentment and revenge pull the strings of the past ever tighter and tie us up into knots, but forgiveness cuts things loose, sets them free of the past. Resentment resolves to "get even," to settle accounts, to balance the books, to hold on tight to the past, never to let it go, unless and until it is paid back. "Don't get mad, get even": that is as vicious, as deeply un-Christian a sentiment as one can imagine, one that never lets go.

So, these medieval ontotheological Christians wanted to know whether God could change the past, make it to be that something in the past was not really past but had never happened, make it to be that such-and-such no longer was true, was no longer something that had happened. For example, could God restore lost virginity? Let us say that a man who lived a long life of lust had a change of heart, that he then turned to God saying "*metanoo*," that he longed to be chaste and to belong to God alone, then could God, who is all-forgiving, restore his virginity? From an ontotheological point of view, one wants to know whether this is a coherent suggestion; but in terms of a hermeneutics of the kingdom, this is a very beautiful, a marvelously metanoetic and evangelical question that arises from a creationistic frame of mind. It is—hermeneutically—the same question that was put to Jesus by the crowds of lame and lepers that swarmed all over him: can you restore this flesh, these withered and distorted arms and legs? Can you make them straight again? And this leprous ulcerated flesh—can you make it whole and wholesome again? And even this dead girl—can you make her live again? Even so, can you restore this wounded heart?

Renovabitis faciem terrae—thous shalt renew the face of the earth—the man with the withered hand, the lame and the leper, the heart of the man who turns to you saying "I have had a change of heart."

Now I ask, by way of bringing this study to a philosophical conclusion, what is the time of the kingdom? What is metanoetic time? What is the time of *metanoia*, of forgiveness, the time of spreading the healing word (*kerysoon*) and of healing (*thera-*

peuon) itself? To put it in very Greek and philosophical terms: what is the being of this time and the time of this being, this being made new, this metanoetic way to be and to temporalize? That is, I think, in a way, the overarching question of Christian philosophy, of thinking out philosophically the being of being-Christian.

Metanoetic time is a time of transformation, or radical metamorphoses, of renewability, alterability. It is not Hegelian time in which a deep historical momentum makes a steady advance by way of a progressive, self-correcting, upwardly moving dialectic. Far more immediate and instantaneous than that, this is a time of the instant, of the *Augenblick*,[20] in which a man or a woman undergoes a transforming change of heart, putting off the old and putting on the new. There is no recourse to mediation, no passage through a mediating state, no dialectically guided passage through opposites. It is all more sudden, more unmediated, and direct than that. The flesh of the leper and of the man with the withered hand are changed, made new, made whole, by the power of God that is with Jesus, in a moment of therapeutic transformation. "Then he said to the man, 'Stretch out your hand.' So he stretched it out and it was completely restored" (Matt. 12:13). In a flash. A man offends you seven times in one day and seven times asks to be forgiven, and seven times you are asked to dismiss his fault. Seven times—that is to say, time and time again, over and over, repeatedly falling and rising up again, until the heart is healed.

This is not an Aristotelian time which runs smoothly across the surface of substances whose potencies pass over into acts for which they were all along being made ready. It is not a time of continuity, of smooth transitions, of potencies passing into act, of acts that simply realize the potentialities that have all along been present, that have slowly and patiently been waiting their

---

[20] The *Augenblick* is a characteristically Kierkegaardian notion—the moment of truth in which the individual, one to one with God, acquires a new mind and resolves upon faith—that has been taken up in a number of places by Derrida, where it means the moment of chance, the opening or breach in the system; for example, see Jacques Derrida, "The Principle of Reason: The University in the Eyes of Its Pupils," trans. C. Porter and E. Morris, *Diacritica*, 11 (1981): 20. Kierkegaard has captured a great deal of what is called here the structure of the temporality of the kingdom, which he opposes to Hegelian history.

turn in the gentle rhythms of genesis and corruption. Metanoetic time is more discontinuous and abrupt, more shocking and surprising; this is a metamorphic, not a hylomorphic, world. Metanoetic time is the time of the surprise, a time in which one is struck by the amazing changes that take place before one's eyes or in one's own heart.

The time of the kingdom is not the time of *ousia*, of the steady beat of presence that rides out every change, that persists and perdures, that presides over the transiencies of particular changes. It is, rather, the time of thoroughgoing upheaval, of a totally transforming renewal. In the kingdom, the assumption is not that things have always been and will ever be thus; rather, the presumption is that one can count on nothing, that one knows neither the day nor the hour, that one can never be sure whether the next moment will not be the last, whether the end will come and that will be that. Let the kingdom come! Let it happen! Let it arrive! Let it come, even though we are not able to see it coming, to predict it, to observe natural signs, the way a red moon predicts a hot summer day. We can only be ready for a moment that could be any moment now.[21]

In the kingdom, time lacks the steadiness of presence, the permanence and the perdurance of *ousia*. This is not an onto-theological world in which the being of time is permanent presence and in which the time of being is to be steadily present. It is a world in which both being and time defer to the power of God, to the power of utter transformation. Being and time are not defined by their own inherent and autonomous qualities that resist alteration from without, that set the terms under which change occurs, terms to which God himself must defer. The world is, contrary to the oldest and fondest faith of ontotheologic, a world without *ousia* and *hypokeimenon*, without *essentia* and *substantia*, without essences following their essential natures which preclude interruption or disruption. On the contrary, the kingdom is a world in which the regularities of *ousia* and *essentia* are suspended, a world that is peculiarly prone to interruption and dis-

---

[21] It is this feature of the experience of temporality in the New Testament, the notion of the *kairos*, that attracted Heidegger's attention in the early Freiburg lectures; see Van Buren, *Young Heidegger*, and Kisiel, *Genesis of "Being and Time."*

ruption. The being of time and the time of being are defined by
their utter transformability, their thoroughgoing vulnerability and
susceptibility to transformation; being and time are radically
contingent, reformable, reworkable, remakable.

Contrary to the most cherished beliefs of onto-theo-logic, such
a world is largely nominalistic; things do not have deep essences
whose essential laws dictate their future destinies. Withered arms
and paralyzed limbs, eyes that cannot see, ears that cannot hear,
feverish and even dead bodies—all are capable of being transformed in a flash, in the blink of an eye, as is the human heart.
No abiding *ousia* dictates the terms under which the power of
God must work; no essential nature lays down the law by which
all things abide. In the kingdom, things seem to be forged from
a fragile, supple stuff that is stiffened neither by essence nor by
nature, that does not obey a natural law or inherent necessity, but
is simply obedient to the power of God, utterly responsive to the
amazing and surpassing power of God to make things whole,
new. In the kingdom, things lack what the Germans call *Selbst-
ständigkeit*, the ability to stand on their own and to persist in
their own subsistence, to subsist by their own persistence. Things
lack standing, self-standing, sub-standing, substance, and sub-
stantiveness. Things are marked, rather, by their readiness for
change, by their instantaneous obedience to a power that over-
takes them, that strikes them down with death and disease, with
paralysis and pain, and then makes them new, restoring and re-
suscitating them, raising bodies up from their graves.

Metanoetic time does not operate according to a rule of recall,
a principle in virtue of which whatever happens is a repetition or
recollection or retrieval of something that has been there all
along. Metanoetic time is not dominated by philosophy's love of
the circle, the Parmenideanism that dictates that we always arrive
at our point of departure, that coming-to-be is coming back to
where we were, that *Wesen* is always *Gewesen*.

Metanoetics does not operate a law of Platonic *anamnesis*, according to which to learn is to remember or to recall something
that must have already been known, on the grounds that knowledge must arise from knowledge, that there cannot be a sheer or
utter coming-to-be from nothing. Plato say in the *Republic* that
learning is not a matter of giving the soul something that it does

not have, of inserting sight into a blind eye (*Republic* 518). Yet that is exactly what it is in the kingdom: giving us what we do not have, putting sight into blind eyes. The Platonic conception is scandalized by change, by novelty and the emergence of something new; it blocks the *renovatio*, the transformation from ignorance to knowledge, from hardness of heart to *kardia*. In the kingdom, novelty is not a paradox or aporia to be explained away, not a symptom of a world that is not really real; it is the rule of the day, of the new day, of the renewal of our works and days.

Metanoetics has nothing to do with Hegelian *Erinnerung*, with an interiorizing memorialization by which the in-itself labors and strains, tested by the powers of negativity to become itself, to become what it already is, to be what it all along has been, to be what it already is. In metanoetics, one becomes what one is not. *Metanoo*, I have had a change of heart, I have been transformed, made into something new. I have not become what I am; I have become something else, something new. Metanoetics is not Heideggerian *Andenken*, according to which thinking forward (*Vordenken*) means thinking back upon or being devoted to what has been, to the oldest of the old, so that what is coming to us from the future comes to us from what has been. In metanoetics, the future has not yet been and we cannot foresee it (even as the past can be undone); we know neither the day nor the hour, and when it comes we will be transformed into something new.

Being and time in the kingdom do not look much like the prevailing conception of being and time in the history of Western metaphysics and the metaphysical theology to which the Church has lent its considerable institutional weight. Things have a less substantial, less essential, more nominalistic, more contingent look. There is little in the kingdom to suggest the hegemonic rule of being, essence, natural law, intellectualism, the primacy of the universal and generic, the rule of law, the primacy of the same over the different, for which philosophy—ontophilosophy, ontotheological philosophy, the metaphysical theology that calls itself "Christian philosophy"—shows such an ineradicable predilection. The kingdom does not seem to be made up of substances running their natural course in time, following up the inner tendencies of their nature according to natural laws, which is a more Greco-Roman and ontotheological way to think about things, for which we do not need and cannot use the New Testament. The kingdom is considerably more "eventualistic," made up of happenings, events, singular constellations, and living in the kingdom means being more sensitive to the singularity of the situation and to the novelty of what is to come. In the kingdom, things seem to happen, so that the best way to describe an event is not to say "It is" but "It happens," *es geshieht, il arrive.* We do better to say "There is," *il y a, es gibt,* and to avoid the substantialistic, ousiological overtones of *is* and *being* and *essence.*

In short, in the kingdom things look rather more like the way the world comes out in postmodern authors like Derrida and Lyotard, in whom we find a philosophy of events, of the *événement,* the happening, and in what one might call the prophetic postmodernism of Levinas, in whom everything is organized around what is otherwise than *ousia.*[22] In the kingdom, things do not have the look of Parmenideanism and ousiology; rather, they take on the accents of a radical creationism, a radical sense of novelty and alterity, of the new and the different, of the other, of the otherwise than *Wesen, ousia,* or *substantia.*

CONCLUSION

Is a Christian philosophy possible today? Might not the resources for such a thing be at hand—and here, now, I must scandalize the ears of the faithful—in the philosophy of différance and alterity in Jacques Derrida, in the radical alterity of Emmanuel Levinas, in the philosophy of events in Jean-François Lyotard, in the most Jewish postmodernism and postmodern Judaism of these Parisian poststructualists?

Is it not possible that an odd thing has happened to Christian philosophy today, that it has for too long kept the company of ontotheologicans and turned a deaf ear to biblical categories, to the philosophical import of biblical categories? Is it not possible that all this talk about the destruction of the history of ontology,

---

[22] For more on this "eventualistic" conception of things, see Caputo, *Against Ethics,* pp. 93–98, 220–27.

of the deconstruction of the metaphysics of presence, and of the end of philosophy, instead of being shot through with the relativism and skepticism, the subversive subjectivism and enervating nihilism that so scandalizes the faithful, who have appointed themselves the defenders of the good and the true—is it not possible that all this *Destruktion* and *déconstruction* is rather an echo, today, of Paul's scolding the Corinthians about the wisdom of God and the foolishness of men? Is it not possible that we might construct a postmodern Christian philosophy out of all this deconstruction?

Is it not possible that the echo of a certain biblical discourse has made its way to Paris?

Is it not possible that, instead of having succumbed to nihilism, postmodern writers have captured something of the biblical world, of its eventualistic, nominalistic, nonessentialistic open-endedness, its prediction for *ta me onta*, and its sense of radical transformability? Is it not possible that, *mirabile dictu*, that is what makes Christian philosophy possible today?

Has the time come for Christian philosophy to have a change of heart?

QUESTIONS AND ANSWERS

Q: You said that what you were doing today was "under the sign" of Derrida. I heard it as actually under the sign of someone else, whom you repudiate at least once, although invoking indirectly: namely, Nietzsche. The problem that I have, just a small one, is how do you first valorize the strategies of what is referred to as *ressentiment*, then take that back and speak on the side that would be against *ressentiment*, the side of forgiveness, from Scheler through Hannah Arendt, in terms of the transformation of the past. For Nietzsche forgiveness is one of the things that counts as the "freezing of the past," for it embodies a claim to power that stands on the side of the disenfranchised. Nietzsche's criticism of the claim to power from the side that is without power is that it, too, seeks power but does not seek power in the name of valorizing or enfranchising those who are on the out and out. Those who are on the out and out are not recognized as out and out; they want to be in. And the point, then, is that there isn't a *difference* in the difference you're looking for here. Nietzsche speaks of blessing and transformation of the past, but that is not what is going on in speaking of a forgiveness that would change the past. For Nietzsche, you change the past by blessing the past. You seem to move between the two, and so I had the sense of terrible sliding.

A: If I were very wealthy, which I assure you I am not, and well ensconced in the halls of power, I would love no one more than one who says, "Love things as they are." *Amor fati.* That's just the way I would vote, to keep things just as they are and love them. As they were and as they are, and as they will be in a perfect circle. The deconstruction of *ressentiment* is to love things as they were. The total transvaluation of all values is to love the whole circle—as they are, as they were, as they will be. The battle that Zarathustra has to wage with himself is that there is nothing new under the sun; he knows it, but he won't say it. That is Greek, that is the circle, that is precisely the opposite of the metanoetics, the philosophy of novelty, which I am defending.

I think that there are many very interesting insights of Nietzsche's into *ressentiment*, and there's hardly any better medicine for religious writers than *The Genealogy of Morals.* I mean, they should take daily doses of that book. But I think the abominable sociopolitical, racial-ethnic, and historical elitism of Nietzsche is not an accidental thing of which we should just say, "Well now, you know, he has his limits." I think that it goes together with a fundamentally elitist conception of being, a contempt of what is ordinary and average, and a hypervalorization of the exceptional. Nietzsche opposes the valorization of everything that is not exceptional and that requires our response, whereas what I am interested in is exactly the opposite.

Now, you say that is a disguised will to power. Well, that's a nice way to get off the hook; then you don't have to do a damned thing. I do think that it's true that those who put themselves in the position of responding to the calls that come to us from others who make claims on us are, in their heart of hearts, liable to be subverted by a hidden and unconscious will to power. I think that is entirely true. I do not think there's any way around that. I think that the ethical relationship is very finite; it is immersed in murky, dark, and obscure motives, and who knows what is going on in my heart. That is no excuse not to respond.

The paradox you bring up is that when someone responds to the powerless it is a concealed form of the will to power. Well, I think that responsibility is vulnerable to that, and I think it is part of the axiomatics of responsibility that one never knows when one thinks one is being responsible, whether one is being dominating. That's right. That's part of the axiomatics of the finitude of the ethical relationship. I think that is completely true. That doesn't relieve me of my responsibility.

I think that Nietzsche has got it all wrong when it comes to giving. Nietzsche thinks of giving as overflowing, as the welling up within of my overabundance, and then my spilling over. In metanoetics, giving is conceived in exactly the opposite terms. The widow in the story gives of what she needs in order to live; she gives of her own "substance." She doesn't give of her overflowing; she gives what she needs. It's exactly the opposite of Nietzsche. Nietzsche, for all his greatness, has a philosophy of a certain kind of autonomy, a certain kind of building up and welling up of the same, which then flows into difference. For Levinas or Derrida, it is not the difference that spreads itself out in many different directions from an overflow; it is the alterity of the other one who lays claim to me. It's not merely *diversitas*; it's *alteritas*, not *diversitas*. It is a long story, but I have tried to tell it in a book called *Against Ethics*.

Q: When you began the essay, you began by talking about postmodernism as a way of being grateful to modernity by being ungrateful, and, in that sense, as being an extension of modernity and not a retreat behind modernity. As the essay went on, though, what I heard at least was the ingratitude side of things coming into focus. Even more than that, dare I say, a discourse of oppositions? It seemed to me not simply an ingratitude, or a grateful ingratitude, but something bordering on—and I choose the term carefully—a discourse of oppositions coming to the fore. Now, let's think for a minute about Jesus deconstructing the Law when he heals the woman on the Sabbath as the Pharisees are looking on. Maybe it is a deconstruction of the Law that's going on, but it's a perfection of the Law at the same time. The Midrash that comes out of the Pharisaic tradition a couple of hundred years later makes it clear that all other Sabbath commandments are subordinate to the needs of life and the demands of life. And so Jesus is actually doing the best thing that could be done for the Law, appearances to the contrary notwithstanding. The deconstruction is drawing on that very source.

I'm wondering (and this is the part of the question I don't have worked out, and it should be the part that's best worked out, so I'm sorry), I am wondering if what I heard, rightly or wrongly, as that oppositional language that I referred to does not mask a sense in which this radical hermeneutic of the kingdom is drawing on the very resources of modernity for its own progress. I wonder if things would not look a little different if the gratitude, as well as the ungrateful part of the gratitude, were acknowledged? And then I wonder if the end of onto-theo logy would not be its annulment, but some kind of preservation of . . .? I'm not sure that I've got the last part of that fully clear.

A: I think I hear you. Let me say two things. First, I insist upon the observation that postmodernism is not antimodernism; that it's an extension of modernity by another means, because I think that it takes up the egalitarianism of modernism. It breaks with the hierarchical, power-on-the-top/powerlessness-on-the-bottom structure of the classical world; and it breaks with the whole model of something coming from above; and it speaks in terms of things coming from below. So a postmodern Christian philosophy would be a philosophy from below, not from above. It pursues the aims of modernity; it pursues the aims of Thomas Jefferson and the democratic ideals, but in a more radical way, because the notion of equality by sameness has now given way to a kind of differential equality. That is, when people are simply hierarchized down, then one way to get them up is to insist on sameness, and that is a crucial moment, which is the moment of modernity. The moment of postmodernity, however, is to push farther, because sameness can also be used as a way of holding people down. So, when you insist on being gender- or color-blind, when you have been bruised by your gender and bruised by your color, then that's just a way of holding people down.

Now, I do think there is a certain moment of *perfectio* in this *destructio.* If you look at a piece that Derrida has written called *The Force of Law*, it's perfectly clear that he thinks the relationship between deconstruction and the law is to make the law better, because the problem with law is that in principle it has to be blind to proper names. You do not want proper names in the law; the law is universal. But there is a point to the law, and the point, I think, is healing, lifting up those who have no power. It is emancipatory. Derrida says, "I can think of no word that is less out of date than the word emancipation." But what deconstruction does not think is that we are moving relentlessly, if gradually, toward a kind of *Aufhebung* or *preservatio* in which things will even out, or the opposites will harmonize. He thinks that we can try to fix this, but then something else will break. The point of deconstructive analysis is to watch out for what's breaking, because something will always be breaking. You may move from one situation to another in which things will not get better, they will get worse. We are not *trying* to make it worse, we are *trying* to fix it, even though something else will break when we fix it. I do not share the modernist notion of synthesis or *preservatio* in the Hegelian sense, but I do think that there is some sense in which there is a *perfectio* in *deconstructio*.

Q: I don't know whether I'm in agreement with what you said, because your discourse can be heard in two ways. One way, I heard you draw some parallels between Derrida and Jesus, and you say they are on the same side, because they defend the wounded flesh against establishment, against the bourgeois, against *ousia*, substance, the sameness of being, the time of presence, and idealism. So, in that case, Jesus would be a good philosopher of today, or maybe not a good philosopher, but anyway a philosopher. It is not enough, however, to defend the dispersion, the other, difference, *me on*, the vulnerable flesh, the marginal, the outlaw, the figures of absence, to be on the side of Jesus. So, my question is, what do you mean by conversion? Is conversion the discovery that there is another dimension than philosophy, that there is another dimension than opposition of *ousia* and *me on*? Or is conversion just to be on the good side of philosophy?

You present Derrida as an overcoming, if I'm not mistaken, of this long tradition of metaphysics, which, according to some people in our time, is a sort of short formula for philosophy. This is a reading of the history of philosophy that I think is a little simplistic and a bit primitive, because we can also write a history of philosophy about those philosophers who from this perspective are considered to be primitive, but who did not consider themselves to be primitive, like Heraclitus, the skeptics, the empiricists, and various other sorts. I say primitive, because I think it is a reduced picture of history when we say that philosophy has always been idealism, has always been a philosophy of totality. I think we can discuss that, but there are many authors who do not fit into this picture. My main question is, of course, whether Christianity points at a dimension different from philosophy or whether we should consider Christianity as the defense of this marginal way of living. I think it is very important, because if Jesus Christ has come for all people, then we should also discover how wounded the establishment is, and how wounded the bourgeois is, and we should also discover that everybody is poor, even, for instance, that Hegel or Kant is poor. The question is which spirit inspires your reading of the history of philosophy. I have always a little suspicion that the spirit can be imitated, and, if I am not mistaken, the enemy of God is the imitator.

A: First of all, the notion that the history of philosophy could be reduced to a simple metaphysics of presence is, I would say, precisely what any careful explication of Derrida's views would avoid. For one thing, Derrida doesn't think that there is such a thing as stepping outside metaphysics; he thinks that metaphysics remains a certain kind of inescapable conceptuality. That is part of what you mean by being a Western person—to speak, and to think in categories that have been deeply set or influenced by Greek conceptuality. Furthermore, the whole point, I would say, of a deconstructionist reading of the history of philosophy is precisely to look for the countertraditions, to look for the moments of dissent, the differences. It is true: Derrida writes about great philosophers; he shouldn't be writing about Plato, Hegel, and Heidegger all the time; he ought to write about Pico della Mirandola, or somebody who is quite less well-known. He ought to find marginal people. When he writes about the great philosophers, he does try to find marginal texts that nobody has read. That is a mistake he makes, even from his own point of view.

What interests him, though, always is the countertradition, and I think that the way to think about the Christian tradition is to think of it in terms, not of the unity of the tradition, but of a very pluriform, multiple, polysemic thing with many, many, many countertraditions. We could embrace a pluralistic and polysemic conception of the Christian tradition or philosophical tradition and look for those sorts of philosophers who are devalorized by the canon. So, I would say that is exactly what deconstruction tries to do, to watch out for canonical, standard readings of the great tradition.

Secondly, I think that it's quite right to say that there is a strategic move in the New Testament which puts the well born and well-to-do at a disadvantage, so it has images like the camel passing through the eye of the needle. That is a strategic move; it is a movement of reversal. It cannot be the final move, because then the kingdom would only be for the wretched of the earth. There are good ways to explain why the well born and well-to-do, the princely, and the powers that be are also alienated and are also meant for the kingdom. The point of the kingdom is precisely its nonexclusionary character. So, I don't mean this to be a philosophy of marginality to the point that if you are in any way hale and whole, if you are physically or mentally well, you are in big trouble as far as the kingdom is concerned. Finally, I would not say that Jesus was a philosopher; I would say we are the philosophers. Jesus couldn't have cared less about philosophy as far as I can tell, and he wouldn't have understood ninety-nine percent of the things that have been said about him by the philosophers ever since. We ought to let philosophy be shocked by the jolt of a prephilosophical experience of the sort one finds in the scriptures, so that the result will be what Derrida, following James Joyce, calls Jew-Greek. I tried to say that ironically by saying what is the being and time of the kingdom, that is, what sorts of revisions and rethinking of our philosophical conceptuality are made possible by revisiting the scriptures, by bracketing the faith/reason distinction and listening and getting a feel for the texture of experience in that world. I must say that I think that Levinas has captured a lot of that. He says something like, "Who is this Jesus? The one who stands by the outcast." So, I think that what we want is a rethinking of our philosophical categories in the light of the unique idiom of the Christian scriptures and of the tradition that follows it.

Q: I think what you said needed to be said. I think it is a whole one-half of the truth, and it's very important. But I think the really living . . .

A: You did say "but"?

Q: Yes. The living truth, I think, is always in the vital tension of opposites which doesn't overcome the opposites. You've dropped one shoe, but there's another shoe to be dropped. After the metanoia, then the Christians wanted to be faithful to the Covenant. The Christian families right away became more stable, much more chaste, keeping the order of families as children and parents. There is a whole order or stability, faithfulness to the Covenant, that is, not always changing. The metanoia is one moment, but it gets back to real stability and peace. After the metanoia, Jesus heals the woman and says, "Go and sin no more." That is, keep the faithfulness of the marriage covenant; that is the whole other side of the metanoia. You then have to live, and maybe that is when and where one can recover the original intention of God in nature, which is now sort of lifted, not destroyed, but lifted up.

A: That's a good point. You know what the Nazis' objections to Heidegger were? This is very interesting. They were worried that, about an hour-and-a-half after the triumph of the Nazi revolution, Heidegger would be on the way to another revolution; that his was such radical questioning that it would question the new order as soon as the new order got to be a few hours old. I thought that was an interesting point. I think that what this sort of radical transformability suggests is a model of interruption, of rhythmic interruption, I would say.

I don't want to think in terms of a moment of revolutionary upheaval in metanoia and change, and then things settle into place. To follow your own example: if we are to believe Elizabeth Schussler-Fiorenza, in the earliest Christian communities, the family was conceived as a community of equals. The families were communal families frequently, and they were conceived as communities of equals in which women had as much to do with running the early local churches as anybody else. Then, Fiorenza says, in the process of trying to get their feet on the ground and hold off the lions, Christianity discovered that the place it was giving to women in the family was a scandal to the Romans, and so it backed off. Hence, the Pauline texts about women obeying their husbands are later than the Pauline texts that say there is neither male nor female. And what Christianity started to do in this moment of stability that you mention was to accommodate itself to the elitist hierarchical order of a patriarchal society, whereas, the more primal Christian impulse was a community of equals.

So, I would worry about settling down too much. If faithfulness means "women be obedient to your husbands," that is not my idea of faithfulness. It would be silly for us to get involved in an argument about the relative merits of stability and instability. The very idea of deconstruction implies structures; if there were not any structures, there would not be anything to deconstruct, simply utter chaos. Deconstruction means, literally, to be parasitic. That is to say, it involves having an organism to prey upon, and Derrida likes that metaphor because it's an unfavorable metaphor. It is not part of the beautiful imagery of Greco-Christianity, of the *theologia gloriae*. But what that means is that you certainly have to have structures in order to get things done. There have to be laws. Justice without laws would be impotent. What you want are good laws that you can enforce, laws that restrain victimizers and release victims. But you need to keep a kind of constant eye on the structures and the stabilities that you are talking about, because it's almost as if there is a moment in structure which marginalizes, and which represses, and normalizes, and flattens out, and that's what postmodernism is all about—exposing the momentum in structures that flatten out, and level off, and exclude, and marginalize, and silence. So, postmodernism in general, not just deconstruction, is a kind of rhythmic intervention in structures that have to be watched, like the law. So Jesus wasn't a wildly anarchistic screwball; he was an interventionist.

9

"Divine Woman/Divine Women": The Return of the Sacred in Bataille, Lacan, and Irigaray

Amy Hollywood

WHILE COMMENTATORS on the work of Luce Irigaray have given some attention to her discussions of the divine, these expositions tend—not surprisingly, given attitudes toward religion among most academic feminists—to be concerned more with making Irigaray's religious references palatable to an a- or antitheological audience than in uncovering their potential contribution to a feminist philosophy of religion or in the related task of situating them within their theoretical, textual, and historical contexts.[1] The Feuerbachian background of "Divine Women" has been analyzed by numerous commentators, as has Irigaray's critique of René Girard's theory of religion, but the more implicit debts of her religious reflections have yet to be brought to light.[2] Here I

---

[1] This is a provisional and fragmentary piece of a projected book-length study on the place of mysticism in twentieth-century French thought and its implications for a feminist philosophy of religion. Irigaray will serve as the organizing center for this study, in that her work brings out the feminist implications of certain trajectories of French philosophy and psychoanalysis. Like Irigaray, moreover, I believe it is important to challenge the unquestioning rejection of religion found in many feminist academic circles. I also believe, however, that it is important continually to question Irigaray. Uncovering her debts—here to Bataille and Lacan—is an important part of both these ventures.

[2] For Feuerbach, see Elizabeth Grosz, *Sexual Subversions: Three French Feminists* (Sydney: Allen and Unwin, 1989), pp. 152–55; Elizabeth Grosz, "Irigaray and the Divine," in *Transfigurations: Theology and the French Feminists* (Minneapolis: Fortress, 1993), pp. 199–214; Margaret Whitford, *Luce Irigaray: Philosophy in the Feminine* (New York: Routledge, 1991), pp. 141–42; Serene Jones, "This God Which Is Not One: Irigaray and Barth on the Divine," in *Transfigurations*, pp. 109–41; and Kathryn Bond Stockton, " 'God' Between

will show that the seminars and writings of Jacques Lacan, in particular *Seminar XX: Encore*, and through Lacan the atheological texts of Georges Bataille provide one context within which Irigaray's return to the divine might be understood.[3] To put the case more strongly: it can be shown that from the often overlooked and misunderstood mimicking of mystical discourse in *Speculum* to her more recent calls for a feminine divine,[4] Irigaray's work is deployed with and against the theories of the divine and the sacred found in Bataille and Lacan. So, while substantial attention has been given to Irigaray's debt to and distance from Lacan's psychoanalytic theory, clarification of the role of religion within his discourse and his relationship to Bataille on the issues of *jouissance* and the sacred will enhance understanding of the meaning and significance of Irigaray's critical appropriations.

Among other issues elucidated, attention to the atheological problematic posed by Bataille in his numerous texts on religion and its psychoanalytic deployment by Lacan in *Encore* will clarify the meaning and intended referentiality of Irigaray's religious language. This will enable us to overcome the impasse evident in recent feminist readings of Irigaray's work on religion, particularly with regard to her apparently uncritical acceptance of the

---

Their Lips: Desire Between Women in Irigaray and Eliot," *Novel*, 25 (1992): 356. On Girard, see Grosz, *Sexual Subversions*, pp. 149–50; and Whitford, *Luce Irigaray*, pp. 145–46.

[3] Lacan is, of course, often discussed, but Irigaray's appropriation and critique of his views on women and the sacred have not been explored. See Grosz, *Sexual Subversions*; Whitford, *Luce Irigaray*; and Margaret Whitford, "Irigaray's Body Symbolic," *Hypatia*, 6 (1991), 97–110. Attention will be given to Irigaray's critique of Lacan's *Encore* in "Così fan tutti," although this text is not the last (or the first) word on their relationship with regard to the divine. See Luce Irigaray, *This Sex Which Is Not One*, trans. Catherine Porter (Ithaca, N.Y.: Cornell University Press, 1985), pp. 86–105.

[4] Grosz, *Sexual Subversions*, p. 151; and Jones, "This God," p. 122; both, I think, misread. The other most sustained discussion of the divine in Irigaray, that by Whitford, does not discuss this text. For brief and suggestive discussions, see Stockton, "'God' Between Their Lips"; Kathryn Bond Stockton, "Bodies and God: Poststructuralist Feminists Return to the Fold of Spiritual Materialism," *boundary 2*, 19 (1992): 141–44; Toril Moi, *Sexual/Textual Politics: Feminist Literary Theory* (London: Methuen, 1985), pp. 135–37; and Philippa Berry, "The Burning Glass: Paradoxes of Feminist Revelation in *Speculum*," in *Engaging with Irigaray*, ed. Carolyn Burke, Naomi Schor, and Margaret Whitford (New York: Columbia University Press, 1994), pp. 229–46.

Feuerbachian claim that religion is a projection and reflection of the ego ideals of its human creators. Irigaray thus argues in "Divine Women" that it is necessary for women to "imagine a divine" in order "to become divine."[5] Whereas Elizabeth Grosz takes Feuerbach's constructivism as a reassurance that Irigaray is not calling for a "leap of faith" or a return to belief and a seemingly apolitical religiosity,[6] Serene Jones has recently pointed to the difficulties that arise for Irigaray if Grosz's interpretation is correct.[7] For Jones, a Christian theologian, Irigaray's concern to protect the incommensurability of the "other" sex against its inscription within a "logic of the same" makes suspect any claim that she is willing to reduce the divine to a newly projected "ego ideal" for women. One might argue that the nature of that ideal—as open, multiple, and indeterminate—effectively undermines the specular logic on which male religion has been based, yet this creates the danger of losing alterity (as Jones suggests) or of repeating the reifying structures of male thought Irigaray herself (psycho)analyzes and deconstructs in "Belief Itself."[8]

Having deconstructed belief in that essay, moreover, Irigaray evokes the possibility of other conceptions or experiences of sacrality created by detachment from faith and the taking of risks. Thus, a Feuerbachian account of religion is unable to account for the multiple valences of the divine within Irigaray's own discourse. As Feuerbach argues, without belief, the divine is merely human, a reversion to the logic of the same and negation of the possibility of radical alterity. Irigaray explicitly rejects belief as it has been constructed within the male economy, yet like Bataille she reinscribes the divine within a language that attempts to subvert the antitheses between immanence and transcendence,

---

[5] Luce Irigaray, *Sexes et parentés* (Paris: Minuit, 1987), pp. 79 and 81; Luce Irigaray, *Sexes and Genealogies*, trans. Gillian C. Gill (New York: Columbia University Press, 1993), pp. 67 and 68.

[6] Grosz, "Irigaray on the Divine," p. 214. Grosz does point to another, "cosmic," dimension of the divine more in line with my readings. See Grosz, *Sexual Subversions*, pp. 180–81.

[7] Jones, "This God," p. 138.

[8] See "Belief Itself," in Irigaray, *Sexes and Genealogies*. I discuss this further in my "Deconstructing Belief: Irigaray and the Philosophy of Religion," *Journal of Religion* 78 (1998): 230–45.

human and divine, self and other.[9] Her divine references, then, cannot be contained within any obviously Feuerbachian mode.[10] Neither theism nor atheism, Irigaray's religious language marks the reemergence of the sacred in a mode reminiscent both of the thought of Bataille and Lacan and of those mystical theologies with which her reflections on religious discourse begin; her language suggests, as Lacan claims, that the mystical is not apolitical. While Irigaray insists that the imaginary and symbolic structures underlying the mystical subversion of duality must be radically rethought, her poetics of the female body itself accepts and elaborates on the problematic of immanence and transcendence central to the thought of Bataille and Lacan. She implicitly follows them in her insistence that the death of the "good old God" enables the return of the sacred, God's "other face." Yet, in following their atheological trajectories, Irigaray consistently undermines their placement of "woman" through her insistence on giving voice to women. Women's voices, she suggests, will further alter accounts of the sacred and its relationship to humanity.

Georges Bataille, like the surrealist movement with which he was sometimes associated and more often in conflict, depicts "woman" as emblematic of the heterogeneous, material, and transgressive alterity with which he wished to counter all idealisms (including that of surrealism itself). In his writings, women

---

[9] Bataille does use the language of radical immanence and atheism, but always with a view to the ultimate subversion of these antitheses through that which is radically heterogeneous and unassimilable to the Hegelian movement of sublation. In his eyes, the greatest threat is posed by idealism; in the present philosophical context, an argument might be made for the dangers of an unreflective materialism (itself idealist, in Bataille's sense, in that it subjects all things to reason). See, for example, Georges Bataille, *Visions of Excess: Selected Writings, 1927–1939*, trans. Allan Stoekl (Minneapolis: University of Minnesota Press, 1985); and Georges Bataille, *Theory of Religion*, trans. Robert Hurley (New York: Zone Books, 1992).

[10] Other readings of Feuerbach are certainly possible. See, for example, Stockton, "'God' Between Their Lips," who emphasized the gap that remains between the individual and the ideal projected onto the divine. While for Feuerbach, the "species being" of humanity bridges that gap, a nonhumanistic appropriation of Feuerbach would depend on its reopening.

are the site of that paradoxical combination of pleasure and anguish—*jouissance*, to use Lacan's term—that transgresses all bounds and undermines rationality. Woman, then, is linked to both mysticism and eroticism. Yet, in his various presentations of a theory of religion, Bataille himself most often occupies this feminized space, and the nature of his religiosity undermines his seemingly stereotypical view of femininity in crucial ways. For while Bataille claims that he was, in the 1930s, "ferociously religious," it is as one without God and hence without a head. "Man will escape from his head as the condemned man from his prison."[11] Like Lacan, as we will see, the "castration" of "woman" is emblematic of the human condition, and thus to be embraced as the site of that joyful anguish Bataille names inner experience.[12]

Here I will focus, however, not on Bataille's explicit discussions of feminization, castration, and women, but rather on the importance for his theory of religion of his account of lacerated human nature. Bataille presents this theory of religion in texts written over the course of four decades and in a variety of genres—often hybrid forms most reminiscent of the oddities of medieval Christian mystical texts. His writings take three primary forms: novels (generally described as "pornographic"), theoretical texts (although often fragmentary), and the mixed genres of the personal yet highly reflective pieces collected in the *Atheological Summa*, written before and during the Second World War.[13] Combining journal entries, theoretical reflections,

---

[11] Bataille, *Visions of Excess*, pp. 180–81.

[12] This is to simplify an enormously complex set of issues in Bataille's writings: namely, the relationship between his pose of "manly castration" and fascination with the phallus, his self-feminization, and women. I can only broach these issues here, although his claim that "man is what he lacks" leads immediately to the question, "And what, then, are women?" For further discussion, see Denis Hollier, *Against Architecture: The Writings of Georges Bataille*, trans. Betsy Wing (Minneapolis: University of Minnesota Press, 1989); Susan Rubin Suleiman, *Subversive Intent: Gender, Politics, and the Avant-Garde* (Cambridge, Mass.: Harvard University Press, 1990), pp. 72–87; and Carolyn Dean, *The Self and Its Pleasures: Bataille, Lacan, and the History of the Decentered Subject* (Ithaca, N.Y.: Cornell University Press, 1992).

[13] The important issue of Bataille's "style" and writing practice is discussed by Michele Richman, *Reading Georges Bataille: Beyond the Gift* (Baltimore: The Johns Hopkins University Press, 1982); and Hollier, *Against Architecture*.

directions for seeking ecstasy, and accounts of ecstatic inner experiences, together with often extended quotations from Christian mystical texts and the writings of Nietzsche, the very fragmentation of Bataille's work is in part exemplary of its content. Like mystical discourse, Bataille's writing constantly denies its own possibility, and his attempts to give a method for interior experience are subverted by his claim that it cannot be attained by systematic means. The more sustained theoretical texts are also extended exercises in contradiction, for in them Bataille attempts to give rational form to that which exceeds and destroys the rational and to encapsulate scientifically that which exceeds all objectification and rationality.[14]

Yet, throughout his writings, although in different forms and by means of different strategies, Bataille provides a coherent and abiding theory of the nature of religion and the sacred. Although attention to the chronology of Bataille's reflections on religion may reveal important shifts in his understanding of human nature, expenditure, sacrifice, and the sacred, for my present purpose I will create a composite picture grounded in the *Atheological Summa* of the 1940s and the posthumously published *Theory of Religion*.[15] For Bataille, religion is always caught in the dialectical movement of immanence and transcendence that marks the specificity of human nature. Taking up from the closing section of Nietzsche's *On the Genealogy of Morals*, Bataille insists that humanity is that which always questions itself. To be human is to ask the meaning of one's suffering and one's being, a self-consciousness alien to the immanence of animal nature. Humanity is always involved in a contradiction, one that Bataille refuses to sublate. Any response to the question of the meaning

These need to be analyzed further in relation to both the mystics and Nietzsche's writing practice.

[14] This is a central issue in Lacan's seminar, *Encore*. See Jacques Lacan, *Le Seminare XX: Encore*, ed. Jacques-Alain Miller (Paris: Seuil, 1975).

[15] Bataille himself points to the continuity of his thought when he writes in the introduction to the collection *Literature and Evil* (trans. Alastair Hamilton [New York: Marion Boyars, 1973], p. ix) "These studies, which are so strikingly coherent, were written by a mature man. Yet they were generated in the turbulance of youth, and they faintly echo this." Bataille's sources for his theory of religion include Alexander Kojève and Émile Durkheim, although he clearly argues against the latter's functionalism.

of being, furthermore, is always itself subject to question, pointing to the endless movement of the dialectic within human existence and thought.[16] While it is constitutive of human nature to question, a mark of its transcendence from the immanence of the natural world, the human being also always desires to return to that lost immanence.[17] Whereas within the world of transcendent, discrete objects rationality comes to the fore, and with it an economy of use and value through which the surrounding world becomes objectified, the religious impulse is precisely the desire to negate this process of objectification and the economy of utility it grounds. Humans desire to return to the realm of immanence. Yet to return to the immanence of the natural world, in which all things are continuous like "water in water," is to remain in a state of animality. Bataille argues that "The constant problem posed by the impossibility of being human without being a thing and of escaping the limits of things without returning to animal slumber receives the limited solution of festival."[18] In the festival, immanence is attained most fully through death, a death enacted on the head of the sacrificial victim. Sacrifice, then, is both an expenditure without return, in which the objectification and utility of the sacrificial victim are overcome, and a return of the immanent—the sacred—through the making sacred of that former object. In this way, Bataille argues, sacrifice brings the sacred into existence through the process of free expenditure.[19]

The sacred engendered through sacrifice is not a limited or objectifiable entity, but precisely a (non)being whose reification has been overcome through its useless expenditure in the act of sacrifice. God arrives on the scene only when human beings confuse the sacred with reason, with that which governs the world of transcendent beings.[20] Through this process, another transcen-

---

[16] See, for example, Georges Bataille, *Guilty*, trans. Bruce Boone (San Francisco: Lapis, 1988).

[17] Here I am following the terms of analysis Bataille uses in his *Theory of Religion*. As Hollier shows, the castrated human being seeks fullness through another act of castration. See Hollier's *Against Architecture*, pp. 138–70.

[18] Bataille, *Theory of Religion*, p. 53.

[19] For discussion of sacrifice in Bataille as it relates to both the father and the mother, see Hollier, *Against Architecture*, pp. 138–70.

[20] "It seemed to me there were two terms to human thought: God and the

dence is posited and the realm of objectifying transcendence re-described as immanence. The desire for immanence, for the return to a state of continuity and fluidity, is now hypostasized as that otherworldly, ultrarational, and instrumental transcendence that religion has become in Western society. Bataille's entire atheological project, then, can be understood as an (always ambivalent and perhaps impossible) attempt to free the sacred from God, to free immanence from transcendence, or expenditure from utility and rationality. Not only is the transcendent other-world, the subject of Nietzsche's polemics, subverted, but also the subject as transcendent to the natural immanence of animal nature. But the latter is not simply a return to animality; it is, rather, a movement through and against the paradoxes of human nature, and one the ambivalence of which Bataille always remains aware—for while humans desire the sacred, they also desire life, and the existence of the sacred seems dependent on the death of the sacrificial victim.[21] Communication is life, but in its essence it demands sacrifice and, hence, death.[22]

While the *Theory of Religion* uses the language of continuity/dis-continuity, immanence/transcendence, and sacred/profane to mark the divisions created by an objectifying (self-)consciousness, Bataille's more personal and evocative texts point to the grounding of experiences of sacrality in a recognition of the lack, laceration, and woundedness of the human subject in the face of his/her question and his/her death. It is through the wound of

---

awareness of God's absence. But since God's just a confusion of the SACRED (a religious aspect) and REASON (an instrumental aspect), the only place for him is a world where confusion of the instrumental and the sacred becomes a basis for reassurance. God terrifies when he's no longer the same as reason (Pascal and Kierkegaard). But if he's not the same as reason, I'm confronted with the last stage of the world, which no longer has anything instrumental about it and furthermore doesn't have anything to do with *future* retributions or punishment. So the question still outstanding . . ." (Bataille, *Guilty*, p. 6). See also, his *Theory of Religion.*

[21] Bataille, *Guilty*, p. 118. This should be compared to René Girard's theory of sacrifice and the scapegoat and then analyzed with regard to Irigaray's critique of Girard. See Irigaray, *Sexes and Genealogies*, pp. 75–88.

[22] Bataille's theory of religion, then, echoes the ambivalent relations between pleasure, death, and reality found in Freud's *Beyond the Pleasure Principle* and analyzed by Lacan in *Encore* and Irigaray in "Belief Itself." This entire discussion should be reread in light of Freud's text and its reinscriptions in Bataille, Lacan, and Irigaray.

existence that humanity is open to its own limits, transgression, and the radical immanence of sacrality. Bataille presents himself as an atheistic mystic who embraces pain, violence, and loss as the site of an expenditure that enables the absolute communication of radical immanence.[23] The chance and contingency of human life mark the meaninglessness of an existence that must recognize the limitations of the reason it has posited in the place of God. Here the lines between Bataille's theory of religion and Lacan's speculations concerning feminine sexuality and the divine become clear. Bataille can be read as the man become woman through recognition of his lack, his symbolic castration, whom Lacan describes in *Encore* (a feminization dependent, Irigaray would argue, on the prior sacrifice of the maternal figure, the castrated mother).[24] For both Bataille and Lacan, woman as "not all," castrated and lacking from the viewpoint of the phallic economy, is an emblem of the truth of human subjectivity; it is through an acceptance of this lack, furthermore, that another divine becomes possible.

A partial exposition of Lacan's seminar, *Encore*,[25] in light of Bataille's theory of religion demonstrates that Lacan was intent on giving a psychoanalytic explanation of the *reasons* for the slide between what Bataille refers to as the sacred and God. Attention to this dynamic will, moreover, clarify and mitigate Irigaray's critique of *Encore* presented in "Così fan tutti." Although, for Lacan, it is the work of psychoanalysis to keep the *objet petit a*, the fantasmatic object of desire and lost plenitude, separate from the A, the Other as site of castration and lack, he also demonstrates the reasons for their repeated coalescence:

> The objective of my teaching, inasmuch as it aims at that part of analytic discourse which can be formulated, or put down, is to dissociate the *a* and the O (*A/Autre*), by reducing the former to what belongs to the imaginary and the latter to what belongs to the

---

[23] Bataille, *Guilty*, pp. 30ff.

[24] Bataille, of course, would agree and then posit the necessity of killing the father as well. See Hollier, *Against Architecture*, p. 166.

[25] For important recent readings of the seminar, see Slavoj Zizek, *Tarrying with the Negative: Kant, Hegel, and the Critique of Ideology* (Durham, N.C.: Duke University Press, 1993); and Teresa Brennan, *History after Lacan* (New York: Routledge, 1993).

symbolic. That the symbolic is the support of that which is made into God, is beyond doubt. That the imaginary is supported by the reflection of like to like, is certain. And yet, *a* has come be confused with S(O) beneath which it is written on the board, and it has done so under pressure of the function of being. It is here that a rupture or severance is still needed. And it is in this precisely that psychoanalysis is something other than psychology. For psychology is the non-achieving of this rupture.[26]

Thus, as for Bataille, it is through the recognition of the lack in one's being, through the admission of the subject's always already castrated and wounded status, that the sacred (the other face of God, in Lacan) is uncovered. Yet, Lacan warns, any understanding of this sacred as the site of lost plenitude marks a reversion to precisely that fantasy of fullness and wholeness marked by the coalescence of the *a* and *A*.

For Lacan, all of this has to do with sexual relations and woman, understood from the standpoint of the male speaking subject as "not all" and hence as outside of the phallic economy of the symbolic register, for insofar as woman is "not all," man is implicitly posited as complete ("la femme" doesn't exist, with the *a* crossed through). To safeguard this wholeness, woman becomes the *objet a*, the part object whose attainment will complete man. Yet, in arguing that the Other and the *objet a* must be separated by psychoanalytic discourse, Lacan reiterates the fantasmatic character of the claim to phallic mastery—one enabled by the centrality of the phallus in Western discourse, but by no means inevitable or necessary.[27] This reading partially answers Irigaray's central criticism of the seminar, for while she accepts Lacan's account of sexual difference as an adequate description of women's place within male-dominate discourse, she questions what she sees as the mastery of psychoanalysis and the apparent inescapability of that which it describes.[28] Throughout the seminar, Lacan explicitly questions and implicitly subverts the claims of psychoanalysis to scientific mastery and argues for the contingency of the phallus as transcendental signifier—the

---

[26] Juliet Mitchell and Jacqueline Rose, eds., *Feminine Sexuality: Jacques Lacan and the École freudienne* (New York: Norton, 1982), pp. 153–54.

[27] Lacan makes this clear in *Encore*, esp. pp. 39–48.

[28] Irigaray, *This Sex*, pp. 99, 102.

support of that conflation of the imaginary and symbolic on which male authority rests. Yet, because of the centrality of the phallus within the existing economy, Lacan argues, women have no fantasmatic support for their subjectivities and claims to mastery. This is both debilitating—the source of her lack of power—and the source of women's greater access to *jouissance*. Like Bataille—one of those men who, presumably, has chosen the side of the "not all" within the phallic economy—Lacan insists on the unknowability and unnamability of this *jouissance*.

A central issue in reading the seminar is how to interpret Lacan's rhetoric. Thus, although he insists on the unknowable character of feminine *jouissance*, arguing that if it could be known, circumscribed, and reduced to the terms of the phallic economy, it would (obviously) no longer be in excess of those terms; at the same time he maintains his right to explain this "something more" insofar as it has to do with God. I believe the claims to "mastery" can be taken ironically, in that they serve always to limit the scope of psychoanalytic claims (that is, the something more is not "fullness of being," what Irigaray refers to as Lacan's assertion of "impotence"). In a similar manner, Lacan undermines his own illusion to Bernini's statue of St. Theresa of Avila. While he begins, as Irigaray stresses, with an apparent reduction of the experience of *jouissance* to biological terms ("you only have to go and look at Bernini's statue of St. Theresa in Rome to understand immediately that she's coming [*jouit*], there is no doubt about it"[29]), he characteristically adds something more (something, moreover, ignored by Irigaray). Charcot and his circle, he writes, "attempt to reduce the mystical to questions of fucking. If you look carefully, that is not what it is all about. Might not this *jouissance* which one experiences and knows nothing of, be that which puts us on the path of ex-istence? And why not interpret one face of the Other, the God face, as supported by feminine *jouissance*?"[30] Charcot, it should be added, attempted to provide a pictorial (and highly eroticized) representation of feminine hysteria, to reduce it to that which

---

[29] Mitchell and Rose, eds., *Feminine Sexuality*, p. 147.

[30] Ibid. The use of Heideggerian language appears in other key sections of the seminar, in particular the closing reappraisal of love. See Lacan, *Encore*, pp. 132–33.

could be seen.[31] Through his allusion to Charcot, Lacan under-mines not only the "simple" male solution to the phenomenon of feminine *jouissance*, but also the allied attempt to reduce it to that which can be captured in an image. And despite the contin-ued complaint by Irigaray and other commentators that Lacan ignores the evidence of the mystics themselves, he explicitly points the reader to them.

Unlike Irigaray, who mimes without citing female-authored mystical texts, Lacan, albeit again rather magisterially, calls his audience's attention to them.

> All the same there is a bit of a link when you read certain genuine people who might just happen to be women. I will, however, give you a hint, one which I owe to someone who had read it and very kindly brought it to me. I ensconced myself in it. I had better write up the name otherwise you won't buy it. It's Hadewijch d'Anvers, a Beguine, what we quaintly refer to as a mystic.[32]

Or again:

> These mystical ejaculations are neither idle gossip nor mere ver-biage, in fact they are the best thing you can read—note right at the bottom of the page, *Add the* Écrits *of Jacques Lacan*, which is of the same order.[33]

Not only does Lacan want his audience to read mystical texts, but he counts his own writings among them, partaking in what

---

[31] See Stephen Heath, "Difference," *Screen*, 19 (1978): 51–112, for refer-ences to Charcot (p. 57) and for criticisms of Lacan on this point (pp. 51–78). See also Irigaray, *This Sex Which Is Not One*, pp. 90–51; and David Macey, *Lacan in Context* (London: Verso, 1988), pp. 66–74, 177–209. Macey points to the importance of the images of hysterical women among the surrealists. See also Rosalind Krauss, *The Optical Unconscious* (Cambridge, Mass.: The MIT Press, 1993). Bataille uses the image of a male torture victim to spark his inner experience, yet one that has been read by some as feminine. See *Guilty*; and, for the images, see Michel Surya, *Georges Bataille, la mort à l'oeuvre* (Paris: Gallimard, 1992).

[32] Mitchell and Rose, eds., *Feminine Sexuality*, p. 146. Many commentators on this text seem to miss this reference. See Alice Jardine, *Gynesis: Configura-tions of Woman and Modernity* (Ithaca, N.Y.: Cornell University Press, 1985), p. 162, where she lists the women mentioned in the seminars and leaves out Hadewijch d'Anvers. See also Elizabeth Grosz, *Jacques Lacan: A Feminist In-troduction* (New York: Routledge, 1990), p. 146.

[33] Mitchell and Rose, eds., *Feminine Sexuality*, p. 147.

Michel de Certeau calls the mystic's *modus loquendi*.[34] To antici-
pate a bit: I think that this is a central aspect of Irigaray's disagreement with Lacan, for in placing his own texts with the
mystics', he asserts the possibility of the (male) psychoanalyst's
occupying the site of feminine *jouissance*. With this move, Irigaray argues, the specificity of the female body is sacrificed and
important political, social, economic, and material differences
are reduced to matters of writing and style.[35]

But before this critique can be elaborating on and evaluated,
the significance of Lacan's claims need to be uncovered. They
must be understood in light of his distinction between that goal
of analytic discourse that is capable of being formulated and the
allusion to some part of his discourse that resists delimitation.
This most obviously refers to the practice of psychoanalysis and
the discourse between the analyst and the analysand. I would
argue, however, that it also refers to a part of Lacan's writing
and performing practice that resists the very terms of analytic
discourse. Like Bataille, whose "scientific" or theoretical language is continually subverted by its own subject matter (that
which is radically other to reason), so throughout *Encore* Lacan
questions the very possibility of scientific psychoanalysis.
Throughout the seminar, Lacan insists on the inadequacy of analytic discourse in the face of feminine *jouissance* and the a. This
symbol, the Other crossed through, marks, in Jacqueline Rose's
formulation, the "place of *signifiance*, Lacan's term for this very
movement in language against, or away from, the positions of
coherence which language simultaneously constructs."[36]
Through this symbol, Lacan marks that which resists the mastery
of psychoanalytic discourse. He claims, moreover, that woman
relates to this place that resists coherence, totality, and meaning.
Within discourse, whether governed by the phallus or not (and
here Lacan argues for the historical contingency of the phallic
economy), there is both a point that fixes meaning (the transcendental signifier) and, allied to it, that which resists the fixing of
meaning.[37]

---

[34] See Michel de Certeau, *Heterologies*, trans. Brian Massumi (Minneapolis:
University of Minnesota Press, 1986).
[35] Irigaray, *This Sex Which Is Not One*, pp. 103–104.
[36] Mitchell and Rose, eds., *Feminine Sexuality*, p. 51.
[37] Catherine Clément, an early biographer of and commentator on Lacan, ar-

It might be argued with Irigaray,[38] then, that analytic discourse plays the role of a kind of negative theology and thus sets the stage for the emergence of feminine *jouissance* within and through language.[39] It works to expose the "false" images (*objet a*) that have become attached to the place of the Other. The fantasizing movement within the phallic economy, as Lacan shows, exists at the expense of women: "For the soul to come into being, she, the woman, is differentiated from it, and this has always been the case. Called woman (*dit-femme*) and defamed (*dif-fame*)."[40] In other words, woman is reduced to nothing at the same time as she serves as the foundation and substance of male immortality, being, the soul (*l'âme*) and love (*l'amour*).[41] The terms "passive" and "active," with which Freud attempts to replace the suspect (because essentialist and biological) *masculine* and *feminine*, like all concepts tied to the acquisition of knowledge, share "in the fantasy of inscribing a sexual tie."[42] Lacan argues that something comes out of this "which makes matter passive and form the agency which brings to life, namely, that this bringing to life, this animation, is nothing other than the *a*

gues: "From the impasse he himself describes, Lacan holds out one hope of exit, doubtless the only one: mysticism, the only legitimate means of transgression." Catherine Clément, *The Lives and Legends of Jacques Lacan*, trans. A. Goldhammer (New York: Columbia University Press, 1983), p. 174. As the abundance of mystical texts attests, this is a means of transgression through language.

[38] Irigaray, *This Sex Which Is Not One*, pp. 89, 103.

[39] The positive result of negation is one reason for the rejection of the term "negative theology" in favor of "apophasis" or "unsaying" by some contemporary scholars. See Michael Sells, *Mystical Languages of Unsaying* (Chicago: The University of Chicago Press, 1994).

[40] Mitchell and Rose, eds., *Feminine Sexuality*, p. 156. I would dispute Macey's claim that this is just another of Lacan's bud puns. Macey disputes any feminist appropriation of Lacan, apparently from the side of feminism. His understanding of the complexities of feminist theory, however, is limited, and his critiques of Lacan are based on misreadings and/or readings of his followers' texts rather than his own. His contextualization of Lacan within early French psychoanalysis and the surrealist movement is, however, important, as are his claims that Lacan must be read historically. If he were willing to see the historical developments within Lacan's corpus, his efforts would be better served.

[41] Lacan engages in a series of elaborate wordplays here, all dependent upon the *a*. Another is developed around the words for mastery and being.

[42] Mitchell and Rose, eds., *Feminine Sexuality*, p. 153. On knowledge as paranoic and as tied to the sexual relation, see Jonathon Lee, *Jacques Lacan* (Amherst: University of Massachusetts Press, 1990), pp. 28–29.

whose agency animates what?—it animates nothing, it takes the other for its soul."[43] The soul, then, that secures man's immortality, comes out of the *hommosexual* and the asexual (so the *a* of *la* is placed under erasure/sacrificed in order to give the *a* to *l'âme*). Thus, it follows that the God of this male economy is in the image of man. By separating the *objet a*, which is supported by the image of like to like, from the Other, the unknowable source and locus of signification and of the paternal metaphor, this identification is no longer possible.

The place of the Other within the symbolic, then, like that of woman within the patriarchal symbolic, is always double.

> Since all of this *feminine jouissance* comes about thanks to the being of *signifiance* [the site of both meaning and its loss], and since this being has no place other than the place of the Other which I designate with a capital O, one can see the cockeyedness of what happens. And since it is there too that the function of the father is inscribed in so far as this is the function to which castration refers, one can see that while this may not make for two Gods, nor does it make for one alone.[44]

Lacan's subsequent allusion to Kierkegaard and his jilted fiancée, Regine Olsen, elucidates the importance of exposing the double character of the Other, for it is only insofar as man recognizes the function of the father (within the phallic economy) as an obstacle and as the place of castration that he is able to renounce the fantasy of totality and sexual relation and move to the place of the woman and feminine *jouissance*.

Although Lacan, in separating the imaginary and the symbolic registers and exposing the fantasmatic character of the male relationship with the *objet a*, lays bare the character of the paternal metaphor as an obstacle to the imaginary unity of like to like, the very naming of that "castrating" principle as the Name-of-the-Father itself perpetuates the fantasy of male totality. This is why, I would argue, Lacan here insists (against his own earlier claims in the *Écrits*) on the contingency of both the phallic and the paternal functions; while the gap or lack at the root of subjectivity will remain (a position Irigaray seems at times to wish to chal-

---

[43] Mitchell and Rose, eds., *Feminine Sexuality*, p. 153.
[44] Ibid., p. 147.

lenge as the last vestige of phallic mastery and refusal of women's other possibilities), the male privilege with regard to fantasy and mastery that is inscribed within the patriarchal symbolic is not necessary to its operation.

The place of what is figured, within phallic discourse, as feminine *jouissance* is both within and beyond language. It belongs neither to the imaginary nor to the symbolic, but to the real (or at least opens up the possibility of the impossible real), which is the source of and result of the tension between these two registers. The coalescing of *a* and *A* is an attempt to reduce this tension, created by the continual disjunction between the lost fullness of imaginary self-presentations and the lack of being that marks humans within the symbolic—that wound, to use Bataille's term, necessary to human communication. Yet, for Bataille, language is precisely that which does not fully or adequately communicate. As Lacan argues, the sexual relation does not exist. The desire for full communication, for the radical immanence and continuity of "water in water,"[45] is, then, both engendered and denied by language and the position of humans within it. This creates the inescapable tension that the subject's confusion of part objects with the Other attempts to allay. This tension, according to Lacan, is the foundation of both the reality and the pleasure principles, which, despite their apparent opposition in Freud's text, work together in the construction of a "reality" always under the shadow of the imaginary. In dissociating the two, Lacan heightens this tension and creates a space for the emergence of the real in and through language, the emergence of a mystical *jouissance*. For Lacan, the gap in our being will always lend itself to the coalescing of imaginary plenitude and the human lack grounded in entry into the symbolic. In language itself, Lacan argues, "There is something of the One," the striving after that point which would fix meaning. While psychoanalytic discourse strives against this fantasy, it also explains it and the contingent form it has taken within a patriarchy governed by the Name-of-the-Father. While god may not be fully two, then, it is never entirely one, suggesting the necessary interrelationship

---

[45] This phrase, a startling precursor of Irigaray's language of fluids and fluidity, recurs throughout Bataille's *Theory of Religion*.

of God as One (or Father, within a phallic economy) and the sacred force of destabilizing *jouissance*. In the same way, although Lacan argues that psychoanalysis challenges the claims to mastery of science, it is also the source of pronouncements of a scientific (albeit primarily negative) form. Though Lacan wishes to argue that it is possible to do so without continuing to "subject women" to the "law of impotence" that marks the phallic economy,[46] this law may have more fully shaped the parameters of his thought than he himself wished to acknowledge.

The possibility of sexual relations—and the communication between persons this relationship symbolizes for Bataille, Lacan, and Irigaray—is, then, according to Lacan, dependent on the refusal of the fantasy of lost wholeness, yet the refusal of that fantasy is itself dependent on the recognition that the sexual relation never occurs.[47] Like many Christian mystical writers, through the deployment of this double paradigm Lacan attempts to subvert the laws of noncontradiction in order to point to or bring into being a new form of consciousness in which the real is manifested. The only possibility for human communication lies in living and writing this contradiction. Lacan's references to mystical texts, including his own, may thus point to a way through this logical and experiential impasse, yet Irigaray's explicit and implicit critiques of his thought suggest that, for her, Bataille, Lacan, and thinkers like them usurp women's voices through their claims to speak from the side of the "not all." Irigaray's concerns are crucial, yet, paradoxically, she is unable to account for history, and the voices of women within history, despite her claims to a greater materialism and concern for the specificity of women's bodies. Lacan, because he argues that both men and women can occupy the position of the male and the female speaking subject, is better able to account for the fact that women have spoken historically, and the multiple ways in which they have done so. What Irigaray's concerns highlight, however, is that when women and men speak from one or the other side of that divide between male and female created by male-dominated discourse, their relation to the penis/phallus—their having or not having it—makes an essential difference.

---

[46] Irigaray, *This Sex Which Is Not One*, p. 103.
[47] Lacan, *Encore*, p. 82.

In addition, Irigaray argues that Lacan's and Bataille's emphasis on castration, lack, and wounding creates a rhetoric of impotence a feminine imaginary might challenge. Put more positively (although Irigaray herself has not done so): it can be argued that she takes up the challenge of *Encore*, attempting to demonstrate how an imaginary grounded in a nonphallic morphology might empower women, serving as a support for their subjectivities, and/or might free all humans from the illusory plenitude (and all too real power) of a symbolic governed by the phallus. For Lacan (and, by implication, Bataille), Irigaray argues, women have no unconscious but are themselves the unconscious of the male symbolic—they serve as voiceless and unknowing emblems for the "truth" of male subjectivity. In giving voice to women's own imaginary, Irigaray seeks to challenge woman's emblematic status and the powerlessness to which it consigns women.

For example, in *Speculum*, a text that both marks her debt to Lacan and was the occasion for her rejection of/by him,[48] Irigaray reads and mimics the mystics much as Lacan does in *Encore*. This chapter, the only one in which Irigaray mimes *women's* voices, is at the center of the work as a whole. Given the chronological ordering followed in the second part of *Speculum*, the mysticism chapter should precede that on Descartes and hence occupy the exact structural center of the work as a whole; instead "La Mystérique" comes after Descartes. This chronological displacement both highlights the chapter's importance and raises issues about the relationship between the feminine imaginary (enflamed mirrors) and the origins of the modern symbolic subject in Descartes. Whereas Lacan insists that the imaginary is a retroactive creation of the symbolic, as in other places throughout her work, Irigaray questions Lacan and reopens the possibility of a presymbolic realm to which the subject might have access. Unlike Lacan (for whom the mystical marks access to the *real*), Irigaray makes clear the limits of these discourses for women (perhaps in part because she reads them as allied with

---

[48] It would be interesting to explore the history of Lacan's excommunications and those he enacted against his followers, including Irigaray. Given the importance of his own excommunications in the development of his thought, it might be that his denial of Irigaray marks the point of greatest respect and a "freeing" by the father from the father.

the *imaginary*). While recognizing the power, voice, and access to *jouissance* women historically have gained through their identification with lack and the wounded Christ, she points to political insufficiency of their challenges to patriarchal Christian culture.[49]

Some critics, of course, have felt that women, and in particular women's bodies, including the mystical bodies that occupy such an important position within *Speculum*, continue to occupy an "emblematic" role in Irigaray's work—and in ways that vitiate the political radicality of her thought.[50] Such readings (although not necessarily their political conclusions) are supported in part by Irigaray's insistence that what is elided in Lacan's usurpation of the place of the "not all" is the specificity of women's bodies. The reasons for this apparent "essentialism" are complex.[51] First, as Irigaray argues in texts like "Divine Women," until women have attained a strong imaginary and corresponding relation to a new symbolic, they will never have real political, social, and economic power. She suggests, furthermore, that because women are culturally identified with their bodies they must move through these (reinterpreted and reevaluated) bodies in order to attain subjectivity. So, secondly, as Margaret Whitford suggests,[52] Irigaray's references to the specificity of the female body—the lips and the mucous membrane—are meant to offer new ways to imagine the subject-in-process without positing woundedness and castration. By creating a new imaginary based

---

[49] Further attention should be given to the reading of Christ and Apollo through Nietzsche in Marine Lover and to the full text of *L'oubli de l'air*, from which portions of "Belief Itself" are taken. These texts question the very possibility of "emblems." See Luce Irigaray, *Marine Lover of Friedrich Nietzsche*, trans. Gillian C. Gill (New York: Columbia University Press, 1991); and Luce Irigaray, *L'oubli de l'air chez Martin Heidegger* (Paris: Minuet, 1983).

[50] I make this argument with specific reference to mysticism in "Beauvoir, Irigaray, and the Mystical," *Hypatia*, 9 (1994): 158–85.

[51] Much has been made, on both sides, of Irigaray's reputed essentialism. On the issue, see the essays collected in *Engaging with Irigaray: Feminist Philosophy and Modern European Thought*, ed. Carolyn Burke, Naomi Schor, and Margaret Whitford (New York: Columbia University Press, 1994).

[52] Whitford, "Irigaray's Body Symbolic." In the larger study, I plan to trace these figures as they are deployed in *This Sex Which Is Not One*, "The Limits of the Transference" in *Sexes and Genealogies*, and *An Ethics of Sexual Difference*, trans. Gillian C. Gill (Ithaca, N.Y.: Cornell University Press, 1993).

on the morphology of the female body rather than that of the male body, Irigaray takes up the challenge posed by Lacan in *Encore*. Through these figures, then, Irigaray's texts reinscribe the dialectic of transcendence and immanence within and on the "mystical" body, creating the possibility of a sensible transcendental.[53]

Certain questions remain, however, ones epitomized in the tension between Irigaray's call for a feminine divine (paralleling that for a feminine imaginary) in "Divine Women" and her deconstruction of belief and its object in "Belief Itself."[54] In Lacanian terms, one is led to ask whether Irigaray's call for the divinization of women does not rest on a denial of the gap between the imaginary and the symbolic similar to that effected by men within patriarchy. Insofar as Irigaray claims that the violence of sacrifice will be overcome through such a reimagining, and insofar as she rejects entirely Lacan's "law of impotence," Irigaray seems to partake in just such a fantasy. Yet, while Irigaray's utopic drive runs this risk, one might argue that there *is* a difference between the "male" desire to fill a gaping wound in being through the death and fetishization of the mother and the openness to communication symbolized by the fluidity of the mucous membrane. The feminine imaginary opens the subject to the possibility of risk without demanding a faith in the closure of a life-threatening wound. Moreover, it might be necessary to risk belief in order to create a new imaginary and symbolic. Perhaps the fantasy of wholeness is *necessary* to women's full subjectivities (even if this belief is subject to eventual deconstruction, as in "Belief Itself"). As I have suggested, a central question is whether there is something in the feminine imaginary that *invites* such deconstruction more readily than the male does—and whether the feminine imaginary is able to function without the subjugation of the other seemingly so necessary to the phallic

---

[53] The Kantian heritage and ramifications of this term need to be further unpacked.

[54] The same tension can be described in terms of that between wonder and self-love, as they are described in Irigaray, *Ethics of Sexual Difference*. See Serene Jones, "Divining Women: Irigaray and Feminist Theologies," *Yale French Studies*, 87 (1995): 42–67.

economy.[55] To pose the question from another angle, we might ask with Lacan whether the new imaginary and symbolic will generate a single divine woman or rather god(s) who are not quite double and yet also not one.

Irigaray accords primacy to the founding of female subjectivity—through a feminine divine—at the same time claiming that subjectivity itself, and by implication divinity, is masculine and must be radically rethought. The sacred as rethought by Bataille and Lacan (and seemingly by Irigaray in certain texts) is also tainted by the masculine economy insofar as it is grounded in an economy of impotence, lack, and sacrifice. Yet clearly a return to the unity of the "good old God" does not fit with Irigaray's ethical and political aims. Rather, Irigaray demands that the imaginary, the symbolic, and the sacred be rethought from the side of women—for whom, she argues, the "not all" is a mark of openness and fluidity rather than lack. Thus, whereas Feuerbach's humanism made him unable to accept the limitations of humanity (hence, his positing of a species being in which divine attributes can unproblematically reside), and Bataille's and Lacan's masculinist imaginary and symbolic posit openness as lack and suf-

---

[55] Attention to the language of vertical and horizontal relations in Irigaray's work generates a graphic account of how this might occur. Within traditional Western religion, hierarchical relations exist among the three:

God
|
man
|
woman

Here God both supports male subjectivity and demonstrates man's lack. Therefore, man must posit woman as the other who is lacking, the part object that fills the lack in his being and/or serves as that against which he is whole.

To subvert this, Irigaray argues that woman should posit herself as a fluid subject-in-process in relation to an open, fluid, noncastrating divine:

God—man—woman

or, perhaps, given Irigaray's insistence that the vertical relation must not be lost:

god—the communication between the two
|
man—woman

Stockton suggests something like this in her readings of Irigaray. See her "'God' Between Their Lips."

fering rather than as possibility, Irigaray inscribes the limitations and fluidity of the human person within an imaginary that divinizes precisely such an always fragile humanity.[56]

According to Irigaray the feminine divine will make sexual, and other, relations possible within an economy grounded neither in use nor in sacrifice, but rather in openness to the demand of (the) other(s).[57] By contextualizing Irigaray's work and beginning to show its relationship to that of Lacan, and through him Bataille (although they are strong linguistic and metaphorical echoes between Bataille and Irigaray as well), we can see one rather unexpected source for Irigaray's insistence on the primacy of sexual difference, one that raises a final question about the political and ethical valence of Irigaray's claims. "The sexual relation," for both Bataille and Lacan (as well as for the surrealist and other avant-garde movements in France with which they were associated), metaphorically serves to represent the (im)possibilities of human communication and community. Insofar as they thought this relationship solely from the side of the masculine, Irigaray attempts to speak the feminine. The potentially radical possibility that difference should not be thought primarily or solely according to the male/female heterosexual couple remains unimagined (and implicitly rejected) in her more recent work.[58]

---

[56] In a larger study, I will give attention to the divergent readings of Christ engendered by these positions. Whereas Bataille celebrates the sacrifice, he deplores the "femininity" of a Christ who accepts his suffering with humility. The remains of a Nietzschean defiance and antifeminism can be seen clearly here, despite Bataille's implicit embrace of a "feminized" position within some texts. Lacan, on the other hand, interprets Christ from the position of the male speaking subject for whom he is feminized, an *objet a* whose death ensures the life of the Father god. Irigaray, while deploring the sacrificial economy in which the figure of (an always feminized) Christ has been inscribed, suggests another reading, in which the possibilities of the incarnation are brought to the forefront. Such a Christ, it could be argued, marks the "death" of the Father God and the emergence of God's "other face"—one pointed to by Lacan as well. See Bataille, *Inner Experience* and *Guilty*; Lacan, *Encore*, and Irigaray, *Marine Lover*.

[57] The theoretical debt to and critique of Levinas will have to be the subject of another essay. See also Grosz, *Sexual Subversions*, pp. 155–58.

[58] Irigaray's early work has been taken as lesbian theory, yet the concern for relations between men and women clearly predominate in the middle and later work. For the relationship between homosexuality and heterosexuality in Irigaray, and a defense of her focus on women as an analytic category, see Elizabeth Grosz, "The Hetero and the Homo: The Sexual Ethics of Luce Irigaray,"

Irigaray implies that to do this once again silences women. But does this have to be the case? And who is silenced by Irigaray's focus on the heterosexual relation? Perhaps thinking both with and against Irigaray may enable us to theorize multiple differences, thereby giving voice to women in all their diversity.

---

in *Engaging with Irigaray*, pp. 335–50. The problems this focus causes with regard to the elision of racial, ethnic, class, and other differences remains.

10

"Christian Philosophy": Hermeneutic or Heuristic?

Jean-Luc Marion

THE REASONS FOR AN APORIA

CONCEPTS ARE MORTAL, TOO. They can die or at least become aporias. Isn't the concept of "Christian philosophy" undergoing this fate today, pointing only to a way that leads nowhere anymore, an abandoned yard, a dead discipline? But do we have to renounce "Christian philosophy" on the simple pretext that we cannot think it anymore? Shouldn't we, instead, increase our efforts to think it afresh?

Before we go any further, let us recall the principal aporia that still characterizes "Christian philosophy" today. It appeared during a debate created between 1927 and 1931 by the position taken by the excellent French historian and philosopher Émile Bréhier. His thesis can be summarized as follows: Christianity has often used philosophies, very diverse ones, but has never created or assimilated any of them, because there is an "incompatibility," or, at least, a radical "separation," between clear and distinct reason and the mystery of a relationship between God and the human person.[1] Both excessive and provocative, this position nonetheless required clarification, once again, of the relation between philosophy and Christian theology—is it an

---

[1] Émile Bréhier, "Y-a-t-il une philosophie chrétienne?" *Revue de Métaphysique et de Morale* (April 1931); and a first discussion in the *Bulletin de la Société Française de Philosophie*, 1932. See the brilliant summary of this debate by Henri de Lubac, "Sur la philosophie chrétienne," *Nouvelle Revue Théologique*, 63, No. 3 (March 1936), 225–53, published in English as "Retrieving the Tradition: On Christian Philosophy," *Communio*, 19, No. 3 (Fall 1992), 478–506.

incompatibility, partial stand-off, or continuity? We might have expected that Catholics (if not all Christians) would uphold, against Bréhier, the theoretical legitimacy and historical reality of such a "Christian philosophy," leaving to nonbelievers the task of challenging it. The distribution of the roles was more complex, however. Some Catholics held that, "in the sense in which we usually understand it, there is no *Catholic philosophy*, any more than there is a *Catholic science*";[2] but this thesis—which was typical of the school of Louvain, for whom Aristotelian Thomism imposes itself on Catholics not because of its Christianity, but because of its strict truth—rediscovered the initial position of Jacques Maritain that only an extrinsic relation exists between the faith of the Christian thinker and his or her philosophy.[3] Even better, it also agrees with the non-Thomistic and non-Scholastic thought of Maurice Blondel: ". . . this term 'Christian philosophy' does not exist any more than Christian physics does."[4] In this way Catholic thinkers managed to reject "Christian philosophy" by using the argument of its non-Christian opponents, from Feuerbach to Heidegger: this is a contradictory syntagma, a "square circle," an "iron-wood."[5] From this it follows that the concept of "Christian philosophy" can appear to be as problematic to believers (non-Thomistic as well as Thomis-

---

[2] Maurice de Wulf, *Introduction à la philosophie néo-scolastique* (Paris: Publisher, 1904), cited in an excellent anthology of the present positions by Étienne Gilson, as an appendix to his first contribution to the debate. See Gilson's *L'esprit de la philosophie médiévale* (Paris: J. Vrin, 1932), p. 430.

[3] See Bréhier's discussion in the *Bulletin de la Société Française de Philosophie* (1932), 59.

[4] M. Blondel, "Les exigences rationnelles de la pensée contemporaine en matière d'apologétique et la méthode de la philosophie dans l'étude du problème religieux," *Annales de philosophie chrétienne* (May 1896), 34. It is true that Blondel evolved on this topic as he did on others.

[5] L. Feuerbach, *Sämmtliche Werke*. VIII. *Vorlesungen über das Wesen der Religion*, ed. Wilhelm Bollin Friedrich Jodl, and Hans-Martin Sass (Stuttgart: F. Fromann, 1903), pp. 58ff.; Martin Heidegger, *Gesamtausgabe* XLVIII (Frankfurt: Klostermann, 1986), p. 162 (see *Dieu sans l'être* ([Paris: Fayard, 1982; repr. Paris: Presses Universitaires de France, 1991] pp. 91ff. = *God Without Being*, trans. Thomas A. Carlson [Chicago: The University of Chicago Press, 1991], chap. 3, pp. 61ff.). There is also Husserl's way of putting God "out of circulation" (*Ideen* I, §58). This thesis was prolonged until recently, for example, in J. Beaufret, "La philosophie chrétienne, in *Dialogue avec Heidegger* II (Paris: Éditions de Minuit, 1973), or "Heidegger et la théologie," in M. Couratier, ed. *Étienne Gilson et nous* (Paris: J. Vrin, 1980).

tic) as to nonbelievers. The question remains entirely open, because the responses do not depend on the theological options. Should we withdraw from it?

ÉTIENNE GILSON'S DEFINITION: "CHRISTIAN PHILOSOPHY" AS HERMENEUTIC

These uncertainties notwithstanding, one formal definition upheld the use of this concept. We owe it to the almost sole initiative of Étienne Gilson: "I call Christian philosophy all philosophy that, while formally distinguishing between the two orders, considers Christian revelation to be an indispensable auxiliary of reason."[6] This definition can, indeed, be understood as having two meanings. Gilson, for his part, often explained that "Christian philosophy" exists whenever revelation makes suggestions to reason, without substituting itself for reason or modifying reason's requirements, in order to broach themes rationally that reason could not handle by itself or even suspect. He gave as an example the concept of creation. But, from this point of view, one might just as well have suggested the concepts of the Eucharist, which became a philosophical theme for Descartes and Leibniz, of grace for Malebranche or Leibniz, of the inspiration of the scriptures for Spinoza, or of Christology as a whole for Hegel and Schelling. Even more, should we not also qualify as "Christian philosophy" all philosophy that opposes itself to Christian revelation and, precisely in order to criticize it in detail, does not stop calling upon revelation as upon an "indispensable auxiliary of reason"? Is this not, essentially, the case with Feuerbach and Nietzsche, who, methodologically at least, are no different from medievalists, insofar they apply reason to the given that is revealed?

It is clear that Gilson intended his definition to have a much more restricted meaning: Christian revelation intervenes as an "auxiliary," not because it would offer to reason themes that otherwise would be unreachable, but because it offers a radically

---

[6] Gilson, *L'esprit de la philosophie médiévale*, p. 33, formula repeated and defended again in *Christianisme et philosophie* (Paris: J. Vrin, 1949), p. 138.

original interpretation of them—that of the revelation of Christ. In other words: in the most well-known thesis of Étienne Gilson, "la métaphysique de l'*Exode*," "Christian philosophy" contends that the quasi-Aristotelian concept of *actus purus essendi* is equivalent to a purely theological and biblical statement, *Sum qui sum* (Ex. 3:14). Let us accept this equivalency as an hypothesis. Let us, then, question the operation, in this very privileged case, that is accomplished by "Christian philosophy." It consists in *interpreting* a philosopheme as a divine name (and the first): but this philosopheme would remain intelligible, and endowed with its meaning, even if it were not interpreted as an equivalent to such a theological theme—*actus purus essendi* could *not* interpret the God from the Exodus, and it has, indeed, not denoted it for all the non-Thomistic Aristotelians, medieval or modern. Inversely, "Christian philosophy" also could *not* interpret the *esse* as the first of the divine names (and replace it with a simple concept as Scotus did), or privilege other transcendentals, such as the *bonum* (according to the prevalent tradition until St. Bonaventure). In short, the assistance from which "Christian philosophy" benefits consists in a theological interpretation of purely philosophical concepts, which is possible but not necessary.

There are, of course, plenty of examples of this kind of "Christian philosophy" which proceeds from a Christian interpretation of philosophical theses: St. Augustine built his entire doctrine of the images of the Trinity within us on the possibility of interpreting the faculties of the soul *memoria/intellectus/amor* as the indication of the Trinity within us; to support the vision of ideas in the Word, Malebranche interprets Cartesian innation in theological terms as innation in the Creator. We know the Christian interpretations of Platonism, stoicism, skepticism, and even Epicureanism well enough to exempt ourselves from demonstrating how the Gilsonian definition of "Christian philosophy" also applies to them. The *preparatio evangelica*, initially reserved for Platonism, can be generalized to all philosophy, depending on the talent of the interpreter. Such has historically been the case. Maurice Blondel has to be regarded as one of the most perfect examples of this process when he pretends always to be able to read transcendence in immanence—"the immanent affirmation of transcendence"[7]—and to extricate the supernatural "necessarily" from nature: "I feel more and more drawn toward the design of showing . . . the natural necessity of the supernatural and the supernatural reality of the natural itself."[8] There is more: it is theology itself that, in one of the richest trends of this century, made the method of immanence its own, and hence the hermeneutics that defines "Christian philosophy" according to Gilson. Indeed, this was the at least tacit presupposition of the dispute about de Lubac's *Supernatural*—(should natural desire be interpreted as a real capacity to see God?), of analogy according to E. Pzywara (should the *analogia entis* be interpreted as a Trinitarian determination?), and, above all, of Karl Rahner's theology (should the passage of the finite being to the infinite being be interpreted as the theoretical place of Christology? should the nonbeliever be interpreted as "anonymous Christian"? does the evolution of "terrestrial realities" allow interpretation of them as "signs of the times," themselves announcers of the coming of the kingdom of God?). These few examples quickly enumerated, but very significant, show sufficiently—if we retain Gilson's definition that "all philosophy that, while formally distinguishing the two orders, considers Christian revelation as an indispensable auxiliary of reason"—that "Christian philosophy" is neither fragile nor marginal in our century. On the contrary, it appears to be the privileged method of a dominant part of Christian and Catholic thought. From de Lubac to Rahner, from Gilson to Blondel—until Lonergan and Moltmann, Mascall and Tracy, even Ricoeur—our century has been, by far, that of "Christian philosophy" as hermeneutic.

THE INDETERMINATION OF "CHRISTIAN PHILOSOPHY"
AS HERMENEUTICAL

As impressive as its partisans are, as important as its results may appear, as venerable as the method of *preparatio evangelica*

---

[7] Maurice Blondel, *Lettre sur les exigences de la pensée contemporaine en matière d'apologétique* (Paris: Presses Universitaires de France, 1956), p. 40.

[8] Blondel, *Carnets intimes* (Paris: Presses Universitaires de France, 1961), pp. 525ff.

which it continues remains, this definition of "Christian philosophy" as hermeneutical nevertheless remains highly controversial. I see at least three arguments that bring it into question.

(1) If "Christian philosophy" can be reduced to a hermeneutic, from the point of view of the revelation of concepts and thus of (supposed) realities already acquired by strict philosophy, it remains secondary, derivative, even elective in comparison with one instance, philosophy, the only original and inventive one. *Actus purus essendi* can also be thought without its interpretation as *Sum qui sum*, since that was the way Aristotle thought it. The triad *memoria/intellectus/amor* can be thought without its Trinitarian interpretation, since that was the way Plotinus thought it. The strictly interpretative definition of "Christian philosophy," therefore, responds to Bréhier's objection only by conceding to it the essential: this supposed "philosophy" limits itself to comment and merely repeats the results of the strict philosophy, which is not Christian. To reduce "Christian philosophy" to a hermeneutic amounts to denying it the level of philosophy.

(2) If "Christian philosophy" is limited to a hermeneutic, even (and mainly) from the point of view of Christian revelation, it becomes subject to the suspicions that weigh on all hermeneutics. Two principles are involved. (*a*) Why privilege the interpretation based on Christian revelation, when others are possible? Marx, brutally but forcefully, made this point: poverty can be interpreted as a virtue, but also as an economic phenomenon linked to the capitalist conditions of production. Why select one interpretation over the other? Why deny the second in the name of the first? The objection is so strong that a good part of Christian theology and of the accompanying "Christian philosophy" is still in the process of responding to it a century after Marx. (*b*) Why take the interpretation based on Christian revelation for what it pretends to be? Every interpretation obeys reasons that differ or may differ in an essential way from those it knowingly invokes. These masked reasons for the interpretation may come forth from unconscious desire (Freud), from "will of verity," that is, the "will to power" (Nietzsche), ideology (Marx), etc. Only the result is important: an interpretation cannot be justified by what it says about itself, but usually by what it does not say. Nietzsche summarized this suspicion in the following principle:

"There are no moral phenomena, only moral interpretation of these phenomena."[9] This applies to the hermeneutics of "Christian philosophy" according to the principle that there is no Christian philosophy, merely a Christian interpretation of philosophy, which then has to justify itself, not because of what it says about itself, but because of what it does not say. From then on, contra-hermeneutics becomes possible, which reverses point by point the hermeneutics of "Christian philosophy." Two examples will suffice: (*a*) the philosophical definition of "God" as "moral God" (Kant, Fichte) can be interpreted as an image of the Christian God or, on the contrary, as what leads to the "death of God" (which is the way Feuerbach, Bauer, Marx, and Nietzsche understood it); (*b*) the definition of "God" as *causa sui* (Descartes) can be interpreted as an image of the Christian God or, on the contrary, as his favorite metaphysical idol (Heidegger). Such contra-hermeneutics results directly from, on one hand, the modern critique of all hermeneutics and, on the other, the definition of "Christian philosophy" as one hermeneutic among others. As a result, the "auxiliary" of revelation is no longer insurmountable. In other words, reducing "Christian philosophy" to a hermeneutic leads to branding it as arbitrary.

(3) The hermeneutic definition of "Christian philosophy" must, according to Gilson, "formally distinguish the two orders" of philosophy and theology, of nature and grace, the known and the revealed. But can it do this? For it to be possible that the interpretation of one be in the light of the other, must it not already be supposed that certain specifically Christian truths are at least already *in nuce* and powerful in the statements of the strict philosophy (or "natural," if one can use that term)? How far can this preestablished convention go? Throughout the history of philosophy the quarrel about the supernatural has never ceased to reappear every time the hermeneutic of "Christian philosophy" succeeds too well: on the topic of double beatitude, the correctness of free will, the disinterested love of God, the intelligibility of divine ends, the meaning of history, etc. In each case, the danger consisted in taking revelation for a simple implication of nature and thus of philosophy. To reduce "Christian philosophy"

---

[9] Friedrich Nietzsche, *Par delà le bien et le mal*, §108.

to a hermeneutic thus exposes it to missing the specificity of creation and, not in the least, of revelation—by locking faith in its *preambula.*

This triple result does not automatically lead us to renounce all "Christian philosophy," not even the definition proposed by Gilson, but it does force us to contest that "Christian philosophy" be defined exclusively as a hermeneutic.

THE DETERMINATION OF "CHRISTIAN PHILOSOPHY" AS HEURISTIC

How else can we define it? When taking into account more precisely the "auxiliary" that distinguishes it absolutely from any other kind of philosophy, Gilson calls it, without more precision, "Christian revelation." This revelation summarizes itself in Christ. But Christ exercises on the world and its wisdom a hermeneutic—by his teaching and, in the end, by his judgment (Luke 24:27)—only because of an entirely different characteristic: his radical newness, his unsurpassable innovation. "Omnem novitatem attulit, seipsum afferens"—He introduced all newness by introducing himself.[10] If Christ reveals what has always been hidden—the mystery of God—and makes all things new—"Now I am making the whole of creation new" (Revelation 21:5)—it is because he himself constitutes all newness, because he comes from God's bosom, from the world that had its being through him, and that, for that very reason, "did not know him" (John 1:10). His revelation introduced realities and phenomena into the world, which never had been seen or known there before him; even the sketches of the Old Covenant would have remained, without his newness, unintelligible—the sanctity, the forgiveness, the resurrection, the communion, etc. With Christ, a newness lives in the world which is not of the world—"the new heavens and the new earth" (2 Peter 3:13). Revelation interprets only in the context of Christ's Trinitarian innovation.

In what does Christ's innovation consist? That he makes manifest that "God is love" (1 John 4:18). This opening, absolutely without common measure among previous representations of di-

---

[10] Irenaeus of Lyons, *Contra Haereses* 4.34.1.

vinity, determines the domain of theology: charity. Charity deploys itself immediately in the character of Christ where it appears carnally, mediately in the Trinity from which it deduces its interpersonal profoundness, and, as a derivative, in the Church where the Son of the Father recapitulates in the Spirit human beings as his adopted brothers and sisters. These are, in the strict sense, the *revelata*, which belong only to theology, and which philosophy, even when it is supposed to be "Christian," need not discuss.

However, apart from its theological use, charity has purely theoretical effects on the horizon of rationality. It opens up, as a new theoretical continent to be explored, what Pascal called the "order of charity,"[11] in opposition to the order of "carnal grandeurs" (all the powers of bodies, politics, economics, the imagination, etc.) and to the order of the "spirits" (the sciences, the arts, etc.). The order of charity, which concerns love in all its facets, dominates the other two and, for that reason, remains less visible and known than they do; indeed, according to an essential paradox, no order can know, or see, a superior order (even if an order knows itself and can see all inferior orders). Charity, the supreme order, thus remains invisible to the flesh and to the spirit, to powers and to sciences. The result is that charity opens a field of new phenomena to knowledge, but this field remains invisible to natural reason alone. That is why philosophy needs an "indispensable auxiliary" in order to gain access to it, revelation: because it is revelation, as the revelation of charity, which offers perfectly rational phenomena to philosophy, although they belong to charity and are as new as it is. We find here again the definition of "Christian philosophy" by Étienne Gilson: all philosophy that, while formally distinguishing the differences of the orders (in the meaning of Pascal), considers Christian revelation (understood as revelation of charity, thus the third order) as an indispensable auxiliary of reason. But from now on, the "auxiliary" brought by revelation not only assists in providing a new interpretation of phenomena that are already visible, but also makes visible phenomena that would have remained invisible without it. "Christian philosophy" is not practiced as a simple

---

[11] Pascal, *Pensées* (Paris: Garnier/Flammarion, 1973), §306.

hermeneutic, eventually ideological, of a natural "given" already accessible to reason without revelation; it offers entirely new natural phenomena to reason, which reason discovers because revelation invents them for it and shows them to it; reason is practiced as heuristic. Étienne Gilson's proposed definition of "Christian philosophy" thus can be understood a second time not as hermeneutic but as heuristic. And, because Gilson did not clearly distinguish the two possible meanings of his thesis, or their profound difference, we will suppose that in going from one to the other we will remain under the patronage of this great philosopher.

As a matter of fact, the heuristic definition of "Christian philosophy" brings up a difficulty that Étienne Gilson often discussed: that revelation—that is, the revelation of charity—would contribute to the appearance of phenomena, which are new and visible only through charity, thus invisible without it. Charity nevertheless would entrust them not only to theology (the science of the *revelata*), but also to philosophy, that is, to knowledge ruled only by natural light. In short, the heuristic of charity would provide phenomena uncovered by revelation to a purely natural philosophy. As a consequence, between theology (supernatural) and philosophy (natural), "Christian philosophy" would introduce a mix: a knowledge that would discuss under natural light facts discovered under supernatural light. All the difficulties of this paradox are concentrated into one: the mix of natural and supernatural, or of revelation and philosophy, does not respect the distinction of the orders. "Christian philosophy" compromises theology as much as philosophy, because its concept is contradictory.

Giving a complete response is, of course, impossible here, but it is possible to give a few examples. Because the question of entitlement to the borders between the disciplines may in the last instance be reduced to questions of rights regarding the real objects of these disciplines; can one justify "Christian philosophy" by its formal object? We will be able to do so if we succeed in describing one or several phenomena given *in* natural experience and not *by* it, but by the "order of charity" or revelation. The most convincing example relates not to God, or the world, but to the human person him- or herself—in other words, the phenomenon of the human being, that is, of his or her natural visibility, which is concentrated in his or her face. One would not deny that this is a phenomenon in its own right, accessible by natural experience to natural reason. But it is not sufficient merely to look at a face in order to see the other that is exposed in it, we see the face of the slave without being able to recognize the other in his or her own right; we also can face another face and coldly kill it; we also can use our own faces to dissimulate ourselves under masks and hide them from visibility; we even can expose our faces only to lie, hurt, or destroy. In short, the face can objectivize itself, hide itself, not appear. This is why it was not sufficient for ancient thought to settle on the term (theatrical or juridical) *persona* in order to obtain access to the concept of person: it lacked the discovery of the primacy, in this unique case, of relation over substantiality, such as only Trinitarian theology conquered. The face becomes really the phenomenon of a human being when it makes a person appear, who is essentially defined as the knot and the origin of his or her relationships. If seeing a face implies reading a net of relationships in it, I will see it only if I experience an "indefinite idea" (Emanuel Levinas), that is, this center of relationships which cannot be objectivized or reduced to me. Experiencing the infinite on the face of another cannot be expressed in a formula; it is a behavior that is experimentally verifiable: facing a face disfigured (by poverty, sickness, pain, etc.) or reduced to its extreme shapes (prenatal life, coma, agony, etc.), I either cannot see it, or any longer recognize another for myself in it, and continue on my way, or I still can *see* in it what I do not see in it naturally—the absolute phenomenon of another center in the world, where my lookalike lives and whose look upon me allows me to live, thanks to him or her. But in this case, to *see* this invisible face, I must *love* it. Love, however, comes from charity, that is, through the "auxiliary" of revelation. Without the revelation of the transcendency of love, the phenomenon of the face, and thus of the other, simply cannot be seen. This is an exemplary case of "Christian philosophy."

In this way, I have attempted to justify the paradox of "Christian philosophy" through its formal object, one of its own phenomena, in order to solve a question of rights (the possibility of an intermediary between philosophy and theology) through a factual answer. It is conceivable that the legitimacy of such a "Christian philosophy" will be guaranteed only by the new phenomena that it would, all by itself, be able to add to the phenomena already treated in philosophy. As a consequence, Christian philosophy would remain acceptable only as long as it invents—in the sense of both discovering and constructing—heretofore unseen phenomena. In short, "Christian philosophy" dies if it repeats, defends, and preserves something acquired which is already known, and remains alive only if it discovers that which, without it, would remain hidden in philosophy.

The Legitimacy of a "Christian Philosophy" as a Heuristic of Charity

Even if one admits that only a heuristic theory of charity can invent concepts such as "person" or "face," one still must examine several legitimate objections to this image of "Christian philosophy." I do not intend to resolve them thoroughly in this essay, but I will at least identify them and outline some responses.

First objection: the above example of "person" or "face" does not prove anything more than a simple tautology. The heuristic that starts with charity discovers some phenomena of charity, of course; but charity only keeps finding itself under other names; and this is why the distance between charity and love matters very little. The heuristic of charity will arrive at real philosophical validity only if it produces concepts of phenomena other than itself. This objection deserves all the more attention when you consider that the response allows you to confirm the heuristic scope of charity. To do this, let us examine three of the many concepts and phenomena that charity has discovered in philosophy.

(a) First, history that is, not only linear and nonrepetitive temporality, which innovates continually by determining irremediable facts forever, but also a temporality free of any fate, when every individual or collective action makes manifest the will of its actor, which judges him- or herself this way in the face of his or her time, the future, and God. Understood in this way, one can risk that history is born as a concept by St. Augustine, who, starting from the History of Salvation of the Christian revelation, discovered in the non-Christian world a history which until then had been ignored by philosophy and was unthought as such.

(*b*) Second, the icon: starting from the revelation of Christ as "icon of the invisible God" (Col. 1:10) and the method of figuration of his elaborated face by Western as well as Eastern painters and sculptors, Christian tradition tended to think and show the paradox of a look, by itself as invisible as any look, which would not be reduced to the level of the object seen, but would imagine the one [look] which looks at him or her: this dialogue in the visible of two invisible looks allows us, then, not only to see prayer, but to enter into it. This is, in other words, the experience of a return look crossing mine. However, beginning with this paradigm, we were able to introduce into phenomenology a concept that was ignored as much by Husserl as by Heidegger and the absence of which precludes almost totally the phenomenology of intersubjectivity—that of contra-intentionality. The intentionality of the *I* can know only objects and objectivizes the other, thus missing it; in order for the other to appear as other, as a nonobject, it would need to be seen as another intentionality, weighing on me; and this contra-intentionality is thought from the icon, the only concept we have to define it; the icon of the face of the other thus becomes an intelligible phenomenon starting from the invention of Christ as icon.

(*c*) As a last example of a heuristic of charity, I shall rely on the authority, uncontested on the matter of rationalism, of Kant, who defines belief (*Glaube*) as "the moral way of thinking of reason in its assent to what is inaccessible to theoretical knowledge." Under these circumstances belief in "what is necessary to presuppose as a condition for the possibility of the final supreme moral goal," he adds a note:

the word *fides* expresses this already; but the introduction of this expression and this particular idea in moral philosophy could seem suspect, because they were first introduced by Christianity, and to imitate them could seem to be a flattering imitation of its language. But this is not a unique case, because this beautiful religion, in the supreme simplicity of its style, has enriched philosophy with moral concepts much more determined and much purer than those that [philosophy] had been able to produce until then; and these concepts, since they are there now, are *freely* approved by reason and admitted as concepts that it could have and should have discovered and introduced by itself.[12]

Nothing needs to be added to this admirable text, except to correct its last sentence: it is exactly because it "should have" rather than "could have" invented these concepts that philosophy had to receive them from the Christian religion, through the intermediary of what we dare call a heuristic of charity.

Second objection: on the supposition that certain phenomena and concepts become accessible to reason only through the "indispensable auxiliary" of revelation, do they really belong to philosophy or to revelation? The response is evident: the concepts and phenomena obtained in the light of revelation remain acquired by philosophy in the strict sense, to the extent that once they have been discovered they are accessible to reason as such; the concepts of face, person, history, faith, and so on, function philosophically even without the Christian convictions of their user. And this is why they may find themselves turned against their origin by non-Christian ideas. The heuristic of charity itself is charitable: what it finds, it gives without confiscating. And in this sense, the whole of philosophy could be called "Christian philosophy," so much is it saturated with concepts and phenomena that were introduced in it, directly or indirectly, by revelation. In this sense, Heidegger, Nietzsche, Marx, or Feuerbach practice as much "Christian philosophy" as Leibniz, Hegel, Schelling, or Husserl does. Recognizing the imprint of Christian revelation on philosophy, and thus the heuristic function of "Christian philosophy" in it, does not depend on a subjective conviction, believing or atheistic: it is about facts, which any competent historian of philosophy knows thoroughly. We can almost sustain the following paradox: the possibility that a "Christian philosophy" nearly comes naturally, whereas that of a philosophy which has absolutely no connection to the Christian revelation seems, in our historical situation, highly problemati-

---

[12] Immanuel Kant, *Kritik der Urteilskraft*, §91 and note 4 ad loc. I owe this reference to de Lubac, "Sur la philosophie chrétienne," 481, which refers to L. Brunschvicg, *La raison et la religion* (Paris: F. Alcan, 1939), p. 166.

cal. In short, how could a philosopher, if he or she really thinks about the major problems of philosophy, not practice "Christian philosophy" (if only to criticize it)?

Third objection: how does this new situation, made in the manner of "Christian philosophy," respect the formal distinction of the two orders, natural and supernatural? The first answer is that the Incarnation results in the questioning of this distinction, which from then on becomes more abstract than real. But the distinction must be maintained at least in regard to the disciplines. Here no confusion is possible: (*a*) theology deploys the discourse of charity from and about the *revelata* in the strict sense, that is, truths that only faith can reach; (*b*) philosophy discusses facts, phenomena, and statements accessible to reason and its workings; and (*c*) "Christian philosophy" finds and invents in the natural sphere, which is ruled by reason, phenomena and concepts that are answerable in the order of charity and that simple reason cannot see or discover. After having formalized them, "Christian philosophy" introduces them into philosophy and abandons them to it. This distinction between the roles demands only one presupposition: that charity, as grace, can be at the same time natural (created) and supernatural (uncreated). Theologians accept this presupposition, whereas pure philosophers apriori cannot forbid what may be proven experimentally.

Fourth objection: does the heuristic determination of "Christian philosophy" reject its more common hermeneutic definition entirely? At this point we know very clearly that the former is not opposed to the latter; on the contrary, the former legitimizes it. Indeed, the major objection to the hermeneutic definition stems from the fact that the proposed Christian interpretation of "terrestrial realities" is arbitrary; why give them a Christian meaning rather than any other? The heuristic definition, on the other hand, permits this response: giving a meaning to "terrestrial realities" departing from charity is justified, because charity discovers and introduces new phenomena into the world itself and the conceptual universe, which are saturated with meaning and glory, which ordain and eventually save the world. Charity does not interpret through and as an ideology, because it gives to the world greater reality and grandeur than the world pretends to have by itself. Thus, we find here again exactly Étienne Gilson's statement, but by basing it on a more complete determination of revelation—as charity which invents, discovers, works. Thus, it becomes clear that this double function of charity, hermeneutic and heuristic, presumes its most radical execution: charity first must give in order to bring reflection. This implies being involved in charitable work and contemplating charity in prayer. It is only in this sense that "Christian philosophy" presupposes faith in Christ.

ABOUT THE POSSIBLE ROLE OF "CHRISTIAN PHILOSOPHY" IN THE CONTEMPORARY SITUATION OF PHILOSOPHY

These answers to a few objections of course cannot suffice to establish a definition of "Christian philosophy" as a heuristic of charity. In the discussion here, it was, indeed, my modest intention merely to contribute a new meditation on Étienne Gilson's formula. It is possible that another point of departure may be preferable—even if this one has the advantage of linking us to a discussion which in its time was very widespread and serious. It is possible, therefore, that the term "Christian philosophy" may turn out to be more of a handicap than an opportunity in the current state of the debate. In conclusion, I would like to suggest two arguments which militate, it seems to me, in favor of its maintenance.

As I understand it, "Christian philosophy" is done by introducing concepts and discovering phenomena which come from charity, inasmuch as charity comes from revelation but inscribes itself in creation. "Even since God created this world his everlasting power and deity—however invisible—have been there for the mind to see the things he has made" (Romans 1:20). As a consequence, Christian philosophy contends that philosophy, in a method which is not directly theological, relates to charity, which is from now on considered as an order, a sphere, or a supplementary (and superior) level of things, and thus of reason. The world can be read in terms of extension (matter, etc.), of spirit (essence, sciences, logic, etc.), and also of charity (love, grace, and their negative correlatives). On the supposition that one accepts this situation of "Christian philosophy," what would be its relationship to the dominant and traditional definition of philosophy as metaphysical science of being as being, or even, after the "destruction of the history of ontology" undertaken by Heidegger, as phenomenology of being as such? Of course, "Christian philosophy" does not at all subscribe to it, or not entirely (in the case of the Thomists). But this irreducibility should not be considered an aberration or weakness, since metaphysics nowadays precisely recognizes its limits by undergoing the "end of metaphysics," while phenomenology pretends nowadays to manifest the "other than being," in multiple modes from elsewhere. By privileging, beyond being, charity as the last scene where the most decisive phenomena manifest themselves, "Christian philosophy" not only could be inscribed in the most renovating developments of contemporary philosophy, but could also contribute in a determining fashion to the overtaking of the end of metaphysics and to the deployment of phenomenology as such.[13]

A second argument comes from the age and rigor of the purely Christian uses of the term "philosophy." Indeed, the Pauline mistrust—"Make sure that no one traps you and deprives you of your freedom by some secondhand, empty, rational philosophy based on the principles of this world instead of on Christ" (Col. 2:8)—has not prevented the most ancient Christian authors (Statius, Clement of Alexandria, Justin "philosopher and martyr"), or the most recent ones (from Gregory of Nyssa to Erasmus), from strongly claiming this term and even the consecrated syntagma of "Christian philosophy." Of course, their interpretation was very different from that of the modern ones: it is not about a science of the world (not even from the Christian point of view), but about the wisdom that Christ gives, by means of life radically different from the wisdom of the world, to attain life in God. Among many examples, Justin: "Philosophy is really a great thing to possess and the most precious for God, God

---

[13] I refer here to my previous work *Dieu sans l'être* (*God Without Being*), particularly chaps. 3–4, *Réduction et donation: Recherches sur Husserl, Heidegger, et la phénoménologie* (Paris: Presses Universitaires de France, 1989), "De la mort de la 'mort de Dieu' aux noms divins," *Laval théologique et philosophique*, 41 No. 1 (1985), and "La fin de la fin de la métaphysique, *Laval théologique et philosophique*, 42, No. 1 (1986).

toward whom it alone leads us and with whom it unites us; and those who apply their spirit to philosophy are in reality saints."[14] In this sense, "philosophy" unites with Christ and sanctifies. Without doubt, this salvific ambition attributed to philosophy in a Christian context finds no echo in recent uses of the term; it is not, however, disqualified, because it is one of the most evident shortcomings of modern philosophy to have lost almost completely one of the original dimensions of the ancient pagan philosophy, from Socrates to Jamblichus. It is to attain the highest good, beautitude, even the immortality of the gods, that one ought to do philosophy. Except for some rare exceptions, metaphysics has renounced this ambition, at the risk of losing one of the primary justifications for doing philosophy. When "Christian philosophy" restores the principle that it knows not only from Christ, but also in order to attain him and beatitude, rather than turn itself away from philosophy as it has done, it rediscovers, after a long errancy of metaphysics, the awareness that original philosophy had of its purpose. Taken as a heuristic of charity, "Christian philosophy" would call, at a time of nihilism, any thought that would like to constitute itself as philosophy back to its forgotten ambition of loving wisdom.

For these two reasons after other arguments, I would suggest that the concept of "Christian philosophy" today may be neither obsolete nor contradictory—nor without a future.

---

[14] Justin, *Dialogue avec Trypho* II, PG 6.475B.

IV
Philosophizing
as a Christian

11

Philosophy and Existence

Jean Ladrière

THE QUESTION OF CHRISTIAN PHILOSOPHY sends us back to the question of the relation between philosophy and Christian faith. Classically, the question has received a very clear answer based on the distinction between reason and revelation, conceived as the two fundamental sources of understanding accessible to man. That distinction itself stems from a classic theological distinction between the order of nature and the order of grace. More precisely, the question that can be raised with respect to philosophy is not, in that context, a question directly concerning Christian faith as such but rather a question concerning theology as intellectual expression of that faith. If there is a problem, it is because philosophy, like theology, appears as an intellectual undertaking aiming at a true understanding of reality and the status of man. And what is meant by "true understanding" is an understanding that is at once intrinsically true, capable of providing the evidence sustaining its validity, and organized according to a systematic scheme. The ideal form of such a scheme is a construction based on fundamental principles that proceeds by deduction from those principles. In the case of philosophy, those principles are presented as expressing basic constraints of reason, thus reflecting the very structure of reason. In the case of theology, they are presented as expressing the basic elements of revelation. As revelation absolutely transcends reason and is, therefore, irreducible to it, the distinction is clear-cut. This thesis about the distinction is complemented and strengthened by the idea of God as the essence and the guarantor of both reason and revelation. Hence, a contradiction between philosophy and theology is impossible, at least if philosophical reason is working in conformity with its natural finality.

This view of the relationship between philosophy and Christian faith rests on several presuppositions concerning, on one hand, Christian faith interpreted primarily as a kind of knowledge, coming under the idea of truth, and, on the other, philosophy, as a system of knowledge constructed according to the Aristotelian idea of science. As a matter of fact, the situation seems to be more complicated. First, a distinction must be made between philosophy as a particular form of life and philosophy as a set of conceptual systems. If philosophy is taken as a form of life, the question it raises concerns its compatibility with Christian faith, itself considered in its practical aspect, as another form of life. If philosophy is considered as a set of conceptual systems, the meaning of such systems has to be made more precise. A philosophical system can be understood as a global interpretation of reality, and then we have the question of the compatibility between that interpretation of reality and the global vision of the real and of human destiny implied by Christian faith and explicated by theology. A philosophical system can also be understood as a reflection of experience upon itself, and then we have a question concerning the scope of that experience: If it includes the kind of experience induced by Christian faith, philosophy becomes a certain form of theology; if it does not include it, philosophy is no longer faithful to its project, which requires it to take account of all aspects and all possibilities of experience.

Moreover, a second difficulty, the role of theology with respect to Christian faith, has to be clarified. Is theology a component of Christian life? What exactly is its role? Or is it a discourse that, by itself, is external to what is effectively lived in the life of faith? Does it play a necessary role in the relationship between philosophy and Christian faith? What kind of mediation is proper to theology in that context? And if theology must actually intervene, is it necessarily in the form of a system that is built according to the model of a science and, therefore, immediately comparable with philosophy, conceived for its part also as a kind of scientific system? These questions and other related ones turn finally around two fundamental questions: one concerning the status of philosophy, the other concerning the mode of the actualization of Christian faith in human existence.

To clarify these questions, we have necessarily to rely upon a certain pre-understanding of what is at stake in them and to make use of certain philosophical concepts to express that pre-understanding. The justification of such a procedure can only be its power of clarification, which can become manifest only through its engagement. If the problem of the relationship between philosophy and Christian faith has some relevance, it must be because, in a sense that must be clarified, there is a place, a *topos* where they meet. According to the classic interpretation, which has been recalled above, that *topos* is the *episteme*, giving to both philosophy and theology their status of rigor and critical validity connected with the idea of science. But it is clear that philosophy, even conceived in this way, is fundamentally connected with a project concerning human destiny, as the word *philosophia* itself indicates. And it is clearer still that theology is only an intellectual exposition of the content of Christian faith, which concerns essentially the salvation of man, not a conceptual truth.

The concept we need to specify the realm of encounter between philosophy and Christian faith must refer to that dimension of man with respect to which the idea of wisdom and the idea of salvation are relevant. What will be proposed here is to have recourse, in this connection, to the concept of existence, not as correlative to the concept of essence, and not as synonymous with reality, but as determining the modality of reality proper to the human being, or, in ontological terms, the specific way in which the human being participates in the realm of being. That ontological modality is characterized mainly by the internal splitting that makes of the human being a question for itself, not primarily under the conceptual form of a problem but as inscribed in the very structure of action.

The mode of self-manifestation that action represents is not simply a kind of adaptive behavior that occurs in a chain of determinations implying each other, but rather an initiative that breaks a continuity, introduces a new perspective, creates new possibilities, gives way to an emergence that affects the world in its meaning. Action necessarily begins in uncertainty, in that kind of consciousness in which existence feels itself enjoined by its situation to take a position in a state of indeterminateness. Consciousness thereby perceives that what is at stake in the answer it is forced to give, even if apparently it is concerned with only some minor affair, is, in the last resort, its own being, or, more precisely perhaps, the quality of its being, as affecting in a certain way the very quality of the world. But the efficacy of action is in the moment of decision, where existence throws itself, so to say, to that uncertainty and from its own resources resolves it in the new determination it gives to itself. The decision is real only precisely through the concrete determination it generates. But in that determination existence is present as such, in the totality of its being, as affecting itself by what its action launches in the world. However, the question that it is for itself remains. The decision, even when it pertains to important matters, is necessarily local; what is at stake in existence is of a global character. The paradox of decision is precisely that, at the same time, through it existence finds its concrete figure, and yet existence is always in excess with respect to the particular determinations implied in decision. Having to assume the weight of its own being, existence discovers again and again that this being escapes its endeavor to answer effectively that demand. Thus, there is in existence an appeal that calls to it from an horizon that transcends every determination and, at the same time, a congenital limitation that prevents it, at least in the order of appearances, from becoming equal in the action it is able to promote, to its very being, present to itself as the task of being really itself.

The question that existence is thus constitutively for itself has often been expressed in terms of "the way." This metaphor suggests that the task of existence is to rejoin its authentic being, to reconcile itself with what it is, to establish in itself the peace of true harmony, to become, finally, what it is promised to be. It presupposes that there is a possible mediation between its present state, which is lived as a disjunction and even as a tearing inscribed in its constitution, and what announces itself in it as a requirement and a hope. That mediation is presented as a path that has to be followed step by step but is not at all representable in advance, like a route drawn on a map. That is a kind of congenital belief that gives the feeling that, although the way exists, it cannot be found by a methodical exploration. The way must give itself: it must reveal from a far-off region, where it is opened up, how to gain access to it; and it shows how it may be followed only to those who are already following it. What existence can do, with respect to the object of its belief, is merely to prepare itself for the announcement in which the way discloses itself. And that implies a concentration of all existential energies, the crouch of the self, trying to make itself fully receptive, not simply in this or that capacity, but in its very being, present at the same time in the actuality and in that distance from which it is calling itself. This expectation is also a self-interpretation. It is the mode in which, in that self-concentration, existence understands its own situation and the question that permeates its being, that decides on the mode in which the announcement of the way will be received. The way bears in itself its own authenticity. But the adjustment of existence to the announcement of the way is not necessarily adequate to the demand of that authenticity.

Philosophy, as it is understood in the Western tradition, is not at all a constitutive dimension of existence, like language, corporeality, or openness to alterity. It is the product of an act of institution, and it remains actual to the degree that this act is renewed through the centuries. It is essentially an historical reality, and it has the relativity of historical facts. Rather than an establishment, it is a project that, at the same time, is able to formulate itself in precise terms, yet remain relatively obscure for itself. The philosophical endeavor is, in part, the attempt to give a strict determination to the project. This attempt can be considered as an historical form of the search in which existence tries to attune itself to the announcement of the way. The term *wisdom*, which has been used by the founders of the philosophical institution, gives an indication about what is sensed as the aim of that search, and it corresponds to a certain presentation of that understanding. The way leads from a form of life in which existence remains foreign to itself to a form of life in which it is in harmony with truth as such—that is to say, with the unfolding of a reality of the self-position of the all-embracing presence that is beyond any determination. Apparently, we have to do here with the idea of an authentic knowledge, as opposed to an inauthentic one. The path along which existence is called to transform itself and to find the reconciliation with its own being seems to be a path leading to an intellectual illumination. But there is more here than the revelation of a more profound truth. What is presented as initiation to a concealed truth is actually the access to a new form of life in which existence is supposed to find the fulfillment of that announcement of itself that is inscribed in its being. In this new form of life, existence is enabled to assume authentically what it is, by recognizing its place and its meaning not simply in the restricted framework of a city but also in the very constitution of the real as such, in all its extension and all its different figures.

That aspect of initiation seems to disappear in what is considered to be the classic form of philosophy, where we have to do very explicitly with the project of a kind of wisdom that can be reached by an adequate form of knowledge. That idea of adequate knowledge is expressed in the concept of science, which itself leads back to the role of principles. Authentic knowledge, source of wisdom, is knowledge of principles and in principles. But the propositional principles, from which all intelligibility derives, are themselves the logical counterpart of the real principles that are at work in the constitution of things and of reality as such. True understanding is understanding on the basis of principles, because such an understanding permits us to see reality not simply as it appears but also as it is constituted. The appearance is not false, but by itself it remains purely factual, not yet intelligible. The search for comprehension tries to connect the appearance with the source from which it comes to appear.

The process in which reality gives itself to be seen and offers itself to be understood can be called the "process of manifestation." This term refers simultaneously to the realm of what is manifest and to the movement by which what is manifest enters into the field of visibility where the real unfolds itself and comes to its proper position in the space of universal presence. Authentic knowledge is understanding of manifestation as such and of what is manifest as giving itself in that very process. The idea of principle, which Aristotle explains by proposing the metaphor of the source, suggests a mode of understanding manifestation as coming from a point-source and moving toward the full exposition of itself, as a kind of uprising from a realm of originality into the proper realm of presence where things are really there for each other and are able to open out their life. The metaphor of the source is close to the metaphor of the way. The process of manifestation is the route that real things follow from an origin to the realm where they are effectively appearing. And the process of understanding follows that process of manifestation, by following the corresponding route in the realm of the concepts. The propositional principles are the reflection of the originary, and the deduction from principles reeffectuates the ascent of the appearances from the originary. By placing itself thus at the heart of the constitution of reality as such, existence puts itself in harmony with that invisible which is, in the visible, the originary force that makes it visible. That harmony is what gives it its authenticity, and in that state it must find the peace which is the signature of wisdom.

Modern philosophy seems to have abandoned the idea of philosophy as knowledge of principles, to the extent that it seems to have renounced proposing a picture of the world. Apparently, the expansion of the kind of understanding which had already been used in Greek astronomy and mechanics, and the extraordinary success of the methods systematically developed in the course of the seventeenth and eighteenth centuries, have constrained philosophy to change its perspectives and reformulate its project in terms of compatibility with what science was doing so splendidly. We could perhaps characterize globally that transformation of philosophy by the rise of transcendental philosophy. By doing so, we must, of course, take account of the displacement that has led from the transcendental conceived as an end to the transcendental conceived as the neutral field of the constitution of experience. The aim now is no longer to give a direct account of the way in which things appear or come into the realm of appearance, but to bring out the conditions of possibility of science and, more generally, of the different kinds of encounter we can have with reality. The reflection is no longer upon the external world, or even reality as such, as it is upon experience as such—that is to say, the field of openness thanks to which we have access to the world, to reality, to being, where encounter is occurring, prior to any interpretation or reconstruction, and from which the life of meaning emerges. In a sense, that inquiry into the structure of experience is still a kind of knowledge, but very different from that objective kind of knowledge provided by science and even from that idea of knowing according to the principles that gave form to the philosophical project in classical times. That classical idea already presupposes the possibility of an objectivation, that is to say, of a separation between the knowing subject and the reality giving itself to be understood. But a radical mode of understanding has to go back to this side of objectivation, to show how the structure of experience makes it possible and to reconstitute the process by which objectivation takes place. What is really primary, and what must be recaptured by reflection that aims at being truly critical, is not a set of first principles but that fundamental field in which the operation occurs by which the very idea of principles is elaborated and by which the principles themselves are formulated and receive their evidence. The unveiling of that field leads, perhaps, to a sort of knowledge, but it is not the representation of an objective occurrence; rather, it is the self-understanding of experience itself, becoming aware in reflection of what it is effectively performing just by being experience. More exactly than a knowledge, that reflection is a deepening of experience, accompanying itself by the word in which it says itself to itself. This word is not external to it, but is called by the very structure of experience, which is by itself that natural light which is at the source of meaning and of understanding and which, therefore, is clarity for itself. Experience is self-consciousness, and, as such, is itself the presence in which it makes itself present. The saying that expresses in words that presence and its different modalities is only the reception in language of what is lived in the natural course of experience. But language is itself a component of experience, and thus, by having recourse to language in order to clarify itself, experience does not leave itself but tries to become more authentically what it is, by unfolding a possibility inscribed in it as the requirement of its self-clarity.

The project of philosophy, in that perspective, becomes the project of the self-understanding of experience. But if there is something like experience, it is because there is an ontological structure that contains precisely the possibility and the demand of that return to oneself from an internal disjunction that occurs in reflection. That structure is what is designated by the term *existence*, such as it has been presented here. We could thus say that the project of philosophy becomes the project of self-under-standing of existence. The bringing into play of this project in-duces a transformation of existence, in the sense that, by virtue of its reflexive discourse, existence passes into a mode of self-presence where it lives its condition in the mode of that articula-tion which is provided by discourse, and thus acquires the sym-bolic possession of its own being. The quest for an ontological harmony, where existence could find its accomplishment and the quiet of the blessed life, takes here the form of a quest for self-understanding, as authentic mode of presence to oneself. The philosophical task, which is devoted to the advent of that onto-logical state, becomes identical with the task that existence is for itself, in such a way that the responsibility existence supports for itself finds its concrete fulfillment in philosophical work. Philos-ophy becomes the highest duty, as the path that can lead exis-tence to a reconciliation with itself.

Apparently, this is not true for a kind of philosophy that has become widespread today and is inspired by the idea of analysis. It can be said that this very idea rests upon some presuppositions concerning the role of language which make the clarification of discourse an objective the validity of which is considered evi-dent. But those presuppositions themselves have to be justified, and the project of such a justification leads us back to the self-reflection of existence. The strength of the analytic position is that it is always able to retort that the discourse in which this project is formulated has itself to be clarified and that, in this last instance, the only acceptable program of self-reflection consists in the self-elucidation of language, because language is the real place where meaning constitutes and shows itself, and the most fundamental process is the springing up of meaning. It remains true, however, that analytic work aims at a dissolution of all illu-sions and misunderstandings, at a transparency of language en-abling meaning to reveal itself without restriction or disturbance, and that what makes such a state desirable is that it is the key to peace of mind. There is a clear indication of that in the *Investiga-tions* of Wittgenstein: when complete clarity is obtained—if that is possible at all—there are no more problems; the mind is in harmony with itself and is able to accept things as they are, in the absolute simplicity of a concrete reconciliation with what there is. We are not very far, here, from the idea of an accomplishment of existence as reconciliation with itself and full assumption of its own being and its destiny. The idea of meaning could be the link between the perspective of existence and the perspective of language. It is true on both sides that what is at stake, after all, is what constitutes the heart of experience: the advent of meaning. On one hand, it is interpreted as the very unfolding of existence; on the other, as the process of the uprising of the word. But existence is, by itself, that uprising, and reciprocally, the uttering of the word is the central *peripeteia* of existence. It remains thus that philosophy, under the variety of its historical expressions, is the instituted undertaking aimed at a transformation of existence so as to give it access to a state of authenticity wherein existence finds finally, with the full understanding of itself, that peace of heart and that kind of self-enjoyment foreshadowed in the idea of the blessed life. Philosophy thus remains faithful to its original project. But more than that, perhaps, it proposes itself as a form of life that is the right way toward salvation.

Christian faith also has an historical character, but not exactly as philosophy does. Like philosophy, it is not inscribed in the being of a man as a constitutive dimension, but neither is it a product of a cultural institution. It understands itself as the acknowledgment of what is announced in the word of God, and the manifestation of the world of God in the word that announces it is an historical event, which gives retrospectively an interpretation of human existence as affected by an internal contradiction which separates it from God and of a participation in the divine life itself. The action of God in the history of mankind gives man access to the possibility of an authentic deification. This possibility is realized fully in Christ, who assumes consubstantially the human condition in his divine being, and it is realized in the members of the Body of Christ by participation in his own condition of eternal Son of God. The reception of the word of God, announcing itself in all the episodes of the Old Testament, becomes, in the New Testament, the recognition of Christ as being himself, in his personhood, Word "who was in the beginning God." Christian faith concerns essentially in man that dimension in which he is called to decide with regard to himself and the meaning of his very being. It proposes not primarily a knowledge which would be the fully authentic one, but a transformation of the very status of man, under the form of a conversion. That is to say, it is a process by which man detaches himself from the dereliction in which he was living to make himself receptive to the action of the grace which must make of him a real resemblance to Christ, a son of God. That transformation affects not some particular capacity or faculty but what is constitutive of the very being of man, namely, existence. It must find its concrete expression in a particular form of life, capable of opening existence to the action of the word of God, more specifically to the action of Christ, as mediated by the sacraments of the Church and primordially by the sacramental history of the Body of Christ. What is thus promised to existence is an accomplishment of itself, not in the line of the full opening out of an institution laid down by itself, but in the mode of a gift, gratuitous and unforeseeable, which existence can only accept in humility and gratefulness, but in which it receives, beyond its own expectation, the full answer to the question that it is for itself. Not only does Christian faith lead to salvation; it is itself the process of the advent of salvation. This advent is the gift of Christ himself. It is already present in the historical events of the life and death of Jesus Christ. And yet it is still to come, announced, expected, sensed already in the waiting of hope, which is itself a gift, in which what is to come, so to speak, precedes itself.

If philosophy and Christian faith both concern existence in its most essential determinations, our question can be reformulated in the following terms: is it possible for existence to assume at the same time the project of philosophy and the calling of Christian faith, and if so, in what sense? At first, it seems that, if philosophy is really conceived and lived as the access to authentic life and, in that respect, as the way to salvation, it is incompatible with the Christian attitude of expecting salvation only from Christ. But this must be considered more carefully. To begin with, it could be suggested that, after all, there are several philosophical projects, and that the word *philosophy* refers (in any case in current Western culture) to very different types of dis-

PHILOSOPHIZING AS A CHRISTIAN

course. Without entering into a detailed classification, two main types can be discerned: (*a*) a kind of philosophy that has, in effect, the pretension of attaining by the sole force of thought an ultimate point of view that would reveal itself as reflecting the position of the absolute, and (*b*) a much more modest type of philosophy, which aims only at a relative clarification of experience, in the conviction that every possible interpretation remains necessarily finite and partial, leaving open the most radical questions. In the first conception, the practice of philosophy must bring about a real transformation of existence, enabling it to place itself in the perspective of the absolute. In the second one, what is expected is only that sort of limited wisdom made up of the dissipation of illusions and the recognition of the real as it is truly. Understood only as an art of clarification, as seems to be the case in the common forms of analytic philosophy, philosophy could be a useful preparation for theology, providing it with conceptual tools theology could use perhaps to elaborate more-refined reconstructions of the classical problems it has to face. But, as has been suggested already, the deep meaning of this idea of clarification is perhaps, after all, so different as to appear to be at first sight, from the radical conception of philosophy, the way to full authenticity. The search for clarity is itself inspired in the last instance by the old idea of wisdom. And there is in that idea a radicality that makes of philosophy an undertaking in which existence is called to decide ultimately on its meaning. And there is in that perspective a kind of pride of spirit which is not reconcilable with the humility required in order to hear the word of God.

But is this really necessarily so? After all, the kind of accomplishment philosophy can provide is only the kind of satisfaction that the mind can find in a discourse, whatever its conceptual force may be. The philosophical discourse is only a discourse, a work of language; it plays with forms, and what it produces by itself is only the representation of the formal aspects of the reality to which it claims to refer. It is not, like scientific discourse, interpretable in empirical terms, which have a local meaning, susceptible to local tests; rather, it signifies only globally, producing its meaning by its own internal organization, making a realm of forms appear, like architecture produces a world of forms by the concrete organization of the materials. Philosophical discourse is a logic, not perhaps in the sense of a formal theory of deduction, but in the sense of a presentation of the categories in which experience can be interpreted. Those categories constitute, so to speak, the intelligible framework that, as representing the principles of an intrinsic constitution, are the apriori conditions of the concrete figures experience is able to show.

This idea of a logic of experience implies a distinction between form and content, as applied to existence. The concrete reality of existence is always a particular commitment of itself in particular actions, in specific attitudes, in determinate projects. But by itself, as an ontological structure, existence is the effectuation, the becoming real of fundamental possibilities that belong to its constitution. The distinction invoked here is between that structural aspect of existence and the concrete realization of itself in which it gives to itself, at each step of its becoming, its historical consistency by the way in which it assumes, under its responsibility, its own being. It could be expressed also as the distinction between the ontological scheme and the efficacy of existence. If this distinction is accepted, it necessarily affects the project of philosophy, in that this project may concern existence in its ontological scheme or in its efficacy. In general terms, it can be said, as has been proposed, that philosophy can be conceived as the reflection of existence in itself. But that conception must be made more precise. That reflection can be understood as being only on the ontological scheme of existence. In this case, philosophy can be characterized as a logic of existence, in the sense explained before. But it can also be understood as contributing, perhaps in a decisive manner, to the efficacy of existence. To make philosophy the realization of the authentic form of existence is evidently to understand it in this second sense. But the first sense, of a logic of existence, does not necessarily entail the second one. And on the basis of the distinction between the two, it becomes possible to think at least as realizable the compatibility between philosophy and Christian faith.

But it is even possible to go further and, while maintaining the compatibility, to take account of the second possible conception of philosophy. It would be difficult, indeed, if philosophy actually concerns existence as such in its fundamental constitution, to maintain that it is neutral with respect to the efficacy of existence. There is a lasting validity in the idea of wisdom, and more precisely in the project of a wisdom brought about by virtue of a specific discourse, be it conceived as the disclosure of the presuppositions of experience or as a methodology of clarification. There is, to be sure, an extreme position according to which philosophy, as a discourse of the absolute, is by itself the authentic realization of existence, in the sense that it enables existence to identify itself with absolute thinking, as thinking of the absolute. Philosophy is then conceived as the recapitulation of the concrete becoming of existence, from its oblivion of itself all the way to its self-understanding as a moment in the absolute life, and as the very self-understanding in which existence discovers the truth of its being and, by being saved from the dispersion in which it was living, receives access to the immutability of the blessed life. But if philosophy is conceived as the logic of existence, it is capable of contributing to the realization of existence, in the more restricted sense in which it gives existence to understand, according to which possibilities it is living, such and such a moment of its efficacy. This understanding is not at all identical with the efficacy of a concrete figure, but it can help such a figure to live itself in a more enlightened consciousness of its meaning and of the possibilities concealed in it.

If we make use of the famous distinction between existential and existentiell analysis, we could say that the logic of existence can take two forms: it can be only a categorical reconstruction of the fundamental structures that belong to the ontological constitution of existence, like temporality or language; but it can also be a description of the existentiell dimension of existence—not, to be sure, describing concrete processes in which existence could be considered as obtaining its realization, but describing the formal aspect of the possible processes in which existence can actually be in search of its realization. The concepts of authenticity and inauthenticity, used by Heidegger in *Being and Time*, are of that type. They do not give indications of the concrete content of an authentic life, but they help clarify the status of the stakes of existence, by showing the opposition between a form of life in which existence, in a sense, would be lost, and a form of life in which existence would become really what it is called to be and would thus obtain its salvation. It thus appears that the distinction between form and content can be refined, thanks to the distinction between existential and existentiell, and that the idea of a logic of experience could perfectly well be understood as covering both a logic of the existential structures of existence and a logic of its existentiell efficacy.

Proceeding along this line: it seems that it is even possible to propose an interpretation of the most radical forms of philosophizing which makes it still compatible with Christian faith. Let us consider such a philosophy. In its explicit terms, it presents itself as a discourse describing a path of thinking leading progressively, through the different levels of the constitution of experience, to the point of view of the absolute and becoming itself at the end of the discursive manifestation of the absolute principle itself. This discourse carries along with itself the efficacy of existence, in such a way that the unfolding of the discourse is, at the same time, the real process in and through which existence arrives finally at its full realization by becoming able to interpret its own being from the point of view of the absolute. Taken as such, in the pretension of its own words, such a philosophy seems, indeed, to be incompatible with Christian faith, as already suggested, in the measure to which it presents itself as the way to salvation. But is it not possible to interpret it as the presentation of a speculative image in which we can find the reflection in a conceptual language of what is effectively lived in religious experience in general, and even perhaps in the specific experience of Christian faith? What makes this possibility acceptable is that, as already underlined, a discourse is inevitably formal, even when it claims to inscribe itself in lived efficacy. In the case of Christian faith, it must be recognized that the efficacy of that faith is a certain form of life, which contains the moment of recognition, where the spirit of the believer, as in the confession of St. Peter, recognizes Jesus Christ the Son of God as the Savior. But there is also the practice, detailed in specific acts, by which the believer is called to imitate Christ and to conform his own life to the evangelical model, according to the precept "Faith without works is a dead faith." That practical aspect is understood not as the simple observance of certain rules or even of certain counsels, but as the concrete efficacy, in everyday life, of a mystical experience in which, through the mediation of Christ and the participation in his life, the believer takes part in the life of the Holy Trinity. That union, in Christian life, between the concreteness of human life and the mystical dimension it receives by grace is, for example, strikingly expressed in St. Paul's question, in the First Epistle to the Corinthians: "Do you not know that your body in the temple of the Holy Spirit?" That form of life, in which Christian finds its efficacy, is actually a progression, inaugurated by conversion, sustained by the sacraments, and moving toward the full realization of the Kingdom of God. It is the process in which and by which man is called to become, as a member of the Kingdom, a real member of the Body of Christ. That process, although made possible only by the spiritual gift which is the fruit of Redemption, takes the human person as it is constituted, according to the possibilities inscribed in the structure of existence. The very ideas of process and progression imply, for example, temporality. And the recognition of Christ passes through the mediation of language. This means that the Christian form of life is itself, as form, a particular actualization of formal dispositions that belong to existence as ontological structure. A logic of existence can try to reconstruct not only formal dispositions as such—this would correspond to the existential aspect of that logic—but also the formal possibilities according to which, in general, those dispositions can be actualized. In operating along this line, the logic of existence would make manifest the structures according to which the concrete process represented by a particular form of life could take place. But if the fundamental existential structures, being prior to any form of actualization, can be expressed in the purely abstract language of categories, the existentiell structures underlying a particular form of actualization, like the form of life proper to Christian faith, cannot be expressed except as presented already in a concrete manifestion.

We have to do here with a theoretical situation narrowly analogous to the situation analyzed by Kant in the case of the metaphysics of nature. There is, indeed, concerning nature, a knowledge which is by pure concepts, which Kant calls metaphysics, and on the other side there is the empirical knowledge of concrete phenomena. But there is also a third form of knowledge, based on what Kant calls "the construction of concepts." That third form, mediating the other two, is given by mathematical physics, in which the pure concepts of metaphysics receive, so to speak, a concrete presentation. We meet there a formal description which gives us to see, in the abstract presentation of the mathematical objects, the concrete meaning of the concepts used, and gives us to understand how they are able to receive their efficacy in the empirical world. Here we have to do with a presentation of the way in which the fundamental existential dispositions can receive their efficacy in concrete life. That presentation is not yet the description of concrete life itself, even as a form of life. But it is already the scheme of concrete actualization of its pure existential possibilities. Philosophy, functioning as an *itinerarium mentis*, and as the progression toward authenticity, is a conceptual creation in which, thanks to the formal aspect of the concepts used (like the concepts of logos, reason, will, and action), an abstract representation of a concrete process can be given. Such a representation can only show a possibility, but it is already related to the concreteness of actual life wherein that possibility receives a particular and effective figure. A philosophical system that could be interpreted along those lines could be considered a symbolic representation, in a conceptual language, of the form of life in which, from the point of view of the individual believer, Christian faith is actually lived, or, correspondingly, of the historical process in which, from the point of view of the announcing of the Kingdom of God, the Body of Christ is progressively constituted. The given representation ought to take account, of course, of the particular type of historicity that is proper to that process and ought, in particular, to reflect in its own language the eschatological character of the history of salvation.

But what is suggested so far is only a possible reading of given philosophical discourses, taken as they are, from the point of view of their compatibility with Christian faith, or even from the point of view of the type of clarification they could provide with respect to the conditions of possibility of religious experience in general and of Christian faith in particular. It is time now to come to the more acute aspect of the question here discussed: is there a mode of philosophizing that would have a specific connection not only with the Christian faith as a possibility but also with the very content of that faith?

The main difficulty that has to be met is that, if the content of the faith is taken explicitly into consideration, it seems that we are no longer in philosophy but in theology. How would it be possible to take account of the content of faith without making explicit reference to revelation as such? It is of vital importance, in treating that question, to remember that Christian faith is based on an historical process and refers by its very content to a reality in the process of becoming, the advent of the Kingdom of God, which not only is a mystical reality but also has its visible aspect in a concrete history. That means that what is revealed is not contained as such in the structure of human existence, such as it is able to understand itself and to reflect its own constitution. On the other hand, revelation is a word of God, addressed to human beings, in terms that must be understood by them even if the terms refer to a reality that transcends the realm of common experience and of what can be discovered by the simple use of human reason. This implies that there must be, in the very structure of existence, a fundamental disposition that enables it to become receptive to the word of God and to understand, on its own terms, what that word signifies. And as existence contains in itself the demand of its own self-understanding, and thus the wish of a resumption of itself in a field of intelligibility, which is reason, the understanding of the word of God implies the endeavor to capture its intelligibility according to the possibilities of reason. The reality disclosed by revelation and thereby making itself accessible to existence, taken in the full integrity of its being, presents itself effectively as offered to the interpretive work of reason as well as to the apprehension of the heart and to the acknowledgment of will. It brings with itself the light in which it can be grasped by the mind; more exactly, it is itself illuminating by its very essence and makes itself understandable by the very fact that it manifests itself.

The endeavor aiming at the understanding of the content of revelation and thus the very object of faith properly constitutes the task of theology. But with respect to that project of understanding, there is a primary task that is relevant for philosophy as such: to try to understand the very possibility of revelation from the part of humans, on one hand, and from the part of the internal content of revelation as such, on the other. There are, thus, two problems in that context. One of them concerns receptivity to revelation. Since revelation announces directly the salvation which is promised to man by God himself, and as salvation concerns existence in its most radical possibilities, that receptivity must consist in the very constitution of existence. The proposition of salvation has a meaning for existence only if existence by itself is in a certain sense expectant of salvation, even if it is has no explicit view of what a true salvation would be. And existence can be that expectation only if it lives itself as affected by a constitutive distress and at the same time as longing for an assistance coming from outside which could deliver it from its state of dereliction. But those two aspects of existence themselves presuppose an ontological constitution for which dereliction and desire are possible.

On one hand, the reception of revelation, as being an answer to the expectation, includes a moment of encounter and a moment of acknowledgment. Again, the possibility of those components of reception must be inscribed in the structure of existence. The occurrence of encounter demands the openness of a common field in which a contact and a kind of reciprocity can be established, the offer of what comes to be encountered having its reciprocal in the attitude of welcoming that receives it. Acknowledgment demands, first, the capacity to perceive, even if it is in relative obscurity, the meaning of what is given in the encounter, and thus primarily a capacity for understanding; and, second, the capacity to go out of oneself, to recognize alterity, and to give one's confidence to the word which gives itself to be heard. The analysis of those presuppositions is not yet the endeavor to understand revelation as such, but is the endeavor to understand how revelation can affect existence. That question is, of course, suggested and even imposed by the fact of revelation. And it is a real question only for those who take revelation as real manifestation of God to man, not as a symbolic representation of a kind of self-understanding of existence. This presupposes already the acceptance of revelation for what it is intrinsically, and in such an undertaking, we have to do with a kind of problematics that can be said to be Christian in its motivation. But the analysis that is required can be based entirely on the way in which existence is present to itself in common experience. And in this sense it is a philosophical undertaking, in the most traditional form. Would it be appropriate to call a philosophical inquiry motivated by Christian faith a Christian philosophy? It seems that the use of such an expression would be misleading, because what is at stake is not, at least directly, the motivation or the use that can be made, for example in a theological context, of such a philosophical analysis but the exact content of that analysis. And this analysis can apply properly to the question proposed only if it refers precisely to structural elements that belong to existence as such and not to a spiritual experience occurring in a particular historical context.

This concerns the question of the receptivity of revelation. There is another problem raised by the fact of revelation, which concerns the very content of revelation, which is the proper object of Christian faith. This content has an intrinsic organization which is reflected in the structure of the *Credo*, where the exposition of the process of salvation is presented as coming from God as creator of every finite reality, finding its efficacy in the Incarnation of the Word of God, his life, his death, and his resurrection, consecrated by the sending of the Holy Spirit, continuing through the course of human history in the life of the Church and called to be fully accomplished in the resurrection of the dead and the advent of eternal life. What is thus proclaimed by the act of faith is not a theory about the nature of God but the unfolding of an immense process in which the totality of humankind, of human history, and even of the created world as a whole is implicated. Believers ratify by his word the reality of that process and assume it for themselves, taking their places, as members of the Body of Christ, through the efficacy of what is said. Thus, we have to make do with a reality that is essentially of the nature of a process, constituted by a sequence of events, and having its meaning precisely as an eventlike reality. The internal life of the Holy Trinity, which is presupposed by the whole process and constitutes the foundation of the *Credo*, is itself made of a processual mode of being, the Son being generated by the Father and the Spirit proceeding from the Father and the Son. The endeavor to understand as far as possible that internal structure of God himself and, on that basis, the whole structure of the salvation in Christ, is the task of theology. But as we have to do here with a reality and even with the most fundamental constitution of reality, the way in which it is presented in revelation gives an indication of what philosophy tries to uncover under the term *foundation*. And at the same it raises a question that is not yet a theological one but one relevant for philosophy in its tradition form: how must we conceive the foundation in order to be able to give an account of the possibility of eventlike reality and of the processual and relational structure of the Trinity? Again, the motivation of that question comes from the faith that receives revelation as the real disclosure of the project of God regarding humans and of the process of salvation as well by God. But the question itself has to be treated according to the method of rational regression by which philosophy has been able to formulate the problematics of the foundation. To be sure, the question makes reference to some fundamental elements of revelation, but it keeps from those elements only what belongs properly to the philosophical project by focusing its attention on the status of event. That concept is analogical, and the way in which it intervenes in the reflection on revelation presupposes a fundamental ontological structure that poses a problem by itself, independent of the particularly strong signification the concept receives in the case of the content of revelation. The analysis of what is thus presupposed constitutes a philosophical task.

There is another aspect of this problematic which is also suggested by the structure of the *Credo*. In its first part it refers to God the Father, "creator of heaven and earth," and in what follows it refers to the Incarnation and to Redemption. We have thus to do there with a duality of perspectives, which nevertheless are connected with each other in a way that is suggested by the order in which they appear. What is invoked first is the event of creation, which gives existence to the realm of the finite beings. And then come the events in which properly God manifests himself, in the person of Jesus Christ, as being at the same time the Son of God and really man. In creation we have to do with the constitution of things. It is properly in that context that the concept of being and the analysis of the different modes of being find their relevance. It could be said also that this context is the proper place of the originary, because in that primordial constitution are already given the possibilities according to which the realm of being will be able to unfold itself. But, with the Incarnation of Christ, the meaning of the originary is completely transformed: a new relation between God and the finite reality, in particular the reality of man, is established.

Here the concept of event takes on a meaning different from that applied to the fact of creation. In the case of creation, we have to do with an ontological event. In the fact of Incarnation and in its consequent facts, we encounter what could be called a soteriological event, opening in its efficacy the process of salvation. Thus, we find inscribed in the structure of the *Credo*, and in the very structure of the reality of salvation, the duality of what is by constitution under the status of the originary and what is by the new initiative of Redemption, which presupposes, to be sure, the primordial constitution, but which opens for us the possibility of a destiny that can be characterized not by reference to an originary, but by reference to an *eschaton*, yet to come, and can be suggested perhaps by the idea of calling. That duality between what is constituted and what is happening unexpectedly, as pure occurrence, has a direct relation to the duality between the existential and the existentiell aspect of existence. The existential refers to the structural constitution of existence, which is posed by the very institution of the realm of being. The existentiell refers to what existence becomes in its efficacy, through the commitments in which it brings into play its own being. The process of salvation concerns existence in that respect, and to that degree in which it is for existence the encounter which changes its perspectives and calls it to become a "new man," opening for it novel possibilities. The duality between the order of constitution, which can be analyzed in terms of structures, and the order of the encounter, which can be analyzed in terms of events, is also an aspect of the philosophical problematics suggested by the content of Christian faith. What must be understood is how the constituted contains the possibility of encounter, of the pure occurrence, how it is of itself open for the surprise of such an arising. This question is also a question about the processual constitution of being. With those questions, a philosophy instructed by Christian faith is called to take up again the old problematics of ontology and to try to reconcile it with what is implied in the dynamics of the life of the spirit, such as it is assumed in the audacity of Christina hope.

We arrive here at the main question concerning the relationship between existence and what can be called provisionally the "universal presupposition," that is to say, the vast possibility of all presuppositions. It is in this question that the two perspectives of receptivity out of the intrinsic content of faith find their unity. By its very internal structure of noncoincidence with itself, existence is openness. And as the guardian of its being, it is open to what is at the most fundamental level of its own constitution, which is also the fundamental level of constitution as such. This openness allows it to be capable of understanding and capable of action. But it must be shown how it is capable of hope. Now, does hope have any meaning unless it be in relation to a personal reality?

Existence becomes aware of itself as given to itself. Its actuality is as the continuing event of a reception in which existence receives its own self-position. What has been called here the "universal presupposition" is the real possibility of such an event as inscribed in the structure of existence. The reality of that possibility must be conceived itself as pure self-position of an actuality not given to itself but giving itself to itself, and capable of posing outside of itself actualities distinct from its own. This pure actualizing actuality is in itself the pure generosity which partakes of its own reality. If existence can interpret itself as the fruit of that ontological generosity, it is effectively able to live the desire which transfixes it as the hope of the fulfillment of that whereof its actuality bears in itself the promise. We find here again, of course, the fundamental themes of traditional metaphysics, evoked in the language of existence. But this is only a sketchy outline of a philosophical task, suggesting a possible philosophical style. It corresponds to the point of view of philosophy about itself. But there is a different question, corresponding to the point of view of Christian faith: what could be the meaning of philosophy for faith, if there is such a meaning at all? Faith contains in itself the demand of understanding, or, correspond-ingly, the claim of its own rationality. That justifies the role of theology as a component of the life of the Church. Philosophy could be considered simply a preparation for theology. It would have, then, simply an instrumental value.

But it has, nevertheless, an intrinsic value. The project on the basis of which it is instituted corresponds not only to a possibility but also to a duty of human reason. It answers a calling, reflecting in the realm of rationality the constitutional vocation of exis-tence. There is a theological conception, insisting on the abstract transcendence of the realm of grace, for which the works of rea-son have no importance from the point of view of salvation. But there is a great tradition fully accepted by the Church, for which the task of reason, deriving from the originary gift of creation, does have a value, even from the point of view of the advent of the Kingdom of God. For that theology, there is a continuity be-tween the order of creation and the order of Redemption—in this sense, that the spiritual dynamism posed by creation has, by des-tination, to be assumed in the dynamism of salvation. This oblit-erates neither the presence of sin in human achievements nor the necessity of conversion. But it belongs to the judgment of God to discriminate between what came from evil and what can be incorporated in the eternal life.

Viewed in that perspective, philosophy must be taken in its ongoing endeavor, with the claims and the demands inscribed in the dynamics of its own problematics, in its historical develop-ment and in the variety of its expressions. The criterion is fidelity to originary inspiration, which reflects a finality. Any work real-ized in that fidelity can be accepted as a valuable contribution. And the work directly inspired by specifically Christian motiva-tions appears, in that perspective, as only a part of a vast under-taking which must be taken in the unity of all its forms. In that polymorphic undertaking, reason is in search of itself, and this search is itself a partial expression of that natural hope which inhabits the human spirit.

Seen in the light of faith, philosophy, as understanding itself as the progressive self-revelation and the coming-to-itself of rea-son, is a mode of celebration of creation, a testimony given, per-haps in obscurity, to the transforming action of the eternal Logos, present in human history by virtue of the Incarnation, and a parable, in conceptual forms, of the illumination given to the human mind by the gifts of the Holy Spirit.

"Every philosophy, in its turn, will be deposited," wrote Whitehead. And Pascal had, in his *Pensées*, that radical judgment: "Descartes, inutile et incertain." Philosophy is submitted, as is every human undertaking, to the temptation of the pride of the spirit. Like man himself, it has to be saved. But its true meaning is eschatological. The life of reason is the hope of reason, And this hope, in the final instance, receives its justification from that hope, given by grace, which is the expectation of eternal life.

QUESTIONS AND ANSWERS

Q: Thank you for this beautiful, inspiring, very complete exposition of the problem and your answer. I have only one question. If philosophy is in a way abstract within the framework of Christian thinking, must not we say that abstractions are always anticipations, and somehow anticipations of that which is beyond the abstraction? So, for instance, you talked about receptivity. Now, if we would try to describe the receptivity that is an element of faith, insofar as it is the disposition that makes it possible for grace to save us, is it possible to say that we can do a phenomenology of receptivity that can be recognized by everybody, or should we say that receptivity itself is already a gift of grace and, therefore, will have some color, some tone, some specificity in the person who believes which is different from the receptivity of a person who does not believe? And would that not mean that the phenomenology of the receptivity in a Christian is different from the phenomenology of the receptivity in a non-Christian?

It is a very difficult question, because there are Christians who are not Christian, and non-Christians who are Christian. But is it not true that there is no general phenomenology of this receptivity, merely one that is already oriented toward and perhaps already a little bit specified for that which comes after it?

A: Yes, the main difficulty in this question of receptivity is that the receptivity concerning Christian faith has to be considered from two points of view: first, from the point of view of the constitution of human existence, and it is this point of view that I have evoked as a problem for philosophy. But, of course, it cannot be forgotten that there is also another essential aspect of this receptivity, which is the grace by which we become able to actually receive the word of God in its originality. And the difficulty is, of course, how to take account of those two components. But, in any case, if grace is necessary to receive the gift of God, it is also true that the gifts of God, and this very grace, are given to man in the measure whereby the human being has a specific constitution that makes it able to receive this grace. But, clearly, this raises a different sort of problem, one that I think is clearly theological. No, the question of the grace of conversion, which is the second aspect of receptivity, is a theological question, because it is a question of grace itself. But what makes possible the reception of the grace in the constitution of human existence— this question belongs to an analysis of existence such as can be performed, let us say, by a phenomenological method. And, in this instance, I don't think there would be a fundamental difference here. What I have suggested is that there is a particular motivation to study this question of receptivity and of the conditions of receptivity.

Now, I have, nevertheless, a hesitation here to which I referred in my talk. It is connected with the possibility of hope. This receptivity of existence, such as it can be analyzed phenomenologically, can give accounts of the possibility of understanding, of the possibility of free action, of the possibility of aesthetic emotion, of the possibility of love, and so on. But the question I raised is: is it possible to give an account of the possibility of hope? And, here again, we have to take account of two levels, because, as I suggested at the end, there is a kind of hope that is inscribed in the very dynamic constitution of reason. I tried to express this by saying that the life of reason is the hope of reason. The constitution of reason is a dynamic one, and for this reason the work of science, for example, appears to itself as a kind of duty, or, in other terms, as finalized by something which is yet to come and which is the objective of the hope. I think that this theme of the hope of reason is fundamental in the second part of the *Critique of Pure Reason*.

But now, of course, there is the theological meaning and reality of hope. Hope is grace, one of the three theological virtues, and this is a gift of God. Nevertheless, there must be in the unity of existence an integration of those two levels of hope. And, again, it seems that it is by virtue of a specific constitution that man is able to receive the grace of hope. There is in the human being a structure, the structure of hope, the hope of reason. There is in the very constitution of the person a structure that makes it possible to receive a grace which is specifically a hope. To take account of this possibility, just as a possibility, can perhaps add something to an analysis which could be made completely in abstraction of any specifically religious faith. Such an analysis can, of course, develop, as Kant has done, a very defined analysis of the hope of reason. But to take account in such an analysis of this further element, which is hope by grace, would perhaps add at least some specific element, without completely transforming the analysis which is proposed. It would, let us say, add an element that is like an openness to what is in the nature of a gift. Finally, we arrive again at this word, because it is necessary to use it when we speak of the relationship of the human spirit with Christian faith.

V
A Concluding
Roundtable Discussion

CONCLUDING ROUNDTABLE
DISCUSSION

MODERATOR: Like Bill Richardson's slide of the painting *The Three Ages of Man*, we have a good visual aid here. We have an abundance of riches—the crowded chairs on the stage attest to that. We also have sort of a physical impossibility, but I hope not a spiritual one. There is no table because we couldn't fit everybody around a table on this particular stage, and I am sure we cannot fit together the pieces of our discussion in these last forty-eight hours. Fortunately, that is not the purpose here. I mentioned the idea of collecting fragments the other day. It seems to me that this time has been too rich and too important to let it end without some sort of an attempt at recollection, an act of memory, a gathering together of the nourishment that we've shared. It is not at all inappropriate, I think, to recognize the obvious Eucharistic significance of what a roundtable session might be thought of as doing. There has been no rehearsal for this, and no prompting in advance, so I relieve the speakers of any necessity for seeming to be prepared to say anything. I will simply ask them now, for the first time, to share with us any impressions, any reflections on what has happened and of what significance they might find that to be. There is no order, no necessity for anyone in particular to speak, but if any of our speakers would like to address themselves to that invitation, we would certainly welcome it.

ROBERT ADAMS: May I take advantage of my possession of the microphone to begin? As a Protestant, and one of predominantly Anglophone training and orientation philosophically, I have found it very interesting to be a participant in a conversation that has been predominantly Catholic and almost as predominantly Francophone philosophically, I would say. As I reflect on that

from my perspective, and as I think about what several participants said about the statements of Emil Brille over sixty years
ago, and their effect in initiating the conversation that has been
going on here, I was reminded of the almost precisely contempo-
raneous and, in some ways, similar stance of Karl Barth, which
affected in some ways—indeed, profoundly affected—the atmo-
sphere in which I as a student first began to think about the relation between philosophy and Christianity.

As I think about our discussion here, one of the things that has
struck me has been the fact that it seems to me that most of the
voices being heard are (as my own is on this subject) integration-
ist and interactionist, and that there has been far less of the insistence on the autonomy of philosophy and theology vis-à-vis each
other than there was sixty years ago (or at least less than I remember from my own student days). And I have been reflecting
on the question of why this is so—and in context that I remember
from student days, a context predominantly Protestant on the
theological side and Anglophone and analytical on the philosophical side—it is clear to me that I remember a situation in
which there was insistence both by the theologians, at least the
Barthians among them, on the autonomy of theology and by the
philosophers on the autonomy of philosophy, an insistence that
indeed makes the term "Christian philosophy" seem somewhat
questionable. It seems quite clear to me that this has changed,
and it has changed in the discussions that I am more familiar
with as well as in the Catholic and Francophone discussions.

If I ask myself why it has changed in the discussions that I'm
more familiar with, there is on the theological side a story that
is rather complicated and perhaps not particularly fruitful for
our discussions here, having to do with some internal weak-
nesses in the Barthian position, which in many ways I have
learned from and admire. But, on the philosophical side, it is
quite clear to me where the changes came from. The analytical
philosophy I first got to know insisted on its autonomy, and the
insistence was based largely on the view it held that philosophy
is linguistic or conceptual analysis which is, of course, a part of
a broader foundationalist view. This view is no longer widely
held, the reason being largely the fact that analytical—or, if we
may be allowed to use the now-favored preposition, postanalyti-

cal—philosophers have become rather skeptical about the analytic–synthetic distinction, and, indeed, about any sort of foundationalism. Though there are still foundationalists among us, there is a lot more antifoundationalism.

My suspicion is—and this is a suggestion I wish to throw out as perhaps a unifying or explanatory theme in the conversation—that it is also true of the European philosophies known as postmodern that they are antifoundationalist, and I wonder to what extent the greater reluctance to insist on an autonomy of philosophy and theology vis-à-vis each other results, quite generally, from an abandonment of foundationalism?

PEPERZAK: I was very much struck by the phrase "audacity of hope" which Jean Ladrière used toward the end of his splendid talk. I particularly enjoyed his emphasis on the unity of the word and person. That is sort of an ideal for me, that we might be able to speak and to think as we are.

When I thought of going to study philosophy and people told me I should go to Nijmegen in Holland, I thought, "Oh no, please! Thomism! I have done that so often already" (at that time it was Thomist). I wrote a letter to Karl Rahner, whom I admired enormously. I had found consolation in his work against the theology I had to study in the manuals, so he was for me a sort of liberation in that time. So, I wrote him a letter, and I said, "Where should I study philosophy? I want to know all the modern and contemporary philosophers. I want to know what is really good today in philosophy, because the theology today is so bad, perhaps we can do something about it by studying twentieth-century philosophy, and not thirteenth-century." Certainly, I do have an enormous admiration for St. Thomas, let me say that. But Rahner wrote me to say he thought that it was not primarily important to study modernity or contemporary philosophy. Of course, you have to do that; but when you really want to be a philosopher, you must think what you are and be what you are. That was very good advice, I think. It has been for me a sort of leading word, which I connect now with the word of Jean Ladrière—audacity of hope. Because in audacity, I hear some new form of the old ideal of autonomy. There is this audacity in which you have to give yourself, but the hope is, of course, only possible in reliance on grace. So that would be my hope: that we would be able to discover together this "audacity of hope."

One final thing: I was very grateful for this conference because I met with people, most of whom I knew already and knew to be fine people, but it became apparent in a most beautiful way that the speakers spoke what they were. The only thing I miss is that those of you attending this Symposium had less opportunity to participate than we speakers did. I am sure that many of you would have a lot of things to say, and I propose that if we have a next conference we have new spiritual exercises that will encompass all of us and give everybody the opportunity to speak.

MARILYN ADAMS: I think the one thing that I appreciated about a number of the talks was a sense of humility. Once we lose or let go of our assumption that somehow we can be certain about things, certain about some things as opposed to others, then a more pluralistic humility opens up, which enables us to recognize that even our non-Christian philosophical colleagues, in their attempt to articulate their vision of value and being, and, because of their gifts and experience, may themselves have insights into who God is. They may not call it that, or name it that way. Nevertheless we may have things to learn from their philosophizing about the nature of God and the human vocation—for example, things said in this conference about love, opening the eyes, and so forth. I think people love different things and are sensitive to different things. In my own soteriology, God is very relentless and tries to get to people however God can; sometimes it is through beauty, sometimes through literary analysis, sometimes through a sensitivity to moral distinctions, or whatever it might be. And I think that the picture that emerges is of our trying to integrate our views of God philosophically, but somehow reality is bigger than any of our integrations, and so it breaks open again, and so we try again. This allows us a kind of flexibility to learn and an openness to our non-Christian philosophical colleagues and a greater sense of community with them in a kind of human project.

LADRIÈRE: Perhaps the most interesting aspect of our meeting was precisely that it took place, that the problem of Christian philosophy is considered a living problem. But it was said that we had to do with this problem as it is today, and we have heard some reflections about the meaning of this today.

I must confess that I remain fixed here on on two questions, because "today" can be considered, let us say, from the interior of Christian faith, that is to say, from the interior of the life of the Church, or it can be considered from the point of view of philosophy and, again, from the interior of philosophy. Regarding the internal concerns of the Church, we could wonder if there are some specific aspects of the present situation of the Church that are calling philosophy to bring its contribution to bear on some particularly pressing issues. I see at least one big problem the Church has to meet today: namely, the plurality of culture and, collaterally, the relationship between the expression of Christian faith and the cultural tradition. Now, this problem of the plurality of cultural traditions and faiths and of the possibility of encounter and genuine dialogue between them—the possibility of dialogue between the Catholic tradition as it has been elaborated in the Western world and, on the other hand, those different cultural traditions—certainly has philosophical aspects. I refer here to the classical notion of universality which has been considered traditionally as one of the main criteria of philosophical and scientific truth; so what does "universality" mean in this context? This is one problem.

Now, as for what specifically concerns philosophy, here in the different contributions we have had insights into that aspect of the question. Nevertheless, there is perhaps a question that remains and is suggested by what has been said, and I refer especially to the contribution of Professor Richardson, who gave us what I consider a diagnosis of the present state of philosophy. The question is this: is there something like a constraint on the way of doing philosophy in the present historical situation? The hypothesis is that we enter into philosophy, that we consider it worthwhile, a valuable and perhaps important undertaking. So, the question is not, philosophy or no philosophy? The question is, if philosophy, then what kind of constraints do we encounter as part of the undertaking today?

Now, those constraints can be purely sociological, and in this case they have not much importance. But the real question is to know if there are rational constraints on the way of doing philosophy, and this question is posed very concretely by what is called postmodernism, to which many references have been made during these sessions. So, what is the meaning of postmodernism with respect to the history of philosophy? And what is the possible constraint that emerges, so to say, through the works attributed to this philosophical movement? Now, this question is connected with perhaps a more general and radical question concerning the historicity of philosophy and the relationship between philosophy and its past. In what sense could it be said or not said, for example, that it is no longer possible to think as we did in the Middle Ages? Again, in what sense could it be said, or not said, for example, that it is no longer possible to think now as in the time of Hegel? And so on.

The kind of relationship between philosophy today and its past is very different from the type of relationship we have in the case of science, because, of course, present science presupposes what went before, but you can do perfectly good work in science without taking account of what occurred before. That is not the case for philosophy. Why? In what sense? What kind of constraint does the history of philosophy—the recent history but also the older history—exert on the present situation of philosophy? And for somebody who decides to work in philosophy, what is the weight, the scope, the meaning of that constraint, if there is a constraint?

The question is still a philosophical question concerning, after all, the fate of philosophy itself and the way in which philosophy understands its own situation and its own task. So, this question was explicitly present in the different contributions and discussions, but I had the feeling that nevertheless it remains a question that must be studied more deeply because it has a direct impact on the problem of Christian philosophy, or, let us say, the problem philosophy has functioning in the framework of Christian faith.

RICHARDSON: I don't have anything profound to say, except to react to what Jean Ladrière has said in the context of how I have tried to think about the problem. When he insists very properly on this constraint that the past imposes on us, given what he has already said about the challenge of postmodernism and all it implies for multiculturalism and the problems that go with it, it seems to me that a vision of the past must see it as the starting point for the mediation of the future. It is in that sense that certainly I formulated the question that served as title to my own presentation. It seems to me that the constraint on our thinking and the constraint on our place in history is imposed upon us from a future that comes through the past. That means that the past—say, the structure of the medieval period, or the structure of the Enlightment with Kant, Hegel, and the rest—has to be for us a mediation of the future. And I think what Christianity offers us is an experience—not simply a philosophical concept, but an experience—of the future as an advent that's still to come. It is in that context that I think of considering philosophy as offering us many approaches, certainly many styles each of which has its validity and many of which have been represented precisely by those who participated in the symposium here. Therefore, in answer to the question "What is philosophy?" I would say that philosophy is many things. Philosophizing is many different ways of trying to approach or to accept the future as coming through the past, as we have experienced it in our own past. That suggests to me a certain positive attitude toward postmodernism, if that's the way to designate the present challenge, but it also suggests to me the danger and the risks of postmodernism.

In listening to Jack Caputo give a very postmodern reading to philosophy, I had a question enter my mind. That was a great presentation in a style we have come to expect from him. But I kept asking myself, Now, who is this Caputo and who is Jack, and how can he talk this way? When, Jack, you talk about postmodernism, you talk with a sense of security, at least you communicate a sense of security, as if you were perfectly comfortable with the challenges and the risks and the shocks that are bound to come—and I always experience in you a certain tranquillity and even joy in the challenge and the freshness that comes out of it. I mean this very sincerely. But it seems to me that you are tethered to a past that assures you a future born, I would think, not of the experience of philosophy but precisely of an experience of the Christian revelation which says, "The truth is still to come."

The risk in this is that those who are not so tethered, who are simply plunged into the maelstrom, do not spontaneously have the sense of security that I think I share with you in playing with these concepts, but a sense of security, if I may speak in the first person, that we have in exposing ourselves to the rigors of postmodernism in all its forms, an assurance that comes not from the philosophy that we are playing with, but from—you mentioned it yesterday, Jack—a sense of *perfectio*, that is somehow ingredient to the dynamism of the postmodern movement. That sense of *perfectio* and that sense of security come, it seems to me, from a future we are assured of simply because we have some experience, however implicit, of what St. John tells us about in the experience of Jesus who is the Christ, and who is reported to us there as saying what he said about the truth.

It seems to me that it's an openness to the future that permits us to find a way of articulating this experience. Jean Ladrière placed us precisely in the presence of that Suffering Servant who is the incarnate truth, put us there in a way that it seems to me (though I realize that this can be challenged) would be impossible except in terms of a conception of philosophy as permeated by the demands precisely of postmodernism. Because when Jean talks about the structures of thought and experience that permit us to talk about an existence which is concretely actualized, these are concepts that come from the thought of postmodernism. It seems to me that it is by reason of concepts that came about in this way, articulating an experience as personal, as profound, and as moving as the one that Jean recounted to us this morning, that there is reason to hope based upon a security that comes not simply from philosophy but from faith as well.

Dupré: I think this conference changed me, changed my opinions rather fundamentally. Unfortunately, it is too early and perhaps too personal yet to say exactly in which way, but two things have become clear to me as they have never been before on the nature of Christian philosophy.

I always considered this in the past as a balancing act that defined itself in an endless ream of discussions in the 1920s and 1930s and of which I was certainly not capable. So, I was then satisfied with being a Christian (or certainly someone who tried to be one), who did philosophy and, at the same time who was so deeply interested in the essentially Christian life that I did something else on the side that could be called perhaps "history of spirituality." This is something I will have to change.

There are two elements here that I think were crucial and that were brought to the fore by my colleagues in a way that I, at least, found convincing. One is the element of conversion that has been repeated by several speakers. In the past, I have always thought of conversion as an exclusively religious term in the narrow sense of the word, but there is, indeed, a conversion to the philosophical way of life, and this morning we have heard it articulated by Jean Ladrière and seen it demonstrated in the most beautiful way before our eyes. So, if it is to be done well, if philosophy is not going to be purely logical exercise but is going to be something that really is serious, then it will have to be a conversion to the spiritual life. And the point that I have never realized so much as during this conference is this: that to do philosophy properly—and my friend Ladrière has explained extremely well how it can be done that way—one must be converted to a way of thinking that is consonant with a spiritual way of living. Reflecting on that, I was recalling a couple of books that appeared quite a while ago and that never sort of rang true to me. One was long ago, a book by Sertillanges, the French Dominican, *La vie intellectuelle*. I thought: Why should a French Dominican write a book on how to study in a way that makes it look like contemplation? Along with this was another book on the classics of Western mysticism, Western spirituality, a book by an English Dominican, Simon Tugwell, in which he discusses Thomas and Albert, the great medieval theologians/philosophers, and the way of study as a way of contemplation. Now I see them both as relevant to what we are talking about.

In other words, the intellectual life is something one has to be converted to as well, as one is converted to a religious life, in the strict sense of the word. And once one is converted to that, then distinctions arise which are and remain essential; so the autonomy of philosophy is to be taken seriously. At the same time, it is I, the person who does philosophy and who moves from one way of life into the other; there is a "breakout" from these constraining factors which makes distinctions possible. And this is another point, a point I learned in a different way from other people here. I learned it from Bill Richardson, from Jean-Luc Marion, and also from Pat Heelan, the fact that I have to, or we have to, expand the notion of Christian philosophy from what it was at its beginnings. This was far too narrow.

The reason why this discussion never got really off the ground in the 1920s or 1930s, or never came to anything conclusive, was precisely that it was too narrowly defined. Here we have redefined it in many ways. For example, last night Marion made it clear that it was a question also of looking at things, a question of hermeneutics, of perceiving things, of seeing things in another light—anything—as long as it is within philosophy. It has been done again on the question of postmodernism, the new kind of questions we raise, and the agreeable conclusion that I could draw is this. I was the first one who should have spoken, I didn't, and now I'm almost the last one to speak, but I'm probably also the one who changed most because I set a stage in my contribution that was extremely pessimistic and, in a sense, remains so. With regard to the break between nature and supernatural, that totally artificial thing, what I conclude now is that even in this brokenness, in this brokenness of our present culture, it is, indeed, possible to return to the life of contemplation and in our way—much more modest I am afraid than in the Middle Ages, or even in the seventh century—to do in the fullest sense of the term *Christian philosophy*. That is what I have learned.

MARION: As Jean Ladrière said, I think the first positive point concerning this conference is the very fact that it took place. It is also obvious that this question of Christian philosophy could raise a sufficient interest to make this conference successful and we have to thank for that not only the energy, but also the very precise insight of Professor Ambrosio, who saw that very clearly; he was right. We can say that now. Christian philosophy remains a crucial issue. This is the first fact.

But the other fact is that this issue is now cast in very different terms than it was when it was initially raised by Brille in, roughly, 1931. And I am struck also by the placement, transformation, and modification of the question. Let me just suggest some ways. First, the question is by no means now a question of a frontier, of a border between philosophy and theology. All the people who gave lectures here seem to agree on that, to some extent. There are, of course, two different methodologies, two different sciences. And because of that, there is no real danger that we can confuse those methodologies when both are brought to bear on the same topics, on the same issues. Those two methodologies can now allow themselves to try to resolve the same difficulties, and we have more a question of, I would say, international cooperation on world issues rather than war over borderlines, and this is a new point.

The second difference is that the content of the term *Christian philosophy* has now changed. The debate is not now confined merely to Scholasticism or Neoscholasticism. Many of us tried to explain the possibility of such a Christian philosophy without referring to the traditional items that are supposed to be related to it, and the fact is that Christian philosophy is not an expression used by the great scholastics, but an expression used by Erasmus or by the first Church fathers, or more recently in a spiritual sense. So, without denying that Scholasticism is a main contribution to Christian thought, of course, it would be completely inappropriate to limit discussion to its possibilities. I think we must emphasize the fact that Christian philosophy is a style of thinking that is a constant feature of Christian faith and is, to some extent, part and parcel of the life of the Church without being limited to this or that school. And so we have to deal with Christian philosophy, I would say, as a charism of the Church. The Church also has the charism of doing Christian philosophy. It is perhaps a charism related to the charism of wisdom, but it is something that is part and parcel of the Christian life and of the Church.

But the third point I would emphasize is the fact that there is a danger in the use of the term *postmodernism*. It is the danger that the precise character of this movement will be lost in a designation that is purely chronological and, therefore, could be viewed as a purely negative eclecticism. The central character of the so-called postmodern movement is, I would say, a question of the end of metaphysics. I think the end of metaphysics is perhaps the best way to name different things that are, for instance, also occurring in postanalytic philosophy. I disagree with this term *postmodernism*. May I suggest that it is not a term used in

France, and it is a typical example of French philosophy for ex-portation. And as you know, as with wine, it is not always the best goods that are exported. So, I would prefer to speak of the philosophy of Levinas, which is not deconstructionist, or of Ri-coeur, or of Derrida, fine, but not of postmodernism as such. It is not precise enough. All this is a question of nihilism and the end of metaphysics, the crisis of rationality and so on, but not this nickname.

So, the new question is that if there is both an enlargement of rationality in diverse rationalities and, on the negative side, a crisis of rationality, both are true. The profession of Christian faith is much more difficult now than it was in previous times. Now the challenge for Christian thought is not, "Are you ratio-nal? Are you as rational as other sciences?" And why not these questions anymore? Because other sciences are now also at odds concerning their own rationality. So, the question now for Chris-tian thought is, can you be rational enough to discuss with other rationalities that also are in crisis? And so it is not an issue of possessing your own territory, or even territory different from other domains, but the question is rather an issue, who is the more rational? And, to that extent, Christian philosophy, and also theology, can give an addition of rationality to some questions which are discussed by everybody in the public square, and the instances of that are very well known. In the history of philoso-phy, of course, I know that in classical philosophy the greatest progress the last twenty years was made by the fact that, for the first time, the historians of classical philosophy admitted that the-ology was a part of their business. But now in phenomenology, it is very clear that in hermeneutics, the Bible, in Derrida, in Levinas, for instance, and also in the question of the gift, the question of faith, which is the first theological issue—all this progress in the common rationality was made in relation to Christian thought and the Christian tradition. So, our challenge is not to defend ourselves against the suspicion of not being ratio-nal. The challenge is to decide and to experience whether we are able to help others be more rational than they are. Are we able to give some more rationality to the open, common debates? And this is, in my opinion, the future of Christian philosophy.

MODERATOR: I think we've reached not only the limit of our time, but also the appropriate place to end. I was struck a few days ago in thinking about this seminar by one of the parables in St. Luke's Gospel, where the servant is coming in after a day in the fields and feels like sitting down to a meal with his master and saying, "Well, we did a good day's work, didn't we? I'm glad it's over." But Christ points out that although this may be the natural expectation, the higher expectation is to realize that first the servant must set the table and serve his master's meal, and then, only after that, will he be able to enjoy his own meal. This parable says to me something about the kind of gratitude that is appropriate not simply to having done a good day's work, which I think we all have—a couple of good days' work—but also the kind of gratitude that is grateful for the opportunity of having done a good day' s work. Perhaps to connect this with something I think, if I understood it correctly, Jean Luc Marion was just saying, we have done nothing more than is expected of us, but that expectation is a gift of love. It allows us to be what we are, to the extent that we all come here wanting to be Christian philosophers.

VI
In Response

Fra Angelico: *The Annunciation.* Convent of San Marco, Florence. Left: the Angel (detail); right: the Virgin (detail).

12

On Seeing Fra Angelico's San Marco *Annunciation:* The Place of Art*

Francis J. Ambrosio

Not yet had we moved our feet on it when I perceived that the encircling bank (which, being vertical, lacked means of ascent) was of pure white marble, and was adorned with such carvings that not only Polycletus but Nature herself would there be put to shame.

The angel who came to earth with the decree of peace, wept for since many a year, which opened Heaven from its long ban, before us there appeared so vividly graven in gentle mien that it seemed not a silent image: one would have sworn that he was saying, "Ave," for there she was imaged who turned the key to open the supreme love, and these words were imprinted in her attitude: "Ecce ancilla Dei," as expressly as a figure is stamped on wax.

—DANTE ALIGHIERI, *Purgatorio X*, 34–45[1]

When you come before the image of the Ever-Virgin take care not to let the "Ave" remain silent as you pass.

—Inscription beneath the San Marco
Annunciation

* I wish to acknowledge the debt I owe to M. Fantoni for his help with many aspects of this study, including insightful criticisms of an earlier draft of the text and valuable guidance for reading in the vast literature on the Florentine Renaissance, as well as for his warm encouragement of interdisciplinary study expressed in his Introduction to volume I of the journal *Italian Culture and History* (1995). An earlier version of this essay appeared in volume III of that journal (1997). Of course, any errors remaining in the final version are entirely my responsibility. Thanks are also due to Georgetown University for support of a sabbatical during which the work of research and writing was accomplished.
[1] Translated by C.S. Singleton, *The Divine Comedy*, 3 vols. (Princeton: Princeton University Press, 1982).

PROLOGUE

THERE IS POWER IN ART: the power of beauty. Beauty's power is mysterious and fascinating; it tends to play favorites. None of this is profound; rather, it is quite commonplace— hardly worth mentioning were it not necessary in order to explain why the following essay has been written, and why written as it has been. Mystery has no "why," so it can be neither comprehended nor explained. Yet, it does happen: mystery takes place in human experience, literally "takes" place, because to experience mystery is to suffer overwhelming power. Whether that power is experienced as benign or malicious is not the issue; what is the issue is that it happens *to* us; it is experienced as an event we undergo, not an action we perform or can control.

Beauty is one of the powers of mystery. While beauty cannot be comprehended or explained, the reality of its happening in the world can be appreciated and to some extent understood, both in its factuality—its "givenness"—and in the manner of its occurrence. The following essay tries to clear a place of appreciation and understanding for the mysterious and powerful beauty that happens as Fra Angelico's fresco of the *Annunciation* in the Convent of San Marco in Florence.[2]

This might well seem a peculiar undertaking here, but the occasion for it is basically academic. For some years I have been asked to lead study groups visiting Florence. At the outset, I suggest to the group members that during the several weeks of their stay they should aspire to become something more than tourists and begin to share in the life of the city in a modest but genuine way, much like welcome guests in another family's home. Occasionally, someone asks what my favorite works of art in the city are, and I generally answer that I have two favorites: Michelangelo's *Pietà* in the Museo del Opera del Duomo and Fra Angelico's

---

[2] For a wide-ranging and suggestive study of one aspect of what I refer to here as the "mysterious power of beauty" as it occurs specifically in the form of images, see David Freedberg, *The Power of Images* (Chicago: The University of Chicago Press, 1989). Freedburg approaches the issue from the perspective of "response." The approach taken here focuses on the phenomenological and ontological dimensions of the issue.

Annunciation in San Marco.[3] Now, after some years of study and reflection on these two works, I have come to believe that this question of "favorites" has an intellectual importance bearing on the issue of methodology in interdisciplinary studies in general and of the Florentine Renaissance in particular. Beyond the strictly personal, the notion of "favorites" offers a clue to understanding how the power of beauty sets itself to work in art and takes place in the world. In other words, in raising the question of the "place of art" in human life and culture, we discover in our ways of speaking about the experience of art—especially about the meaning it has for us—that the particular and the general, the immediate and personal, as well as the intellectual and theoretical forms of the question are deeply interconnected. No doubt, some of the interest this realization held for me is idiosyncratic, a result of my academic training and professional practice in the discipline of philosophy. But this brings us back to the metaphor of being "at home" in places that are not strictly speaking one's own home, whether personally, academically, or culturally. In the end this essay is written in the hope that the efforts to understand and, to some degree, explain the experience of profound recognition and deep personal inclination toward a favorite work from which one is, paradoxically, separated by temporal and cultural distance will shed light on how art takes place in human life and

---

[3] One striking difference between these two works is immediately evident in the context of the present discussion and bears comment: the *Annunciation* is still located in the spot in which it was first created and for which it was intended; the *Pietà* was intended by Michelangelo to be located on his own tomb, though it is now in the Museum of the Works of the Cathedral in Florence. It is commonplace to observe that today much of the art that we see is "out of place," for example, when we see a work in a museum. But what is lost, or at least likely to be misplaced, when a work has been collected involves more than its removal from its "original" physical location. The loss extends much further and reaches to those larger dimensions of meaning upon which its creator endeavored to allow it to open by including its "location" in the event of imagination in which the work originated. Before art works were produced to be sold, as long as art was still typically commissioned, its creation almost always involved at least some general determination of the type of place the work would be given: a church, a public building or square, a private home or garden. Works of art are not imagined for museum spaces; nor are they made to be collected. To say that art has a place in human living is to say that the intended location of the work is as much an element of its meaning as pigment, marble, subject matter, artist, or viewer.

culture by embodying a revelatory event of truth occurring as a spectacular and fascinating vision of beauty.

INTRODUCTION

From a theoretical perspective, the concern of this essay is to elaborate a hermeneutic understanding of the experience of appreciating a work of art, using a favorite work, Fra Angelico's *Annunciation*, to focus and magnify our observations. How does mystery yield meaning in and as appreciation?

The treatment here will be theoretical, not abstract or purely formal, precisely in the sense that, because it seeks to understand an experience of meaning which occurs originally as appreciation, the structure of that experience can be articulated and its significance clarified only upon reflection. Therefore, to achieve a truthful understanding, the study must have constant recourse to the "original" in two senses: the work and the experience, while we keep in mind that ultimately these two "objects" of reflection are inseparably linked in a still more original relationship, however mysterious that may be. For the purpose of this study, then, this threefold sense of originality can be stated thus: our appreciation of the extraordinary beauty of the *Annunciation* centers itself in the experience of its being in its own original place, uniquely proper to itself. From this appreciation of the unique propriety of beauty's way of taking place in this work, we can hope to gain a clearer understanding of the way beauty takes place in all art.

The study will follow a threefold hermeneutical procedure, employing *categorial*, *disciplinary*, and *thematic* perspectives on its subject matter. Each of these perspectives derives from and is related to the others through the notion of *place*. Schematically, their deployment and interrelation can be tabularized as follows:

	Categorial	*Disciplinary*	*Thematic*
(1)	site	historical	tradition
(2)	position	literary	memory
(3)	situation	theological	incarnation
(4)	space	philosophical	contemplation
(5)	place	existential	meaning

Because of the relative complexity of the procedure we will be employing, it will be useful to give a working definition of the term "place" as it is used technically here, and then to state, initially and provisionally, the main point of each element of the analysis in summary form, in anticipation of the argument as a whole.

Definition: "Place" denotes the unique existential index of the meaning of an event within the continuous field of human experience that we call the world.

Summary of Elements:

(1) The *site* of a work of art refers to all the environing conditions of its material and physical embeddedness in the world as an expression of the living cultural *traditions* that converge upon it and are transformed in it.

(2) The *position* of a work of art refers to its setting in the narrative and dramatic patterns that articulate the dynamism and vitality of cultural traditions. The work of art *memorializes* these patterns by giving them imaginative expression in the form of stories.

(3) The *situation* of the work of art refers to its involvement in the ways of life of the persons who habitually dwell with it. The situation of all art is ultimately *religious* and specifically *liturgical*.

(4) The *space* of a work of art refers to its function of demarcating and opening up a *contemplative* horizon of meaning within the world. This contemplative function implies that all art is originally *decorative* in character.

(5) Finally, the *place* of a work of art refers to its origin in and as an event occurring in human existence as the experience of beauty's power to excite and satisfy the desire for *meaning*. The work of art takes place in the world as the fulfillment of desire expressed in terms of finding oneself (or not finding oneself) *at home in the world*.

I

Fra Angelico's painting of the San Marco *Annunciation* was a focal event of unique importance in the history of the Florentine

Renaissance. This study's first task, then, is to do a rough survey of the historical topography[4] of that event: that is, trace the major contours of the cultural forces that were at work in shaping the site of that event and converge upon that site as a point of focus, achieving there a kind of maximum intensity of tension between vectors of continuity and stability, on one hand, and innovation and change, on the other. It is this tension-laden convergence of cultural forces which confers upon the event of the painting a mass and magnitude of meaning great enough to challenge our capability to take the measure of its site accurately.

The site of the San Marco *Annunciation* is the Dominican convent attached to the Church of San Marco, which until 1436 was under the supervision of Silvestrine monks. In that year, partly at the instigation of Cosimo il Vecchio, Pope Eugenius IV ordered the Silvestrines to exchange churches with a group of Dominicans from the Convent of San Domenico in Fiesole who had recently taken over the small, rather remote Church of San Giorgio alla Costa across the Arno. Quite apart from the strategic significance of this move in the political master-plan of Cosimo, recently returned to Florence from exile in Venice and eager now to solidify his de facto control of the machinery of civil government in Florence through an alliance with the pope which culminated in the spectacular staging of the Council of Florence in 1439, this gambit had its own valence in the internal politics of the Dominican Order in central Italy. Since the establishment of the Dominicans in Florence at Santa Maria Novella in 1219, that

---

[4] It should be clear that I am including "art" here among the cultural dynamics that shape history, and thereby subsuming "art history" into that larger category. Of course, I recognize that this methodological choice involves a sacrifice of much analytic precision and nuance that would properly attend a strictly art historical treatment of this work, and must rely on the benefits of an attempt at a "interdisciplinary" study to redeem that loss in some fashion. Furthermore, there is no suggestion that the type of survey made here could be comprehensive from the perspective of the professional historian, who will undoubtedly note with concern the absence of reference to many standard works that the canons of professional scholarship in the discipline of history would require. The only claims that can be made for the "scientific" character of the present study are that the effort has been made to survey the multiple facets of the subject matter in the scholarly literature sufficiently to avoid genuine mistakes either of commission or omission, and, beyond that, to call attention to some particular issues and insights that in the view of the author shed valuable evidential light on the main line of argument put forward here.

convent had been the Order's center of power and influence in the city. By the beginning of the fifteenth century, however, a reform movement known as the Observance had arisen within the Order. Its goal was a return to the full vigor of the charism of the founder, which the leaders of the movement took to be embedded in the specific precepts of the Constitutions of the Order, as they had been laid down by St. Dominic himself. The initiating figure of this movement in Florence was Fra Giovanni Dominici, a friar of Maria Novella who founded San Domenico in Fiesole in 1406. Therefore, when the Dominicans moved to San Marco in 1436, they brought with them the particular cast of Dominican spirituality associated with the Observance.

Perhaps this brief background account of the way Cosimo came to be linked with the renovation of San Marco is sufficient to allow us to identify at least three of the principal sight lines which must guide our survey of the site of the *Annunciation*. First, the transformation of Florentine culture which manifested itself in the fifteenth century, of which the San Marco renovation is one episode, is a complex event that can be adequately denominated only by the term "Christian Renaissance." Second, the *Annunciation* itself must be viewed as part of a larger program of fresco decoration, the extent and coherence of which is uniquely noteworthy in that the decoration was specifically intended to illustrate and reinforce the spiritual revitalization ambitioned by the Dominican Observance and was the religious justification for the physical renovation and enlargement project. Third, the scope of Cosimo's patronage of the project signals the full emergence, after a period of gestation, of a new source of spiritual, social, and artistic inspiration in Florentine culture, the lay Confraternities, one of which in particular, the Compagnia de' Magi, was closely identified with San Marco and shaped the specific character of Cosimo's relationship with it as a religious center.

The nexus of these three lines of influence makes it plausible to claim that, from an historical perspective, the placement of the *Annunciation* on the site of the renovated Convent of San Marco is an essential element of its beauty. Let us examine each of these factors in turn before considering how together they might support this claim.

In his splendid introduction[5] to an important collection of essays, Timothy Verdon articulates an intellectual perspective which not only outlines a method of historical scholarship sharing the basic assumptions of the approach taken here, but also frames that method within the context of a larger attempt to understand the meaning and significance of images and the religious imagination holistically from within the lived experience of the historical culture by which they were made. Such an attempt goes far toward realizing in concrete detail the intellectual commitments that guide this discussion of the *Annunciation*.[6]

Verdon locates this attempt to provide a more adequate framework for Renaissance studies within the movement in recent scholarship away from the Burckhardtian tendency to interpret the Renaissance primarily in terms of the cultural categories of modernity. The set of essays he introduces as a whole take "Christianity and the Renaissance as equal coefficients."[7] He goes on to say:

> Indeed, . . . to have called this collection "Christianity *in* the Renaissance," or "Renaissance Christianity," would have suggested subordination—of the ancient religious system to an intellectual and artistic movement in the first case, or of the astonishing vitality of this movement to established religion in the second. It was a question here, as in all areas of historical interpretation, of weighing tradition against innovation: of evaluating the respective influence of things that had always been and things that were new. For Renaissance studies the issue is critical, since imbalance in either direction not only distorts but tends to negate the object of study. . . . This book sees the historical reality as more subtle: an equilibrium of stimuli—precarious, but at the same time dynamic in its tension between continuity and change.[8]

---

[5] Timothy Verdon, "Christianity, the Renaissance, and the Study of History," in Timothy Verdon and John Henderson, eds., *Christianity and the Renaissance: Image and Religious Imagination in the Quattrocento* (Syracuse: Syracuse University Press, 1990), pp. 1–37.

[6] Although I am grateful and indebted to Timothy Verdon for the clarity and synthetic vision of the approach to Renaissance studies which his essay formulates, and I believe that there is a deep affinity between his position and the approach taken here, I hasten to make clear that the responsibility for the use made here of such an approach, especially for any missteps in its employment, is strictly my own.

[7] Verdon, "Christianity, Renaissance, History," p. 2.

[8] Ibid.

Drawing on methodological categories developed by twentieth-century historians like Huizinga and Focillon and philosopher Michael Polanyi, Verdon argues for the necessity to "put on
the mind" (cf. Phil. 2:6), of Renaissance Christian believers and
penetrate the "logic of faith"[9] that structures their imaginations:

> The most basic challenge to historians of religious culture is to
> articulate for those who may not have "heard the call" the pat-
> terned set of properties which made it seem wise to those who did.
> . . . the importance of this integrative approach is especially clear
> for the history of art, since religious artifacts are concrete expres-
> sions of the beliefs that shape lives. But where a Renaissance artist
> could take lived faith-experience for granted—his creative process
> presupposing a correlative recreative process in his public—
> modern historians have to feel their way back into that way of
> "seeing things," cautiously reassembling the apparatus of imagi-
> nation which first gave plastic and pictorial images their power to
> stir feeling and elicit response. Nevertheless, only such a grasp of
> the specific emotional gravity of their subject allows scholars to
> analyze the relationship between form and content central to the
> creative process.[10]

Obviously, all this applies directly to any attempt to understand the historical site of the work of Fra Angelico and the Florentine religious culture in which it was embedded: the Christian
Renaissance imagination from which it emerged is as much a
datum of its art historical setting as the date of its execution.

The second element of our survey of the site of this work
touches on the individuating element of Fra Angelico's artistic
imagination—its formation in the crucible of the reform spirituality of the Dominican Observance. It is the surpassing merit of
William Hood's masterful work, *Fra Angelico at San Marco*,[11]
to have demonstrated conclusively the strict necessity of recognizing that all the fresco works done by the painter as part of the
renovation project in the convent, including the *Annunciation*,

---

[9] St. Anselm uses this phrase to describe his *Monologion.*
[10] Verdon, "Christianity, Renaissance, History," p. 9.
[11] W. Hood, *Fra Angelico at San Marco* (New Haven, Conn.: Yale University
Press, 1993); see also a preliminary version of the main lines of Hood's argument in his essay, "Fra Angelico at San Marco," in Verdon and Henderson,
Christianity and the Renaissance, pp. 108–31.

form a unified program that was specifically intended by him, guided by his religious superiors and their theological consultants, to illustrate and teach the charism of St. Dominic as articulated in the Constitutions of the Order which the founder himself had drafted, and this as read through the scrutinizing lenses of Observant practice.[12]

Having entered the order at the Convent of San Domenico, Piero Guidolino, born in Vicchio in the Mugello country north of Florence in the late 1390s, took on the identity of Fra Giovanni, a son of St. Dominic of the Observant branch of the family. He thus became an inheritor not simply of the Dominican spiritual patrimony, but of the particular legatical effects associated with the Observance. Principally and schematically, these were three: within the broader emphasis on intellectual labor to combat heretical distortion of sound doctrine, a preferential option for preaching as opposed to scholarship and writing as their mode of apostolic labor; a stricter and more literal application of those prescriptions in the Constitutions touching on material poverty; and, finally, a dedication to liturgical contemplation, including fidelity to an unabridged oration of the Hours of the Divine Office in common, as well as the daily Chapter of Faults and the addition of the Little Office of the Virgin, the Salve procession, and other Marian devotions.[13]

The significance of each of these Observant emphases for the spiritual imagination of Fra Giovanni as exercised in his ministry of painting will be resumed later. For now, it is important to note that, while Dominican practice universally retained the central place of preaching, poverty, and liturgy in the life of every friar and convent, a member of the San Domenico and San Marco convents like Fra Giovanni could be distinguished from his con-

---

[12] Beyond Hood's book, the bibliography on Fra Angelico is too extensive to survey here. Therefore, I limit myself to a selection comprising those works that contributed directly to this study: the standard reference is J. Pope-Hennessy, *Fra Angelico*, 2nd ed. (London: Phaidon Press, 1974); Umberto Baldini, *Beato Angelico* (Florence: Edizione d'Arte il Fiorino, 1986); Georges Didi-Huberman, *Fra Angelico: Dissemblance and Figuration*, trans. J. Todd (Chicago: The University of Chicago Press, 1995).

[13] Hood discusses the background and essential characteristics of the Dominican Observant movement in chapter 1 of his book, "The Myth of Original Perfection and the Ideals of the Dominican Observance."

frères at Santa Maria Novella by the degree of prominence and rigor of devotion with which these spiritual rubrics were integrated into his daily routine. Unlike the Franciscan movement, there did not arise a formal institutional division within the Dominican Order between the "progressive" faction who more freely adapted the letter of the Constitutions to accommodate changing conditions and demands of their ministerial situation and the more "conservative" or traditional faction who formed the Observance. Nevertheless, the differing degrees of emphasis characterizing the two Dominican groups are, as will be seen, certainly significant enough to merit serious attention for one who seeks to understand precisely the sense in which Fra Giovanni's painting in general, and the San Marco *Annunciation* in particular, could have been created only within the imaginative horizon of the Dominican Observance.

The third element of this survey of the historical forces that converge on the site of San Marco is the interplay of the lay patronage of religious art in fifteenth-century Florence and the expanded arena for active involvement of the laity in the spiritual life of the Church which the Confraternities provided.[14] For present purposes, the issue here is straightforward: what would have induced Cosimo to spend the enormous sum of more than 40,000 florins[15] for the convent project, thereby providing the occasion and setting the stage for the exceptionally ambitious program of frescoes which Fra Giovanni was commissioned to carry out? Not surprisingly, any adequate answer to this question, like all

---

[14] For a helpful study of the phenomenon of artistic patronage in general in the religious life of Florence in this period, see Richard Fremantle, *God and Money in Renaissance Florence* (Florence: L. S. Olschki, 1975); on the role of lay patronage in the Observant movement, see N. Rubenstein, "Lay Patronage and Observant Reform in Fifteenth-Century Florence," in Verdon and Henderson, eds., *Christianity and the Renaissance*, pp. 63–82; many of the diverse elements in the transformation of lay spirituality are surveyed in the essays included in Part Two of the same volume. On the involvement of the Medici in the Compagnia de' Magi and its association with San Marco, see R. Hatfield, "The Compagnia de' Magi," *Journal of the Warburg and Courtauld Institutes*, 33 (1970): 107–61; finally for an attempt to analyze the complex interaction of these and other social forces in the creation of artistic images, see Martin Wackernagel, *The World of the Florentine Renaissance Artist*, trans. Alison Luchs (Princeton, N.J.: Princeton University Press, 1981).

[15] Wackernagel, *World of the Florentine Renaissance Artist*, p. 229.

questions of human motivation, is anything but straightforward. But precisely in that fact lies its significance: Fra Angelico's painting is caught up in a web of individual and social currents which connect it to the cultural world in which it originates, and which in turn pulsate throughout our experience of the painting. We encounter not simply the painting, but the painting embedded in its world.

As patron, Cosimo would have been moved by pangs of conscience over "many political acts of violence,"[16] the stigma of usury, the unquestioned obligation of the great families to use their wealth for the cultural aggrandizement and religious edification of the city, as well as the need to demonstrate the scope of the power and influence that he commanded. But beyond all this, the growing Confraternity movement was teaching the laity that, as individuals, their actions could play a role not only in their own salvation, but also in the mission of the Church in the world. As a result, Cosimo's personal piety and his partiality to the Dominican Observance led him to see a symbolic significance in the family's involvement in the San Marco project which well suited the evolving sense of destiny he envisioned for himself, the Medici, and Florence. Hatfield puts the matter thus:

> Cosimo's interest in San Marco was not unconditional but dependent on his favour towards the order. Probably it was incidentally, as the new benefactors of San Marco, the symbolic locus of Bethlehem on each Epiphany Day, that Cosimo and his family adopted the cult of the three kings—and with it the *Compagnia de' Magi*. . . . From a letter written by his wife Contessina to their son Giovanni, it emerges that Cosimo took part, dressed in a fur cloak, in the *Festa de' Magi* on Epiphany Day, 1451, and that in those of previous years he had worn a gown of gold. Besides the famous frescoes by Benozzo Gozzoli in the chapel, there were at least four other paintings and a wall-hanging representing the Magi in the Medici Palace when an inventory was taken of it possessions in 1492.[17]

To summarize: Cosimo's motivation for the San Marco project is best understood as a symbolic expression not just of his own

---

[16] Ibid.

[17] Hatfield, "Compagnia de' Magi," 135–37.

many-faceted identity, but also of the role a person like him could and should play in the coming-to-be of a genuinely new cultural world. In this symbolic expression we can read, I believe, the declaration of a new way of locating the place of art in the lives of the inhabitants of that world, and the site of that declaration is the Convent of San Marco. For, while the "site" of an art work comprises every material and physical dimension of the aesthetic coordinates that locate the observer's experience of it, physical and material conditions are not abstractions: they too have histories, and while history is not reducible to empirical "facts," such facts are the groundwork of history and the site of historical meanings. It is in this sense that I would suggest that it is cultural traditions, dynamic processes of transformative tension between continuity and innovation, stability and change, which best express how to understand the coordinates by which this most basic level of our experience of a work of art is located in the world.[18]

II

As the friars of the Convent of San Marco passed along the north corridor of the dormitory between their cells, which doubled as private studies during the day, and the many other areas of the convent and church upon which their liturgically punctuated daily routine unfolded, they would frequently pass the spot where the *Annunciation* was frescoed on the corner of the corridor's inner wall. After vespers, on their way to bed, they would directly confront the fresco's scene as they rounded the final corner of the stairway leading up from the main cloister. How does this positioning affect our understanding of the painting's meaning and our appreciation of its beauty?[19] What dimension does

---

[18] For a detailed exposition and argument in support of this dynamic use of the world "tradition," the reader is referred to Hans-Georg Gadamer's discussion of an hermeneutical understanding of history in Part Two of *Truth and Method*, 2nd rev. ed., trans. Joe. Weinsheimer and Donald G. Marshall (New York: Crossroads, 1989).

[19] Hood notes that by virtue of its position in the north corridor, the *Annunciation* is outside the convent enclosure and therefore would be seen by members of the laity who might visit the library, for example, or certainly by Cosimo on

consideration of the position of a work of art add to our experience of it beyond what is given in its site-location?

"Position" is characterized above as the art work's setting in the narrative and dramatic patterns that articulate the dynamism and vitality of the cultural traditions in which it is embedded. The work of art "memorializes" these patterns by giving them imaginative expression and recalling the "story-context" from which the work's subject matter is drawn.[20] The suggestion offered here is that a clue to the significance of a work's position can be discovered by attending to the role of memory in such an experience as the Dominican confrères of Fra Angelico can be imagined to have had daily as they repeatedly viewed the painting.

Beyond its obvious universal significance for human experience in general, the role of memory, particularly the memory of persons, takes on particular importance for those responding to a religious vocation. For vocation refers to an event of "calling," and as such is essentially interpersonal and communitarian. To remember who one is means to recall the relation of self and other in the dynamics of past formative encounters, as well as the identity shared with those who have experienced similar encounters. While memory can be viewed as a cornerstone of any formalized and institutionalized religious identity, the role of memory was especially emphasized and fostered in the spirituality of the Dominican Observance. Novices were taught not simply to keep the memory of the founder in mind, but also to remember him by imitating his actions and way of living, even to the point of being schooled in the bodily postures and gestures the saint was recorded as employing when at prayer, thus embodying his spirit again in themselves.[21] Memory, then, can provide

---

the way to the suite of cells reserved for him at the opposite end of the corridor; see Hood, *Fra Angelico*, p. 260. This fact only extends rather than changes the significance of its positioning.

[20] I would wish to argue that this sense of "position" as related to a narrative context is not limited to "representational" art alone, but extends even to subject matter which would be termed "abstract." An explanation of this assertion cannot be undertaken here, but it would be along the lines of a distinction between realistic and phenomenological epistemological approaches to the notion of meaning.

[21] See Hood, *Fra Angelico*, chap. 9, pp. 195–208.

the connection between the material and physical facts of the *Annunciation*'s location in time-space and its position in the original viewers' daily encounters with it, and ultimately, our own as well.

It has been widely remarked by art historians both that there is a marked difference between what might be loosely referred to as Fra Angelico's "public" and "private" styles of painting, where "public" refers to works intended for display in churches (altarpieces, for example), and those intended specifically for his Dominican confrères living in the convent; and that the plan of his private works in San Marco, executed as part of Cosimo's project of renovation and aggrandizement of the convent, had a specifically didactic purpose to play in the life of the community. The ambitious goal of their didactic function, however, reached beyond mere illustration either of general truths of Christian belief as embodied in the life of Christ portrayed in the Gospel, or even of definite principles of the Dominican Constitutions which set forth the rule of life through which Dominic's followers attempted to preserve and activate in their lives the unique spiritual charism of the founder. Rather, Fra Angelico believed that both before and beyond the "imitation of Christ" or the discipline of the rule lies the way of the disciple, and that the origin of discipleship lies in an experience of conversion and calling which occurs in the imagination as a transformation of one's way of seeing the world and envisioning one's place in it. For the disciple, this process of transformation, this "metanoia" or "change of mind," is a growth into the identity of being a witness and bearing testimony to God's Incarnate Word revealed in and as the human person of Jesus. It is, in other words, a transformation of one's personal identity into the way of living properly understood as contemplative.

Contemplation is the most fundamental form of discipleship, and religious life in all its forms, whether monastic, conventual, or secular, has as its explicitly avowed purpose the ordering of all the circumstances and activities of an individual's life so that they might most effectively conduct the "follower of the rule" to the envisioning of that love which is the habitual home of contemplation. From this perspective, the friar's physical home, the convent, easily comes to be viewed as a "school of contemplation," in just the same sense as the parental home should be the child's first and best school of virtue. But just as the evangelical counsels of chastity, poverty, and obedience envision a contemplative identification with Christ which goes beyond the limits of the moral imagination and its proper virtues, so too the "home-making" of the conventual school of contemplation envisions the creation of images which bring the revealing light of embodiment to the mysterious works of the Spirit of God at the heart of human history. This, then, is the "didactic spirit" of Fra Giovanni's program which inspired the "private" style of the frescoes of San Marco: to serve his confrères by helping to make them at-home in the mystery of God's Incarnate Love and see their way clear along the path of discipleship first traveled by St. Dominic.

In executing this program, however, Fra Angelico was also remembering two other spiritual and creative guides, Giotto and Dante, who, though not members of the nuclear Dominican family, belonged to another branch of the extended clan, the Franciscans, who shared with the Dominicans the closest bonds of religious kinship. The artistic influence of Giotto and Dante on the work of Fra Angelico is to be discerned not so much in elements of style or subject matter as in the shaping of the artist's imagination in the contemplative tradition of the Christian West. To fully explicate the effective dynamism of this heritage and, in particular, of the role of Giotto's and Dante's work in the style of Fra Giovanni's frescoes in San Marco would both require and merit a more detailed study than is possible here, but some of the more important features of that legacy can be suggested by concentrating on the notions of memory and the site of a work of art mentioned earlier.

First, we must note that Giotto, like his contemporary and colleague Dante, was profoundly affected by the spirit of St. Francis and its Incarnational sensibility. Like Dante, Giotto was a "tertiary Franciscan," that is, a lay person who committed himself to live the life of the Franciscan rule without taking formal religious vows. Like Giotto, whose birthplace was within a few miles of Piero Guidolino's near Vicchio, the latter was an icon painter. This fact calls attention to a kinship between them that is effective more in shaping the imagination than in determining style or genre. Giotto, as the forerunner of the "new" style of painting "according to nature," had begun to depart in many ways from the dominant Byzantine iconographic style of his master Cimabue and his Sienese contemporary Duccio. Yet, at the level of artistic intention, he remained a child of this tradition in viewing iconic painting as a window onto mystery, the religious mystery of God's salvific love. The iconic face,[22] especially in the gaze of the eyes, presented a visage which fixed the viewer in a movement of invitation that approached him or her out of the space of the divine. This visage, itself contemplative, solicited a recognition and response in kind, an entering into a mutual gift-giving in which total self-donation, springing up in gratitude, was the occasion for an experience of intimate union, the fruits of which were peace, freedom, and the integrity of genuine fulfillment. This contemplative experience, whether properly mystical or natural according to its grace, was understood to be a foretaste of the "beatific vision," the enjoyment of perfect self-possession which is complete identity of essence with existence in God, and in which the angels participate to an exemplary degree.

Of course, Giotto was not a theologian, nor need we think of him as a religious mystic, though nothing prevents us from so imagining him, or, for that matter, Dante or Fra Giovanni as well. But because they are artists their contemplative character reveals itself in and through their presentation of nature, both in the sense of the world of nature, as embodying the splendor of God's creation, and in the sense of human nature as the stage upon which salvation history, the drama of human freedom with Christ as the central actor, works itself out. This intuition, and the dramatic shift of artistic emphasis and stylistic demands which it occasioned, are ultimately traceable to the impetus for renovation of the spirit of lived Christianity and the institutional life of the Roman church which proceeded jointly from the Franciscan and Dominican movements, whose influence spread so swiftly and irresistibly in the thirteenth and fourteenth centuries. From this intuitive reshaping of the religious imagination into a specifically

---

[22] For a stunningly insightful phenomenological treatment of the iconic face, see Jean-Luc Marion, *God Without Being*, trans. Thomas A. Carlson (Chicago: The University of Chicago Press, 1991), chap. 1, pp. 7–24.

Incarnational form, the principal stylistic innovations attributed to Giotto sprang directly. His attention to the natural and historical setting of scenes from the life of Christ, the Virgin Mary, and St. Francis, the full spatial density and weight of the human body, and especially the representation of the place of human emotions, primarily located in the gestures of the body and the expression of face and eyes, are accounted for by a contemplative vision which is continuous with the spirit of Byzantine iconography, but reimagined through the eyes of an Incarnational spirituality that for a variety of historical reasons had been effaced for more than a thousand years. In other words, Giotto's painting, like Dante's poetry, as we shall see, continues to adhere to the contemplative purpose of art in the service of discipleship but at the same time gives itself over, with the enthusiasm and energy that would later flower into what we now refer to as the Renaissance, to an unprecedented reimagining of its possibilities through an increasing attention to observing in detail the way of nature's own original self-presentation, and most especially in the study "from life."

As visibly striking as the legacy of Giotto is in the private style of Fra Giovanni, however, the spiritual and artistic bonds of relation to Dante's poetic vision are even more deeply rooted in the imagination at work in the San Marco *Annunciation*. The central metaphor of the *Divine Comedy*, the figure of Beatrice, essentially distilled in the image of her eyes and her smile, is the iconic memorial in the poem of the central metaphor of St. Francis's conversion, his spiritual marriage to "Lady Poverty," the feminine aspect of the Crucified who spoke to him first in San Damiano and with whom Francis became one flesh in the total intimacy of the La Verna experience, betokened by the Stigmata. For Dante, Beatrice is Lady Poverty, Sister Death, and, finally, the incarnate image of Mary. Sister, lover, wife, mother, and Queen: the roles come together unmistakably in Dante's recounting of St. Francis's story, narrated, significantly for our present considerations, by the Dominican theologian Thomas Aquinas as a part of an iconic diptych that portrays St. Francis in his historically inseparable companionship with St. Dominic. Dante's portrayal of St. Francis identifies him as Lady Poverty's "second spouse," whose spiritual marriage to her was consummated at La

Verna in a mystical and metaphorical reenactment of its exemplar, when at Jesus's crucifixion "she leapt with Christ upon the cross when Mary stayed below."[23] Cross and marriage bed are effectively seared into and transform the religious and artistic imagination of a cultural epoch. This is the key image that unlocks for us the rich contemplative beauty and opulent human meaning of Fra Angelico's San Marco *Annunciation*. The angel, the iconic messenger, is the envoy from the divine realm, who mediates and ministers to the marriage of the mystery of original Love, creative and redemptive gift-giving, with the mystery of human freedom embodied in the receptivity of acceptance in the Virgin's "fiat," flesh become word. For the contemplative and cultural imagination of Fra Angelico's epoch, this is the original image, the "first scene" in which we come to see what the truth is regarding sin and grace, pride, the original sin, and forgiveness, the fulfillment of freedom in love.

This is Dante's insight as expressed in the passage quoted at the beginning of this study: Dante's *Purgatory* reveals the truth of every religious house insofar as its function is to serve as a "school" of contemplative discipline and discipleship: its first and best preceptor is Mary Annunciate.

As soon as he has passed through St. Peter's Gate, Dante the pilgrim begins the ascent of the seven storey mountain. His forehead has been marked with the wounds of the seven-fold "P" representing the seven capital sins, which are the roots struck deep in the soul of every blossoming act of sin and which must be rooted out and wound healed—the work of Purgatory. Dante the poet, through the voice of Vergil, has already explained that this ascent is governed by the "Law of the Mountain": the souls in Purgatory may pursue the work of repentance, for which they ardently yearn, as long as the day lasts, but when night comes they are enjoined to take no further step upward; rather, they must rest. For the poet, Purgatory is the school of contemplation, which must be learned, or rather recollected, in the soul, in order to be at home and embark upon the true adventure of education in love which is Paradise. The Law of the Mountain is this school's primal lesson, the discipline of time. The mountain is

---

[23] Dante, *Paradiso*, XI, 72.

the place of sinful freedom and its inner structure, its law, is freedom's time. Time is the peculiar rhythm of freedom's mutuality, its exchange of gifts, and the extent of gift-giving demarcates the space in which freedom's dramatic history takes place. Literally, then, the first scene of the drama which Dante the pilgrim is given to contemplate is that of the Annunciation; divine art, which exceeds Nature's, which in turn exceeds human art marks the beat of freedom's graceful approach in the angel's annunciative arrival, engraving it in the almost living marble flesh of freedom's space, so that it can speak silently. In that original contemplative silence, Mary fulfills the responsibility of her freedom in acceptance of the gift announced, "Hail, full of grace," through her acceptance embodied in her words, "Let it be done unto me according to your word." The marriage is consummated; the Incarnate Word, conceived.

Surely, now we can recognize Dante, the pilgrim-poet standing before the first image of divine art, as the antecedent of Fra Angelico, standing before the still-blank wall at the head of the stairway leading to the friars' dormitory in San Marco, imagining his role as apprentice to the Divine Artisan in the work of rendering this element of the time–space of his community an effective testimony to the place it should hold in the curriculum of the house as school of contemplation. Did he, perhaps, have Canto X of the *Purgatorio* specifically in mind when he chose the subject for this wall? Are we to see the stairs leading to the dormitory with the *Annunciation* at their head as the first flight of the seven storey mountain of which the convent was the base? The dormitory was the night-place where in the rest of sleep after the day's labors below, another time of "soul-work" would occur: the dreamwork of each friar watched over by the individual icon frescoed by Fra Angelico or his assistants in each cell, each one gathering an immeasurable depth of meaning against the contemplative horizon which the prime scene of the Annunciation opened up? It seems to me quite probable on the basis of the internal evidence of the unique appropriateness of such a choice, but, of course, it could still be attributed to providential grace or even fortunate happenstance. Finally, it matters little to the point of this reflection. I am not aware of any information regarding Fra Angelico's specific knowledge of Dante, though for a Dominican born in the Mugello, educated and trained in Fiesole and Florence in the fifteenth century not to have read and meditated upon the *Comedy* often seems almost unthinkable. Some minor but pleasing circumstantial evidence adds a further aura of plausibility to the surmise that Fra Angelico did have Dante in mind.

> During the course of his research for the first edition of the *Lives*, published in 1550, Vasari interviewed a lay brother at San Marco named Fra Eustachio. He passed on the anecdotal details that enliven the narrative of Vasari's life of Fra Angelico. Said to have been able to recite prodigious quantities of Dante by heart, Fra Eustachio was famous for his memory. However, Vasari failed to learn more about the dormitory frescoes than that they were scenes from the New Testament. Perhaps this is all the old man knew, or perhaps this is all that he thought Vasari would understand. At any rate, it seems that Fra Angelico himself was more important to Fra Eustachio than were the paintings at San Marco.[24]

Fra Eustachio did not, of course, know Beato Angelico personally, and there is no implication that the latter knew "prodigious quantities" of Dante by rote as the former did. Rather, Hood's point is that the *memory of persons*, both actively remembering and being held in memory, is an essential element of the Dominican Observance, as the living Dominican vine that frames the Chapter Room Crucifixion shows so clearly. Furthermore, the fact that Beato Angelico almost never depicts St. Dominic in a group scene without placing St. Francis by his side indicates that the Dominican memory reflexively moved toward its extended family, of which none were closer that the sons of Brother Francis, despite the well-known and very real strife of sibling rivalry.

Our argument here has been to show that Dante and Giotto figure prominently in the memory of the Dominican family, not just iconographically, but contemplatively, so that the shape of their imaginations, itself formed by St. Francis and therefore so congenial and complementary to that of St. Dominic, was deeply patterned into the spiritual and artistic vision of Beato Angelico. In this sense, the jointure between Dante's Annunciation in Canto X of the *Purgatorio* and the dormitory *Annunciation* provides the authentic framework that alone demarcates precisely

---

[24] Hood, *Fra Angelico*, p. 275.

the position of the latter work in the continuum of contemplative time–space, effectively extended in the memory of persons. In other words, the fresco is positioned there to memorialize the event in which past and present intersect to form a single ongoing narrative episode in one of the oldest story-traditions of European civilization: the contemplative. The next two sections will explore the dual roots of this tradition.

III

Just as the "memory of persons" offered a clue to understanding the significance of its position, the inscription that Fra Giovanni himself placed beneath the painting offers a clue into a third dimension of the *Annunciation*'s beauty, its situation. "Situation" here refers to the interactive relation of the work with those who allow themselves to be properly engaged by it. In other words, an art work's situation refers to the efficacy in the beholders' lives of its initiative and their acceptance of its capacity to "set itself to work" and infiltrate the patterns of meaning that constitute their existence and identity. In these terms, one can identify the *Annunciation*'s situation as "liturgical," in the sense that its beauty comprises the theological drama that it both depicts and instigates in the daily lives of its Dominican witnesses. It is a liturgical icon of the mystery of the Incarnation and of the miraculous role of Mary as the exemplar of human freedom accepting her vocation to play the key supporting role in that drama.[25] The

---

[25] It is important to note the signal importance of images of Mary in the iconography of the Florentine artistic imagination. Certainly, images of Mary were ubiquitous in Christian Europe. But the particular history of miraculous images of Mary in Florentine religious and civic experience situates the production of another major representation of the Virgin as the centerpiece of such an ambitious and "high-profile" a public project as the San Marco renovation in a context of immensely heightened liturgical drama. Not only had Florentines been long used to venerating no less than three miraculous Madonnas, the column figure of the Virgin near the Oratory of Or San Michele, the tavola Madonna in Impruneta, and *Annunciation* in the Servite church of SS. Annunziata, but the physical proximity of the latter image to the site of San Marco could not but guarantee that Fra Angelico's work would immediately be viewed as a candidate for inclusion in the network of pious veneration which surrounded these other images. This situation alone assured that this latest and innovative

title that Christian theology gives to this drama is Incarnation, the "passion play" of God's Word of Love setting itself to work on the stage of human history, with the Annunciation as the first scene of its central episode.

Recall the inscription that Beato Angelico himself placed in the frescoed framework of the *Annunciation*, "When you come before the image of the Ever-Virgin take care not to let the 'Ave' remain silent." Regarding it we know the following:

> This [inscription] means that the beholder's verbal if unspoken response to the image was expected to mimic Gabriel's words in the angelic greeting, and, like the angel in the painting, Dominican custom expected the friar to genuflect as he said the words. In this way the north-corridor *Annunciation* was as much a part of the liturgy of the Dominican Constitutions as was the altarpiece in the Church. Thus the friar's entire action—the action of his body and the silent action of his mind as he prayed—exactly imitated the angel's action in the painting.[26]

In Dante's *Purgatorio*, the repentant proud who labor on that cornice must pass by the scene of the Annunciation bent over double by the huge weight of the boulder of their pride which they struggle to carry on their back. Dante instead views the image straight on, because he bears the task of the poet to express the meaning of the entire scene by viewing the work in its proper situation in the contemplative economy of purgation. Dante suits his posture to his role and the inscription enjoins the friars to do likewise, because their identity as members of the Order of Preachers requires that they assume the instrumental role of the angel in annunciating the offer of incarnational grace to the faithful Church, of whom Mary is the type. And as they pass by on their way to sleep or to work, their liturgical action punctuates the transformation of their spiritual identity back and forth between the identity of Gabriel in the day and the identity of Mary in the night, integrating in themselves the two dynamics of contemplative time–space: initiative and receptivity.

---

work would have a power of fascination that reached beyond the walls of the convent to the entire city.

For an insightful study of the broad cultural significance of images of the Virgin in Florentine religious sensibility, see R. Trexler, "Florentine Religious Experience: The Sacred Image," *Studies in the Renaissance*, 19 (1972): 7–41.

[26] Hood, *Fra Angelico*, p. 272.

Joining in the rhythm of the dance of time, Beato Angelico's brothers are invited to take in their hands and turn "the key to open the supreme love," and enter into the perspective of the painting, transgressing its frame, there to play the dual role of Gabriel and Mary who are inclined toward each other and regard each other with gesture of hands and eyes that bespeak the intimacy of a marriage that can be consummated only within the womb of the contemplative soul. Thus, we discover here another clue to the true place of a work of art from within its own perspective, a perspective that is situated within the larger horizon of time–space which occurs as a "fusion of horizons"[27] between the painting's inner perspective and the perspective of its engagement with the lived existence of it witnesses. The investigation of this clue, its "space" understood as horizon, will be carried out in Section IV of this study. The immediate task, however, is to articulate the dynamism we have discovered to be the painting's situation: namely, the life of contemplation, with Mary as its exemplar, and the manner in which the painting sets itself to work in that situation, that is, liturgically.

Fra Giovanni, of course, did nothing novel in according primacy to the Annunciation scene within the pedagogical schema he developed in executing his mission to adorn the convent in a manner befitting its domestic function as a school of contemplation. On the contrary, as a son of the Observance he would have been particularly eager to reverence the traditional centrality universally afforded to Mary as the "Mediatrix of all grace" by Christian spirituality in general and by the monastic tradition in particular. As noted earlier, the mendicant movement initiated by Sts. Francis and Dominic, which, viewed with hindsight, appears as a significant modification of the already 700-year-old tradition of monastic life, was in fact viewed by both founders and followers alike simply as an adaptation of the essential spirit of that tradition to the needs of changing cultural contexts. That spirit, in fact, was the cultivation of the contemplative life, which was

---

[27] Gadamer uses this term to indicate the process of hermeneutical understanding that occurs as the establishment of "common ground" between the world in which a work emerges and the world in which an interpreter of that work stands forth to encounter it; see *Truth and Method*, pp. 265–380, and, in particular, pp. 306–307, and 374–375.

ordered hierarchically toward three ends: (*a*) the worship and adoration of God; (*b*) charity toward the neighbor and service to the Church through prayer; and (*c*) the salvation of the individual monk's soul. In this sense, ordered as means to a threefold end, the contemplative life must be understood, not as opposed to the active life, but as being a radical form of action. Hence, when St. Benedict instructed his monks that *laborare est orare* and *venit hospes, venit Christus*, he was instructing them in the diverse modalities and rhythms of a rule of life that envisioned a transformation of every detail and circumstance of the monk's way of living into a single, organically integrated prayer, which is most properly styled "contemplation-in-action."

The mendicant movement, while renovating the circumstances and routines of contemplative life, remained rooted in an awareness of its spiritual and theological source. The contemplative was to be a disciple who constantly sought to identify him- or herself with Christ through an ongoing act of historical imagination which envisioned the beholder mystically integrated into the redemptive events of the Savior's life, passion, death, and resurrection. Thus, the spirituality of the monastic and mendicant orders was ultimately an extension of the theology of the sacraments: that is to say, contemplative life, like the sacraments, was a repetition or reenactment of the uniquely privileged historical event of divine revelation, the Incarnation. Like the sacraments, the contemplative life was understood theologically to be not merely symbolic or memorial, but to effect a real bond of identification between the faithful disciple and the Incarnate Word of God, mediated by the material reality of the word of Scripture for the contemplative as by the material species of the sacraments—water, bread, wine, oil, exchange of vows, confession, and absolution. Perhaps the clearest and most direct illustration of this sacramental theology and spirituality is found in the Eucharist and the liturgy of the Mass, so that monastic life centered on the celebration of the Eucharistic liturgy. From its origins, however, monasticism demonstrated an extraordinary power of imagination at interweaving the properly sacramental, liturgical, and contemplative elements of the Christian spiritual tradition to form a seamless tapestry of rare richness and aesthetic artistry. It is natural enough, therefore, that the liturgical presence of

Mary in monastic life should be second only to that of Christ and should constitute the monks' privileged path of access to the source of grace. Mary was the first and paradigmatic contemplative-in-action, in that she first "gave body" to the Son of God and did so in a manner that modeled the highest possible degree of human freedom in that event of total receptivity to God's Word of Love, the Annunciation.

If the mendicant movement can in any sense be understood not simply as an adaptation of monastic life, but as a genuine renewal and reform of its original charism and vigor, we must look for the root and impetus of that movement even further back in its history than Francis and Dominic, back, in fact, to St. Bernard of Clairvaux, founder of the Cistercian reform of the Benedictine tradition. The Cistercians were perhaps the single most effective promoters of the dramatic rise in popularity of Marian devotion in the eleventh and twelfth centuries. So significant was St. Bernard's influence on both Franciscan and Dominican spirituality that Dante chose him as a sort of baptized and spiritually transformed image of Vergil to be the pilgrim's final guide and sponsor in his journey to God. There Bernard's role is specifically to intercede for Dante with Mary, who in turn necessarily must be the one to plead that Dante be allowed the fulfillment of his heart's first and final desire: a true vision of God in a mystical revelation of the divinity in both its Trinitarian and its Incarnate reality. It must be remembered that in Dante's artistic imagination the distinctive elements of both Franciscan and Dominican spirituality were interwoven in a seamless pattern, an achievement made possible in large part by the centrality of Mary to both traditions. The nuptial imagery in Marian devotion enters Franciscanism through the lifelong cultivation of Francis's self-identification as the spouse of Lady Poverty, under the influence of the courtly love tradition spread by the troubadour-poets, whom Dante also greatly admired and imitated in La Vita Nuova, and who, in a loose but nonetheless relevant sense, sprang up from the same rich cultural soil as St. Bernard. No less than St. Francis's, St. Dominic's religious imagination was shaped by St. Bernard and the Cistercian movement. Hood puts the matter thus:

Perhaps most important for a study of Fra Angelico is to remember that the Cistercians were the primary devotees of the Virgin Mary.

Through Albert the Great and his pupil Thomas Aquinas, the Dominicans usurped this prominence in the thirteenth century, but theirs was a continuation of Cistercian tradition, not a break with it. Like a beehive, a Dominican priory owed its security to the members' placing their individual agendas second to the common good. And like a honey bee every friar had his place in the collective at whose heart was the Virgin Mary, the legal abbess of every Dominican convent, or by extending the metaphor one could even say its queen. Dominican notions of the common good were thus founded on internal domestic harmony centered on an abiding if invisible female presence, appropriated from the Cistercians' emphasis on the centrality of Mary's motherhood, on her intercession with a sometimes wrathful God, and most of all on the monks' attempts to model their own orientation to the masculine Christ according to Mary's example of yielding, willing acquiescence.[28]

Hood's comment highlights in its final observation an aspect of Marian devotion that will be relevant (Section IV) in considering how it is that Mary, particularly in the Annunciation scene, came to be taken as the iconographic emblem *par excellence* of the perfect exercise of human freedom: a "yielding, willing acquiescence" to the initiative of Divine Love in the form of a contemplative vocation of which Gabriel is the envoy. For now, this consideration of the theology of the contemplative life which forms the framework that situated Fra Giovanni's painting in the daily life of the Convent of San Marco might well conclude with a brief sketch of the distinctive form that Dominican contemplative prayer took in the paraliturgical practice of the friars' private meditation, as exemplified by St. Dominic himself.

In the Constitutions, the saint proposes a maxim, very much in the spirit of the Benedictine *laborare est orare*, which was intended to encapsulate epigrammatically the apostolic orientation of the friars' private meditative prayer: *contemplata aliis tradere*, to pass on to others the things contemplated. This passing on, of course, preeminently took the form of preaching, emphasizing that the friars' meditation on the mysteries of faith revealed in Scripture and furthered by their theological study should be ordered first to their salutary communication to the faithful in the

---

[28] Hood, *Fra Angelico*, p. 21. It is interesting that Dante used the similar image in *Paradiso*, XXXI, but note the exchange of roles.

form of sound doctrine and the reproof of heresy, rather than to the spiritual edification of the friars themselves. This relatively detached and intellectual emphasis in Dominican prayer stood in sharp contrast to the Franciscan pursuit of direct affective engagement in the mysteries contemplated and the resulting increase in spiritual ardor and apostolic fervor. This, in turn, would have its own ministerial efficacy, through St. Francis's admonition to his followers to preach more by their example, especially in the embrace of outward poverty and the performance of charitable works, than by their words.

Notwithstanding the characteristic Dominican intellectuality of meditative prayer, there was a corresponding emphasis, equally original and deeply rooted in the charism of the founder, on bodily posture and physical gesture that offered a counterpoint to meditation's inner orientation toward verbal expression and suggests yet another dimension to the liturgical situation of the *Annunciation*. In the treatise *De modo orandi*, written by an anonymous confrère of St. Dominic's, the founder is described as habitually employing seven specific combinations of posture and gesture which he chose as uniquely appropriate to the intention or spiritual purpose of the particular episode of prayer in which he was engaged, characteristically before a crucifix. The treatise recounts St. Dominic's conviction that prayer, even when oriented primarily toward intellectual meditation, should both solicit and respond to grace by means of physical gesture and that these methods were indispensably important as aids to achieving authentic contemplative disponibility of the whole person, body and soul, to the initiative of divine grace sought in prayer. Obviously, this disposition toward liturgical and paraliturgical ritual should be viewed as the horizon against which the depth of meaning resident in the inscription which Fra Giovanni placed beneath the *Annunciation* should be understood: the friar's genuflection and silent "Ave" are the prayerful gestures of response to the mysterious reality of grace that the painting commemorates sacramentally within the paraliturgical ritual of the convent's daily life, thereby opening out a new contemplative horizon into which the friar is continuously invited to enter and fuse his own situation with that of the figures portrayed. Liturgy, then, moving beyond its narrower conventional meaning, can be understood as naming every element of physical, verbal, and performatory ritual by which persons effect an embodiment of the contemplative attitude which is the center of the universal religious dimension of human existence. Human life is situated in the midst of mystery; mystery is the horizon against which human existence is profiled. Liturgy comprises every human gesture of acknowledgment and solicitation of mystery's interruptions of and intervention in those lives. Art is one such element of liturgy, and it is in this sense that, explicitly or implicitly, all art is religious.

IV

The claim that all art is fundamentally religious properly demands a philosophical justification in terms of the kind of human experience in which a work of art can be appreciated. More specifically, because such a justification will necessarily presume a way of understanding human existence as a whole, it requires an ontological hermeneutic of the way in which human existence takes place in the world.[29] Clearly, the attempt to offer such an explanation in full terms would, to borrow Dante's phrase, "swamp the fragile bark"[30] of the present venture. But something must be said, if only by way of suggesting a direction. To facilitate this, a schematic outline of the argument we shall attempt to offer will be useful:

---

[29] Here I am most closely following Gadamer's hermeneutics of human understanding as it applies to the work of art. First, Gadamer recognizes the necessity of profiling his way of thinking in this area against that of Heidegger, especially as presented in the latter's revolutionary lecture, "The Origin of the Work of Art," in *Poetry, Language, Thought*, trans. Alfred Hofstadter (New York: Harper & Row, 1971); my own use of some of the leading ideas in that text will be obvious to the reader familiar with Heidegger's lecture. Gadamer also acknowledges, however, that he finds it necessary to depart from Heidegger and reinterpret the project of articulating the ontology of the work of art in terms of its centering in language, making clear that at this primary level, "language" includes every form of symbolic expression. This effort is sustained throughout Gadamer's work as a whole, but some of its key elements can be found in *Truth and Method*, Part One, and in the essays collected in his *The Relevance of the Beautiful and Other Essays*, ed. Robert Bernasconi (Cambridge: Cambridge University Press, 1986).

[30] The "piccioletta barca" of *Paradiso*, II, 1.

1. Religion basically means *"mystery-dealing."*

2. The liturgical element of religion deals with the need to imagine the human story against an *open horizon* which allows the major events of that story to articulate their full dimensions, that is, to take on genuine depth of meaning. Horizonal depth of meaning is the *sacred space* in which all forms of art stand and against which they figure forth. This implies that all art in its proper liturgical function is *decorative*.

3. The philosophical notion of *contemplation* articulates the Greek cultural imagination's most developed response to the human religious need for depth of meaning. The function of contemplation as the goal of the philosophical way of life (contemplation-in-action) is to enable human existence to make itself at home in the sacred space of the world through the practice of the properly philosophical genre of art, *"theory-making."*

4. In the liturgical art of philosophical theory-making, the ideals of truth, freedom, and beauty emerge as *conceptual icons*, decorating the horizon of sacred space and demarcating the limit-possibilities of the field of depth of human meaning. The contemplative philosophical imagination envisions the realization of these ideals as *integrity of personal identity*. The appropriation of the Greek contemplative ideal by the Judaeo-Christian tradition constitutes a fusion of horizons which opens up the proper space of Western European culture in which Fra Angelico's *Annunciation* stands.

1. Religion basically means "mystery-dealing." First steps are always tension-laden; most anticipated, least certain. The argument begins in mystery, with the word itself. In Greek, *musterion* is derived from two roots: *muthos*, word, speech, and generally, anything delivered by word of mouth—hence, story or narrative, as in myth; and *steresis*, privation or lack, not in the sense of something accidental which could or could not be present but happens to be missing, but, rather, in the sense of something necessary for things to be whole or complete, which, however, is absent, as for example, the heliotropic response of a plant reveals its need of light. Mystery is the necessary absence of the words that are needed for the whole story to be told. What story? The story of origins and destinies; the story that tells the secret meaning of what is happening. This is the center of religious experience: the instinctive human need and desire to tell the whole story. Most literally, *musterion* refers to religious rites that are secret, that is, not to be spoken of precisely because their true meaning cannot be spoken or understood in words. This "excess" of meaning in relation to language is the origin of the distinction between the sacred and the profane: the sacred is the horizonal boundary-space of mystery upon which the uninitiated must not tread, because it is set apart in reserve for the liturgy which embodies what words cannot say and which can be experienced only by participation. Hence, to the uninitiated, the mystery is literally meaningless and shows itself only in the tension of a question of meaning in which they must participate in order to experience understanding.

To begin and end in mystery is to begin and end in silence. Mystery is the silent deprivation of the words necessary to let the story unfold itself and show its meaning. It is not only the absence of the needed words, however; it is their necessary absence. *Steresis* is not *stasis*, the static or still. Silence is tense, restless, stirring; it is the *eros* of language, the wanting of words and meaning. Mystery means the presence-in-absence of the word. Early Greek philosophy recognized this in a way we anachronistically refer to as the "problem" of the one and the many, or, better perhaps, as the question of relation: why, and how, does silence need words and words silence. Meaning is relation: to be human is to need meaning, to be in need of the whole story about the way silence and speech belong together in language. Language is the way human existence happens in the world; history is the story of this happening, but a story without beginning or end. History begins and ends in myth.

So, let mystery be the starting point of our argument, insofar as mystery gives a way to begin and allows religion to emerge as the history of human existence in the world finding itself mysteriously situated in need of language. The fundamental religious question expresses the radically human need for meaning in the face of the real possibility of absurdity. We have said that meaning is relation, and, by extension, absurdity is the radical denial of relation. Explicit religious faith and belief arise from a basic trust in the possibility for human existence to be at home in the world in a familiar way, that is, to be allowed to participate in telling the story that begins and ends its history. Denying this possibility means finding the human in a situation of irremediable alienation, of always being a stranger and of suspecting that the human relation to the world, other human beings included, is marked either by basic hostility or by, at best, indifference. It is to expect an original and final betrayal of the human need for relation. In this situation, existence, in need of a word, would be absurd. To be human is to be situated in the question of meaning or absurdity, to be in need of words for a story in such a way that the need encompasses and surrounds existence as a whole from beginning to end. To be human is always to be dealing in the mysterious, sacred necessity of language, the tension of the need for both silence and speech; it is to worship the sovereign necessity of language or to blaspheme its exilic destitution. Religion means always to exist in the middle of the question of meaning or absurdity, to be dealing with the necessary story of the need that initiates history, to be dealing with the need to participate in the properly religious question of the storyteller—to trust in meaning to tell the tale or to suspect the absurdity of a sterile silence.

2. **Liturgy deals with the need to imagine the human story against an *open horizon* that allows the events of the story to articulate their full dimensions, that is, to take on genuine *depth of meaning*. Horizontal depth of meaning is the *sacred space* in which all forms of art stand and against which they figure forth.** The necessity of participation in liturgical ritual as a privileged form of mystery-dealing has already been stated. Now we must see how art plays its part in the religious liturgies which open up the horizon of the human need for meaning in full depth. This role can be stated summarily: the liturgical function of all art is decorative, in the strictest etymological sense; that is, art makes space fitting and proper for the sensuous and dramatic experience of the sacred in the midst of the profane as a means of invoking a divine revelation of the secret beauty that lies veiled and hidden in the casket of the mortal body and its world. Because "decoration" is a strictly religious need and all art is religious, all art is oriented toward a revelation of the beauty of a possible divine epiphany of meaning in the sensuous experience of flesh and blood. Therefore, the interplay of light and dark, music and si-

lence, dance and rest, eating and fasting, offering and immolation are the most basic elements of liturgy's endeavor to make the space of worship decorous for sacrifice, which is the central activity of religion. Sacrifice is the ritual enactment of the rhythms of the revelation of mystery. In conceptual terms, this rhythm can be stated as the unbreakable tension in opposition of finitude and transcendence as coordinate dimensions of meaning that demarcate the space of the human story, setting foreground off against horizon. Without such decorous demarcation, the episodes of the story remain dimensionless, shallow, flat, and insipid. They disappoint, even betray, expectation and end in despair. Bathed in the lights, smells, sounds, tastes, and textures of the liturgy of divine revelation, the story is transformed into the glorious spectacle of the fulfillment of the immemorial secret promise that evokes every human hope.

Art plays the role of decorating sacred space for the sacrificial liturgies that solicit divine revelation, and decorating is a necessary element of mystery-dealing. Therefore, it is important to be clear about how the coordinate dimensions of finitude and transcendence become experientially determinate in the flesh-and-blood experience of decorating. One way of suggesting how such experience occurs is to remind ourselves of the formulation that the Greek imagination gave to this dynamic: the doer of deeds must suffer; by suffering one learns. As Hans-Georg Gadamer has observed,[31] this maxim is rooted in the most profound depths of the Greek cultural experience, precisely because it identifies the necessity of sacrifice as the price of revelation. The doer of deeds, including the deeds of art, whether as actor or initiate-spectator, must suffer, because the structure of all human doing begins and ends in the necessity of suffering mystery: it arises in the need of meaning and ends in the unfathomable revelation of the excess of divine dispensation to the dimensions of human existence. Mystery is the sole origin and destiny of every human doing and suffering. To know this experientially is to be wise with the wisdom of the original and final divine commandment: nothing in excess. "Excess" is the sacred, secret precinct of the divine. Divine revelation, therefore, comes only at a price.

---

[31] Cf. Gadamer, *Truth and Method*, pp. 346ff.

Because revelation is always excessive, the doer of deeds, prompted by divine madness, must be willing to participate in the liturgy of sacrifice as the price for entering upon sacred ground. *Hubris*, the original sin, is the violation by humans, even if unwittingly, of the space of the sacred, heedless of the strictures enjoined upon those initiated into the mysteries. It is ultimately the "tragic flaw" of the one who fails in the attempt at self-knowledge, which is why the prohibitive form of the commandment is ritually and spatially linked to its hortatory opposite—know thyself. So, for example, we must see that Socrates in his visit to the oracle at Delphi discovers the origin and destiny of his philosophical vocation while standing upon the same sacred space as Orestes and Oedipus did. Caught in the no-man's-land of judgment, caught in the middle point of intercourse between life and death, suspended between the command of the father and the injunction of the mother, they learn the awful truth that opens up the mystery of their identity and places it in their own hands. The father commands: be King, sovereign over thyself, under the yoke of necessity alone, to which even the gods must bend their neck; know and possess thyself alone, at whatever price. The mother enjoins: nothing in excess, submit to the necessity of the blood knot; be ready to sacrifice yourself to redeem the blood-bond.

Art decorates the sacred space upon which mystery sheds the dark excess of light and secret beauty that bodies forth and confers an unfathomable depth of meaning upon the events of human living; deeds done and passions suffered, both stretched out and imaged in the dramatic liturgy of the mating-dance of life and death, in the rhythms of whose intercourse all stories begin and end.

3. The philosophical conception of *contemplation* articulates the Greek cultural imagination's most developed response to the human religious need for depth of meaning. The function of contemplation as the goal of the philosophical way of life (contemplation-in-action) is to enable human existence to make itself at home in the sacred space of the world through the practice of the properly philosophical genre of art, "*theory-making*." Rooted as it is in the Greek religious, mythic, dramatic, and scientific traditions, the philosophical way of life is oriented toward a fulfillment of the soul's need for an expression in depth of the meaning of the whole human story. The culmination of philosophy in contemplation must be understood as a life commitment centered on mystery-dealing and oriented toward allowing human existence to make itself at home in the sacred space of divine revelation. The properly philosophical art of theory-making is, like all art, essentially decorative, in the sense of making the world a fitting and appropriate space for the celebration of the communion at table of the divine and human ways of being. Participation in philosophical dialogue is the table-liturgy in which the intercourse of gods and mortals is consummated following the ritual dance of sacrifice and revelation which embodies the mysteries of life and death.

The contemplative tradition is arguably the supreme legacy of Greek culture to Western civilization. Together with the Christian Gospels, it demarcates the horizon against which the art of Fra Angelico, and most especially the San Marco *Annunciation* figures forth its beauty. Just as Jesus incarnates the revelatory word of the Gospel story, Socrates incarnates the dialogical word of philosophy. The Gospel story comprises the subject matter of every painting Fra Angelico crafted. Socrates appears in none of them, yet is present in absence as the "patriarch" who dictates all the structural dynamics and liturgical rubrics that guide Fra Angelico's artistic enterprise of decorating his family home to render it a fitting space in which to conduct a school of contemplation. To illustrate, rather than to explain and argue, this assertion and the several others which immediately precede it here regarding the origin and orientation of the contemplative tradition, two hasty profiles of Socrates, sketched in broad strokes, might bear scrutiny in the hope of catching the family resemblance.

The first is of Socrates in the *Phaedo*, celebrating his deathday by composing in dialogue with his friends an original funeral liturgy, a swan-song served up in the form of a feast of arguments for the "immortality of the soul" and set out on a table constructed in the shape of a theory of two worlds—or two families—to both of which the soul is related. The fare is rich, the drink potent, and the guests suspicious of their host's anticipatory instinct toward festivity. Should Socrates once falter in his enthusiasm or encouragement for the party game to which the guests had skeptically challenged him, to play the bard to the soul's whole story from the beginning to the end, their faintheartedness might well have turned to despair, the death of the soul, as Socrates intimates in his plea to Phaedo not to cut off those boyish curls, whose loss Socrates says he would mourn far more grievously than that of his seventy-year-old body. And why would he mourn? For the golden freshness of their beauty!

The second profile appears as a kind of inverse image in the *Symposium*. Taken together with the first, they form a diptych, much like the familiar masks of tragedy and comedy. A different table, another sort of feast: a drinking party in celebration of Agathon's victory for his work of *poiesis*, art-making, at the drama festival. When Socrates takes the floor for another tour-de-force performance of theory-making, he evokes the memory of an Orphic priestess, the only female character to occupy center stage in Plato's work. In her name, Socrates recites the liturgy of an initiation ritual into the erotic mysteries of Beauty. But the profile of interest here is the one of Socrates given as interruption of Socrates's serious theory-craft by the drunken Alcibiades, he of the keen but wayward erotic eye. The profile is presented in caricature style, with Socrates likened to Silenus, in satyr form, half-animal, half-man. Parodying the four stages of Socrates's rendition of Diotima's initiation rite, Alcibiades recounts the episodes of his cross-purposed entanglements with Socrates's peculiar personality and his eccentric way of life. Alcibiades has been left in the discomfitted position, unparalleled in his experience, of being the rejected, jealous suitor. He is bewildered, resentful, and, most of all, ashamed. And yet, he is compelled to bear witness, to testify that he still finds Socrates surpassingly beautiful. Returning to the image of Silenus and the statue replicas of that character often used as a kind of shrine in Greek homes to house small votive statues of the tutelary gods of the family, he says that if you open Socrates up, like the doors on the statue, that is if you really get inside of his arguments, which express his living soul, you find them to be the only ones that make any sense. Seen in this light through Alcibiades's loving, if grudging, eyes, Socrates reveals himself to be full of tiny golden icons of shining virtue, shimmering images of all that is divine in human life. In contrast to the sharp focus of this mystical intuition of Socrates's true identity, Alcibiades sees himself in the light of another divine revelation, the revelation of all that is opposite to the beautiful, the *kalon*: he experiences himself exposed as embodying the humanly ugly, the *aischron*, all that is unfit to be looked upon, all that is indecorous and shameful, alien and estranged from the sacred. Thus, Alcibiades's sketch of Socrates opens up an horizon of divine revelation of the depths and dimensions of meaning, both ideal and actual, brilliant and shadowed, in human existence. Furthermore, that revelation is given precisely in terms of Beauty manifesting itself as a field of force, a relationship of tension-in-opposition that must be understood explicitly through its human embodiments, the *kalon* and the *aischron*.

This key discovery of the Platonic dialogical style of philosophizing is reenforced at the very end of the *Symposium*, where Plato joins the frame of the diptych he has crafted in these two dialogues by adding a small footnote of his own to Alcibiades's major portrait. After Alcibiades has gone, the party degenerates until Socrates has drunk his companions under the table, literally and metaphorically, and caps off his victory in the bout of wine-heady words they have been contesting by demonstrating that one artist can indeed write both comedy and tragedy. The diptych reveals the identity of that person who is able to hold comedy and tragedy, life and death, finitude and transcendence, intellect and eros, sanity and madness, theory and practice, divine and human together in the integrity of a personal identity. For Plato, Socrates embodies human excellence (*arete*) as the capacity to make oneself at home in the world, knowing who one is by knowing one's way around in the circle dance of life and death and knowing how to tell the whole story from beginning to end in that new form of *poiesis* called philosophy. For *poiesis* is, in the first instance, neither creativity nor fabrication, but self-knowledge that expresses itself through craft as art. The craft of philosophy, which expresses the self-knowledge of its way of living and dying, is theory-making in dialogue with the questions that make us human by situating us in relation to divine mystery and soliciting a response which fulfills itself in the integrity of identity of the philosopher-king, the contemplative in action, in the figure of Socrates. This person is festival celebrated in language: in the solidarity and community of his conversation, meaning plays itself out to the full depth of its horizon by setting question and response to work to construct out of their own substance an altar-table for ritual sacrifice and meal and to transform themselves into food and drink, bread and wine. In the person portrayed in these profiles we see the "soul" wherein the sacred marriage festival is celebrated and consummated, and gods and mortals at table sat down, for the altar-table is also always marriage bed, centering, through its transformation, the field of tension around which the circle-soul dances.

4. In the liturgical art of philosophical theory-making, the ideals of truth, freedom, and beauty emerge as *conceptual icons*, decorating the horizon of sacred space and demarcating the limit-possibilities of the field of depth of human meaning. The contemplative philosophical imagination envisions the realization of these ideals as *integrity of personal identity*. The appropriation of the Greek contemplative ideal by the Judaeo-Christian tradition constitutes a fusion of horizons which opens up the proper space of Western European culture in which Fra Angelico's *Annunciation* stands. It remains only to link the Greek contemplative tradition of craftsmanship in home-making, represented by Socrates, with the Dominican style of painting employed by Fra Angelico working to decorate San Marco. That endeavor, which might seem at first a lyric leap or flight of fancy, is reduced to the more manageable, though still breathtaking, proportions of human artistic imagination once we recognize the craft they share: both are icon makers.

It has already been observed that Fra Angelico's work exhibits a freedom of imagination that ranges across the field of tension characteristic of the transition in painting from the medieval Byzantine style to the representational style "according to nature," which emerged with eruptive power in the work of his contemporary Masaccio, in the Church of Santa Maria Novella, and in the Brancacci Chapel. Fra Angelico's artistic vision is no mere eclecticism of borrowed elements from two divergent imagistic vocabularies, however. It is a genuine transformation of the iconic tradition in which works of art function as media of contemplation serving the specific religious liturgical purpose of schooling initiates into the mysteries that nourish and nurture the way of life proper to the vocation of the new conventual Orders.

But the philosophical craft of theory-making is also basically iconic in character. The ideal entities that decorate the realm of the Platonic *eide*, the so-called "Forms," must be understood as imaginative visions of the contemplative soul which is stretched out in the care-filled tension of the field of force between the "two worlds" of which human existence finds itself a citizen: the ideal world of things as they should be if human desire hopes to be fulfilled with enjoyment of the "Good," and the actual world of things "as they are" when perceived in the time–space of the "body," the realm of "bare facts," not simply empirical but also political, economic, religious, and artistic, when all such actualities are not set off and figured forth against the horizon of their full depth of possible meaning. Through the theory-craft of philosophical contemplation the sacred space of human existence in the world is decorated with works of artistic imagination in the form of the ideals of truth, freedom, and beauty, while the dynamics of the field of force of which they are the foci are traced according to the patterns of a way of living guided by the "knowhow" of caring for the center of human existence, the need for meaning, conceptualized iconically as the "soul." In the decorous world of contemplation-in-action we see in reflection "golden images of virtue" like the ones Alcibiades saw when he opened up Socrates, and we recognize the images as icons inviting us to see through them the beauty of the truth of human existence, which makes persons free to enjoy their being at home in the sacred space of the world.

How the living spirit of the Greek contemplative tradition was handed down through Neoplatonism and stoicism until it reached St. Augustine to be integrated with the Christian kerygma and expressed in a new form in the discipline of the Augustinian canonical rule; how it was mediated by the Benedictine monastic rule so as to survive the dissolution of the civilization of the Roman Empire and preserve its essential vision; how this tradition was again transformed and renewed in the late medieval world by the inspiration of Sts. Francis and Dominic—all this is another story which cannot be told from beginning to end here. Nonetheless that story is certainly the horizon of the imaginative space in which Fra Angelico painted his San Marco *Annunciation*.

V

Finally, we are in a position to frame the question that has guided this attempt to appreciate the beauty of the *Annunciation*. Implied throughout has been the expectation that a work of art might in some sense have a proper and appropriate place (or places). Yet, equally relevant, has been the issue of what "place" might mean in reference to a work of art. Having identified site, position, situation, and space as determinants of that meaning, we now must consider how the elements fit together to form a whole that is more meaningful than merely the sum of the parts. Thus the question becomes, "How does the meaning of the painting set itself to work as beauty so as to take its proper place in the world?" In other words, we must ask, "Where does meaning occur?" The response we make is that it is in *metaphor*, understood as a *meeting place* created in the symbolic expression of language in all its forms, a place of communion where an event of freedom occurs in the story of human existence which transforms that story so as to give it a new truth and reveal the beauty at play in the festive dance of gift-giving and -receiving that celebrates a wedding of personal identities, consummating their transformation into a living icon of the mutuality and intimacy of relationship which is the secret promise buried in the human need for meaning: love. Beauty is the aura of love experienced as the fulfillment of the human desire for meaning, and metaphor is its body.[32]

This meeting takes place and its meaning occurs in the experience of the work of art as metaphor. Metaphors are the "soul" of human existence and the "fabric-tissue" of culture, so that we can now say that the place of art is in the soul of the person who participates sacramentally in the integrity of gift-giving and

---

[32] Clearly, the sense in which the term "metaphor" is being used here vastly exceeds the narrow scope of its technical definition as a rhetorical trope in the form of an "implied comparison." Rather, it names one of the two most basic dynamisms of all language, the other being narrative. Narrative is the power of language to extend meaning into story; metaphor is the power of language to intensify and focus meaning in narrative to give it integrity of identity. It is in this sense that we shall argue in what follows that the human person is the root-metaphor of all language. All meaning is rooted in human personal existence.

-receiving which the work of art occasions and by which it takes its proper place in the world. Art gives time by providing an occasion and gives place by preparing a meeting-ground for the fulfillment of human existence in love. The San Marco *Annunciation* illustrates in a paradigmatic way how the work of art takes place in human existence because in it a mysterious completeness of identity is accomplished between the event it represents metaphorically and the event it sacramentally occasions. We turn now to a consideration of the story-event the painting illustrates so as to prepare ourselves to understand the experience it metaphorically occasions.

The painting illustrates the Gospel story of the Annunciation. The interpretation of the story to be proposed is this: The story illustrates that home-making in its many forms is the basis of all human activity, because home-making is contemplation-in-action and as such is the first responsibility and the basic discipline of freedom. We shall consider each of the major elements of this proposition in turn: (*a*) the question of freedom; (*b*), contemplation-in-action as freedom's first responsibility; and (*c*) the disciplined practice of home-making as the proper environment in which to discuss ethical issues.

(*a*) The Catholic tradition has from the beginning accorded a privileged evidential role in regard to questions concerning human freedom to Mary, the mother of Jesus. So, it is to Mary, as the embodiment not only of what it means for a human being to be entrusted with the care of a child, but, even more, of what it means for a human being to be free, that we look to give direction to our reflection. In particular, because we are looking for a place to begin, it seems appropriate to look to Mary as we find her in the Gospel story referred to as the Annunciation, where the source of her freedom and the initial step in the forming of her identity-in-freedom appear most clearly. Despite the story's familiarity, or rather because of it, we should listen again now.

In the sixth month the angel Gabriel was sent by God to a town in Galilee called Nazareth, to a virgin betrothed to a man named Joseph, of the House of David; and the virgin's name was Mary. He went in and said to her, "Rejoice, so highly favored! The Lord is with you." She was deeply disturbed by these words and asked herself what this greeting could mean, but the angel said to her,

"Mary, do not be afraid; you have won God's favour. Listen! You are to conceive and bear a son, and you must name him Jesus. He will be great and will be called Son of the Most High. The Lord God will give him the throne of his ancestor David; he will rule over the House of Jacob forever and his reign will have no end." Mary said to the angel, "But how can this come about, since I am a virgin?" "The Holy Spirit will come upon you," the angel answered, "and the power of the Most High will cover you with its shadow. And so the child will be holy and will be called Son of God. Know this too: your kinswoman Elizabeth has, in her old age, herself conceived a son, and she whom people called barren is now in her sixth month, for nothing is impossible to God." "I am the handmaid of the Lord," said Mary, "let what you have said be done to me." And the angel left her [Luke 1:26–38].

Gabriel and Mary are engaged in this story in a search for a language of freedom they can share. In their conversation we have a privileged opportunity to observe how the meaning of freedom occurs and is understood. What we discover is that it occurs as original and mutually open relation, in which neither member possesses existential meaning apart from the initiative or response of the other because both are radically in need of each other. Meaning is relation, and freedom means the original, mutual need of and openness to identification within the bonds of relation.

Gabriel, angelically efficient channel of truth that he is, announces the issue with unmistakable clarity in the first words of his greeting, "Rejoice, so highly favored [full of grace]! The Lord is with you." Mary has the good sense to be deeply disturbed by this and to ask, though only to herself, what it means. Few of the rest of us would be that quick to the question. The question is this: what can it possibly mean to say that the realm of divine mystery, of origins and destiny, draws near to the realm of existence in time; that the critical boundary of the finite is somehow extended out beyond itself into the open so that, through the intimacy of this meeting, the two might come to belong together in the integrity of one person? What indeed can this mean, or, rather, how does this event come to happen to her?

Gabriel is the voice of need; the need which is mystery, the mysterious need which knows no why except the freedom of love. The freedom of love is gift-giving, and its mysterious *kenosis*, its transformation into need, is the silent source of all meaning. The angel speaks of the rejoicing born of the wonder of all wonders, the wonder of existence—Mary's, her nation's, all the nations, and soon, of her son's; he speaks of favor and grace, not just to her, but of original grace, the graceful favor of existence as a free gift beyond all reason—"All is grace." He speaks of nearness—the Lord is with you, because he has need of you, because he has entered into the need which *is* you. Gabriel is speaking the language of freedom, of original open relation. Mary is learning to understand what it means, and so must we if we wish to discuss ethical issues well. We cannot undertake here to work out a full semiotics of this language, but some fragments of a primer of ethical terms might suggest the shape of the whole. They are offered without explanation, their meaning to be understood primarily through the person who interprets them by embodying what they mean, Mary.

1. Freedom means giving and receiving life as a gift.

2. Freedom is essentially relational: its structure is a mutual exchange of gifts.

3. Freedom is essentially mysterious: it arises in an original acceptance of need beyond all necessity. This mystery of *kenosis*, transformation into need, is the silent source of the meaning of freedom.

4. Human freedom is essentially responsive: we first receive life as a gift from beyond ourselves; we can, in turn, freely give what we have freely received.

5. Because freedom has its origin in a relationship of mutuality, it is essentially both finite and transcendent.

6. Human freedom is essentially both erotic and rational.

7. Human freedom is essentially both passionate and active.

8. The highest achievement of freedom is the commitment to identify oneself with the freedom of another at every possible level, including that of the bond to original mystery. This commitment to identify with the total freedom of another as one's own is love.

9. Love is the complete meaning of freedom.

But there is one more word to be added to our primer, the

meaning of which can be understood as a unifying theme running through all its more specific elements. It is *contemplation.*

(*b*) We have seen that the angel's salutation is an invitation to Mary and, in and through her, to all persons to learn the meaning of freedom, to rejoice in the wonder of life given as a gift. We have also seen that the realization that our very existence is the work of freedom, that we *are* freedom, is deeply disturbing to Mary, prompting her to question herself about its meaning. The angel's next words take notice of her situation, addressing her now individually by name: "Mary, do not be afraid; you have won God's favor. Listen!" These are the words of vocation, of that calling from the realm of divine mystery that beckons human existence to emerge and stand out as an individual in the open space of free identity where the truth of who we are is uncovered. What the angel calls Mary to, the vocation he offers, is to be contemplative.

Notice that vocation here is not a role that an individual plays; it is a way of being oneself, an identity. Mary's role will be as mother, but her identity is to be contemplative, to listen to God's word with her whole being throughout her whole life. Contemplation is the ontological structure of human freedom, and as such is the structure of every vocation to take up an individual identity-in-freedom. We are all called with Mary to be contemplative, for to be human *is* to be called into existence as free, as originally open to receive the gift of life individually in the form of an invitation to play some definite role in the history of God's drawing near. This is the freedom that is always contemplative, that always begins with the challenge to put off the anxiety of being what we are, finite, not the source but the recipients of gracious favor without cause or reason, and to "Listen." This is the identity of every contemplative, to await a word of calling, to listen for a word of vocation addressed in timely fashion to him or her alone in the silence of attention. Mary recognizes her vocation unerringly in the angel"s words and responds appropriately, "I am the handmaid of the Lord." Her response interprets her identity by saying how she stands before God: the meaning of my existence is to wait on the Lord, to attend to the event of his having need of me, to listen for his call. Mary had been well-brought-up; she had learned the language of readiness and responsiveness from the psalmists, "My soul waits for the Lord, like the watchman for day-break." "The eyes of the maid are on the hand of her mistress," to see what she will do.

"What will you do?" The question expresses the silent stretching out of the attentive soul toward God, opened wide to receive the gift that will be its own. "Let what you have said be done to me." Here freedom expresses itself authentically and resolutely, and Mary takes upon herself the fullness of contemplative existence. What begins as attentive openness, listening for a word, must be accepted as the event of its historical accomplishment. Contemplative existence fulfills itself in acceptance by allowing the events given by God to happen. Contemplation, fulfilling itself in acceptance, is the original responsibility of freedom and, as such, the source and purpose of every more particular responsibility and of every responsible action. Contemplation, embodied in the free human existence of Mary, shows us the truth of who we are: those whom divine favor approaches to ask attendance and allowance for its gift-giving.

One final observation of Mary's portrayal of freedom. As the acceptance of a gift, Mary's allowing the event of God's giving to happen has its full meaning as gratitude. But gratitude here is not a feeling or even an attitude, but a disposition, a way in which our existence is disposed to care for and cherish the gift received. The gratitude that is appropriate to the gift of life is the disposition to take care of the needs of life, to nurture life, and so to allow it to grow. Acceptance issuing in gratitude gives birth to new life. Perhaps the most striking thing about our passage is that it portrays human freedom as the contemplative response to a vocation to share in the giving of life by accepting the need to care for a child in gratitude. What the angel asks Mary to listen to is instruction about how to care for the child who she will allow to be the incarnational event of divine gift-giving. How is she to show gratitude as care? ". . . you must call him Jesus." Beyond conceiving and bearing, there is naming; the parent gives the child a name in a sacramental act of bearing witness to the identity-in-freedom that this child will have in the history of his people. The care of the parent in gratitude is to bear witness to the freedom, to the life given as gift, that *is* the child. The nurture that is parenting is accomplished by giving testimony to the way the child's life will receive its meaning in attentive, responsive acceptance of the vocation that is addressed to it. The care of the parent is to bear witness to the truth of who the child is. Contemplative gratitude bears witness to freedom through acceptance of the child's need for care, in whatever way that need expresses itself, great or small, satisfying or frustrating, heart-warming or heart-breaking. One can recognize a contemplative heart only through a watchful eye and a steady hand. The contemplative eye lingers over the texture and detail of things; it is taken up in its identity to be a careful witness to what is happening before its eyes. The living out of this contemplative identity of bearing witness to the freedom of the child through care for its need in a love born of gratitude—this I call *home-making*. Home-making is the disciplined practice of the vocation to be contemplative.

(*c*) This leads us back to the third element of our initial proposition: namely, that the practice of home-making, as the most fundamental responsibility of freedom, is the proper place to raise issues about the place of art in human existence. I want to ask what is required to make a proper home in which the need of freedom for meaning can be cared for lovingly through the beauty of art? Against that backdrop, I want to ask further what place do the issues that we properly call "aesthetic" have in such a home. Put differently: I would like to ask now what the relation is between contemplation practiced as home-making and the place of art in human existence.

The standard move at this point is to say that it is beyond the scope of an essay such as this to work out fully the nature of this relation. Be that as it may, we can perhaps discern at least two clues to an understanding of it. The first is this. However one chooses to explain precisely what the role of the virtues is in human living, Aristotle makes two things about them abundantly clear: that they are in support of the contemplative life, and that friendship is the necessary intermediate step between a life of moral virtue and the full happiness of contemplation. The moral virtues, in other words, support the contemplative life through the mediation of friendship, understood, as Aristotle does, as an expansion of the moral capacity to take increasing pleasure in rational activity. Friendship, as it were, doubles our capacity for happiness, because it allows us to take the same pleasure in the good activities of our virtuous friend as we take in our own, because in both cases they are chosen and enjoyed for their own sake and not for the advantage or pleasure of anyone in particular. The second clue makes a very similar (perhaps the same?) point from a very different perspective. The clue is to be found in the various Gospel scenes in which Jesus commends to us what are generally called the evangelical counsels and are identified as poverty, chastity, and obedience. As with friendship in Aristotle's schema, these counsels have a different status from the moral virtues in that they are situated, as it were, closer to contemplation. As Jesus makes clear, they are not obligatory; they cannot be commanded by the law. Rather, they are offered as counsels to freedom in its individuality to help it in directing its capacity for contemplative attention to that open, clear space in its existence in which the richest gifts could be given. The counsels are the inner supporting structure of the contemplative life. They are best understood, I believe, as disciplines of freedom and can be distinguished from the virtues in this regard. The virtues support rational activity within the limits of human potential; the counsels understood as contemplative disciplines support passionate acceptance of the limits of existence as a gift given by the divine mystery. In this sense, the counsels are more fundamental, closer to the source and the goal of freedom, than are either moral virtues or obligations. This accounts for their supersedence of universality, their inablity to be universalized; they can only be offered.

But what is it that is being offered as a gift in the counseled disciplines of poverty, chastity, and obedience, and what is their connection to the Aristotelian discussion of friendship? Clearly, it lies in understanding the counsels as the disciplines through which a genuine, though limited, bond of mutuality prevails in a free relation. As the inner structure of contemplation, the counsels come into play, as does contemplation itself, in the experience of vocation, of the calling into existence of an individual identity-in-freedom. Like contemplation itself, therefore, poverty, chastity, and obedience will be the structure of every vocation, not of some as opposed to others. What they offer is recollection, that deep remembrance that arises from the depths of the soul and, preceding it, turns consciousness toward the horizon against which will appear whatever is to be given into our care. They offer, in other words, the gift of attention as a fundamental disposition. Chastity as a discipline disposes our freedom to fidelity; that is, it disposes us not to run away from the intimacy of free relation, from that kind of drawing near that is naked of every meaning and purpose other than the nearing itself. Most of the chasing-after of unchaste behavior, whether explicitly sexual or not (for chastity has to do, not with sexuality specifically, but with intimacy), is a fleeing from intimacy with another human freedom, with our own freedom or with God's. We cannot bear the primitive terror that something, be it good or bad, will happen to us. The work of chastity as a discipline is to remember that the terror is the angel's voice announcing the arrival of the gift. Poverty disposes our freedom to kindness, that is, to every form of gentleness and tenderness in caring for the vulnerability that accompanies the powerlessness of mutual belonging to another. Poverty remembers that to be in relation is to be needy and exposed, and it remembers what it is to be hurt. Finally, obedience disposes freedom to docility, to that special kind of willingness that remembers that it is dedicated to the work of responding in gratitude to the gift of existence it has received by participating in the giving of that gift anew. Obedience is the eagerness of attentive care to be directed toward need; it is that anterior submission of one's right to choose without which the exercise of authority must become oppression.

Mary, who as contemplative embodies the discipline of the counsels, bears witness to all this. In our story, she asks, "But how can this come about, since I am a virgin?" Gabriel's answer demonstrates the particular kind of efficacy that the counsels have in turning our attention away from what we choose toward what God gives. "The Holy Spirit will come upon you, and the power of the Most High will cover you with its shadow." Granted the formulaic, indeed archetypal, character of the images here, we can at least say that Mary is being told that something literally tremendous is going to happen to her in the having of this child, but not much beyond that, in the way of either explanation or reassurance. Mary's virginity, whether as a physical fact or chosen state, only provides her the occasion to realize what intimacy with the mystery of divine freedom must mean in her life and to remember what chastity asks in every human life: that we stay and abide the drawing near of God despite our terror. The living out of her chastity, as well as of her poverty and obedience, is marked in the story by the laconic eloquence of its conclusion, "And the angel left her." What does this mean? He was sent to offer a gift. It has been received and accepted, so he leaves the gift now in its proper place. He leaves her; she is the witness to and the appropriate place of grace. Her vocation, accepted freely as her own, makes her who she is now, mother to a child. To be a parent is to bear witness to the gift given, to participate in giving the gift by making a home for it. At home with her, this child will learn to remember what it is to be faithful, kind and docile in receiving and giving, in revealing, in *being* God's gift, God's grace. She embodies what the vocation of having a child means, what it means to make a home, what it means to be free.

The place of art in human existence can be understood by analogy to the place of the child in relation to parents' role in homemaking. More precisely, the beauty of art needs the attentive disciplined witness of contemplative human freedom in order for the truth of its beauty to be given its proper name and its living capacity to grow in meaning, to be carefully nurtured and loved.

EPILOGUE

The true place of Fra Angelico's *Annunciation* is at the top of the stairs leading to the dormitory of his family home, on the site of the Convento di San Marco of the Dominican Observance. He chose that location as the position for the painting so as to situate it in the decorative scheme which he elaborated to serve the needs of the liturgical rituals employed by the community of friars in carrying out the apostolic mission of the convent to function as a school of contemplation. In this he was responding to his vocation as a Dominican friar to preach the Gospel and as an artist to provide an occasion and prepare a place for the revelation of divine mystery as beauty. This was his way of home-making and of caring for his soul, the souls of his confreres, and all souls who would accept the invitation to enter upon the sacred space that his painting opens to them and to meet at its table to celebrate sacramentally what it portrays metaphorically.

ABOUT THE AUTHORS

MARILYN MCCORD ADAMS is the Horace Tracy Pitkin Professor of Historical Theology at Yale Divinity School, where she teaches medieval and reformation theology and philosophical theology. For twenty-one years before, she taught medieval philosophy and philosophy of religion at UCLA. She is the author of a two-volume work about William Ockham and of a forthcoming book, *Horrendous Evils and the Goodness of God*, as well as of many articles in medieval philosophy and theology and philosophy of religion.

ROBERT MERRIHEW ADAMS is Clark Professor of Moral Philosophy and Metaphysics at Yale University. He has also taught philosophy at the University of Michigan and the University of California, Los Angeles, and is a past president of the Society of Christian Philosophers. He is the author of numerous articles on the philosophy of religion, ethics, metaphysics, and the history of modern philosophy and of *The Virtue of Faith* (1987), *Leibniz: Determinist, Theist, Idealist* (1994), and *Finite and Infinite Goods: A Framework for Ethics* (1999).

FRANCIS J. AMBROSIO is Associate Professor of Philosophy at Georgetown University. He has published widely in scholarly journals, writing on hermeneutics, especially the work of Hans-Georg Gadamer, and has contributed essays on Gadamer's thought to *The Specter of Relativism* (1995) and *The Philosophy of Hans-Georg Gadamer* (1997). In addition, he is the editor (with Michael J. Collins) of *Text and Teaching* (1991).

JOHN D. CAPUTO, Cook Professor of Philosophy, Villanova University, is the "Perspectives in Continental Philosophy" Series Editor for Fordham University Press. His most recent works include *Deconstruction in a Nutshell: A Conversation with Jacques*

Derrida (1997) and *The Prayers and Tears of Jacques Derrida: Religion Without Religion* (1997). Professor Caputo is a past president of the American Catholic Philosophical Association and past Executive Co-Director of the Society for Phenomenology and Existential Philosophy.

Louis Dupré was born and educated in Belgium. He taught philosophy at Georgetown University from 1958 to 1972. In 1973 he became the T. Lawrason Riggs Professor in Religious Studies at Yale. He concentrates on philosophy of religion and of culture. He is the author of fourteen books, the most recent of which are *Passage to Modernity* (1993), *Metaphysics and Culture* (1994), *Religious Mystery and Rational Reflection* (1998), and *Symbols of the Sacred* (1999).

Patrick A. Heelan, S.J., Ph.D. (geophysics), Ph.D. (philosophy), is The William A. Gaston Professor of Philosophy at Georgetown University. He has taught philosophy of science at Fordham University and at the State University of New York at Stony Brook. His philosophical interests center on the works of Edmund Husserl, Martin Heidegger, Maurice Merleau-Ponty, and Bernard F. Lonergan, S.J., and their relevance to the philosophy of physics and perception. Among his scholarly publications are *Space-Perception and the Philosophy of Science* (1983).

Amy Hollywood teaches religion at Dartmouth College. She is the author of *The Soul as Virgin Wife: Mechthild of Magdeburg, Marguerite Porete, and Meister Eckhart* (1995) and various essays on medieval mysticism and contemporary theory. She is currently working on a book-length manuscript "Sensible Ecstasy: Mysticism and Sexual Difference from Bataille to Irigaray."

Jean Ladrière, born in Nivelles, Belgium, studied philosophy and mathematics at Catholic University of Louvain (now at Louvain-la-Neuve). He was professor at the Higher Institute of Philosophy of that university from 1952 through 1986 and has been emeritus since then. He has worked in epistemology, philosophy of science, social philosophy, and philosophy of language. He is a member of the Royal Academy of Belgium and of the International Institute of Philosophy. His publications include *Les limitations internes des formalismes* (1957, reprinted 1992), *L'articulation du sens* (2 vol., 1970 and 1984), *Les enjeux de la rationalité* (1977), and *L'éthique dans l'univers de la rationalité* (1997).

Jean-Luc Marion received the Philosophy Award of the French Academy for his oeuvre in 1992. He was professor at the University of Poitiers (1981–1988), at the University of Paris X-Nanterre (1988–1995), and since then at the University of Paris IV (Paris-Sorbonne). He is director of the collection "Epiméthée." His publications include *Sur l'ontologie grise de Descartes* (1975, 1981, 1992), *L'idole et la distance* (1977, 1989, 1991), and *Dieu sans l'être* (1982, 1991).

Adriaan T. Peperzak, who is Arthur J. Schmitt Professor of Philosophy and Director of the Center for the Advanced Study of Christianity and Culture at Loyola University, Chicago, received his Ph.D. from the Sorbonne in 1960. He has published five books on Hegel, two on Levinas, and approximately 150 articles. Among his recent works are *Before Ethics* (1997) and *Platonic Transformations* (1997) and articles on the intersection of philosophy with faith and theology.

William J. Richardson, Ph.D., is the author of *Heidegger: Through Phenomenology to Thought* (Preface by Martin Heidegger) and co-author (with John P. Muller, Ph.D.) of *Lacan and Language: Reader's Guide to the Écrits* and *The Purloined Poe: Lacan, Derrida, and Psychoanalytic Reading.* He has writtten widely on issues concerning the relationship between psychoanalysis, philosophy, and religion. A graduate of the William Alanson White Psychoanalytic Institute (New York City), he was formerly Director of Research at the Austen Riggs Center (Stockbridge, Massachusetts). He is now Professor of Philosophy at Boston College and engaged in the private practice of psychoanalysis (Newton, Massachusetts).

David Tracy is the Andrew Thomas Greeley and Grace McNichols Greeley Distinguished Service Professor of Theology at the Divinity School, University of Chicago, where he has taught since 1969. Among his recent works are *Plurality and Ambiguity: Hermeneutics, Religion, and Hope* (1987), *Dialogue with the Other* (1990), and *Naming the Present* (1995). He is scheduled to give the Gifford Lectures in Edinburgh, Scotland, in the spring of 2000.